SECURE TECHNOLOGY PROJECT MANAGEMENT

2nd Edition

SECURE TECHNOLOGY PROJECT MANAGEMENT

2nd Edition

AI-Aware Security by Design, Secure SDLC, and ADDIS Gate Governance

Dr. Alemayehu Hailu, CISA, CISM

ISBN: 9798295526718
Printed in the United States of America

Dedication

To all the professionals who stand at the crossroads of innovation and responsibility.

To the project leaders who choose discipline over speed, governance over convenience, and security over shortcuts.

And to the next generation of digital stewards who will shape a safer, smarter, and more resilient world.

Acknowledgements

This book is the result of many years of professional practice, research, and collaboration across technology, cybersecurity, governance, and project management disciplines. I am grateful to the many colleagues and professionals whose insights strengthened the ideas presented in this book. Their experience across governance, cybersecurity, and digital transformation shaped both the structure and depth of this work.

My appreciation extends to the global institutions and research communities whose frameworks and guidance continue to advance our field. Their contributions provided the foundation on which much of this book stands.

Finally, I thank my family for their support throughout this journey. Their encouragement, patience, and belief in this work made its completion possible.

About the Author

Dr. Alemayehu Hailu is a cybersecurity governance specialist, technology risk advisor, and project governance strategist with extensive experience in digital transformation, enterprise security, and emerging technology oversight. He holds professional certifications including CISA and CISM and has built a career at the intersection of governance, cybersecurity, and structured project execution.

His work focuses on integrating Security by Design, governance frameworks, and risk management into enterprise technology programs. Dr. Hailu has worked and advised organizations across multiple countries on cybersecurity governance, digital risk management, and secure technology implementation.

He is the creator of the ADDIS Framework, a governance-centered project methodology designed to unify strategy, cybersecurity, risk, and execution across the full digital lifecycle.

"Evidence Beats Confidence, Every Time."

♦

Use gates to turn uncertainty into decisions.

♦

Use evidence bundles to make decisions defensible.

♦

Treat Security by Design as execution work, not final inspection.

Preface to the Second Edition

When the first edition was written, technology projects were already complex, already multi-vendor, already exposed to escalating cyber risk. That reality has not softened. It has intensified. Cloud ecosystems have expanded, software supply chains have stretched across borders, and threat actors have become faster, more specialized, and more financially motivated. The difference now is that artificial intelligence has entered the delivery environment as both an accelerator and a destabilizer.

AI speeds up development, analysis, testing, documentation, and operations. It also introduces new categories of failure. A project can be on time and on budget; yet still ships a system that behaves unpredictably in production, leaks sensitive data through unintended pathways, or amplifies risk through automated decisioning. The uncomfortable truth is that AI does not merely add features. It changes the trust boundary. It changes how we validate quality. It changes what "secure by design" must mean in practice.

This second edition keeps the original intent intact: to bridge the gap between traditional project management discipline and the security realities of modern technology delivery. The book still treats security as a lifecycle commitment, not a closing checklist. It still treats governance as a practical mechanism, not an organizational slogan. It still emphasizes that deliverables are not paperwork, they are evidence.

What is new is the clarity and pressure applied to "evidence-driven delivery." In the AI era, a team must show proof that the solution is not only functional, but also safe, controlled, monitored, and governable. This aligns with NIST's emphasis on governance and risk communication in the Cybersecurity Framework 2.0 (NIST, 2024b). It also aligns with modern secure development expectations as defined in the Secure Software Development Framework, and its community profile for generative AI and foundation models (Souppaya et al., 2022; NIST, 2024a). For organizations adopting AI systems, it aligns with a risk management posture that is structured, repeatable, and measurable (NIST, 2023).

If you are leading a Project Management Office (PMO), managing a program, or delivering a project, the goal is not to slow innovation. The goal is to keep innovation from becoming an unpriced liability. The second edition therefore makes one central argument: the most successful technology organizations do not separate delivery from protection. They fuse them.

The Path to Success in the Age of AI and Emerging Technology

Technology is not simply changing how we work; it is changing what systems are. Digital platforms now blend software, data, identity, and business operations into a single organism. That shift is already transforming how people live, work, and communicate, and it has made technology project management more difficult because complexity multiplies across vendors, dependencies, and attack surfaces. The first edition captured that reality clearly. The second edition extends it to the AI era.

Here is the challenge that many teams still underestimate: traditional project controls were built for deterministic systems. In a deterministic system, if you test the same input, you expect the same output. In an AI-enabled system, outputs may shift based on model updates, retrieval data changes, prompt patterns, drift, user behavior, and operational context. Even when a model is not “learning” live, its performance can degrade when real-world conditions evolve. This creates a new delivery risk. You can achieve successful implementation and still fail after go-live.

That is why security and governance must be embedded into every phase of the lifecycle, not attached at the end. The ADDIS approach already recognizes this by weaving security-by-design processes into the lifecycle and requiring deliverables and control gates to confirm readiness before proceeding. This edition strengthens that logic for emerging technologies, especially AI, by introducing "AI overlay controls" that activate when AI is in scope. The overlay does not replace the baseline secure SDLC discipline. It reinforces it with additional evidence requirements around data governance, model risk, evaluation rigor, and monitoring.

In many environments, the technology challenge is compounded by ecosystem constraints. Across African contexts, the success barriers are not only technical. They can include limited localized capacity, weak standards enforcement, inadequate planning, insufficient appraisal of alternatives, difficulty estimating impact, and gaps in knowledge transfer. These realities magnify risk, particularly when solutions are imported, rushed, or adopted without disciplined governance. In such settings, a project's security posture is often shaped more by procurement decisions and vendor behavior than by internal engineering choices. This is why the method in this book treats system development and system acquisition as equally important paths, both requiring structured deliverables, verification, and control gates.

Project management remains essential, but it is not sufficient by itself. Many mainstream project practices still emphasize schedule, budget, and scope, yet devote limited attention to the security controls and cyber-specific obligations that must be handled with strict diligence. The second edition confronts this directly. It treats security as a set of continuous engineering and governance activities that produce evidence. It treats risk acceptance as a documented decision, not a quiet assumption. It treats every gate as a point where leadership must choose, with eyes open, whether to proceed, proceed conditionally, or stop.

NIST Cybersecurity Framework 2.0 adds practical weight to this approach by elevating governance and emphasizing that cybersecurity outcomes must be communicated and managed as enterprise risk, including across supply chains (NIST, 2024b). The SSDF reinforces that secure development must be a set of practices integrated throughout the lifecycle, not a final scan before release (Souppaya et al., 2022). For AI systems, NIST's AI RMF formalizes how organizations can frame, measure, and manage AI risk, shifting AI governance from abstract ethics to operational controls and accountability (NIST, 2023). These are not academic references. They are modern expectations. Increasingly, regulators, auditors, customers, and boards treat them as evidence of due care.

So, what does "the path to success" look like now?

It looks like an organization where the PMO is not only a scheduler, but a governance engine. It enforces disciplined delivery standards, ensures security deliverables exist, and ensures gate reviews are real decisions backed by evidence. It looks like project teams that understand the SDLC they are using, and can integrate secure SDLC practices into it, whether their approach is agile, hybrid, or procurement driven. It looks like leadership that treats emerging technology adoption as a strategic bet that must be defended through risk management, compliance alignment, and operational readiness, not just enthusiasm.

In this edition, you will see that philosophy implemented through a simple discipline: at the end of each phase, deliverables become inputs to the next phase, and the project cannot move forward until appropriate authorities confirm readiness through quality and gate reviews. That discipline is the difference between "we built it" and "we can operate it safely."

In the age of AI, project success is measured not just by delivery, but by delivery that is governed, secure, and demonstrably under control.

How to Use This Book

This book is designed to be fully usable on its own. It explains the ADDIS lifecycle, Gate Governance, and the secure SDLC expectations that define what defensible evidence looks like at each decision point. Reusable templates and structured evidence aids, when offered, are intentionally maintained as a separate ADDIS Toolkit publication so the core book remains platform-neutral and durable across different delivery environments. Whether your organization relies on spreadsheets, ticketing systems, document repositories, or integrated delivery tooling, the governance requirement remains the same: capture consistent, reviewable evidence for risk, quality, compliance, and security outcomes, then make that evidence easy to validate during Quality Reviews and Gate Reviews.

This book is built to be used, not simply read. Think of it as a field guide for leading technology initiatives where delivery pressure is high and risk is real. Each chapter connects project management discipline to Security by Design practices, so security is treated as part of execution, not a closing event. That approach aligns with modern expectations that cybersecurity is governed as enterprise risk and managed through measurable outcomes and accountability (NIST, 2024b).

Start by deciding what kind of work you are leading. Is this an in-house build, a vendor acquisition, or a hybrid program with both tracks? Is the solution purely deterministic software, or does it include AI components that change how behavior, validation, and monitoring must be managed (NIST, 2023)? Those two questions shape how you apply the method. They also determine what evidence you must produce to demonstrate due diligence and readiness.

Approach the book in three deliberate passes. The first pass builds shared language. Read the opening chapters to align on roles, decision rights, and the lifecycle model you will use. This is where you eliminate common confusion early, such as who owns risk acceptance, who approves control intent, and who is accountable for secure outcomes. The second pass is execution focused. Follow the phase chapters in order and treat each phase as a working sprint with defined outputs. The third pass is assurance focused. Revisit the gate sections and confirm your evidence bundle is complete, consistent, and defensible. This "read to align, read to execute, read to assure" routine keeps teams from skipping hard work and calling it progress, a pattern that becomes costly in later phases.

The most practical way to use this book is to treat each phase as a contract. Each contract has four elements: input, required activities, deliverables, and a gate decision. That structure mirrors proven secure development thinking, where secure outcomes depend on practices being integrated throughout the lifecycle rather than appended at release time (Souppaya et al., 2022). In the early phases, the book pushes you to define the real problem, clarify requirements including security requirements, and identify risk and compliance obligations while change is still cheap. In the middle phases, it forces you to translate intent into architecture, controls, and testable designs. In the later phases, it emphasizes operational readiness, monitoring, and governance maturity so the solution remains safe after go-live, not only during deployment.

Pay special attention to gates. Gates are not meetings to review slides. They are decision points where leadership decides whether to proceed, proceed with conditions, or stop. When gates are weak, teams learn to hide uncertainty until it becomes a production incident. When gates are strong, the organization becomes faster over time because it reduces rework, prevents security debt, and improves confidence in releases. This governance posture is consistent with enterprise governance principles that demand clarity of accountability, decision authority, and oversight across technology investments (ISO, 2015).

To make gates real, you should use evidence bundles. An evidence bundle is a curated package of deliverables that proves the phase outcomes are complete and that risks are understood and treated. For traditional software projects, evidence bundles include items such as requirements with security requirements, architecture decisions, threat models, security testing results, remediation closure, and operational runbooks. For AI-enabled projects, the evidence bundle expands because the system's behavior depends on data, model artifacts, evaluation results, and runtime monitoring. That is why this book integrates an AI overlay. When AI is in scope, you must add evidence related to data provenance, evaluation thresholds, human oversight, and post-deployment monitoring for drift and misuse (NIST, 2023). The overlay is not a new methodology. It is a disciplined expansion of Security by Design for systems whose behavior cannot be validated by traditional test cases alone.

If you are a project manager, use this book to drive execution discipline. Your job is to turn uncertain work into structured work. Use the phase guidance to plan activities and use the deliverables expectations to prevent scope drift and hidden risk. Your success is not only delivering on schedule; it is delivering with traceable decisions and clear risk ownership. If you are a PMO leader, use the book as an operating model. Standardize minimum evidence expectations by project risk tier and institutionalize a gate cadence that rewards clarity over optimism. This is how a PMO becomes a governance engine rather than an administrative office. If you are a security leader, use the book to embed security requirements into planning, design, acquisition, and deployment. This aligns with secure development guidance that expects organizations to define, implement, and continuously improve secure development practices across the lifecycle (Souppaya et al., 2022). If you are an executive sponsor, use gate decision records to ensure risk acceptance is explicit, not assumed, and that security and compliance obligations are funded and scheduled as real work.

As you apply the guidance in this book, keep one principle in mind: artifacts are not bureaucracy when they reduce uncertainty and create evidence. They become bureaucracy when they exist without decisions or accountability. The goal is not to produce documents. The goal is to produce proof. This mindset matches the direction of modern cybersecurity governance, which emphasizes measurable outcomes, supply chain accountability, and decision-making structures that connect cybersecurity to enterprise objectives (NIST, 2024b). It also aligns with widely used governance and control frameworks that stress clear governance objectives, management practices, and responsibility structures across technology delivery (ISACA, 2018; ISO, 2015).

Finally, use this book to build organizational memory. Each phase and gate produces lessons learned. Capture them. Feed them back into your operating procedures, governance routines, and delivery standards. Over time, your organization should not only deliver projects, but it should also become a learning system that improves its security posture, delivery predictability, and governance maturity with every implementation. That is what secure technology project management looks like when it is practiced as a discipline, not performed as a ceremony.

“In a digital economy, speed without governance is not agility, it is exposure.”

TABLE OF CONTENT

Professional and Legal Disclaimer

This publication does not constitute legal, regulatory, financial, or cybersecurity advisory services. Readers should consult qualified legal, regulatory, and security professionals before implementing any frameworks, controls, or methodologies described herein. The author assumes no liability for actions taken based on the material contained in this book.

INTRODUCTION

This book begins with a simple observation: technology projects no longer fail quietly. When a modern project fails, it rarely fails in isolation. It fails in public, sometimes in regulatory filings, sometimes in customer churn, sometimes in operational disruption, and often in the one place leaders cannot afford to lose ground or trust. In earlier eras, delayed implementation could be treated as an internal inconvenience. Today, a rushed release can become a breach headline, a compliance event, or a multi-day outage that exposes the true fragility of the enterprise. That shift is not a matter of fear; it is a matter of physics. Digital systems are more connected, more dependent, and more automated than ever, and AI has accelerated both capability and risk. That is why secure technology project management is no longer an optional specialty. It is a leadership discipline, and it is now inseparable from how value is delivered.

A second observation follows quickly. Most organizations do not suffer from a lack of frameworks. They suffer from a lack of translation. They can cite standards. They can purchase tools. They can create policies. Yet many still struggle to convert security intent into delivery reality. The gap shows up in familiar places. Requirements are approved without clear security acceptance criteria. Architecture decisions are made without a credible threat model. Third-party dependencies enter the environment without enforceable security obligations. Testing happens, but evidence is incomplete. Operational readiness is treated as a final checklist rather than a design constraint. Projects become stories rather than proofs. People say, “We believe we are ready," when the enterprise actually needs to know, "What can we prove, and what risk are we knowingly accepting?"

This second edition was written to close that gap. It is built for the leader who is tired of hearing that security slows delivery, while watching avoidable incidents consume months of recovery work. It is built for the project manager who is expected to deliver outcomes in an environment where threat actors move faster than committee calendars. It is built for the product leader who wants speed but also wants to protect customer trust and brand credibility. It is built for the security professional who is asked to "review quickly" at the end, even though the most important control decisions were made months earlier. It is also built for executives and board-facing leaders who must justify technology decisions with evidence, not optimism, especially as regulatory and disclosure expectations around cyber risk management and incident reporting continue to sharpen accountability (U.S. Securities and Exchange Commission, 2023).

The title "Secure Technology Project Management" is intentional. It does not mean "project management for security teams." It means the discipline of managing technology projects so that security, resilience, compliance, and operational readiness are treated as core delivery outcomes, alongside functionality and schedule. It is project management that respects the reality that a product is not truly delivered until it is safe to operate, observable under stress, governable through change, and supportable through incident conditions. It is project management that treats security by design as an engineering approach and a governance approach, not a slogan on a slide. It is project management that treats AI as a delivery reality, not a future add-on, because AI changes the behavior of systems, the shape of threats, and the expectations placed on governance.

The timing of this edition is not arbitrary. The cybersecurity landscape has matured into an enterprise risk reality, and leaders are increasingly expected to show how governance drives cybersecurity outcomes. NIST Cybersecurity Framework 2.0 reinforces this by explicitly elevating governance as a core function and by framing cybersecurity as a set of outcomes that organizations can use to understand, assess, prioritize, and communicate their risk posture (NIST, 2024b). That framing matters because it shifts conversations away from tool inventories and toward decision accountability. It also aligns naturally with project delivery since projects are where many of the most consequential technology risk decisions are made.

Secure delivery also now demands software supply chain discipline. Modern systems are assembled from open-source components, managed cloud services, third-party APIs, and vendor platforms. Vulnerabilities and misconfigurations can arrive through dependencies, and changes can be introduced outside the organization's release schedule. In this reality, secure delivery must be designed as a lifecycle system, not a one-time review. NIST's Secure Software Development Framework (SSDF) captures the practical implication: many SDLC models do not address software security in enough detail, so secure practices must be integrated into each SDLC implementation (Souppaya et al., 2022). The SSDF is not merely guidance for engineers. It is guidance for project leaders, because it implies that secure development is a planned, resourced, and verified activity, and that project governance must demand evidence that these practices were actually executed.

Then AI arrived and changed the delivery contract again. AI-enabled solutions behave differently than traditional deterministic systems. They can drift overtime. They can be manipulated through input. They can leak sensitive information through retrieval pathways. They can influence decisions in ways that create safety, fairness, privacy, or compliance consequences. In response, organizations need lifecycle AI governance that is practical enough to apply during delivery. The NIST AI Risk Management Framework (AI RMF 1.0) provides a risk-based structure organized around Govern, Map, Measure, and Manage, emphasizing that governance applies across all stages of AI risk management processes (NIST, 2023). NIST's Generative AI Profile further recognizes that generative AI introduces novel or exacerbated risks and provides a companion profile for applying AI RMF outcomes to generative AI contexts (NIST, 2024b). Together, these sources point to a clear delivery requirement: if a project includes AI, then evaluation, monitoring, and guardrails must be treated as deliverables, and proof of those deliverables must be part of release readiness.

So, what does this book do differently?

First, it treats governance as a delivery system, not an overhead function. A gate in this book is not a ceremonial meeting. It is a decision point with defined outcomes and evidence requirements. Projects do not "present progress." They present proof. That proof is packaged into evidence bundles that can be independently reviewed, audited, and reused for operational handover. This approach aligns with modern governance expectations across cybersecurity, operational resilience, and enterprise risk management. It also supports the practical reality that risk decisions must be documented and accountable, not implicit and forgotten.

Second, it treats roles and decision rights as security controls. Many breaches and outages trace back to unclear ownership. The project team assumed security would handle something. Security team assumed the product team would implement it. Operations assumed it would be addressed before handover. Procurement assumed a vendor's marketing claims were sufficient. In secure delivery, assumptions are liabilities. This book therefore emphasizes role clarity across project management, product management, program leadership, PMO governance, security, architecture, operations, legal, and compliance. The objective is not bureaucracy. The objective is to ensure every major risk has an owner who can act, escalate, and accept or reject residual risk with authority.

Third, it treats secure SDLC and DevSecOps as execution engines rather than slogans. Many teams talk about "shifting left," but the real measure is whether security requirements, testing, and policy enforcement are embedded in the delivery workflow, supported by automation, and producing repeatable evidence. NIST guidance on DevSecOps implementation for cloud-native systems emphasizes pipelines that take source code through stages such as building, testing, packaging, deployment, and operations, supported by automated tools and feedback mechanisms (Souppaya et al., 2022). That pipeline mindset matters because it turns security into a mechanism. Instead of asking people to remember security, the delivery system enforces security.

Fourth, it recognizes that compliance is not a post-project documentation exercise, it is a design constraint. Whether or not an organization pursues formal certification, ISO/IEC 27001 provides a clear message that information security must be managed through a systematic management system, oriented around risk assessment, treatment, governance, and continual improvement (ISO, 2022). AI governance is also becoming formalized, and ISO/IEC 42001 specifies requirements for establishing, implementing, maintaining, and continually improving an AI management system (ISO, 2023a). These standards reinforce the same principle: trustworthy systems require disciplined management systems, not ad hoc heroics. This book translates that principle into project delivery practices that are realistic and repeatable.

Fifth, it is written to be used. The chapters build toward practical execution. Templates, checklists, and evidence bundle libraries are not decorative extras. They are operational tools. They are designed to reduce the effort of doing the right thing and to eliminate the "we will figure it out later" behavior that turns into incident reports.

This edition is also anchored in a delivery philosophy that aligns with modern project management thinking. PMI's principle-based approach emphasizes stewardship, value delivery, systems thinking, tailoring, and accountability, which naturally supports secure delivery leadership (PMI, 2021a). A secure technology project is an exercise in stewardship. You are a steward of customer data, business continuity, operational safety, and organizational reputation. That stewardship requires you to ask harder questions and to demand clearer evidence. It also requires you to accept that speed and security are not opposites. The real conflict is between speed and rework. Evidence-driven delivery reduces rework, which is how mature teams move fast without gambling.

At the center of this book is ADDIS 2.0, the methodology that organizes delivery into five phases: Analyze, Design, Develop or Acquire, Implement, Sustain. The phases are familiar, but the intent is sharper. ADDIS 2.0 is a control spine. It is designed to work across agile, hybrid, and traditional approaches, and across build and buy tracks. It introduces gates that function as decision checkpoints, each supported by an evidence bundle. The gates are where governance becomes real. They define what must be true before the organization invests further, increases exposure, or transitions into operations.

The gate mindset is simple to describe, yet difficult to practice without discipline. Before you move forward, you must be able to answer, with evidence, a small set of high-stakes questions. Are we solving the right problem and do we understand the risks of the solution? Is the architecture defensible and designed for control effectiveness? Have we proven security controls through testing, not just intention? Are we operationally ready, with monitoring, incident response pathways, and recovery plans? Have we formally accepted residual risk at the right level of authority? If you cannot answer these questions, you are not late, you are exposed.

A short, realistic conversation often reveals why gates matter.

- Product Lead: "We need to release this quarter, competitors are moving."
- Security Lead: "Understood, show me the evidence that the controls work."
- Project Lead: "We completed development and ran tests."
- Operations Lead: "What happens at 2 a.m. when it fails, and who owns recovery?"
- Executive Sponsor: "What risks are we accepting, and can we defend that decision later?"

When governance is weak, these questions feel like friction. When governance is mature, these questions feel like protection. They keep the enterprise from confusing urgency with readiness.

This book does not argue for perfection. It argues for proportionality. Not every project needs the same rigor. A low-risk internal tool should not be forced through heavyweight ceremony. But a high-risk customer-facing system, a regulated data platform, or an AI-enabled decision system absolutely requires deeper assurance. That is why this book repeatedly emphasizes risk tiering, tailoring, and evidence scaling. The structure stays consistent, the depth changes with risk.

It is also important to clarify what "AI-aware Security by Design" means in this edition. It does not mean that every project must build its own models or implement advanced AI governance tooling. It means that project leaders must recognize how AI changes threat models and accountability. If your system uses AI, you must consider adversarial inputs, prompt injection, data leakage through retrieval, model drift, and misuse cases that exploit the system's behavior. You must also define evaluation baselines and monitoring signals that can detect degradation and abuse. The NIST AI RMF and the Generative AI Profile support this lifecycle viewpoint, pushing organizations to treat AI risk management as continuous, context-driven, and governance-led (NIST, 2023; NIST, 2024b). This book turns that into deliverables, gate criteria, and evidence requirements that teams can execute.

This is why the book is organized into parts that reflect a logical progression from reality, to foundations, to governance mechanics, to phase playbooks, to AI overlay, to case studies.

Part ሀ explains the new reality of secure technology project delivery, including how AI and emerging technologies alter both risk and expectation, and how digital trust becomes a measurable delivery outcome. Part ለ establishes roles and operating models, because without decision rights and accountability, secure delivery collapses into confusion. Part ሐ introduces ADDIS 2.0 and gate governance, defining the control spine, the evidence bundle discipline, and the decision outcomes that prevent preventable failure. Part መ provides phase playbooks and gate reviews, with clear expectations for tasks, deliverables, quality review preparation, and pass or fail decision logic at each gate. Part V adds the AI governance overlay, because AI requires additional lifecycle controls that must be integrated into the same delivery spine. Part ረ provides practical execution tools, common pitfalls, and case studies, because leaders learn quickly when patterns are visible and reusable.

If you are reading this book as a project leader, the invitation is direct. Treat security, resilience, and compliance as delivery outcomes, not constraints. Use the templates and gates to structure conversations early, when change is cheap, not late, when change becomes crisis. If you are reading this as a security leader, the invitation is equally direct. Shift from late-stage approval to early-stage enablement but preserve independent assurance through evidence-based reviews. If you are reading this as an executive or board-facing leader, the invitation is to demand an evidence culture. Ask what is proven, what is assumed, what risks are accepted, and who owns them. These are governance questions, and modern governance increasingly expects them to be answered clearly (NIST, 2024b; U.S. Securities and Exchange Commission, 2023).

Finally, a word about tone. This book is intentionally practical. It is written to be used in real programs, with real constraints, and with real tradeoffs. It recognizes that delivery leaders live in the tension between urgency and discipline. It also recognizes that the enterprise cannot afford to treat security as a luxury item. If anything, secure delivery is the only way to make progress sustainable. When you build systems that are governable, observable, and resilient, you do not just reduce breaches. You reduce churn. You reduce downtime. You reduce rework. You improve decision quality. You increase confidence. You build an organization that can innovate without breaking trust.

That is the promise of secure technology project management in the age of AI and emerging technology. Not that you will never face incidents or surprises, but that when the storm comes, you will not be improvising in the dark. You will have a spine. You will have evidence. You will have accountable decisions. And you will have a delivery system designed to protect value, not merely produce features.

> "Buying technology does not transfer accountability."

ADDIS is the governance **spine,** **SDLC** is the execution ***engine.***

"ADDIS tells you when to decide, SDLC tells you how to build."

Practical takeaways

- **ADDIS controls progression.** Defines phase outcomes, evidence intent, and decision thresholds.
- **SDLC produces proof.** Builds, tests, scans, and validation results become gate-ready evidence.
- ***Security is designed, not appended.*** Controls are placed early and validated throughout delivery.
- **Evidence replaces reassurance.** *Confidence is not a control, verification is.*

When governance and execution are aligned, delivery becomes ***repeatable, not heroic.***

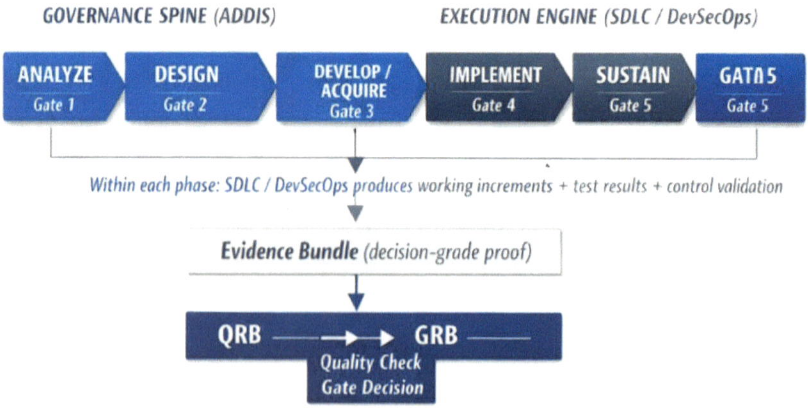

U

SECURE DELIVERY TODAY

INTRODUCTION

Part *U* exists for one reason: the ground has moved. Technology projects used to be judged by a familiar triangle of time, scope, and cost. That triangle still matters, but it no longer tells the truth on its own. A project can land on time and still fail in the only ways that matter now. It can break customer trust. It can expose regulated data. It can create an outage that spreads across business units like a domino line. It can ship a feature that becomes a liability because its controls were assumed, not proven. In the age of AI and hyper-connected ecosystems, the cost of "almost secure" has become too high to hide behind optimism.

Modern delivery lives inside a new operating reality. Your systems are no longer isolated products. They are ecosystems. They rely on cloud services, open-source components, third-party APIs, data pipelines, identity providers, and vendors whose update cycles are not aligned to your release calendar. This means your risk perimeter is not your network boundary, and your accountability cannot stop at your org chart. That is why secure technology project management is no longer a specialist discipline that shows up near the end. It is a delivery system. It is a governance posture. It is a set of evidence-driven habits that must be present from the first framing conversation to the first day of operations, and then through the life of the product.

The shift is also cultural. Organizations are being pushed toward clearer cybersecurity governance expectations from regulators, boards, and customers. In the United States, public companies face explicit expectations around cybersecurity incident disclosure timing and governance transparency, which changes how leaders treat readiness, detection, and response as board-level concerns (U.S. Securities and Exchange Commission, 2023). SEC In the European Union's financial sector context, DORA emphasizes operational resilience and ICT risk management as mandatory disciplines, including oversight of third-party ICT risk, which further forces projects to treat resilience, testing, and vendor accountability as part of delivery rather than post-delivery cleanup (European Insurance and Occupational Pensions Authority, n.d.). EIOPA These pressures are not just legal matters. They change the internal logic of project success. A project that cannot demonstrate control effectiveness, monitoring readiness, and response capability is not truly ready, even if the feature works.

That is where Part *U* begins. It establishes the reality you are delivering into, so the practices in later parts do not feel like bureaucracy. They will feel like survival, and more importantly, like disciplined value creation.

A new definition of "secure delivery," from intention to proof

Security by Design is often treated like a slogan. In a modern delivery environment, it has a stricter meaning. It means you design controls into the solution early, and you produce proof as you go. Not promises. Proof. That proof becomes the project's currency at governance gates, in audit conversations, and during incident response. It is the reason this book consistently uses the language of evidence bundles, decision outcomes, and review boards.

The NIST Cybersecurity Framework 2.0 provides a useful lens because it emphasizes outcomes that any organization can use to understand, assess, prioritize, and communicate cybersecurity efforts, and it expands attention to governance through the Govern function (NIST, 2024b). That message is highly practical for project leaders. It implies that cybersecurity is not only a technical control set. It is a management system that shapes priorities, decision rights, and accountability. A secure delivery leader therefore needs two competencies at once. The leader must understand enough technical security to ask hard questions and must also understand governance well enough to ensure those questions become decisions, actions, and measurable outcomes.

Secure delivery also requires secure engineering discipline. When security is bolted on late, it turns into expensive rework, friction with stakeholders, and "exceptions" that quietly become permanent. NIST's Secure Software Development Framework (SSDF) reinforces a basic truth: secure practices must be integrated into development, not treated as a separate activity that occurs after development (Souppaya et al., 2022). In project terms, that means security is not a milestone. It is an execution method. It is embedded in requirements quality, architecture decisions, coding practices, testing evidence, and release readiness criteria.

Now add AI. AI does not simply introduce new features; it introduces new uncertainty. AI systems can be correct today and drift tomorrow. They can behave differently across contexts. They can be manipulated through inputs that look harmless. They can expose data through retrieval pathways that were not designed as access control systems. That is why Part U treats AI as a delivery reality, not a future chapter. The NIST AI Risk Management Framework emphasizes managing AI risks across the lifecycle and improving the ability to incorporate trustworthiness considerations into design, development, use, and evaluation (NIST, 2023). For project leaders, the key implication is simple: if you are delivering AI-enabled capabilities, you need lifecycle controls and lifecycle evidence, not a one-time review.

AI also forces a more explicit conversation about misuse and abuse. OWASP's Top 10 for LLM applications is not merely a security list. It is a reminder that AI-enabled applications create new failure modes such as prompt injection and insecure output handling, which can turn a helpful feature into an exfiltration channel or an execution pathway if not constrained and tested (Open Worldwide Application Security Project, 2023). The moment AI output influences decisions, workflows, or code paths, you must design guardrails, define validation rules, and produce testing evidence that proves those guardrails work.

This is the heart of modern secure technology project delivery. You are not managing tasks; you are managing trust. Trust is earned through evidence.

What Causes Today's Project Failures

It is tempting to explain project failure as poor planning, weak communication, or changing requirements. Those still matter, but they do not capture the deeper failure patterns that dominate modern delivery. Many modern failures are systemic. They occur because governance is weak at the seams, where systems integrate with vendors, cloud services, data pipelines, and identity platforms. They occur because teams treat risk as a document rather than a decision mechanism. They occur because security is measured by activity rather than outcome. They occur because operational readiness is treated as an afterthought. They occur because organizations assume they can handle incidents, until the first incident proves otherwise.

The pressure is amplified by digital trust expectations. Customers assume that systems will keep working, keep data private, and keep business processes safe even when something goes wrong. Regulators increasingly assume the same. This shifts the burden onto project delivery leaders. Readiness is no longer "feature complete." Readiness is "safe to operate."

That is why this book insists on governance gates that evaluate evidence bundles, not slide decks. A gate decision is a decision about whether an organization is prepared to absorb the risk that comes with moving forward. If the project cannot show control effectiveness, monitoring readiness, and accountability, the right decision is not to proceed quickly. The right decision is to proceed safely, or not at all.

This is also why the book uses delivery governance constructs such as QRBs and GRBs (Quality and Gate Review Board). Quality review and governance review are not the same activity. Quality review is about completeness, internal consistency, and readiness for scrutiny. Governance review is about decision rights, risk posture, accountability, and whether the organization is willing to accept the residual risk that remains. Those disciplines keep projects from drifting into the danger zone where they are too far along to stop, but not safe enough to release.

AI forces a more explicit contract between project leaders and the organization. In traditional systems, requirements are often stable enough that you can define acceptance criteria and build deterministic tests. In AI-enabled systems, performance and behavior are influenced by data, prompts, retrieval content, user context, and model updates. The system is therefore not just code; it is a behavior pipeline. This changes how you scope, test, and govern.

First, AI introduces new assets that must be governed. Prompts become configuration. Retrieval indexes become access control surfaces. Evaluation datasets become quality baselines. Logs become sensitive because they may contain prompts and outputs. This is where data governance and security governance converge, and it must be handled intentionally.

Second, AI introduces new risks that are not captured well by traditional threat models unless you extend them. Prompt injection is one example, where untrusted input can manipulate behavior. Insecure output handling is another, where output is trusted without validation and becomes an exploitation pathway (Open Worldwide Application Security Project, 2023). Overreliance is another, where humans trust AI output beyond what is safe, creating operational and compliance harm. These risks are not theoretical. They show up in real systems, especially when AI tools are integrated into workflows with privileges.

Third, AI introduces the need for continuous evaluation and monitoring as a governance requirement. The AI RMF reinforces the need to manage AI risks across the lifecycle and to operationalize trustworthiness considerations (NIST, 2023). In project terms, this means a "done" definition must include monitoring signals, thresholds, incident pathways, and change control for models and prompts. Without those elements, an AI-enabled system is not governable.

Part *U* sets these expectations early because later chapters depend on them. If you treat AI risk as an add-on, your gates become ceremonial. If you treat AI risk as part of the delivery contract, your gates become protective.

Governance as a Delivery Requirement

A common mistake in technology organizations is to treat compliance as an external constraint rather than an internal design input. That approach fails under modern expectations. Compliance obligations often translate directly into control requirements, evidence requirements, and operational practices. ISO/IEC 27001 is a widely used standard for information security management systems, emphasizing an organized approach to managing information security risks through requirements that support continual improvement (ISO, 2022). When organizations align delivery with a management system mindset, they stop treating security as a checklist and start treating it as a system of accountability.

Regulatory expectations also increasingly reinforce operational resilience. Digital Operational Resilience Act (DORA), for instance, is intended to strengthen digital operational resilience in the EU financial sector, explicitly emphasizing the ability to withstand, respond to, and recover from ICT disruptions and cyberattacks (European Insurance and Occupational Pensions Authority, n.d.). Even if you are not in scope for DORA, the logic is spreading. Customers, boards, and insurers increasingly expect operational resilience as a default attribute of modern systems. That attribute must be built and verified, and it often must be demonstrated with evidence.

Disclosure expectations reinforce the same pressure. The SEC's cybersecurity disclosure rules require material incident disclosure in a defined timeframe after a materiality determination, which increases the importance of detection, assessment, documentation, and governance clarity (U.S. Securities and Exchange Commission, 2023). This does not mean every project must be governed as if it is a public company initiative. It does mean that project leaders should assume a future where incident handling, evidence quality, and governance transparency matter more than they did in the past.

Part *U* therefore frames governance, risk, compliance, and resilience as a delivery system. Not because it is fashionable, but because it is now the cost of entry for trustworthy digital operations.

Part *U* is designed to recalibrate how you define success. It does not replace project management fundamentals. It upgrades them for a reality where threats are adaptive, dependencies are external, systems are interconnected, and AI introduces new behavior uncertainty.

Chapter 1 will establish the modern landscape. It will show how AI and emerging technologies change project delivery assumptions, how digital trust becomes a measurable outcome, and why Security by Design must be treated as architecture and governance, not a slogan. It will also set the tone for how this book treats gates. Gates are not bureaucratic hurdles. They are decision points that protect the organization.

Chapter 2 will focus on the failure patterns that matter. It will translate cyber risk into delivery consequences, and delivery weaknesses into cyber outcomes. It will show why organizations repeat the same failure patterns, and how evidence-driven governance breaks those cycles. It will also introduce the idea of risk tiering, because not every project needs the same level of scrutiny. What matters is proportionality, which is a hallmark of mature governance.

Chapter 3 will anchor the system. Governance, risk, and compliance are often described as overhead. In modern delivery, they are the steering wheel. Chapter 3 will show how to treat Governance, Risk, and Compliance (GRC) as a delivery system that enables speed safely. It will connect frameworks such as CSF 2.0 and SSDF to practical governance behaviors, including accountability, evidence requirements, and operational readiness expectations (NIST, 2024b; Souppaya et al., 2022).

By the end of Part *U*, you should have a sharper definition of what "secure technology project management" means in practice. You will also have a clearer rationale for why later parts of the book insist on structured deliverables, gate evidence bundles, and review board decisions. You will understand that the book is not adding paperwork. It is building a trustworthy delivery spine.

The rest of the book then provides the machinery and operating model needed to execute that governance spine, with evidence expectations and practical guidance that translate intent into action. Part *U*, however, gives you the reason. It makes the case that in today's environment, the only sustainable speed is governed speed, and the only credible governance is governance proven by evidence.

Secure Projects in the AI Era

Technology projects used to be difficult because they were large and expensive. Today, they are difficult because they are deeply interconnected. A single delivery effort may depend on cloud identity services, third-party APIs, external data sources, distributed teams, and vendors whose code becomes part of your production environment. In that reality, project success cannot be measured only by schedule, scope, and budget. It must also be measured by trust, meaning whether the solution can be operated safely, defended under attack, and sustained without constant emergency work. This is consistent with modern cybersecurity governance thinking, where cybersecurity outcomes are treated as enterprise risk outcomes and must be prioritized, communicated, and governed like any other critical business risk (NIST, 2024b).

Artificial intelligence intensifies the situation in a specific way. It accelerates delivery while simultaneously expanding the risk surface. Teams can use AI to draft requirements, generate code, triage defects, and summarize security findings, which can be valuable when time and expertise are constrained. At the same time, AI-enabled systems introduce new categories of operational uncertainty, especially when model behavior changes across context, when outputs are probabilistic, or when a solution relies on evolving data and model versions. This chapter sets the foundation for the 2nd edition by explaining why AI changes the definition of a technology project, why partial security fails faster in this era, and why a gate-driven secure delivery method remains the most practical way to deliver value without turning innovation into an unpriced liability.

Traditional software projects are usually validated through deterministic expectations. Requirements describe expected behavior, tests confirm that behavior, and release criteria emphasize stability and functional completeness. AI-enabled systems challenge that assumption because outputs can vary based on prompt phrasing, retrieval context, model configuration, data drift, and user interaction patterns. This variability does not automatically make a system unsafe, but it does change what "verification" and "readiness" must look like in a real delivery environment. The NIST AI Risk Management Framework positions this issue directly by emphasizing that AI risk must be governed and managed across the lifecycle through structured activities that map, measure, and manage risk, rather than relying on informal assumptions or one-time validation (NIST, 2023).

In practice, AI introduces a set of delivery dependencies that must be treated as first-class project constraints. Data becomes a primary project dependency, not just an input. If a team cannot explain where training or retrieval data came from, whether it is lawful to use, how it is classified, and how it is protected, then the system's trust boundary is undefined. That uncertainty is not a technical detail; it is a governance failure. It undermines risk ownership and weakens the organization's ability to make defensible gate decisions. This fits the CSF 2.0 emphasis that organizations need a consistent way to understand, assess, prioritize, and communicate cybersecurity efforts, including those that span supply chains and external dependencies (NIST, 2024b).

AI also changes the nature of "testing." A system can pass functional test cases and still fail operationally if the AI component produces harmful outputs under realistic conditions, if it leaks sensitive data through unintended interactions, or if it behaves inconsistently when exposed to edge-case prompts. This is why the 2nd edition treats testing and validation as behavior assurance, not only feature confirmation. It also explains why a model's acceptance criteria must be defined early and measured consistently, because ambiguous acceptance criteria usually lead to ambiguous risk ownership. The AI RMF supports this orientation by emphasizing lifecycle evaluation and continuous risk management rather than static assumptions of correctness (NIST, 2023).

Finally, AI changes accountability. When a model influences a business outcome, accountability does not disappear, it becomes more urgent. Someone must own the decision to deploy, someone must own the monitoring strategy, and someone must own the mechanism to intervene when behavior deviates from safe expectations. If those responsibilities are not explicit, the organization eventually discovers the gap during an incident, a customer complaint, or an audit. The 2nd edition therefore treats role clarity and evidence bundles as governance tools that protect both the business and the delivery team.

The first edition makes a strong statement that security must be compulsory and integrated, not partial, and cosmetic. In the AI era, partial security fails faster because trust boundaries expand and uncertainty increases. A single weak control can become an amplification point. For example, weak access control on prompts and logs can expose sensitive data. Weak monitoring can allow drift to degrade outcomes silently. Weak supplier governance can allow insecure dependencies or model services to introduce unmanaged risk. These are not future problems; they are present-day failure patterns that appear quickly once a system is used at scale.

CSF 2.0 reinforces the practical reality behind this point. It describes cybersecurity management as an enterprise effort with governance at the center, and it highlights the need to communicate and prioritize cybersecurity outcomes for different stakeholders, including leadership and external parties when relevant (NIST, 2024b). When governance is weak, projects tend to substitute optimism for evidence. They rely on slide-based confidence, last-minute scanning, and informal risk acceptance. Those behaviors create the illusion of progress, but they often produce expensive rework and operational instability later.

From the development side, the Secure Software Development Framework makes the same argument in operational terms. SSDF describes a core set of secure development practices that should be integrated into any SDLC implementation, precisely because many SDLC models do not address security in sufficient detail by default (Souppaya et al., 2022). In other words, secure delivery is not an event at the end of the project, it is a discipline embedded throughout. When AI is in scope, this discipline becomes even more important because the system's risk profile includes both software vulnerabilities and model-behavior weaknesses. NIST SP 800-218A extends SSDF thinking specifically to generative AI and foundation model contexts, reinforcing that secure practices must be adapted to AI model development and AI system usage patterns (NIST, 2024a).

The four guiding principles of the 2nd edition

The 2nd edition applies four principles consistently, not as slogans, but as practical controls that appear in phases, artifacts, and gate reviews.

The first principle is that security is an architectural requirement, not merely a test result. When security is treated as an end-stage scan, it becomes a negotiation against deadlines. When security is treated as design intent, it becomes part of the project's definition of done. SSDF supports this principle by emphasizing secure practices integrated into the lifecycle, including requirements planning, secure design, secure coding, and verification activities that produce evidence (Souppaya et al., 2022).

The second principle is that governance is a delivery capability. Governance exists to define decision rights, enforce accountability, and make risk ownership visible. CSF 2.0 reinforces that cybersecurity outcomes need governance context so organizations can align priorities, communicate expectations, and manage risk consistently across the enterprise (NIST, 2024b). This is why the book treats gates as real decision points supported by evidence bundles, not ceremonial reviews.

The third principle is that evidence beats confidence. A progress update is not proof. Evidence is what allows leadership to make defensible decisions, and evidence is what supports organizational learning after release. Evidence bundles also reduce variance across projects because teams follow a repeatable structure for producing, packaging, and reviewing deliverables.

The fourth principle is that AI raises the assurance baseline. When AI is in scope, teams must add controls around data provenance, evaluation rigor, monitoring readiness, and model change governance. The AI RMF exists precisely because AI introduces distinct risks and requires an explicit risk management posture that spans design, deployment, and ongoing operation (NIST, 2023).

Why ADDIS and Secure SDLC remain the right response.

The ADDIS methodology remains central to this book because it turns delivery into a disciplined sequence that produces measurable outputs. It creates a common operating picture across technical teams, governance boards, and business sponsors. It also gives the organization a practical mechanism for saying "not yet," which is one of the most valuable governance capabilities in high-pressure environments. The method's gate discipline aligns with CSF 2.0's focus on governance-driven risk management because both require structured communication of risk posture and readiness, not informal optimism (NIST, 2024b).

Secure SDLC provides the execution layer that makes lifecycle discipline meaningful. It ensures security requirements, threat modeling, secure coding, verification, and sustainment controls are embedded throughout the lifecycle. SSDF strengthens this approach by providing a high-level set of practices that can be integrated into any SDLC implementation, which is especially important because many SDLC approaches do not natively define security requirements at sufficient depth (Souppaya et al., 2022). When AI is introduced, SP 800-218A further clarifies how secure practices should be adapted for AI model development and generative AI system contexts, so the organization can maintain evidence-driven discipline even as the technical paradigm changes (NIST, 2024a).

This is where the 2nd edition introduces the AI overlay concept. The overlay does not replace baseline gates or baseline secure SDLC practices. It adds AI-specific evidence requirements when AI is part of scope. In analysis, that means clarifying data readiness, provenance, lawful use, and oversight expectations. In design, it means defining misuse cases, evaluation criteria, and guardrails. In implementation, it means validating monitoring, rollback, and intervention mechanisms. In sustainment, it means enforcing drift monitoring and controlled change governance. The AI RMF provides a structured foundation for this approach because it frames AI risk management as a lifecycle responsibility rather than a one-time certification event (NIST, 2023).

"In the AI era, 'works' is not enough, 'controlled' is the standard."

3

Cyber Risk and Project Failure Patterns

Technology projects do not fail in the abstract. They fail in predictable ways, and most of those failures can be traced back to weak governance, unclear accountability, and late security integration. In the first edition, the message was already clear: cyber risk is inseparable from delivery risk. In the second edition, that truth becomes even sharper because today's systems are more connected, more dependent on external services, and more exposed to fast-moving threats. In practical terms, cybersecurity is not merely a technical domain. It is an enterprise risk outcome that must be governed, prioritized, and communicated as part of business management, which is exactly the posture emphasized in the NIST Cybersecurity Framework 2.0 (NIST, 2024b).

A useful metaphor is this: a technology project is not only building a house, it is building a house on a busy street while traffic keeps changing. You can have perfect interior design, but if the doors do not lock, if the wiring is unsafe, and if the foundation is unstable, the house is not livable. In modern delivery, the "street" is the threat landscape, the vendor ecosystem, and the regulatory environment. You cannot pause it. You can only design and govern your project to survive inside it. That is why secure technology project management must treat security as a design constraint and an operational requirement, not a late-stage inspection (Souppaya et al., 2022).

Many teams still treat cybersecurity incidents as interruptions that happen to projects. The more accurate view is that cybersecurity risk is part of the project's physics. It shapes architecture, data flows, identity controls, testing strategy, rollout sequencing, and operational readiness. When you adopt that view, security stops being the "department of no," and becomes part of engineering reality. This aligns with secure development expectations described in the Secure

Software Development Framework, which emphasizes integrating secure practices across the lifecycle, so risk is addressed early and continuously, rather than only near release (Souppaya et al., 2022).

This shift matters because modern systems rarely operate alone. A project may rely on cloud identity, hosted databases, SaaS platforms, managed CI/CD (Continuous Integration / Continuous Delivery) pipelines, and third-party libraries. Every dependency extends the trust boundary. Every integration increases the number of places where misconfiguration, weak access control, or insecure defaults can become a breach path. The NIST Cybersecurity Framework 2.0 explicitly recognizes this kind of risk reality by placing governance at the center and emphasizing enterprise-wide and supply-chain considerations as part of managing cybersecurity outcomes (NIST, 2024b).

Digital trust is the confidence that a system will behave safely and reliably, even under stress. Customers experience trust as availability, privacy, correctness, and transparency. Executives experience trust as reduced volatility and fewer reputational shocks. Regulators experience trust as compliance, accountability, and evidence. Engineers experience trust as systems that can be monitored, defended, and maintained without constant firefighting. These perspectives differ, but they converge around one requirement: proof.

That is why this book repeatedly returns to evidence bundles, gate reviews, and traceable decisions. In a high-trust environment, teams do not simply say, "we are secure." They show that controls were designed, tested, and validated, and they show that risk acceptance was explicit rather than accidental. This is consistent with the SSDF's emphasis on demonstrable secure development practices and with CSF 2.0's governance-centered framing of cybersecurity outcomes (Souppaya et al., 2022; NIST, 2024b).

AI increases the stakes of trust because it can change how decisions are made and how outcomes are produced. When AI influences an operational workflow, a project must prove not only that the feature works, but also that behavior is monitored and bounded. The AI Risk Management Framework reinforces this lifecycle posture by emphasizing structured risk management across governance, measurement, and ongoing management activities (NIST, 2023). In other words, trust in AI systems is not a one-time certification. It is an operating discipline.

Common Tech Project Failures Across Industries

Technology projects fail in many forms, but the root causes are usually the same. Secure technology project management is not about eliminating all risk. It is about preventing avoidable breakdowns and making the remaining risks explicit, owned, and managed. The issues highlighted below matter most because they repeat across organizations, escalate fast, and create expensive downstream impact when they are ignored.

A common failure pattern is weak identity and access governance. Teams focus heavily on application features and give less attention to identity design, privileged access, role segmentation, and operational access workflows. Then the project reaches implementation, and the environment is "temporarily open" to meet a deadline. Temporary becomes permanent, and the system goes live with excessive permissions. This is not merely a technical oversight. It is a governance breakdown because it indicates that release readiness was declared without proof of control readiness. CSF 2.0 supports treating these outcomes as enterprise governance concerns, rather than isolated security tasks (NIST, 2024b).

Another common failure pattern is unclear data control design. Projects often treat data classification, retention, and deletion as documentation tasks instead of engineering requirements. The result is that sensitive data becomes widely accessible, logs capture confidential content, and integrations replicate regulated information across environments. This risk becomes more severe when AI is introduced because prompts, retrieval contexts, and model outputs can unintentionally expose sensitive material if design controls are weak. The AI RMF emphasizes data and context as central to AI risk and highlights the need for governance and management practices that address those risks throughout the lifecycle (NIST, 2023).

A third failure pattern is supply chain blindness. Teams adopt third-party libraries, vendor services, and SaaS platforms without fully defining security expectations, audit rights, incident notification requirements, and configuration responsibilities. This creates a fragile system where the organization assumes security exists but cannot prove it. The SSDF was developed precisely because organizations need repeatable practices to reduce this kind of risk, including managing third-party components and integrating secure practices into the lifecycle (Souppaya et al., 2022). CSF 2.0 also reinforces the importance of governance and supply chain outcomes, which aligns with why this book treats acquisition as a first-class delivery path, not a secondary track (NIST, 2024b).

A fourth failure pattern is "testing without meaning." Many teams run tests, but the tests do not reflect real-world behavior. They validate functionality but not resilience. They validate performance but not abuse paths. They validate happy paths but ignore adversarial and edge-case conditions. Secure technology project management corrects this by ensuring that threat modeling, test planning, and validation are treated as phase deliverables rather than optional add-ons. This is consistent with the SSDF's orientation toward integrating verification and validation activities into secure development practices (Souppaya et al., 2022).

A fifth failure pattern, increasingly common now, is unmanaged AI adoption. It appears as shadow AI tools used in development, unapproved AI integrations in business workflows, or rushed deployments where evaluation criteria were never defined. The dialogue below captures the pattern:

A project sponsor may say, “We need an AI feature to stay competitive.” The delivery team responds, “We can integrate it quickly.” Then governance asks, “How will you evaluate behavior, prevent data leakage, and monitor drift?” If the answer is silence, the project is not missing a feature, it is missing a safety case. The AI RMF exists because this gap is widespread, and it formalizes how organizations can move from excitement to structured risk management (NIST, 2023).

Security by Design as a delivery discipline

Security by Design is often spoken about as a value statement, but in practice it is an execution discipline. It requires that security requirements are treated as real requirements, that architecture decisions are made with threat modeling, that secure engineering practices are enforced, and that release readiness includes operational controls. This is why the SSDF is highly relevant to project delivery, even when teams think of it as a “software security” document. Its central message is that secure development is achieved through repeatable practices integrated across the lifecycle, producing evidence that controls were applied (Souppaya et al., 2022).

The ADDIS method reinforces this discipline by converting it into a lifecycle model with gates. Gates create structured moments where leadership must decide whether the project has earned the right to proceed. In a mature environment, gates prevent “late truth,” meaning the discovery of risk after the organization has already committed resources, integrations, and operational change. CSF 2.0 supports this governance posture by emphasizing that cybersecurity outcomes require governance structures, accountability, and communication at the enterprise level (NIST, 2024b).

When AI is in scope, Security by Design must expand to include AI-specific safeguards. That does not mean replacing the baseline security discipline. It means adding controls for data provenance, evaluation rigor, monitoring, and change governance. The AI RMF supports this integrated posture by framing AI risk management as a lifecycle activity, not a one-time decision (NIST, 2023).

How This Chapter Improves Delivery Discipline

This chapter improves delivery discipline by increasing precision in how teams define readiness and how leaders make decisions. When you can recognize the failure modes that repeat across projects, you can design governance that prevents them instead of reacting after damage is done. That starts with language. Digital trust is not a slogan. It can be translated into measurable expectations, such as control effectiveness, auditability, and operational reliability. Once trust is expressed as outcomes, it can be supported by artifacts, test evidence, and decision records. In the same way, cyber risk is not an interruption to delivery. It is a delivery constraint. When it is treated as a constraint from day one, security work becomes planned work, and schedules become more realistic.

The chapters that follow convert these principles into practical execution controls. You will see ownership clarified through governance structures, decision rights, and RACI models that eliminate orphan risk. You will see lifecycle discipline enforced through the ADDIS phases and gate reviews that require evidence, not reassurance. You will also see evidence bundles used to make decisions repeatable and defensible across teams and vendors. This approach aligns with modern guidance that treats cybersecurity as a governed business outcome and secure development as an integrated lifecycle practice, while accounting for AI risk as a structured category of enterprise risk (NIST, 2024b; Souppaya et al., 2022).

GRC for Technology Delivery

Many organizations still treat Governance, Risk, and Compliance as a separate function that runs parallel to project delivery. The project team builds, and then "GRC" reviews near the end. That separation looks convenient because it preserves speed and avoids friction early. In reality, it pushes risk discovery into the most expensive moments of the lifecycle, when architecture choices are already locked, vendors are already selected, and deadlines have already hardened. The outcome is familiar, delivery becomes fragile, security requirements become last-minute negotiations, and compliance turns into a scramble for documents instead of a disciplined confirmation of readiness.

This second edition treats GRC as something more practical and more powerful. GRC is the delivery system that makes security, quality, and trust repeatable across projects. It defines decision rights and minimum control expectations, it forces accountability to be visible, and it creates evidence that supports defensible Go or No-Go decisions. This approach aligns with modern cybersecurity governance guidance that positions governance as a central outcome and frames cybersecurity risk as enterprise risk rather than a narrow technical concern (NIST, 2024b).

Governance, risk, and compliance

A simple way to understand GRC is to translate it into three operational questions. Governance answers why the organization is taking a specific technology risk and who has the authority to accept it. It clarifies strategy alignment, accountability, escalation paths, and the boundaries that teams must not cross. Risk answers what could go wrong, how severe the impact could be, how likely it is, and which controls reduce exposure to an acceptable level. Compliance answers how the organization proves that required controls were implemented, reviewed, tested, and maintained. When these three elements are integrated, the project does not merely "move forward." It moves forward with clarity and traceability.

This is where many teams get the relationship wrong. Governance is not a committee calendar. It is a decision mechanism. Risk is not a spreadsheet. It is a prioritization tool that shapes design and execution choices. Compliance is not paperwork. It is evidence discipline. ISO/IEC 27001 reinforces this management-system mindset by expecting organizations to operate information security through defined responsibilities, controlled processes, and continual improvement rather than one-time efforts (ISO, 2022). When teams adopt this mindset, they stop asking "How do we satisfy compliance at the end?" and start asking "How do we produce proof as we build?"

When GRC is treated as external, the project learns the truth too late. Controls are identified after the design is already chosen. Data handling requirements are clarified after integrations are built. Vendor obligations are discovered after contracts are signed. At that point, the project has limited options. It can accept risk quietly, it can delay go-live and absorb cost, or it can deploy and hope the system behaves well in production. None of these choices are mature governance. They are forced compromises created by timing failure.

The symptoms often appear as "surprises," but they are predictable. The project reaches implementation and discovers that privileged access is poorly designed, logging is incomplete, encryption is inconsistent, incident response is not integrated, or third-party responsibilities are unclear. These are not minor technical issues. They are governance failures because they indicate that decision-makers allowed progress without verified readiness. The NIST Cybersecurity Framework 2.0 emphasizes governance and accountability as essential to managing cybersecurity outcomes, especially in environments that rely on external relationships and supply chains

(NIST, 2024b). In other words, the framework is not asking for more meetings. It is asking for better decisions supported by clearer accountability.

A practical GRC model can be understood as three layers that reinforce each other. The first layer is policy and minimum standards. These standards define what “acceptable” means for identity, access control, data protection, logging, vulnerability management, secure configuration, and vendor obligations. Without a baseline, each project creates its own interpretation of security, and the organization cannot scale assurance. The baseline also protects project teams. It reduces negotiation and ambiguity. It sets a clear minimum so teams can focus on delivery instead of re-litigating fundamentals.

The second layer is project-level risk execution. This is where the project translates minimum standards into phase deliverables and engineering work. It includes risk analysis, threat-informed design, security requirements, testing plans, and operational readiness activities. It also includes exceptions. Exceptions will occur in real environments, especially when budgets, legacy constraints, and vendor limitations collide. Mature organizations do not pretend exceptions do not exist. They make them visible, document their rationale, assign owners, and require compensating controls or closure dates. This is how risk acceptance becomes an explicit leadership decision rather than an accidental project habit.

The third layer is evidence and oversight. This is the layer that converts good intentions into defensible outcomes. It includes quality reviews, gate reviews, and decision records that capture what was reviewed, what risks remain, and why leadership decided to proceed. Evidence is also what makes learning possible. When incidents occur, the organization can compare what it believed at the gate with what actually happened in production, then improve standards and templates. This is consistent with secure development guidance that emphasizes producing demonstrable outcomes through repeatable practices integrated across the lifecycle (Souppaya et al., 2022).

How gates operationalize GRC inside ADDIS

ADDIS turns GRC from abstract expectation into lifecycle enforcement. Each phase produces outputs that become the next phase's inputs, and each gate requires proof that readiness has been achieved before the project proceeds. This design directly addresses the most common GRC failure, which is late truth. Gates force truth early.

From a governance perspective, gates do four things that matter. First, they force timing. Security and compliance cannot be postponed indefinitely because a gate requires evidence now, not later. Second, they force ownership. A risk register becomes useful only when risks have owners and treatments. A gate decision makes ownership explicit because the decision record identifies who approved, who accepted conditions, and who is responsible for closing gaps. Third, gates force consistency. When the same gate evidence bundle pattern is applied across projects, leadership can compare projects, auditors can evaluate controls more reliably, and the PMO can detect drift in execution quality. Fourth, gates force learning. Every gate becomes a checkpoint that produces feedback, and that feedback becomes improvements to templates, standards, and training.

The quality of a gate depends on the quality of the evidence behind it. This is why the book treats evidence bundles as a core delivery asset. An evidence bundle is not a deck. It is a structured package that includes artifacts, test results, approvals, and updated risk status. This logic aligns with secure development practice guidance that emphasizes integrated security tasks and verifiable results rather than end-stage security theater (Souppaya et al., 2022). It also aligns with the governance-centered posture emphasized in CSF 2.0, where accountability and prioritization support defensible risk decisions (NIST, 2024b).

AI raises the assurance bar, but it does not change the core logic of GRC. Governance still defines who can approve, who is accountable, and who can accept residual risk. Risk management still identifies exposures, ranks them by impact and likelihood, and drives the selection of controls. Compliance still requires proof that commitments were met and that controls operate as intended. What changes with AI is the set of risks that must be managed actively, and the depth of evidence required to justify production use with confidence.

AI systems depend on more than code. They depend on data quality, data provenance, and the conditions in which they are used. If training data is incomplete, biased, outdated, or poorly labeled, the system can behave unpredictably even when the engineering is strong. AI also introduces failure modes that do not look like traditional software defects. A feature can pass functional testing and still cause harm by producing misleading outputs, revealing sensitive information, or behaving inconsistently across user groups and contexts. Because of this, readiness cannot be proven only by "the system runs" or "the test suite passed." Readiness must include proof that the organization understands the intended use, can define unacceptable use, and can detect harmful behavior quickly when real users interact with the system.

This is why gate readiness needs stronger evaluation discipline when AI is in scope. Evaluation criteria must be defined in advance and tied to measurable thresholds. Testing must represent realistic use cases, including edge cases, adversarial prompts where relevant, and high-impact workflows where errors could create safety, financial, or compliance consequences. Evidence bundles should show what was tested, what results were achieved, what risks remain, and what conditions were imposed to manage residual risk. Just as important, gates must confirm that monitoring exists after go live. For AI, monitoring is not optional. It is how the organization detects drift, degradation, unexpected failure patterns, and misuse. In practical terms, decision-makers should be able to answer two questions at every gate: What could this AI capability do wrong, and how will we know quickly when it starts doing it?

This is where the AI overlay fits naturally. The organization does not create a competing governance track or a special lane that only AI projects follow. Instead, it activates additional evidence requirements inside the same gates. The lifecycle remains consistent. The decision forums remain consistent. What changes is the evidence depth when AI is present. That approach reduces confusion across teams, vendors, and reviewers. It also prevents AI risk from being treated as a lightweight ethics exercise, rather than as an operational control requirement that must be designed, tested, monitored, and governed.

Governance is the "*why,*"
risk is the "*what,*"
compliance is the "*proof.*"

ʌ

DELIVERY ROLES AND FOUNDATIONS

INTRODUCTION

Part ʋ described the new reality. Part ʌ is where that reality becomes executable. This section is not about collecting more frameworks, it is about building an operating model that can actually deliver secure outcomes, repeatedly, under pressure. The modern project environment is noisy. Stakeholders want speed. Threat actors want opportunity. Regulators want accountability. Operations teams want stability. Customers want trust, and they will withdraw it quickly if you give them a reason. When the room gets loud, the teams that succeed are not the teams with the most slides. They are the teams with clear roles, clear decision rights, and a delivery model that turns intent into evidence.

A useful way to think about Part ʌ is to treat it like the foundation of a building. You can decorate the top floors all you want, but if the foundation is weak, the whole structure sways when the first storm hits. Secure technology project management is that storm season. AI has accelerated development cycles and expanded what is possible, but it has also expanded what can fail. Cloud ecosystems and vendor dependencies have made delivery more scalable, but they have also made the blast radius wider. DevOps has made release frequency higher, but it has also made control drift easier. The only sustainable response is to make governance and security part of the operating model, not a side process that shows up at the end.

Modern standards and guidance point toward this same conclusion, even when they use different language. The NIST Cybersecurity Framework 2.0 is built around outcomes that help organizations understand and manage cybersecurity risk, and it explicitly emphasizes governance as a first-class concern, not an afterthought (NIST, 2024b). NIST's Secure Software Development Framework similarly frames secure development as a set of practices that must be integrated into the software development life cycle, rather than bolted on after the code is written (Souppaya et al., 2022). PMI's modern direction reinforces another critical idea: projects exist to deliver value, and the organization must treat delivery as an interconnected system rather than isolated work streams, which makes governance, accountability, and tailoring essential for success (PMI, 2021a; PMI, 2021b).

Part ٨ takes those high-level ideas and turns them into practical mechanics. It answers questions that determine whether your secure delivery approach will work in the real world. Who owns risk decisions, and who only advises. Who can approve an exception, and who must remediate it. Who defines acceptance criteria, and who verifies them. Who decides whether the system is safe to operate, and who will carry the pager when it is not. Without clarity, security becomes a debate. With clarity, security becomes a decision system.

At a human level, you can feel the difference between a project with role clarity and one without it. In the unclear environment, meetings become negotiations. People speak in cautious language. Risks are described but not owned. You see phrases like, "We should probably," "It would be good if," and "Security will review later." In the mature environment, the language shifts. People say, "This is the control owner," "This is the evidence required," "This is the go or no-go criterion," and "This is the operational handover condition." Those phrases may sound rigid at first, but they are actually what enables speed. They reduce rework, reduce friction, and reduce the number of surprises that arrive after the point of no return.

This part also reframes a quiet truth that only experienced practitioners say out loud: most security failures in projects are not caused by a lack of security tools. They are caused by a lack of operating discipline. Controls are not implemented because responsibilities are fuzzy. Testing is skipped because schedules are unrealistic. Exceptions are granted because decision rights are unclear. Monitoring is missing because operations was not involved early. Vendor risk becomes a late scramble because procurement and security were not integrated from the start. The technology is rarely the only problem. The operating model is the problem.

Roles are not job titles, they are risk controls.

One of the most dangerous myths in technology organizations is that "we have a CISO, so security is covered." Leadership matters, but leadership alone cannot carry delivery. Security by Design requires distributed accountability, and that accountability must be expressed through roles that map to decisions and evidence. When roles are treated as job titles, the project will still drift. When roles are treated as risk controls, the project stays aligned.

Start with a simple premise: every critical risk must have an owner who can act. That owner may not fix everything personally, but they must have the authority to drive remediation, to escalate, and to refuse unsafe progression when evidence is weak. NIST CSF 2.0 emphasizes cybersecurity as an organizational risk management discipline that must be understood, prioritized, and communicated, which implicitly requires clear accountability across the enterprise (NIST, 2024b). In practice, that means the project leader, the product leader, security, architecture, operations, and sometimes legal or compliance must share a structured responsibility model, not a vague agreement.

PMI's principle-based approach supports this mindset. Principles such as stewardship, systems thinking, risk, quality, and value are not abstract ideas, they imply behaviors and responsibilities that must be assigned and sustained throughout delivery (PMI, 2021a). PMI If a project claims to value stewardship but has no clear owner for data handling decisions, it is not practicing stewardship. If a team claims to care about quality but has no mechanism for independent validation, quality is a slogan, not a discipline. If a project claims to manage risk but treats risk logs as paperwork, risk management is theater.

Part ٨ therefore clarifies the roles that commonly exist in technology delivery and draws sharper boundaries between them. Project management, product management, and program management are often blended in practice. That blending can be healthy when it is intentional, and the organization understands who holds which decision rights. It becomes harmful when it is accidental and nobody can tell who is accountable for outcome, risk acceptance, and operational readiness. A project manager may be accountable for schedule, coordination, and gate readiness packaging. A product manager may be accountable for value outcomes, customer needs, and prioritization tradeoffs. A program manager may be accountable for cross-project dependencies and portfolio-level outcomes. A PMO may be accountable for enforcing governance standards, stage criteria, and evidence quality. Security and architecture are accountable for defining and validating control expectations, and operations are accountable for running the system safely after release. Those distinctions are not academic. They prevent the most common failure mode in secure delivery: the assumption that someone else is handling it.

This section also makes a point that matters even more in the AI era. AI introduces new assets that behave like code but are not always treated like code. Prompts, retrieval indexes, evaluation datasets, model configurations, and monitoring thresholds all influence behavior. When they are not assigned owners, they become orphan assets. Orphan assets become exploit paths. The NIST AI RMF emphasizes lifecycle risk management for AI systems and the need to incorporate trustworthiness considerations into design, development, use, and evaluation (NIST, 2023). That is a direct call for role clarity. If no one owns the evaluation baseline, drift becomes invisible. If no one owns prompt governance, injection becomes "someone else's problem." If no one owns data provenance, the organization cannot explain why the model behaves the way it does.

So, Part ʌ treats role clarity as a security control. It is one of the cheapest controls you can implement, and one of the most effective.

Many organizations design operating models as if they are organizational charts with meeting schedules. That approach fails in modern delivery because it does not address the real issue. The real issue is decision flow. Who decides, based on what evidence, at what time, with what accountability, and with what escalation path.

A mature operating model answers these questions early and then enforces them consistently. It integrates value delivery with risk governance. PMI frames value delivery as a system, not a single project activity, which means portfolios, programs, projects, product operations, and enabling functions must interact through structured information flows (PMI, 2021b). That framing aligns with secure delivery because cybersecurity and resilience are not produced by one team at the end. They emerge from coordinated decisions across the system.

IT governance frameworks reinforce the same idea. ISO/IEC 38500:2024 provides guiding principles for governance of IT, aimed at effective, efficient, and acceptable use of IT across the organization, which is another way of saying governance must shape decisions, not merely observe them (ISO, 2024). COBIT, as a governance and management framework for enterprise information and technology, similarly emphasizes aligning technology with enterprise objectives through a holistic governance system (ISACA, 2019). You do not need to adopt every component of these frameworks to benefit from their message. The message is that governance exists to enable value while optimizing risk, and it must be designed as part of how the enterprise operates.

Part ٨ therefore focuses on practical operating model patterns that work. It clarifies how a PMO can evolve into a "security and value office," not by taking over security work, but by enforcing consistent delivery governance, evidence standards, and gate readiness expectations. It shows how architecture and security functions can operate as enabling partners rather than late-stage auditors, by participating earlier in requirements and design while still preserving independent assurance. It shows how operations can be engaged as a first-class stakeholder so that monitoring, incident response, and handover readiness are built into the definition of done, not discovered when the system hits production.

This is where the book's gate governance philosophy becomes important. Gates are not only control points. They are operating model rituals. If you design gates well, you create predictable decision moments where the organization can pause, examine evidence, and either proceed safely or correct course. If you design gates poorly, they become rubber stamps. Rubber-stamp gates are worse than no gates because they create false confidence.

Operating models also determine how you handle exceptions. Every technology organization has exceptions because reality is messy. The question is whether exceptions are controlled. A controlled exception has a documented rationale, a risk owner, a time limit, compensating controls, and a revalidation date. An uncontrolled exception is a permanent hole in your control fabric. Role clarity and board governance are the difference.

Secure Delivery Execution Model

Once roles and operating models are clear, you need an execution engine. That engine is your SDLC, and in modern organizations it is increasingly expressed through DevSecOps practices. Many teams say "we do DevOps" but still treat security as external. That is not DevSecOps. DevSecOps means security is embedded into the pipeline as code, automation, and repeatable checks, and it produces evidence that can be used for assurance and governance.

NIST's SSDF provides a structured set of secure software development practices that can be integrated into any SDLC model, which is exactly what modern organizations need because they rarely operate in a single development approach (Souppaya et al., 2022). Some teams use agile. Some use hybrid. Some use phased delivery for regulated systems. Some acquire vendor solutions and integrate them. SSDF does not force one method. It provides practices that must exist regardless of method.

DevSecOps makes those practices operational. NIST SP 800-204C provides guidance on implementing DevSecOps primitives for cloud-native applications, describing pipelines that take source code through stages such as build, test, deployment, and operations with automated feedback mechanisms (Chandramouli, 2022). This guidance matters to project leaders because it turns security from a meeting into a mechanism. The pipeline becomes the place where security testing, artifact integrity checks, and policy enforcement live. Evidence becomes a byproduct of doing the work correctly, not an after-the-fact reconstruction.

This is also where reliability becomes inseparable from security. Modern systems must remain dependable under stress. Site Reliability Engineering literature emphasizes designing and operating systems with a mindset where reliability and security reinforce each other, and where operational practices and automation help sustain production quality (Beyer et al., 2016). In practice, this means secure delivery is not finished when code merges. It is finished when the system can be operated safely with monitoring, incident response capability, change control discipline, and clear ownership.

AI once again increases the stakes. AI features are often delivered as integrations with external model services, internal model endpoints, or retrieval systems connected to enterprise data. This expands the number of interfaces and the number of trust boundaries. It also expands the importance of identity, authorization, logging, and validation controls. When the organization chooses DevSecOps practices and a secure SDLC approach, it gains the ability to enforce consistent controls and produce consistent evidence even while moving quickly.

Part ለ therefore frames secure delivery foundations as a three-part structure. First, choose an SDLC model or combination of models that fits the organization's work. Second, integrate SSDF-aligned secure development practices into those models so that security is embedded, not appended. Third, operationalize those practices through DevSecOps automation where possible, so that security becomes repeatable, measurable, and auditable.

What This Part Delivers

Part ለ prepares you to execute the rest of the book without confusion. It builds the human and organizational mechanics required for ADDIS gate governance and evidence bundles to work in practice.

Chapter 4 clarifies the distinctions and overlaps among project management, product management, program management, and the PMO. It treats these not as competing disciplines, but as complementary roles that must be designed intentionally to reduce risk and increase value delivery.

Chapter 5 expands the view to portfolio governance and reframes the PMO as a security and value office. This does not mean the PMO becomes a security team. It means the PMO becomes the engine that enforces delivery discipline, including gate criteria, deliverable quality, evidence traceability, and accountability alignment across projects.

Chapter 6 brings the execution engine into focus, comparing SDLC models, secure SDLC expectations, and DevSecOps as a modern delivery mechanism. It anchors the discussion in practices that are supported by widely recognized guidance like SSDF and DevSecOps implementation references, so your approach does not depend on institutional memory or local preference (Souppaya et al., 2022; Chandramouli, 2022).

By the end of Part ለ, you should be able to look at any project and quickly diagnose whether it has a delivery foundation capable of producing secure outcomes. You will know whether decision rights are clear. You will know whether evidence expectations exist. You will know whether the PMO and governance boards are structured to help or structured to delay. You will know whether security is embedded in the SDLC and operationalized in pipelines, or whether security is still waiting at the end of the line.

If Part ሀ was the warning that the weather has changed, Part ለ is the construction plan for building a house that can withstand that weather. Then Part ሐ, መ and Part ሠ will give you the gate governance spine and the phase playbooks, turning this foundation into a repeatable delivery system. Part ረ will layer AI governance explicitly on top of it, and Part ሰ will give you Case Studies and Practical Execution to make it real.

In secure technology project management, the details are not decoration. They are the difference between a successful launch and a painful lesson. Roles, operating models, and secure delivery foundations are those details, and they are where disciplined organizations separate themselves from hopeful ones.

Roles make governance *real.*

"Controls fail most often when ownership is unclear."

Practical takeaways

- **Decide ownership before you decide design.** If risk acceptance, control ownership, and operational ownership are unclear, the project will move fast in the wrong direction.
- **Treat decision rights as a control.** A clear RACI and escalation path prevents "silent approvals" and protects the organization when pressure rises.
- **Make gates enforce accountability.** QRB validates completeness and quality, GRB makes the decision and records who owns remaining risk and conditions.
- **Operational ownership is not a handoff event.** The operating team must be identified early, involved throughout, and equipped with runbooks, monitoring, and authority.

From Roles to Decisions to Evidence

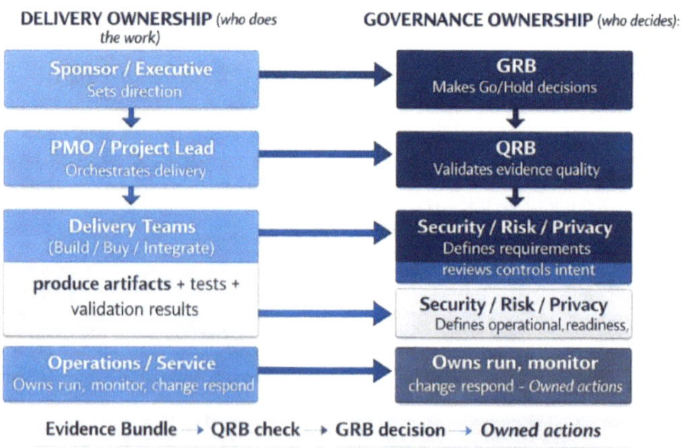

A delivery model is only as strong as its ***decision rights****, ownership clarity, and evidence discipline.*

Delivery Roles and the PMO

Organizations rarely fail at technology delivery because they lack intelligence or ambition. They fail because responsibility is blurred, decision rights are unclear, and the operating model is inconsistent. In one meeting, a leader says, “This is a project.” In the next meeting, another leader says, “No, it is a product.” A third person insists it is a program, because it involves multiple workstreams and vendors. The words are familiar, yet the meaning shifts like sand underfoot. When language drifts, accountability drifts with it. That is when security requirements become optional, risks are accepted quietly, and the delivery team loses the ability to separate urgent pressure from responsible readiness. In modern environments, this confusion is not just inconvenient. It is dangerous, because digital trust is now part of business value, and it can be lost quickly when a system is released without clear ownership and disciplined governance (NIST, 2024b).

This chapter establishes a clear operating picture. It distinguishes project management, product management, and program management in a way that is practical rather than theoretical. It then explains the role of the PMO as a governance engine that reduces delivery variance, enforces minimum standards, and turns “we think we are ready” into “we can prove we are ready.” The chapter also addresses a modern reality that every leader must now accept. AI has accelerated delivery capacity, but it has also expanded the surface area of responsibility. It can increase speed, yet it can also increase unmanaged change if roles, controls, and decision rights are not sharpened. That is why this chapter treats governance as a delivery capability rather than an administrative overlay, which aligns with the governance-centered posture emphasized in CSF 2.0 (NIST, 2024b).

Most organizations are familiar with the classic triangle of scope, schedule, and cost. Those are still necessary constraints. Yet they are no longer sufficient constraints for technology delivery. A system can be on time and within budget and still fail the business because it cannot be operated safely, monitored reliably, or defended under realistic threat conditions. The discipline of delivery must therefore include outcomes that were previously assumed to be "security team concerns," including identity integrity, data protection, resilience, auditability, and operational readiness. When these outcomes are not owned explicitly, they become the orphan responsibilities that no one sees until something breaks. Governance frameworks increasingly reflect this reality by emphasizing accountability, enterprise risk management, and communication as foundations for cybersecurity outcomes (NIST, 2024b).

Portfolio management, program management, product management, and project management serve distinct but interconnected purposes within modern technology organizations.

Portfolio vs. Program vs. Product vs. Project

	Portfolio	Program	Product	Product	Project
Purpose	Manage investments	Coordinate investments	Deliver product value	Achieve defined results	Achieve defined results
Horizon	Long-term (years)	Mid-term (1–2 years)	Iterative (quarterly/feature-based)	Short-term (months)	Short-term (months)
Success Metrics	Strategic alignment, ROI, capacity	Program goals, benefits, budget	Product KPIs, user satisfaction	Project requirements, schedule, budget	Project requirements traceability
Artifacts	Business cases, roadmap	Program charter, roadmap, policies	Product backlog, roadmap, MVP	Product plan, requirements traceability	Project plan, requirements traceability
Decision Cadence	Quarterly, annually	Monthly or quarterly	Sprint or release/demo	Sprint or release/demo	Weekly or bi-weekly

Shared Operating Layer (applies to all four)		
Governance	Metrics	Stakeholder Alignment

This layer is where the PMO sets decision rights, standards, reporting cadence, and gate accountability.

Each discipline operates over a different time horizon, focuses on different success measures, and follows a different decision cadence, even though they often involve the same stakeholders and resources. Confusion among these roles leads to misaligned priorities, ineffective governance, and delivery risk, particularly when security, compliance, and emerging technologies are involved. The following comparison clarifies how these disciplines differ, where they intersect, and how shared governance, metrics, and stakeholder alignment enable coordinated and accountable technology delivery.

A helpful way to begin is to reset the mental model. Project management is not a lesser form of product management. Product management is not a modern replacement for project management. Program management is not a bigger project. They are different instruments in the same orchestra, each designed to produce a specific kind of control. A conductor who does not know which instrument is playing will not produce harmony, no matter how talented the musicians are. In delivery terms, harmony means aligned goals, stable decision rights, consistent execution, and security embedded as a design constraint. Without that harmony, organizations become noisy. Work multiplies, defects accumulate, and risk decisions become reactive.

Project management exists to deliver a defined outcome within defined constraints. A project is temporary, it has a start and an end, and it produces a unique result, even if that result is an enhancement to an existing system. The project manager's role is to turn intention into execution. That includes defining scope boundaries, building realistic plans, coordinating dependencies, managing stakeholders, controlling changes, and ensuring quality and risk are handled with discipline. Modern PMI guidance continues to emphasize that project management is a structured approach to delivering outcomes through planning, execution, and control, with a strong focus on managing uncertainty and enabling value (PMI, 2021b). The security implication is straightforward. If the project manager cannot enforce clear scope and change control, security requirements tend to become the first casualty. The team begins to treat controls as negotiable, because delivery pressure is constant and governance is weak.

Product management exists to maximize value over time. While projects are temporary, products are persistent. A product has a lifecycle, an evolving user base, a roadmap, and an ongoing responsibility for performance, reliability, and adoption. Product management therefore prioritizes what to build next, what to stop, and what tradeoffs are acceptable across usability, growth, cost, and risk. In digital organizations, product managers often serve as the voice of outcomes. They understand user pain, market pressure, and adoption barriers. They also shape the definition of success beyond delivery completion. A project manager may declare success when the release is completed. A product manager may declare success only when adoption is real, errors are controlled, and the system is producing value without constant escalation. When both voices are present and respected, the organization is more likely to deliver solutions that are both usable and safe.

The tension between project and product management is not a problem. It is a feature. The problem arises when the organization forces one discipline to pretend it can replace the other. If an organization uses only project thinking, it may ship functionality on time but fail to sustain it because product ownership is weak and operational learning is ignored. If an organization uses only product thinking, it may pursue continuous change without adequate delivery control, leading to unstable releases, uncontrolled scope creep, and incomplete security verification. The healthiest organizations use project management to provide delivery discipline and product management to provide value direction. They do not allow the disciplines to compete for authority. They design the operating model, so each discipline owns the decisions it is best suited to own.

Program management sits above this level when the organization needs coordinated outcomes that multiple projects cannot deliver alone. A program is a structured collection of related initiatives designed to achieve benefits that require alignment across workstreams. A program may include application build, vendor acquisition, data migration, process change, training, cybersecurity controls, and operating model transformation. Each project can succeed in isolation and still fail the program if the pieces do not integrate into a usable outcome. Program management exists to prevent that fragmentation. It coordinates dependencies, manages inter-project risk, and ensures the organization's benefits case is realized. In practice, program management becomes essential when the initiative touches multiple business units, multiple technical domains, and multiple vendors. It becomes even more essential when the initiative introduces shared capabilities like identity platforms, monitoring infrastructure, or data governance. Those capabilities cannot be designed five different ways by five different teams. Program management enforces convergence.

When roles are unclear, failure patterns become predictable. One pattern is the "handoff trap." A project team delivers a feature and declares completion, then an operations team inherits a solution that is difficult to support and difficult to monitor. Another pattern is the "governance gap." A product manager drives rapid enhancement, yet no one owns the risk acceptance and gate readiness decisions. A third pattern is the "shadow decision." A vendor contract is signed, or a tool is adopted, without clear accountability for the security obligations and configuration responsibilities that come with it. These patterns are not merely operational annoyances. They are risk multipliers. They increase the attack surface and reduce the organization's ability to prove due care, which is why modern guidance emphasizes governance as a foundational outcome rather than an optional process layer (NIST, 2024b).

A short dialogue illustrates the real-world cost of role confusion. A sponsor asks, "Who approved that we can store customer data in that third-party platform?" The project manager replies, "Procurement handled the contract." Procurement replies, "Security reviewed the questionnaire." Security replies, "We flagged risks and asked for compensating controls." The sponsor pauses, then asks the only question that matters, "So who owns the decision?" Silence follows. That silence is the governance gap. It is the space where risk becomes unmanaged. A mature operating model prevents that moment by making decision rights explicit and by ensuring that gate decisions are recorded, owned, and defensible (NIST, 2024b).

The PMO is the organizational mechanism that prevents this confusion from repeating. Many PMOs were originally built to standardize templates, collect schedules, and provide executive reporting. Those functions are still useful, but they are not sufficient in modern digital environments. Technology delivery has become too complex, too vendor-dependent, and too exposed to cyber risk for the PMO to operate as a passive administrative layer. The PMO must become a delivery governance engine. It must create repeatability, enforce minimum standards, and ensure that risk and quality controls are built into the lifecycle. When a PMO operates this way, it becomes the institution that protects the organization's ability to scale delivery without scaling chaos.

A governance-oriented PMO does several things that are easy to describe but difficult to execute without discipline. It defines the delivery lifecycle and the required artifacts. It establishes gates and readiness criteria, then it enforces them consistently. It clarifies decision rights so that risk acceptance cannot happen quietly. It also creates escalation pathways when projects drift. This is where governance stops being theory and becomes a practical capability. The CSF 2.0 perspective supports the idea that governance is central to managing cybersecurity outcomes as enterprise outcomes, which reinforces the PMO's role in shaping delivery practices that produce defensible results (NIST, 2024b).

The PMO also reduces delivery variance. Delivery variance is the difference between what one team does and what another team does, even when both teams claim they are following the same methodology. Variance is not always bad. Some customization is necessary. Yet uncontrolled variance is a quiet threat. It leads to inconsistent testing, inconsistent documentation, inconsistent risk handling, and inconsistent vendor governance. Over time, it creates a portfolio where leadership cannot compare projects reliably and cannot enforce minimum security expectations consistently. The PMO's value is therefore not only efficiency. It is standardization with purpose. It creates a shared operating picture, so teams can move quickly without reinventing foundational controls.

This is also where the governance of IT, as defined in high-level governance standards, becomes relevant. Governance of IT emphasizes that technology decisions should align with business objectives, that responsibilities should be clear, and that performance and conformance should be monitored through accountable oversight (ISO, 2015). While such standards are not project manuals, they reinforce a principle that projects often forget. Decision rights must be clear. Oversight must be real. Accountability must be assigned. These are governance fundamentals, and the PMO is often the most practical place to operationalize them inside delivery.

A mature PMO does not only publish templates. It runs a system. It defines the minimum set of deliverables that prove readiness at each phase. It ensures that those deliverables include security-by-design outcomes such as clear requirements, architecture controls, testing evidence, and operational readiness. It also ensures that the decision process is stable, meaning the same types of projects follow the same types of gate reviews, and exceptions are recorded rather than normalized. This stability enables learning. It allows the organization to refine what “good” looks like over time. It also allows the organization to defend decisions under audit and after incidents because evidence exists and accountability is traceable.

The PMO’s operating model should fit the organization’s maturity and risk exposure. In some organizations, the PMO acts as a supportive function, offering coaching and light governance. In other organizations, it acts as a controlling function, enforcing standards, artifacts, and gates. In high-risk environments, it may act as a directive function, directly managing delivery leadership and assigning project managers to critical initiatives. The point is not to choose the most rigid model. The point is to choose a model that matches risk reality. As digital risk increases, the PMO must shift from advisory posture to enforcement posture. That shift does not have to create bureaucracy. It can create clarity. It can reduce late-stage rework and protect the organization’s reputation by ensuring that minimum security outcomes are not negotiable.

Clarity of decision rights is where many PMOs struggle, yet it is where they provide the most value when they get it right. Decision rights should be explicit across scope change authority, risk acceptance authority, control design ownership, operational readiness ownership, and vendor accountability. If these rights are not clear, the project becomes a negotiation environment, where the loudest voice wins rather than the evidence. A good PMO makes it difficult for vague decisions to survive. It requires that important decisions be made with evidence, recorded with ownership, and reviewed at the right governance level. This approach aligns with enterprise governance principles and with the governance emphasis embedded in CSF 2.0 (NIST, 2024b; ISO, 2015).

The relationship between the PMO and product management is especially important. In many modern organizations, product teams operate continuously. They deliver enhancements in short cycles and respond to market feedback quickly. This can create friction with traditional PMO models that were built for large, sequential projects. The solution is not to abandon governance. The solution is to modernize governance so it fits continuous delivery. A mature PMO can support product teams by defining lightweight but consistent evidence expectations. It can embed security-by-design requirements into the product lifecycle, so that rapid delivery does not become rapid risk. It can also define how gates work in iterative environments, which may mean gates occur at major release boundaries, at architectural changes, or at risk-trigger events. The discipline remains the same. Evidence supports decisions. Risk acceptance is explicit. Operational readiness is validated.

Program management becomes a partner in this model. Programs often span both project and product work. For example, a digital transformation program may include project delivery for foundational capabilities such as identity modernization and data platform migration, and it may also include product delivery for customer-facing applications that evolve continuously. Program governance ensures the foundation supports the products, and it ensures that cross-cutting controls are consistent. Without program discipline, each workstream can drift into its own definition of security, testing, and readiness. That is how fragmentation becomes institutional.

AI introduces a new layer of pressure on all these disciplines, and it does so in two directions. It increases speed, and it increases the risk of uncontrolled change. AI tools make it easier for teams to generate code, generate documentation, and accelerate development. That can be beneficial, especially when teams are understaffed or when deadlines are strict. Yet AI also increases the likelihood of shadow adoption. A team may integrate an AI service into a workflow because it appears easy. Another team may begin using an AI coding assistant without clear policy. A third team may deploy an AI-enabled feature without clear evaluation criteria. These actions are not always malicious. Often they are simply the byproduct of pressure and convenience. Still, they introduce risk that the organization cannot manage if decision rights and governance are weak.

In the AI era, the difference between project management and product management becomes even more important. Product leadership must define acceptable use and unacceptable outcomes. It must define where automation is allowed and where human oversight is mandatory. It must clarify what trust looks like for users. Project leadership must ensure that the delivery plan includes evaluation, testing, monitoring readiness, and operational controls. The PMO must ensure that AI-related controls are not treated as innovation extras. They must be integrated into the same lifecycle discipline that governs all critical technology delivery. CSF 2.0's governance framing supports this integrated approach because it emphasizes governance, accountability, and enterprise risk management as foundations for cybersecurity outcomes across the organization (NIST, 2024b).

A practical way to think about these disciplines is through the metaphor of a ship at sea. Product management decides where the ship should go and why it matters. Project management ensures the ship is built correctly and launched safely. Program management coordinates the fleet when multiple ships must move together. The PMO is the navigation system and the rules of the sea. It enforces the standards that prevent collisions, and it ensures that the crew follows procedures that make the journey survivable. AI adds a faster engine. It can help the ship move quicker. Yet if navigation rules are weak, a faster engine simply accelerates the ship toward the rocks.

To make this operating model real, organizations must design clear collaboration patterns. Project managers should not be the sole owners of risk. They should be the orchestrators of risk visibility. Product managers should not be the sole owners of value. They should be the stewards of value within defined guardrails. Program managers should not only manage timelines across workstreams. They should manage integration readiness, shared control consistency, and benefit realization. The PMO should not only collect status reports. It should enforce the discipline that makes delivery consistent and defensible. When these collaboration patterns are explicit, governance becomes less political. Decisions become less emotional. Security becomes less negotiable because it is embedded into the definition of readiness.

As you move through the chapters that follow, you will see these roles translated into lifecycle mechanics. You will see how the PMO enables gates and evidence bundles, and how governance reviews are structured as real decisions rather than ceremonial meetings. You will also see how the ADDIS phases reinforce accountability by requiring specific deliverables at each stage. The key insight is that roles and governance do not exist to slow delivery. They exist to prevent avoidable failure and to protect digital trust. In a world where systems are connected, vendor-dependent, and increasingly AI-enabled, a disciplined operating model is no longer a maturity aspiration. It is a survival requirement (NIST, 2024b).

In summary, project management provides delivery control and execution discipline. Product management provides value direction and continuous outcome ownership. Program management provides cross-workstream convergence and benefit realization. The PMO provides standardization, governance enforcement, and evidence-driven readiness. When these functions are aligned, the organization gains speed with stability. It can deliver faster without turning risk into an invisible passenger. When they are misaligned, the organization may still deliver, but it will deliver inconsistently, and it will eventually pay the price through rework, incidents, or loss of trust. This chapter therefore sets the foundation for the next step, which is to translate these roles into portfolio governance and PMO operating models that enforce secure, compliant, and sustainable technology delivery at scale.

Secure delivery means governance is lived daily in every role.

Practitioners overlap in **responsibility.** They strengthen delivery when they overlap in **understanding.**

Portfolio Governance and the PMO

Portfolio governance is where strategy becomes real. It is also where organizations quietly decide what they will protect and what they will leave exposed. Most executives do not wake up and choose risk, yet risk is chosen every time a portfolio is funded, every time a roadmap is accelerated, and every time a "must deliver" date is set without funding the controls required to deliver safely. This is why portfolio governance must be treated as more than a prioritization meeting. It is the enterprise mechanism that aligns value, risk, capacity, and accountability, then keeps that alignment intact as conditions change. In the modern environment, where systems are interconnected, vendor-dependent, and increasingly AI-enabled, portfolio governance is no longer optional discipline. It is the control plane for digital trust, which is consistent with the governance emphasis in the NIST Cybersecurity Framework 2.0, where cybersecurity is managed as enterprise risk and governance is a core outcome (NIST, 2024b).

Many organizations still manage portfolios with a narrow lens. They focus on business cases, cost estimates, project schedules, and resource availability. Those inputs matter, but they do not capture the full reality of technology delivery. A portfolio is not simply a list of investments. It is a living system of dependencies, shared platforms, data flows, and risk exposures. If one initiative changes the identity architecture, five other initiatives inherit that change. If a data platform is redesigned, downstream analytics and reporting initiatives inherit the ripple effects. If a vendor is selected for a customer workflow, security, privacy, resilience, and compliance obligations are inherited as well. Portfolio governance exists to see those connections early, then to manage them intentionally rather than accidentally.

In modern digital organizations, the PMO must operate as more than a delivery coordination function. It serves as the enterprise mechanism through which value realization, risk control, and security assurance are continuously enforced. Acting as a Security and Value Office, the PMO defines delivery mandates, establishes governance structures, builds enforceable standards, enables tooling, and embeds assurance checkpoints across the lifecycle. This operating cycle ensures that every initiative passing through the ADDIS gates is not only delivered efficiently, but is governed, controlled, and demonstrably secure through measurable evidence and accountable decision-making.

The second edition introduces a sharper claim: portfolio governance is the first and most powerful form of Security by Design. That may sound surprising because Security by Design is often discussed at the engineering level. Yet the truth is simple. Security cannot be "engineered in" if it is never funded, never prioritized, and never required as a condition for approval. Portfolio decisions determine whether security is embedded or treated as a late-stage scramble. They determine whether projects will be allowed to proceed without evidence, and they determine whether the organization will accept unmanaged digital risk as the price of speed. A mature organization does not let those decisions happen informally. It designs governance structures that make risk visible, make accountability explicit, and make evidence a normal output of delivery.

The governance of IT has long emphasized that decision rights must be clear, that responsibility must be assigned, and that performance and conformance must be monitored as part of organizational governance. ISO/IEC 38500 expresses this at the board and executive level by framing governance as guiding and monitoring the use of IT, with clear accountability and alignment to organizational objectives (ISO, 2015). In practical portfolio terms, that guidance becomes very concrete. It means the organization must be able to answer, at any time, what initiatives are approved, why they are approved, what risks they introduce, which controls are required, who owns those controls, and how leadership will know whether those controls exist before go-live.

A portfolio that cannot answer these questions is not a portfolio. It is a queue of activity. It may still produce outputs, but it will not reliably produce outcomes. The organization will be busy, yet fragile.

Portfolio Governance, Strategy to Execution

Portfolio governance begins with a simple premise. Resources are finite, risk is unavoidable, and priorities change. The portfolio must therefore be governed as a dynamic set of choices. This is where many organizations get trapped. They attempt to create a perfect annual plan, then they treat the plan as fixed. When the environment shifts, they force work to continue according to an outdated script. This can look disciplined, yet it is actually a form of unmanaged risk. The portfolio becomes misaligned with business reality, and security decisions become reactive because new threats or new regulatory expectations were not incorporated into governance decisions quickly enough.

A better approach treats portfolio governance as a routine . The routine is not chaos. It is structured adaptation. Strategy informs the portfolio, the portfolio informs program and project execution, and execution feedback informs strategy adjustments. The Standard for Portfolio Management emphasizes that portfolio management is about aligning components with organizational strategy and balancing value, risk, and resource constraints, rather than simply administering a list of initiatives (PMI, 2017). The practical implication is that portfolio governance is not merely selecting projects. It is continuously ensuring that the organization's limited capacity is applied to the work that best advances strategic objectives, while managing exposure to acceptable levels.

This is the point where cybersecurity must be integrated as a portfolio lens. Security is not a "feature" that can be added on demand. It is a risk management discipline with requirements that affect schedule, architecture, tooling, and vendor choices. If the portfolio governance process does not incorporate security risk early, the portfolio will overcommit. It will approve timelines that do not include security tasks. It will approve budgets that do not fund control implementation. It will approve acquisitions without requiring the contractual obligations and verification steps that make vendor assurances real. Later, when security gaps are discovered, the organization will either delay delivery or ship risk. Both outcomes create cost, and the second outcome creates a silent liability that can surface as an incident.

A governance-centered framework like CSF 2.0 reinforces the need to manage cybersecurity risk as enterprise risk and to communicate and prioritize cybersecurity outcomes across stakeholders. It also emphasizes that the framework supports understanding, assessing, prioritizing, and communicating cybersecurity efforts (NIST, 2024b). That language fits portfolio governance perfectly because portfolios are, at their core, prioritization systems. The portfolio decides what will be done, what will be delayed, what will be stopped, and what risk will be accepted as part of those choices. When cybersecurity is treated as an enterprise outcome, portfolio governance becomes the natural place to integrate security priorities, not as obstacles, but as conditions of sustainable execution.

One of the most practical outcomes of portfolio governance is the ability to differentiate "important" from "urgent." Urgency is often emotional. It is driven by deadlines, competitor moves, and internal pressure. Importance is structural. It is driven by strategic alignment, systemic risk reduction, and long-term capability building. Security investments often struggle because they look less urgent than feature delivery, even though they may be more important for long-term trust. A mature portfolio model corrects this by making risk reduction and resilience explicit value categories. It treats initiatives that reduce systemic exposure as strategic work, not as overhead.

Portfolio governance must also manage dependencies intentionally. A portfolio is full of invisible connections, and those connections are where failure often starts. If one program depends on a shared identity platform upgrade, and that upgrade slips, multiple initiatives are impacted. If one product depends on a data governance uplift that is not funded, the product will likely accumulate data risk and later face compliance friction. If an AI initiative depends on clean labeled datasets and monitoring infrastructure, and those dependencies are not funded, the project will either degrade its assurance standards or delay its release. The portfolio, not the individual project, is the best level to see these dependency chains. It is also the best level to fund shared controls and shared platforms that reduce repeated effort across teams.

This is where an enterprise governance framework such as COBIT can be useful conceptually, even when a project team never mentions it. COBIT 2019 frames governance and management objectives for enterprise IT, emphasizing a system of governance that aligns technology with enterprise goals and integrates risk considerations into decision-making. It provides a structured vocabulary for thinking about governance, performance, conformance, and accountability at scale (ISACA, 2018). Portfolio governance benefits from that mindset because it forces leaders to see technology not as isolated projects but as a governed capability system.

The PMO as a Security and Value Office

The PMO is often positioned as a delivery support function. In a mature environment, it becomes something stronger. It becomes the operational engine of portfolio governance. It is the place where strategy is converted into executable standards and where execution produces evidence that informs governance decisions. This chapter calls that evolved PMO model a Security and Value Office, not as a rebranding exercise, but as a description of its true responsibilities.

A Security and Value Office does not replace cybersecurity leadership. It does not replace architecture or engineering. It does not replace compliance. Instead, it orchestrates the delivery system so security and value are not competing forces. It makes them compatible through governance design. It does that in three ways. It sets the minimum delivery standards that every initiative must follow. It enforces lifecycle control points through gates and evidence bundles. It provides portfolio leadership with transparent insight into risk, readiness, and capacity so decisions are made with clarity rather than optimism.

The difference between a traditional PMO and a Security and Value Office shows up in day-to-day behavior. A traditional PMO asks, “Is the project on track?” A Security and Value Office asks, “Is the project on track, and is it safe to proceed based on evidence?” A traditional PMO tracks milestones. A Security and Value Office tracks readiness. A traditional PMO can be satisfied by a schedule. A Security and Value Office demands proof that the schedule is built on controls, testing, and accountable decisions. This orientation is consistent with a governance-centered cybersecurity posture because it treats cybersecurity as an enterprise responsibility and integrates governance into how decisions are made and monitored (NIST, 2024b).

To make this real, the PMO must operate with a small number of non-negotiable artifacts. These artifacts are not meant to create paperwork. They are meant to create evidence. They include an approved business case and scope definition, a risk register with owners, a security requirements baseline, an architecture assurance record, a testing and validation plan, an operational readiness plan, and a gate decision record that captures the outcome and conditions. The specific templates can be tailored to organizational size. The principle should not change. If the organization cannot produce evidence of readiness, it cannot credibly claim readiness.

This is where portfolio governance and ADDIS gates become mutually reinforcing. Portfolio governance decides what is funded and prioritized. ADDIS gates ensure funded work proceeds responsibly through the lifecycle. The PMO sits between them, translating strategic priorities into delivery standards and translating delivery evidence into governance insight. When that translation is weak, leadership receives status updates that sound confident yet hide risk. When the translation is strong, leadership receives decisions supported by evidence, along with clear options for handling residual risk.

The Security and Value Office model also changes how the PMO interacts with product teams. In many modern organizations, product teams deliver continuously. They release features in iterative cycles and respond quickly to user feedback. If PMO governance is rigid and document-heavy, product teams will bypass it. They will adopt tools and methods that seem faster, then governance will become reactive again. A mature PMO avoids this by modernizing its controls. It does not ask for unnecessary ceremony. It asks for consistent evidence. It defines a lightweight governance routine that fits continuous delivery, then enforces minimum standards at the moments of highest risk, such as major architectural changes, production environment changes, vendor onboarding, or releases that introduce new data flows or AI features.

The same logic applies to AI-enabled delivery. AI can create rapid feature acceleration, yet it also creates risk acceleration when governance is weak. Teams may adopt AI services for customer workflows or internal decision support without defining evaluation criteria, monitoring readiness, or rollback controls. A Security and Value Office anticipates this. It does not attempt to ban innovation by default. It integrates AI oversight into the same portfolio and gate mechanisms that already exist. It requires that AI work be classified appropriately in the portfolio, that AI dependencies be funded, and that AI evidence be produced at gates. This keeps the organization consistent and reduces the chance that AI becomes "shadow capability" that is difficult to govern after it is already embedded in operations.

Portfolio Decisions That Prevent Failure

A portfolio governance model is only as good as its decision mechanics. Many organizations hold portfolio reviews, yet the decisions are driven by politics or urgency. The meeting feels active, but the criteria are unclear. This is where a Security and Value Office provides leverage. It helps the organization adopt simple, repeatable decision criteria that make prioritization defensible.

One useful approach is to require each portfolio candidate to be scored on a balanced set of dimensions. These dimensions should include strategic alignment, economic value, regulatory and compliance exposure, cybersecurity risk impact, dependency complexity, operational readiness burden, and organizational capacity. The scoring does not need to be perfect. It needs to be consistent. Consistency is what allows leadership to compare investments and to explain why certain work is prioritized. It also allows the organization to see when it is underinvesting in foundational risk reduction.

This type of balanced decision approach aligns with portfolio management thinking that emphasizes balancing value, risk, and resource constraints across portfolio components (PMI, 2017). It also aligns with governance standards that emphasize guiding and monitoring technology use and performance with clear accountability (ISO, 2015). When cybersecurity is included as a scoring dimension, it becomes part of the portfolio's definition of value rather than an afterthought.

Another essential decision mechanic is the use of portfolio-level risk appetite statements. Risk appetite is often discussed in enterprise risk management, yet it is rarely translated into portfolio language. A portfolio risk appetite statement clarifies what types of risk the organization is willing to accept to achieve growth and what types of risk are not acceptable, such as unmanaged exposure of regulated data, uncontrolled privileged access, or unverified third-party services. When this appetite is explicit, portfolio decisions become simpler.

Leaders can say yes faster when an initiative fits the appetite and can say no faster when it violates it unless compensating controls are funded.

Portfolio governance must also enforce "stop rules." Many portfolios accumulate zombie initiatives. Work continues because it started. The business case is outdated, yet no one wants to stop the project. Stopping feels like failure, even when stopping is the responsible choice. A mature portfolio treats stopping as governance discipline. It uses clear triggers to revisit approval, such as major scope drift, persistent inability to meet control requirements, unacceptable risk exposure, or repeated gate failures. These stop rules protect organizational capacity and reduce the chance that sunk-cost thinking turns into operational liability.

The PMO as a Security and Value Office plays a central role here. It provides visibility. It surfaces evidence that the initiative is not meeting readiness thresholds. It clarifies whether failure is due to underfunding, poor execution, unrealistic expectations, or unresolved dependencies. It then presents leadership with options that are honest and defensible. Continue with additional funding and revised scope, pause until a dependency is resolved, or stop and replan. This is governance doing its job.

A particularly important portfolio mechanic is the management of shared capabilities. Security and resilience often depend on shared platforms, such as identity and access management, centralized logging and monitoring, vulnerability management tooling, data governance platforms, and incident response integration. If each project funds these capabilities independently, the organization wastes money and creates inconsistent implementations. If the portfolio funds them as shared capabilities, projects can move faster and with higher assurance. Portfolio governance must therefore distinguish between product features and capability foundations. Features create visible value quickly. Foundations create invisible stability and long-term trust. Both matter, yet foundations are often underfunded because their benefits are harder to market internally. A mature governance model corrects that imbalance by explicitly funding foundations as strategic investments.

This is where a governance framework like COBIT is useful again because it encourages organizations to design governance systems that fit enterprise needs and to integrate governance objectives with enterprise goals. It reinforces the idea that governance is a system, not a set of disconnected processes (ISACA, 2018). Portfolio governance is one of the most visible places where that system must work.

Many organizations operate in third-party delivery environments. They buy platforms, integrate services, and rely on external providers for critical capabilities. In these environments, portfolio governance must treat acquisition decisions as high-impact governance decisions, not as procurement transactions. Vendor selection is a portfolio choice because it shapes the solution approach, control capability, and long-term operational dependency. It also introduces contractual and compliance obligations that can be difficult to unwind later.

A Security and Value Office ensure that acquisition initiatives follow the same governance discipline as in-house builds. It requires that vendor risk be assessed early. It requires that contracts include security obligations, audit rights, incident notification requirements, and data handling clauses aligned to organizational standards. It also ensures that implementation plans include verification steps, not just deployment tasks. Without this discipline, organizations often inherit risk through contracts, then spend years trying to compensate with internal controls.

Portfolio governance also needs to recognize that vendor risk is not uniform. Some vendors provide commoditized services with low switching cost. Others become deeply embedded in the enterprise operating model. The portfolio must treat these differently. High-embed vendors require stronger governance because switching later is expensive and disruptive. This is another reason why portfolio decisions should include risk and dependency dimensions. It prevents the organization from selecting a solution that looks attractive in the short term but creates long-term exposure.

How to know portfolio governance is working

Governance is sometimes judged by how many meetings occur. That is a misleading metric. Governance is working when delivery outcomes become predictable, risk becomes visible early, and decision-making becomes less emotional.

A strong portfolio governance system produces several observable effects. First, initiatives are more clearly aligned to strategy. That does not mean every initiative is perfect. It means the organization can explain why it chose each initiative and how it contributes to objectives. Second, the portfolio has a clear view of capacity and does not continuously overcommit. Third, the organization sees risk earlier, because the PMO requires early evidence, not late reassurance. Fourth, the quality of gate decisions improves, because gate inputs are based on structured evidence rather than narrative confidence. Fifth, the organization learns. Templates improve. Standards refine. The portfolio becomes smarter with each cycle.

This is where CSF 2.0's language about helping organizations understand, assess, prioritize, and communicate cybersecurity efforts becomes practically relevant. Portfolio governance is the mechanism that operationalizes those verbs, especially prioritization and communication (NIST, 2024b). A portfolio that prioritizes cybersecurity outcomes explicitly and communicates them through funded initiatives and evidence-based gates is a portfolio that treats digital trust as a strategic asset.

ISO/IEC 38500's focus on governance principles and the model for guiding and monitoring IT also becomes relevant here, because it reinforces that governance must exist at the highest level, and that the organization must monitor performance and conformance rather than assume them (ISO, 2015). A portfolio governance system that does not monitor conformance is not governance. It is permission.

Key Takeaway

Portfolio governance is where organizations decide whether they will deliver value with stability or deliver value with hidden liability. It is the control point that shapes what gets approved, what gets funded, and what gets protected. When portfolio governance is weak, the PMO becomes a schedule tracker that measures activity without shaping outcomes. When governance is strong, the PMO functions as a decision engine. It helps leaders prioritize the right work, fund the right controls, and stop or reshape initiatives before they become expensive failures.

This chapter emphasized that portfolio decisions are not neutral. They determine whether security is treated as a design constraint or pushed into late-stage remediation. They also determine whether risk is managed transparently or quietly absorbed until it becomes an incident, an audit finding, or an operational crisis. In the AI era, these choices matter even more. Speed is easier to obtain because tools and platforms accelerate delivery. However, safe speed is harder to sustain because AI increases complexity in behavior, data dependence, and monitoring demands. That is why portfolio governance must evolve from approving projects to governing outcomes.

A Security and Value Office PMO makes that evolution operational. It creates repeatability by standardizing how initiatives are evaluated, classified, and routed through gates. It reduces delivery variance by defining evidence expectations and requiring evidence bundles that show readiness rather than confidence. This approach strengthens leadership decision-making because it converts uncertainty into visible signal. Leaders gain a clearer view of risk exposure, capacity constraints, control readiness, and the true cost of delay or rework.

Over time, the organization becomes faster because it reduces reversals, avoids avoidable security debt, and invests earlier in the controls that prevent downstream disruption.

Portfolio governance also reinforces accountability. It clarifies who owns tradeoffs, who approves residual risk, and who is responsible for ensuring that funding covers both delivery and assurance. This is what turns governance from policy into practice. It is also what allows the PMO to function as a stabilizing force in environments where delivery pressure is high and risk is real.

The next chapter shifts from the mechanics of portfolio governance to the mechanics of execution. It explains how SDLC choices and Secure SDLC discipline shape the way teams actually deliver, whether they use agile sprints, hybrid programs, DevSecOps pipelines, or vendor-led implementation. This transition matters because delivery models change, but the need for Security by Design does not. Portfolio governance sets direction. It decides what work is authorized, what outcomes are expected, and what level of risk the organization is willing to carry. Execution discipline then determines whether those decisions turn into results or turn into drift.

A well-chosen SDLC gives teams structure for planning, building, integrating, and releasing in a repeatable way. Secure SDLC adds the controls, evidence capture, and validation steps that keep speed from becoming exposure. When governance approves work without a delivery method that can produce proof, projects rely on optimism. When SDLC discipline is strong, teams deliver with traceable decisions, predictable quality, and operational readiness that holds up under real-world change.

Secure SDLC and DevSecOps

Technology delivery is often described as a methodology choice, yet in practice it is a governance choice. The SDLC model you select shapes how decisions are made, when risks are discovered, and whether security becomes a built-in discipline or a late-stage negotiation. Many organizations believe they have standardized on a single model. Then reality intrudes. One team works in agile sprints, another follows a vendor's implementation playbook, a third uses a hybrid approach because procurement and compliance require formal approvals, and a fourth is quietly releasing changes through CI/CD pipelines without calling it "release management." The result is not innovation. It is fragmentation. Fragmentation is expensive because it multiplies rework, weakens evidence, and produces inconsistent controls across the portfolio.

This chapter treats SDLC selection and Secure SDLC execution as a practical operating system. It explains how common delivery models behave under real constraints, including regulatory requirements, vendor dependencies, and modern attack patterns. It also clarifies how DevSecOps transforms secure delivery from periodic inspection to continuous assurance. The chapter's central message is simple. Speed is not the enemy. Blind speed is. Mature organizations keep speed, but they attach it to disciplined evidence and accountable gates. This approach aligns with the governance-centered posture emphasized in the NIST Cybersecurity Framework 2.0, which treats cybersecurity as enterprise risk and governance as a foundational outcome, not a technical side conversation (NIST, 2024b).

At the heart of SDLC choice is a question many teams avoid because it exposes tradeoffs. When do you want to learn the truth? Every SDLC model learns the truth at different times. Some models discover design flaws early. Others discover them when code is already built. Some models discover security gaps during architecture review. Others discover them after deployment when systems are already connected to production data and real users. Security by Design is not a slogan that can compensate for a poor lifecycle choice. It must be operationalized through practices that match how work is actually executed. That is why NIST's Secure Software Development Framework exists. SSDF outlines secure development practices that can be integrated into any SDLC, precisely because many SDLC implementations do not address security rigorously by default (Souppaya et al., 2022). In other words, the SDLC is the pathway. Secure SDLC is the discipline that makes the pathway safe.

Many teams also misunderstand what Secure SDLC means. They assume it is a new SDLC model, like agile or waterfall. It is not. Secure SDLC is the security and integrity layer applied to any SDLC. It ensures that security requirements are treated like real requirements, that secure design principles are applied, that code is developed with secure practices, that testing includes security verification, and that operations include monitoring and controlled change. SSDF reinforces this integration posture by framing security activities as repeatable practices that produce evidence across the lifecycle, not as a one-time "security review" near the end (Souppaya et al., 2022). This evidence mindset is also consistent with the ADDIS method's gate philosophy, where deliverables and proof of readiness are required before advancing to the next phase.

An effective SDLC strategy therefore has two parts. First, choose a delivery model that fits the project's constraints. Second, integrate secure development practices in a way that produces consistent evidence, regardless of whether the team is building, buying, or implementing. When organizations succeed, they do not argue about labels. They align reality, discipline, and proof.

Choosing the right SDLC in a world of constraints

Waterfall is often criticized, and sometimes unfairly. The waterfall model can work well when requirements are stable, when the system is well understood, and when the organization needs formal stage approvals. It also works in environments where traceability is a priority, such as regulated systems and safety-critical domains. The main strength of waterfall is structure. Its weakness is late learning, particularly when the project includes complex integrations, vendor dependencies, or evolving user needs. In waterfall, teams may complete planning and design in detail before building. That can reduce ambiguity early, yet it also creates risk when assumptions are wrong. Security suffers when early design assumptions do not reflect real threat conditions, or when the architecture must change later under schedule pressure.

The V-model can be viewed as a structured refinement of waterfall. It emphasizes verification and validation by pairing each development phase with a corresponding test phase. This pairing creates a disciplined test strategy that can improve quality and traceability. The risk is that teams may treat verification as a compliance exercise rather than meaningful assurance. Secure SDLC practices can strengthen the V-model by ensuring that security requirements are paired with security verification activities, and that design decisions are paired with threat modeling and architecture assurance. SSDF supports this pairing mindset by stressing that secure development requires integrated tasks and verifiable outcomes, not informal "best effort" security activities (Souppaya et al., 2022). When implemented well, the V-model can help organizations demonstrate control maturity, yet it still requires governance discipline to ensure that test evidence is meaningful and that security is not merely documented.

Iterative and incremental models emerged because organizations needed earlier feedback and earlier learning. They allow teams to build in slices, validate assumptions sooner, and adapt the plan as real constraints become visible. These models reduce the cost of being wrong because you discover wrongness earlier. For security, iterative delivery can be beneficial when it includes continuous threat modeling, continuous security testing, and controlled releases. When those controls are absent, iterative delivery can produce a rapid accumulation of small insecure decisions that eventually become systemic risk. The speed feels productive until the system becomes too complex to secure without major refactoring.

Agile delivery is an evolution of this iterative thinking. It is often described as a mindset, but its operational value is in how it reduces time-to-feedback. Agile delivery emphasizes collaboration, incremental delivery, and responsiveness to change. Those features can support security when security is embedded into the backlog and treated as a product attribute. Yet agile can also harm security if teams treat security work as non-functional overhead that can be deferred. In many real projects, security tasks are postponed because they do not demonstrate immediate user-visible value. The result is predictable. The project reaches a release milestone and discovers that security controls are incomplete, evidence is weak, and risk acceptance becomes a political negotiation. Mature governance prevents this by requiring evidence at gates, even in iterative delivery. This is consistent with CSF 2.0's emphasis on governance and accountability for cybersecurity outcomes, because governance must exist regardless of delivery style (NIST, 2024b).

Hybrid delivery has become the default in many organizations, even when they do not admit it. Hybrid means combining predictive controls where necessary with agile execution where possible. Procurement processes, budget approvals, and regulatory obligations often require formal artifacts and stage gates. At the same time, engineering teams want iterative development and continuous integration. Hybrid succeeds when it is intentionally designed. It fails when it is accidental. Accidental hybrid delivery produces the worst of both worlds. It creates bureaucracy that slows feedback, yet it still lacks the discipline that makes predictive delivery safe. A well-designed hybrid model, by contrast, can allow agile teams to iterate while still producing the artifacts, evidence, and decisions needed for portfolio governance and audit readiness.

DevOps takes the conversation further. DevOps is not only a set of tools. It is a delivery culture that integrates development and operations to reduce friction, improve release cadence, and increase operational learning. DevOps can be a powerful enabler of secure delivery because it creates opportunities to automate control checks, enforce configuration standards, and integrate monitoring early. Yet DevOps also increases risk if release speed outpaces control maturity. That is why DevSecOps matters. DevSecOps is DevOps with security integrated as a continuous discipline, meaning security controls and verification are embedded into pipelines, code review practices, infrastructure provisioning, and monitoring.

This is where the language of SSDF becomes especially relevant. SSDF emphasizes that secure development should be achieved through a set of practices integrated into organizational processes and workflows, including secure coding, vulnerability management, secure build environments, and verification. It also emphasizes the need to produce evidence that these practices are performed (Souppaya et al., 2022). DevSecOps is one of the most practical ways to operationalize that idea because it enables security to be enforced repeatedly, automatically, and consistently. Instead of relying on a single late-stage security scan, DevSecOps integrates control checks throughout the lifecycle. The goal is not perfection. The goal is early detection, repeatability, and traceable assurance.

Selecting an SDLC model is therefore not an academic exercise. It is a risk decision. The model determines when design decisions are reviewed, when security is tested, and how quickly changes reach production. It also determines whether evidence can be produced consistently. The PMO and governance bodies should treat SDLC selection as part of project intake and planning, not as a team-level preference that happens quietly. When SDLC selection is left informal, the organization cannot enforce minimum standards consistently. It also cannot compare project readiness across the portfolio reliably. Governance loses visibility, and security loses leverage.

A practical selection approach begins with constraints. If requirements are stable and formal approvals are mandatory, a structured model such as waterfall or V-model may fit, provided it integrates secure practices and meaningful testing evidence. If requirements are uncertain and stakeholder feedback is essential,

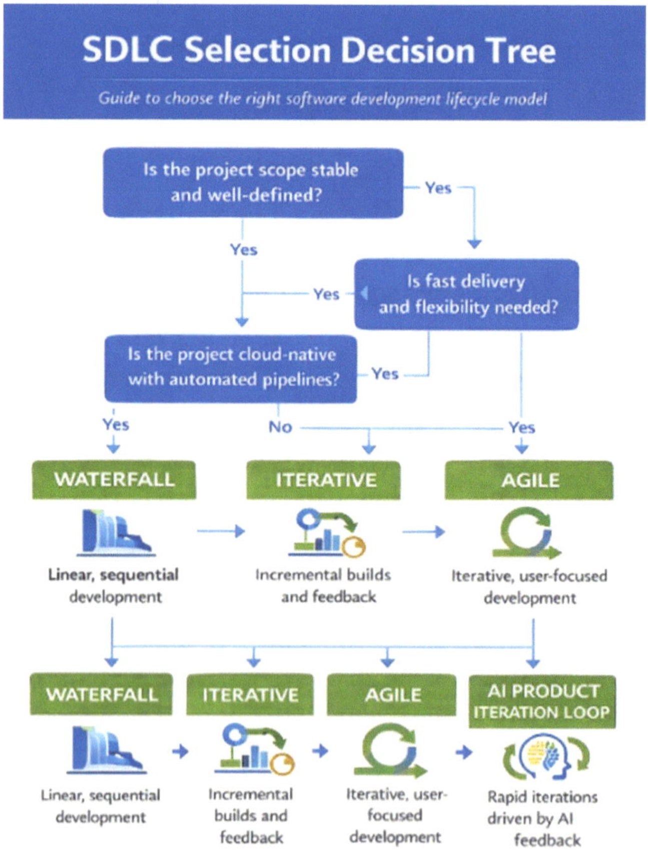

iterative, and agile approaches are more suitable, provided security work is embedded in the backlog and enforced through evidence-based gates. If the organization needs rapid releases and continuous improvement, DevSecOps becomes essential, provided the release pipeline includes automated security controls and monitoring readiness. In each case, the delivery method must still produce evidence that readiness exists. This is the connective tissue between SDLC choice and the ADDIS gate discipline.

Regardless of the SDLC model selected, all delivery activities remain governed by the ADDIS phases and Gate Reviews. SDLC models determine how work is executed, while ADDIS determines when decisions are made, what evidence is required, and how risk is governed.

Secure SDLC as the discipline that makes any model safe

Secure SDLC begins with a mindset shift that many teams resist. Security is not a separate workstream. It is part of the definition of done. This does not mean every feature requires heavy ceremony. It means every feature and every system change must satisfy minimum security expectations appropriate to its risk. A secure SDLC operationalizes this through explicit practices and artifacts, which is the approach SSDF formalizes. SSDF describes practices such as preparing the organization, protecting software, producing well-secured software, and responding to vulnerabilities. These practices are not dependent on a specific SDLC model. They can be integrated into agile, hybrid, or predictive delivery (Souppaya et al., 2022). This flexibility is exactly why SSDF is useful as a stable anchor for secure delivery governance.

A secure SDLC starts in requirements. Requirements should include security and privacy outcomes, not just functional outcomes. This includes data classification assumptions, access control expectations, logging requirements, regulatory constraints, and availability targets. In AI-enabled systems, it also includes requirements for monitoring, safety guardrails, and acceptable use boundaries. When security requirements are not captured early, teams often "discover" them later. Late discovery becomes late rework. Late rework becomes schedule pressure. Schedule pressure becomes risk acceptance. The pattern repeats because the lifecycle failed to force early clarity.

After requirements, secure SDLC moves into design discipline. Design is where the trust boundary is defined. Trust boundaries are not diagrams for documentation only. They are the practical description of where data flows, who can access it, what identities are trusted, and which external systems are allowed to interact. Threat modeling becomes a design tool in this stage. It helps teams think like adversaries and identify how the system could be misused. It also helps teams identify where compensating controls are required. In modern environments, design assurance must also account for supply chain and vendor dependencies, because those dependencies often define the real attack surface.

Secure SDLC then becomes engineering practice. Secure coding, peer review, dependency management, and secure build environments are not optional when systems handle sensitive data or critical operations. Here again, SSDF provides a stable anchor because it frames secure development as integrated practices that should be performed routinely and consistently, rather than as ad hoc best effort. It also emphasizes the importance of securing the build environment and managing third-party components, which is essential in modern software supply chains (Souppaya et al., 2022). Engineering teams cannot claim secure delivery if they cannot demonstrate how they manage dependencies, how they control access to build systems, and how they validate that code changes do not introduce known weaknesses.

Testing is where many organizations still fail, even when they believe they are mature. They test functionality thoroughly, yet they test security superficially. Secure SDLC requires security verification as part of the test strategy. It includes static and dynamic testing approaches, vulnerability scanning, configuration validation, and abuse case testing. The purpose is not to guarantee that vulnerabilities never exist. The purpose is to reduce the probability of predictable failures and to ensure that security findings are addressed in a controlled way before release. DevSecOps strengthens this by embedding security checks into pipelines so testing is continuous, rather than concentrated near release.

Deployment and operations complete the secure SDLC picture. Release readiness is not only about whether the feature works. It is about whether the system can be operated safely. This includes monitoring, alerting, incident response integration, backup and recovery readiness, and access control governance. A secure SDLC therefore extends into sustainment. The organization must be able to patch, respond to vulnerabilities, and manage configuration changes without introducing uncontrolled risk. This lifecycle responsibility aligns with the governance framing in CSF 2.0, which emphasizes that cybersecurity outcomes are not one-time achievements, but ongoing responsibilities managed through governance and risk management (NIST, 2024b).

In AI-enabled delivery, secure SDLC must also address new categories of assurance. The system must be evaluated for behavior, not only for functionality. Monitoring must include indicators of misuse and degradation. Change control must account for model updates and dependency changes that can alter outputs. This is why NIST has developed an SSDF community profile focused on generative AI and foundation models, which extends secure development thinking into AI contexts (NIST, 2024a). The broader point is not that AI requires an entirely separate lifecycle. The point is that secure development practices must evolve to account for AI-specific risk patterns, while still remaining evidence-based and integrated.

DevSecOps as continuous assurance, not continuous chaos

DevSecOps is often described as "shift left," yet the more accurate description is "build security into the flow of work." When security is built into the flow, teams do not have to stop the world to address it. Controls are applied repeatedly, and evidence is produced naturally through the pipeline. This is the difference between security as an event and security as a discipline.

A DevSecOps model typically includes pipeline controls that enforce coding standards, run automated tests, scan dependencies, validate infrastructure configurations, and promote artifacts through environments only when evidence thresholds are met. These controls are valuable because they reduce human variability. They also support audit readiness because the pipeline becomes a traceable record of what was tested and what passed. SSDF supports this orientation by emphasizing repeatable practices and the production of evidence. DevSecOps makes those practices operational at scale (Souppaya et al., 2022).

Yet DevSecOps is not a magic shield. Organizations can implement CI/CD tooling and still be insecure if governance is weak. A pipeline that promotes code quickly without meaningful assurance simply accelerates risk into production. That is why DevSecOps must be governed. Release criteria must be clear. Exception handling must be controlled. Break-glass access must be restricted. Monitoring must be integrated. These requirements align with CSF 2.0's emphasis on governance and risk management as foundations for cybersecurity outcomes, because continuous delivery must still operate under accountable oversight (NIST, 2024b).

In practice, DevSecOps success depends on balancing automation with decision rights. Automation should handle routine control enforcement. Human decision-making should handle risk acceptance and tradeoffs, especially when conditions are unusual. This balance becomes especially important during incidents or urgent fixes. Mature organizations define what can be released automatically and what requires explicit approval. They also define what evidence is mandatory at each stage. Evidence is the fuel of governance, and DevSecOps is one of the most effective ways to produce it consistently.

A strong DevSecOps program also requires investment in shared platforms and shared controls. Identity and access management, secret management, centralized logging, and vulnerability management tooling are not project-specific luxuries. They are foundational capabilities. This links directly back to portfolio governance. If the portfolio does not fund foundational platforms, projects will implement their own ad hoc solutions, which creates inconsistency and increases risk. A PMO operating as a Security and Value Office should therefore treat DevSecOps enablement as a portfolio capability investment, not as a single project deliverable. This reinforces the idea that secure delivery is an organizational system, not a team-level preference.

Applying SDLC to Acquired Systems

Many technology projects are not pure engineering builds. They are acquisitions and implementations. The organization selects a vendor platform, integrates it into existing environments, migrates data, configures workflows, and trains users. In such cases, some teams mistakenly believe that SDLC discipline does not apply because the solution is "already built." That belief is a costly error. Even when software is acquired, the organization still performs an SDLC. It may not write the code, but it still performs requirements definition, design of integrations, configuration, testing, deployment, and sustainment. It still owns the operational consequences. It still owns the risk.

Secure SDLC in acquisition contexts therefore focuses on three areas. The first is vendor governance and assurance. The organization must define security requirements for vendors, include them in contracts where appropriate, and verify that vendor claims match reality. The second is secure configuration and integration design. Many breaches occur not because vendor software is inherently flawed, but because implementations are misconfigured, privileges are excessive, or integrations expose data improperly. The third is operational readiness. Even the best vendor platform can become a burden if monitoring is weak, incident response is unclear, and support models are immature.

SSDF remains relevant here because its principles apply to the lifecycle outcomes, not only to coding. The organization must ensure that software is used in a way that produces secure outcomes, that vulnerabilities are managed, and that supply chain risks are addressed. In acquisition contexts, the evidence may look different, yet the discipline is the same. The organization must be able to show what it required, what it validated, what it accepted, and how it will maintain control over time.

This is also where ISO/IEC 27001's management system perspective is helpful. ISO/IEC 27001 expects organizations to define processes, responsibilities, and controls that maintain information security as an ongoing management responsibility (ISO, 2022). Acquisition and vendor implementation projects are precisely where this management system posture is tested, because control responsibilities are shared across internal teams and external providers. Without clear responsibility assignments and evidence of control execution, the organization becomes dependent on assumptions. Assumptions are not controls. They are blind spots.

SDLC Discipline Aligned to ADDIS Gates

SDLC discipline can become overwhelming if organizations treat it as unlimited checklist activity. The solution is not to abandon discipline. The solution is to structure it through gates and evidence bundles. This is where ADDIS provides a practical pathway. Each phase has a purpose, and each gate requires proof of readiness. The SDLC model determines how work is executed within each phase, yet the gate discipline ensures that readiness is validated before advancing. This provides a stable governance structure that works across delivery styles.

For example, in agile delivery, the team can deliver incrementally. Yet at key transition points, such as moving from design into development of core capabilities or moving into production deployment, gates still require evidence. The evidence may be produced incrementally, yet it must still be packaged and reviewed. In DevSecOps delivery, the pipeline produces continuous evidence. Gates still matter because they force explicit decisions for major releases, architectural shifts, and risk acceptance. In acquisition delivery, the vendor provides certain assurances and artifacts. Gates still matter because they force the organization to validate configuration, integration design, and operational readiness. In every case, the lifecycle discipline remains consistent. Evidence supports decisions.

This approach supports governance clarity, which CSF 2.0 emphasizes as foundational to cybersecurity outcomes. Governance is not optional because delivery style changed. Governance must hold across delivery styles, otherwise the portfolio becomes ungovernable and risk becomes unmanaged (NIST, 2024b). A PMO that enforces gate discipline therefore protects the organization from methodology chaos. It allows teams to use different SDLC models where appropriate while maintaining consistent control expectations and consistent evidence standards.

Summary and Next Steps

The SDLC is not just how teams build. It is how organizations learn the truth. It determines when risks are exposed, when controls are validated, and how quickly changes reach production. Secure SDLC ensures that security is embedded as a lifecycle discipline, producing evidence rather than promises. DevSecOps operationalizes this by integrating security into the flow of work and by enabling continuous assurance through automation and repeatable controls. This is especially critical in environments that rely on vendors, cloud services, and interconnected ecosystems, where supply chain exposure and configuration risk become dominant risk drivers.

The message of this chapter is not that every organization must adopt the same SDLC model. The message is that every organization must adopt consistent secure development practices, consistent evidence expectations, and consistent governance discipline across whatever SDLC model it uses. That posture is aligned with SSDF's lifecycle integration approach, with ISO/IEC 27001's management system expectations, and with CSF 2.0's governance-centered framing of cybersecurity as enterprise risk (Souppaya et al., 2022; ISO, 2022). It also supports the broader direction of secure development guidance for AI-enabled systems, where security and assurance must evolve as the technical paradigm evolves (NIST, 2024a).

In the next chapter, the book transitions from delivery engine fundamentals to the ADDIS methodology overview, and then into gates and evidence bundles. That transition matters because the SDLC explains how work is performed, while ADDIS and gate governance explain how readiness is proven and how decisions become defensible. Together, they create a delivery system that can move fast without moving blind.

ሐ

ADDIS AND GATE GOVERNANCE

INTRODUCTION

Part ሀ made the case that the world has changed. Part ለ translated that change into roles and operating foundations. Part ሐ now turns those ideas into a repeatable delivery system, one that can survive complexity without drowning teams in ceremony. This is the moment in the book where secure technology project management stops being a philosophy and becomes a mechanism. It becomes a control spine, a routine of governance checkpoints, and a discipline of evidence that makes decisions defensible.

Most organizations already have some version of governance. They have committees, review meetings, sign-offs, and templates. Yet the same organizations still ship systems that are difficult to operate, fragile under stress, and porous under attack. That contradiction usually has one root cause. Governance is present, but it is not integrated into delivery. It floats above delivery like a weather report, describing conditions without changing what people do next. ADDIS 2.0 and gate governance are designed to fix that. They bring governance down from the balcony and place it inside the work, where it can shape decisions, enforce accountability, and demand evidence before the organization commits to irreversible steps.

Think of modern delivery like building a bridge while traffic is already flowing beneath it. You cannot pause the river. You cannot stop the wind. You cannot assume the materials will arrive perfectly labeled. Yet you still need engineering discipline, inspection rigor, and a decision process that prevents the next beam from being bolted into place when the prior beam is not sound. Gate governance is that inspection rigor. Evidence bundles are the inspection record. The control spine is the structural blueprint that makes inspection consistent across projects, teams, and technologies.

The language of NIST CSF 2.0 helps here because it is organized around outcomes and it elevates governance, not as an administrative accessory, but as a core function that establishes and monitors risk management expectations and policy (NIST, 2024b). When you apply that idea to project delivery, the meaning is straightforward. A project is not simply an execution effort. It is a risk-taking act on behalf of the enterprise. The job of governance is to make that risk-taking explicit, proportional, and continuously managed, rather than accidental, hidden, or discovered after harm occurs.

A second anchor is the NIST Secure Software Development Framework. SSDF emphasizes that most SDLC models do not address software security in enough detail, so secure development practices must be integrated into each SDLC implementation (Souppaya et al., 2022). That statement is more disruptive than it looks. It means security is not a separate lane. It is an attribute of how the lane is built. It also means secure delivery requires a system that forces security practices to appear as deliverables, tests, and proofs, not as good intentions. Gate governance is where those proofs become non-negotiable.

Now add AI, and the need for a disciplined delivery spine becomes even more obvious. The NIST AI RMF organizes AI risk management around the functions Govern, Map, Measure, and Manage, and it is explicit that governance applies across the entire AI risk management lifecycle (NIST, 2023). The NIST Generative AI Profile further highlights that generative AI introduces novel or exacerbated risks and provides a companion profile for applying the AI RMF to generative AI systems (NIST, 2024b). In practical project terms, AI multiplies the number of assets and decisions that must be governed. Prompts, retrieval sources, datasets, model versions, evaluation baselines, and monitoring thresholds become part of the production system. If they are not governed, the system is not controllable. If the system is not controllable, you cannot claim it is ready.

Part ꝺh introduces ADDIS 2.0 and gate governance as a response to these realities. It is not presented as a competing framework to established standards. It is presented as an execution model that helps teams operationalize standards, produce evidence, and make decisions that are consistent with enterprise risk appetite.

ADDIS as a Delivery Framework, not a Checklist

ADDIS stands for Analyze, Design, Develop or Acquire, Implement, Sustain. Many readers will recognize the routine . It resembles classic delivery phase models, and that familiarity is intentional. The difference is in how it is used. ADDIS 2.0 is not a linear checklist. It is a control spine that works across multiple delivery approaches, including agile, hybrid, DevSecOps, and vendor acquisition. Its purpose is not to slow teams down. Its purpose is to prevent teams from accelerating into preventable failure.

In real projects, phases overlap. Discovery continues during design. Design decisions continue during development. Implementation planning starts early. Sustainment requirements should shape architecture. The value of ADDIS is not that it pretends these overlaps do not exist. The value is that it forces critical decisions to be made with the right evidence at the right time. It creates "decision gravity" around moments that otherwise drift, such as approving scope that introduces unacceptable data risk, approving architecture that cannot be monitored, or approving deployment without a recovery plan.

This is why Part ሐ introduces the idea of the control spine. The control spine is the minimum set of governance expectations, security practices, and evidence requirements that must exist in every project, regardless of size. Larger projects add more rigor. Higher-risk projects add deeper assurance. But the spine stays consistent. That consistency is what makes governance scalable.

The principles behind enterprise governance frameworks align with this idea. COBIT describes governance as a system that includes processes, organizational structures, policies, procedures, and information flows, and it frames governance as the mechanism that helps ensure stakeholder value while optimizing risk (ISACA, 2019). ISO/IEC 38500 similarly positions governance of IT as a domain of organizational governance and provides principles to guide responsible and acceptable use of IT across the organization (ISO, 2024). These sources reinforce the same message. Governance is not a meeting. Governance is a system of decision rights, information quality, and accountability.

ADDIS 2.0 takes that governance-system idea and fits it to delivery. It defines what information must exist, what decisions must be made, and what evidence must be produced, so that the organization can proceed with confidence. The gates make that confidence real, because the organization must confront evidence instead of relying on assumptions.

Gates That Enforce Decisions

Many organizations have gates in name, but not in practice. They call them approvals, steering committees, or sign-offs. Yet teams pass through them with incomplete testing, unresolved risks, and unclear operational ownership. That is not gate governance. That is ceremonial motion.

Gate governance in this book means something stricter. A gate is a decision point where leaders evaluate readiness using an evidence bundle and a defined set of pass, conditional pass, or fail criteria. The gate is not only a control mechanism. It is a risk management mechanism. It prevents the organization from spending more money and accumulating more dependency on a path that is not safe to continue.

The logic is consistent with how effective stage-gate models are described in innovation governance. Stage-gate systems are structured around stages of work separated by go or no-go decision points, designed to manage risk and guide investment decisions. While ADDIS is not a product innovation method, it shares a governance truth with stage-gate approaches. You need explicit decision points where leadership says, "Show me the proof, then we proceed."

In cybersecurity, the need for explicit decision points becomes sharper because threats do not wait for your project timeline. Attackers exploit weak seams and rushed releases. Misconfigurations become breaches. Unverified assumptions become incident reports. This is why NIST incident response guidance increasingly frames incident response as integrated into broader cybersecurity risk management practices rather than treated as a standalone emergency activity (NIST, 2025). When incident response is integrated, the implications for project governance are clear. Projects must produce readiness evidence that supports detection, response, recovery, and continuous improvement, not merely feature completion.

Gate governance also counters a dangerous human tendency. Under schedule pressure, teams become storytellers. They tell a story of readiness. They show green status on slides. They highlight progress. They minimize unresolved issues. They mean well, but the story becomes the product. Gate governance breaks that tendency by requiring evidence that is independently reviewable. It changes the conversation from "We believe we are ready" to "Here is what we can prove."

This is where a short dialogue can capture the difference:

- Project Lead: "We are ready for release."
- Reviewer: "Ready means what, exactly?
- Project Lead: "All features are complete."
- Reviewer: "That is functionality. Show me safety. Show me resilience. Show me how you will detect failure. Show me how you will recover. Show me your open risks and who accepted them."

Gate governance makes that reviewer's question normal, not confrontational. It makes it part of the operating language of delivery.

Evidence bundles, the currency of accountable decisions.

If a gate is the decision point, the evidence bundle is what makes the decision credible. An evidence bundle is a curated set of deliverables, test results, risk records, and operational proofs that demonstrate readiness. Evidence bundles prevent two common failure patterns. First, they prevent vague claims. Second, they prevent last-minute scavenger hunts where teams scramble to assemble artifacts after decisions have already been made emotionally.

Evidence bundles also support audit readiness. ISO/IEC 27001 emphasizes establishing, implementing, maintaining, and continually improving an information security management system, which implies disciplined documentation, traceability, and evidence of control effectiveness (ISO, 2022). Whether an organization is formally certified or simply aligned, the ability to produce consistent evidence matters. It matters to regulators. It matters to customers. It matters to internal oversight. Most importantly, it matters during incidents, when leadership asks what was known, what was decided, and what controls were in place.

In ADDIS gate governance, evidence bundles are structured and repeatable, yet flexible enough to be tailored. That flexibility is essential because projects differ in risk and complexity. A simple internal workflow tool may not require the same depth of penetration testing evidence as a customer-facing banking platform. An AI-enabled decision support tool that influences credit eligibility requires deeper assurance than a chatbot that answers generic FAQs. The governance system must therefore be risk-tiered.

The NIST AI RMF and the Generative AI Profile encourage organizations to manage AI risks based on context, use case, and impact, which supports this proportional approach (NIST, 2023; NIST, 2024b). The same proportionality is implied by CSF 2.0's emphasis on organizational profiles and tailoring cybersecurity outcomes to organizational needs. In other words, evidence bundles should not be identical across all projects. They should be consistently structured and consistently governed, with depth scaled to risk.

This book's gate governance model also treats evidence as an engine of learning. When projects collect evidence early, they discover gaps early. When they discover gaps early, remediation is cheaper. When remediation is cheaper, teams can move faster without gambling. Evidence creates speed by preventing rework. It is the paradox that mature organizations learn to love. The faster you want to go, the more you should invest in proving you are on a safe path.

Gate Decision Outcomes, Pass, Conditional, Fail

Gate governance only works if the outcomes are meaningful. This book uses three primary outcomes: pass, conditional pass, and fail.

- A pass means the evidence demonstrates readiness, residual risks are within tolerance or formally accepted, and operational ownership is clear.
- A fail means readiness is not proven, critical risks remain unmitigated, evidence is incomplete, or the system cannot be operated safely.
- A conditional pass is the most abused outcome in poorly governed environments. Teams treat conditional pass as a polite

> way to say yes. In this book, conditional pass has teeth. It is a controlled commitment with explicit conditions, owners, deadlines, and verification steps. A conditional pass without enforcement is a silent breach of governance. It is an organizational promise that will not be kept.

This is where the "control spine" concept matters. A control spine defines which conditions cannot be waived without senior risk acceptance, and it defines which evidence must exist for a gate to proceed. For example, if a system handles regulated data, access controls and logging cannot be "done later." If a system introduces an external dependency, third-party risk controls and contractual security obligations cannot be "assumed." If a system is AI-enabled and uses retrieval from internal content, the authorization model for retrieval cannot be "we will figure it out." These are not preferences. They are structural requirements.

Regulatory pressure strengthens the need for disciplined decisions, but the discipline is valuable even without regulatory scope. Modern incident disclosure expectations and operational resilience expectations force organizations to treat readiness as a governance issue rather than a project issue. That is why NIST incident response guidance now more explicitly aligns incident response capabilities with broader risk management practices tied to CSF 2.0 (NIST, 2025). A mature gate system anticipates incidents and demands that projects prove they can detect, respond, and recover.

What Part ሐ covers, and why it is the hinge of the book

Part ሐ contains three chapters, and they are the hinge that makes the rest of the book practical.

Chapter 7 introduces the ADDIS methodology overview and the control spine concept. It explains how ADDIS 2.0 works across build and buy tracks, across agile and traditional delivery, and across AI-enabled and traditional systems. It also defines the minimum governance expectations that keep delivery aligned with enterprise risk tolerance.

Chapter 8 explains phase gates, decision outcomes, and evidence bundles. It gives you the mechanics for designing gates that work, and it explains how evidence bundles should be structured so decisions are repeatable and defensible. It also clarifies how to scale rigor based on risk tier and impact.

Chapter 9 introduces governance review boards, quality reviews, and accountability through the QRB and GRB model. This is where the operating model becomes visible. Quality reviews protect the gate by ensuring deliverables are internally coherent, complete, and review-ready. Governance reviews protect the enterprise by ensuring the decision is made at the right level with the right authority and risk ownership.

This distinction between quality review and governance review is essential. Quality review is about workmanship. Governance review is about accountability. If you only do quality review, you may build something that is well-crafted but still misaligned with risk tolerance. If you only do governance review without quality discipline, your gate meeting becomes a chaos session where leaders debate incomplete artifacts. The QRB/GRB model gives structure, and structure is what allows speed without recklessness.

Part ሐ also prepares you for Part መ, where each ADDIS phase becomes a playbook and each gate becomes a formal review with a distinct end-of-phase package. In Part መ, you will see the gates applied repeatedly, and you will see how evidence bundles evolve from early framing and feasibility in Analyze, to architecture assurance in Design, to build or buy readiness in Develop or Acquire, to production readiness in Implement, to continuous assurance in Sustain. But none of that works unless Part ሐ is understood and adopted. Without Part ሐ, later chapters can be read as templates. With Part ሐ, later chapters become a living system.

Finally, Part ሐ sets up the AI governance overlay in Part ሠ. AI governance is not an isolated topic, it is a layer on top of the same gate governance system. The AI RMF and the Generative AI Profile reinforce that AI risks must be governed and managed across the lifecycle (NIST, 2023; NIST, 2024b). That is exactly what ADDIS gate governance is designed to do. It makes lifecycle governance concrete. It makes it measurable. It makes it auditable.

If Part ሀ was the diagnosis and Part ለ was the foundation, Part ሐ is the operating system. It is the disciplined logic that transforms secure delivery from aspiration into repeatable execution. It does not promise perfection. It promises clarity. Clarity about what must be true before the enterprise invests further. Clarity about who owns which decision. Clarity about what evidence is required. Clarity about how the organization learns and improves.

The modern enterprise does not fail because it lacks talent. It fails because it lacks a reliable mechanism for turning talent into safe outcomes. ADDIS 2.0 and gate governance provide that mechanism. They create a cadence of proof. They convert risk into decisions. They keep the organization from confusing motion with progress. They help you deliver technology that is not only functional, but trustworthy.

7. ADDIS Overview and Control Spine

Most organizations already have "a way of doing projects." They have templates, a few approval meetings, and a familiar tempo of kickoff, planning, build, test, and go-live. The problem is not that these elements are wrong. The problem is that they are often disconnected. Decisions happen without evidence. Evidence appears late, usually when delivery pressure is highest. Security work becomes a side quest that competes with schedules instead of shaping the schedule. Then the organization acts surprised when a release is unstable, when a vendor implementation creates hidden exposure, or when a system goes live without operational readiness. In the first edition, this book argued that secure technology delivery requires discipline. In the second edition, that argument becomes sharper because systems are now more interconnected, more vendor-dependent, and more AI-influenced than ever. In this environment, the methodology is not just a delivery preference. It is the operating logic that determines whether the organization can produce trust on purpose, or whether it hopes trust will appear after release.

ADDIS is introduced in this book as a practical delivery system designed to keep value and security moving together. ADDIS stands for Analyze, Design, Develop or Acquire, Implement, Sustain. At first glance, it looks like a typical lifecycle model, and that is intentional because organizations do not need novelty for novelty's sake. What they need is a method that makes risk visible early, forces accountable decisions at the right moments, and produces evidence that supports those decisions consistently. ADDIS is not meant to compete with agile, DevOps, or hybrid approaches. It is meant to govern them. It gives the organization a stable lifecycle spine, while teams select an execution style that fits the work. The method also aligns naturally with the idea that cybersecurity is an enterprise governance outcome, not merely a technical activity, which is consistent with governance-oriented guidance in modern cybersecurity frameworks (NIST, 2024b).

The simplest way to understand ADDIS is to picture a bridge. The business is trying to cross from an idea to an operational capability that people depend on. Most organizations build the bridge while walking on it. That can work when the river is shallow and the stakes are low. Yet when the river is deep, when compliance and reputation are on the line, and when the solution connects to critical data and external services, you need a stronger structure. ADDIS provides that structure, and the "control spine" concept is the steel inside the bridge. It is the set of governance controls that remain consistent across phases, even as the project's activities change. The control spine prevents the team from improvising fundamentals every time pressure rises, and it gives leaders a predictable way to ask, "Are we ready, and can we prove it?"

The control spine has four core ideas. The first idea is that each phase produces outcomes that become inputs to the next phase, and those outcomes must be visible, reviewable, and owned. The second idea is that readiness is proven through evidence, not through confidence or enthusiasm. The third idea is that risk acceptance is a decision, not an accident. The fourth idea is that security is embedded across the lifecycle, which matches the secure development posture that emphasizes integrating security practices into every stage of software development, not only at the end (Souppaya et al., 2022). These ideas are simple, yet they are powerful because they convert leadership intent into enforceable behavior.

In practice, the control spine is expressed through a small set of consistent governance elements that appear in every phase. There is always a scope boundary that is defined, maintained, and controlled. There is always a risk view that is updated, owned, and reviewed. There is always a set of security and compliance requirements that apply, and those requirements are treated as real constraints. There is always a quality and assurance plan that defines what will be tested and how proof will be produced. There is always an operational readiness lens because a capability is not truly delivered until it can be supported and defended in production. When these elements are present, teams move with clarity. When they are missing, teams move with velocity but without control, and the cost of that weakness arrives later in the form of rework, incidents, and loss of trust.

ADDIS also serves another purpose that organizations rarely admit they need. It gives the organization permission to say "not yet" without becoming political. Many technology failures are not caused by lack of talent. They are caused by the inability to slow down at the exact moments when slowing down would prevent a far larger failure. ADDIS creates defined moments where leadership must decide whether the work has earned the right to proceed. This is not meant to create bureaucracy. It is meant to create courage, because courage in technology governance is not saying yes quickly, it is saying yes responsibly.

A short dialogue captures the difference between weak governance and a controlled spine. A sponsor says, "We need to launch in four weeks, marketing already announced it." The project team replies, "We can hit the date if we reduce testing and tighten scope." A mature governance leader asks, "What are the conditions for safe release, and what evidence do we have today?" That question changes the entire conversation. It moves the team from urgency to readiness, and it moves leadership from pressure to accountability. This is exactly why a governance-centered approach treats cybersecurity and operational resilience as outcomes that must be guided and monitored, rather than hoped for (NIST, 2024b).

The ADDIS phases as a lifecycle of clarity

The Analyze phase is where the organization decides what problem it is actually solving, and why it is worth solving. Many projects fail because they skip this discipline. They begin with a solution and then search for justification. Analyze corrects this by demanding a clear problem statement, a value hypothesis, a feasibility view, and early risk framing. In secure delivery terms, this is where you identify what data is involved, what regulatory obligations exist, what threat exposure is likely, and what the major dependencies are. Analyze is also where you establish ownership, because a project without a real sponsor and a real business owner becomes a drift vehicle. It keeps moving because work is happening, not because outcomes are being achieved.

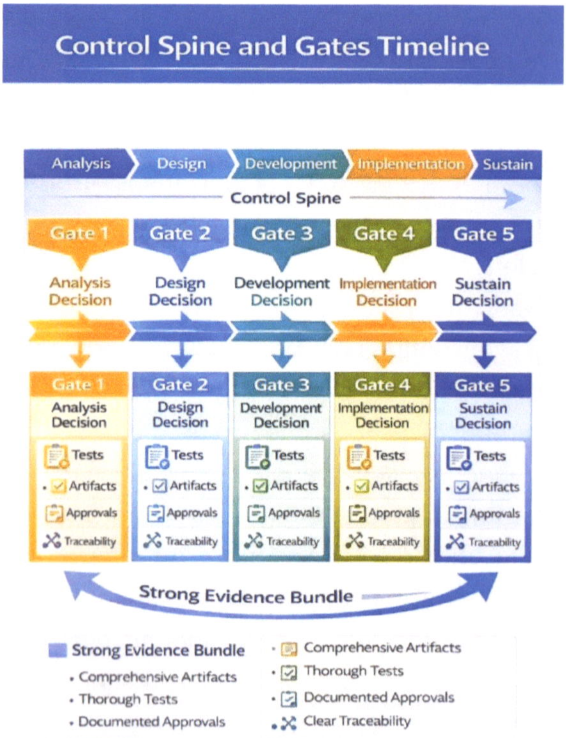

The most important output of Analyze is not a document. It is alignment. Alignment means the organization agrees on scope, constraints, and success criteria. In the second edition, Analyze also takes on a new urgency because AI and emerging technologies can create "illusionary feasibility." A prototype can look impressive, yet remain ungovernable in production if data governance, monitoring, and accountability are unclear. Analyze therefore includes a realism check. It asks whether the organization can support, secure, and govern what it intends to deploy. This is not innovation resistance. It is innovation maturity.

The Design phase is where the organization makes decisions that are expensive to reverse. Design is not just how the system will look. It is how the system will be trusted. This is where architecture defines trust boundaries, identity flows, data flows, and control placement. It is also where the organization chooses patterns for integration, logging, key management, and resilience. In many organizations, design is rushed because building feels like progress and design feels like delay. Yet skipping design discipline usually delays the project anyway, because weak design creates defects that multiply during implementation. Secure development guidance reinforces that security should be built into design and development practices, and that organizations should plan for secure outcomes rather than treating security as a last-minute verification task (Souppaya et al., 2022).

Design in ADDIS is also where testing becomes meaningful. Testing is often treated as a phase at the end. In mature delivery, testing is a strategy defined early. The test strategy includes functional validation, but it also includes security verification, performance validation, resilience testing, and operational readiness validation. When AI is in scope, the design phase must also define what "acceptable behavior" means, how evaluation will be conducted, and what monitoring and intervention mechanisms will exist. That is not an ethics discussion. It is an operational design requirement.

The Develop or Acquire phase reflects a reality that many methodologies treat poorly. Organizations do not only build. They often acquire, configure, integrate, and customize vendor platforms. ADDIS treats build and buy as two tracks inside the same lifecycle because both tracks require disciplined governance. If you build, you must manage secure engineering practices, dependency control, secure builds, and verification evidence. If you acquire, you must manage vendor obligations, shared responsibility boundaries, configuration risk, integration testing, and assurance evidence. In both cases, the organization still owns the outcome. A vendor contract cannot carry operational accountability for you.

This phase is where many projects accumulate hidden security debt. Development teams may push features quickly without maintaining secure coding discipline. Acquisition teams may trust vendor claims without verifying control implementation in the deployed environment. ADDIS addresses this by requiring that assurance work is embedded into the phase deliverables. It also requires that findings are managed as part of delivery, not postponed until the end. This aligns with a secure development posture that emphasizes repeatable practices and evidence of execution across the lifecycle (Souppaya et al., 2022).

The Implement phase is where the solution enters the real world. It is the moment when the organization discovers whether the system is truly ready, not only functional. Implementation includes deployment, migration, integration validation, stabilization, user readiness, and operational handover. In secure delivery, implementation is also where you validate that controls work under production conditions. Identity integration must behave correctly. Logging must capture meaningful events. Monitoring must generate actionable signals. Incident response must be integrated. Backup and recovery must be real, not theoretical. Implement is the phase where many organizations learn an uncomfortable truth. They delivered a solution, but they did not deliver an operable capability. ADDIS treats that gap as unacceptable because the goal is not delivery theater. The goal is sustainable operation.

The Sustain phase is where delivery maturity proves itself. Sustain is not "maintenance." Sustain is governance in motion. It includes continuous monitoring, vulnerability management, patching, change control, incident readiness, periodic assurance, and continuous improvement. In the second edition, Sustain also includes the governance of emerging technology behavior over time, especially for AI-enabled systems. Systems change. Threats change. Data changes. Dependencies change. A system that was safe at go-live can become unsafe later if monitoring and change governance are weak. This is why governance frameworks treat cybersecurity as an ongoing enterprise outcome, not a one-time project achievement (NIST, 2024b).

ADDIS and SDLC: How They Relate

Technology projects succeed when teams can clearly separate two essential ideas: how work is governed and how work is built. This section is written to explain that distinction by defining the ADDIS model and the SDLC model, then showing how they relate, how they differ, and how they are used together to manage modern technology delivery. The aim is to give readers a practical, repeatable way to apply ADDIS as the governance and decision spine, while using SDLC and DevSecOps as the execution engine that produces working increments and the evidence needed for quality and gate decisions.

This book uses ADDIS as the delivery and governance spine, and it treats SDLC as the execution engine inside that spine. This distinction matters because modern delivery is not just shipping code. It is managing risk, producing defensible evidence, and creating operational trust across the entire lifecycle. That is why ADDIS and SDLC must be understood together, but they should not be treated as interchangeable (PMI, 2021; ISACA, 2019).

ADDIS is a structured project delivery operating model. It organizes work into phases, Analyze, Design, Develop or Acquire, Implement, and Sustain, and it uses gates as formal decision points. Those gates require evidence bundles, not opinions, and they clarify who has decision rights, what must be proven, and what risk can be accepted before moving forward. In short, ADDIS is how the enterprise governs technology delivery from idea to operation.

SDLC, by contrast, is the engineering lifecycle used to design, build, test, and release a system. SDLC can be executed in multiple forms, such as waterfall, iterative, Agile, or DevSecOps. It defines how work flows through engineering activities and how increments are delivered. Secure SDLC and DevSecOps strengthen SDLC by integrating security requirements, secure engineering practices, and continuous validation into daily delivery activities (NIST, 2022).

If ADDIS is the map of the territory and the rules of travel, SDLC is the vehicle and the driving technique. You can drive a sports car or a truck, on a highway or on a dirt road. You still need a destination, traffic rules, and checkpoints. That destination, rules, and checkpoints are what ADDIS supplies.

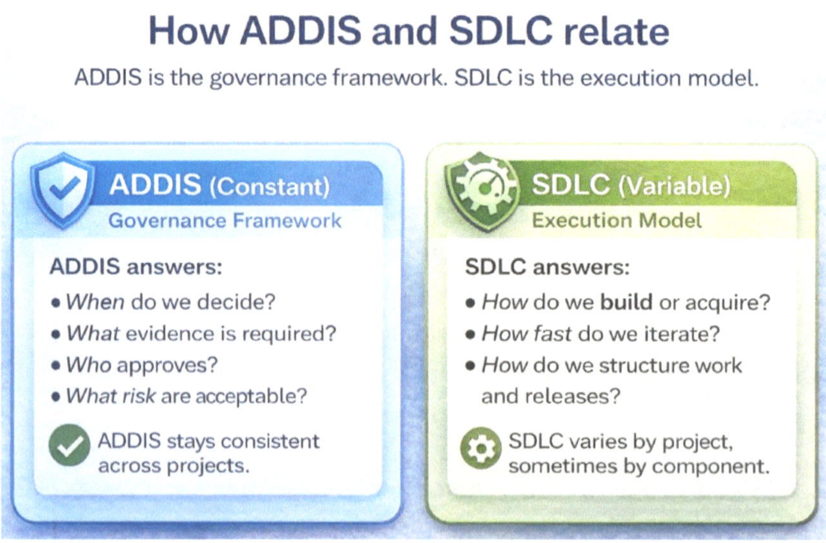

The relationship model: control spine and execution engine

A useful mental model is to think of ADDIS as the outer operating system and SDLC as the inner execution engine. ADDIS defines phase intent, governance objectives, decision points, and evidence expectations. SDLC defines the daily work mechanics that generate the evidence, such as requirements decomposition, design elaboration, coding, code review, pipeline checks, testing, release packaging, and deployment validation.

Gates are the bridge between the two. Gates are where leadership asks, "What did we produce, what did we test, what did we approve, and what risk remains?" That evidence is generated by SDLC activities and quality practices, then packaged and governed through ADDIS gate readiness. This is why "we are Agile" is never a substitute for "we are governable." Agile can accelerate delivery, but it does not automatically create defensible risk decisions. ADDIS is the mechanism that turns fast delivery into accountable delivery (PMI, 2021; ISACA, 2019).

In practice, ADDIS does not replace SDLC. It orchestrates SDLC. It tells SDLC what must be true at each point where the organization must decide. The SDLC then produces the artifacts and proofs needed to satisfy those conditions.

How ADDIS and SDLC differ

They differ in purpose, scope, cadence, outputs, and success measures. ADDIS is decision-centric. It exists to protect value, prevent unmanaged risk, and ensure the organization can defend its choices. It covers business feasibility, governance, compliance, vendor obligations, security-by-design, operational readiness, and continuous assurance. It includes the work that is not "engineering," such as funding decisions, vendor selection, architecture assurance, risk acceptance, handover approvals, and sustainment governance.

SDLC is execution-centric. It exists to build and evolve the product or system. It governs the flow of work through engineering stages and the technical discipline required to deliver stable increments.

ADDIS cadence is anchored to gates and governance reviews. SDLC cadence is anchored to delivery cycles, iterations, sprints, or release trains. SDLC can run weekly or daily. Gates do not need to happen daily. Gates should happen when decision rights must be exercised and when risk exposure changes materially.

ADDIS outputs are evidence bundles and decision records. SDLC outputs are working software, infrastructure, configurations, automated test results, and release packages. Both outputs matter. Working software without governance evidence invites hidden liability. Governance evidence without working software is theater.

Finally, ADDIS success is measured in risk-managed value delivery. SDLC success is measured in quality increments delivered efficiently. A mature organization measures both, because trust and velocity are not enemies. They are partners when governance and execution are properly aligned (ISACA, 2019; NIST, 2022).

Who uses which, and why that matters

Different stakeholders use these models for different reasons, and clarity here reduces conflict. Executives and boards primarily consume ADDIS outcomes, such as gate decisions, risk posture, audit readiness, material third-party exposure, and operational resilience. They should not be asked to interpret sprint burndown charts as evidence of compliance or cyber readiness. Their job is decision accountability.

The PMO or PPMO (Project or Project Portfolio Management Office) is the steward of ADDIS. It ensures that decision rights are applied consistently, that evidence bundles follow standards, that gates are not bypassed, and that conditional approvals are tracked to closure. The PMO also ensures that teams do not confuse "busy" with "ready."

Product management lives inside both worlds. Product leaders shape outcomes and value hypotheses, but they must operate within ADDIS decision points when risk, compliance, or investment exposure is high. They depend on SDLC to deliver increments, and they depend on ADDIS to keep delivery defensible.

Program and project managers orchestrate the integration. They translate gate expectations into actionable work plans. They work with engineering to ensure SDLC produces the evidence required for gate readiness. They also coordinate reviews, approvals, stakeholder sign-offs, and risk decisions.

Engineering and DevOps teams primarily use SDLC and DevSecOps practices. Their responsibility is to produce quality increments and reliable evidence. Their artifacts, such as test results, pipeline logs, deployment validation, and configuration baselines, become key inputs to gate evidence bundles (NIST, 2022).

Security, risk, and compliance teams use both. They define control expectations and assurance requirements and they validate that risk decisions are explicit. Security shapes what "done" means at every gate and helps teams build evidence continuously rather than scrambling before review (ISO/IEC, 2022; ISACA, 2019).

How to use both in a real project

A practical way to run a technology project is to pick an SDLC model that fits the solution, then govern it through ADDIS.

Start in Analyze by selecting a delivery approach. If the problem is stable and regulatory requirements are heavy, a more sequential approach may be appropriate. If the problem is exploratory and customer feedback is central, iterative, or Agile delivery may be more effective. If you need continuous security validation and frequent deployment, DevSecOps is often the right execution engine. Regardless of which SDLC you select, the organization still needs gate decisions tied to evidence, such as feasibility, architecture assurance, security readiness, and operational readiness.

Then, treat each phase as a governance objective, not as a paperwork milestone. Analyze should validate value, feasibility, and risk framing. Design should validate architecture, controls, data handling, and test strategy. Develop or Acquire should validate build evidence or vendor controls and contract obligations. Implement should validate production readiness and safe deployment. Sustain should validate continuous assurance and operational governance.

At each gate, the team should produce a small, structured evidence bundle that answers the same hard questions. What did we intend to do, what did we build or procure, what did we test, what did we approve, and what residual risk remains. This aligns naturally with secure software delivery practices where evidence is produced as part of development, not appended after the fact (NIST, 2022; ISO/IEC, 2022).

ADDIS governs the journey; SDLC executes the work within each phase.

What changes for Build vs Buy

Build and Buy can use the same ADDIS gate structure, but the evidence differs. In Build, evidence comes from engineering practices, secure coding, pipeline controls, and technical tests. In Buy, evidence comes from vendor due diligence, contractual controls, product security documentation, testing rights, integration validation, and ongoing third-party monitoring. ADDIS prevents a common failure pattern, where organizations treat procurement as a shortcut and discover too late that they purchased risk.

Gate 3 is especially important here. For Build, Gate 3 is readiness to deploy based on engineering evidence and assurance closure. For Buy, Gate 3 is readiness to onboard and deploy based on contractual enforceability, integration controls, and security evidence that can be validated and monitored over time.

What changes for AI systems

AI intensifies confusion because AI delivery is not a one-time ship event. AI introduces a lifecycle loop, data, model development, evaluation, deployment, monitoring, drift detection, and retraining. Teams can still use SDLC practices, but they also need lifecycle controls that are continuous. That is why ADDIS works well for AI systems. It gives you governance checkpoints and decision rights, while the AI lifecycle loop produces evolving evidence.

For AI-enabled projects, evidence must include risk tiering, data governance, evaluation metrics, monitoring and drift, misuse and abuse testing, and audit-ready logs. This aligns with AI risk management practices that emphasize governance, measurement, and ongoing monitoring, not one-time certification (NIST, 2023; ISO/IEC, 2023). It also aligns with the concept that evidence is an operational asset, especially where AI decisions can create safety, legal, or reputational exposure.

Common failure patterns when teams confuse ADDIS and SDLC

One common trap is the sentence, "We are Agile so we do not do gates." That is like saying, "We drive fast so we do not need traffic lights." Agile delivery can reduce waste and accelerate learning, but it does not replace decision rights. Gates can be lighter in Agile environments, but they still exist as decision points where risk and readiness must be proven.

A second trap is, "We passed a gate so security is done." Security-by-design is never a one-time gate. Gates confirm readiness at a point in time. Sustainment confirms whether controls still work when reality changes, such as new vulnerabilities, vendor changes, cloud configuration drift, or new AI misuse patterns (ISO/IEC, 2022).

A third trap is, "We have an SDLC so governance is covered." SDLC can produce great engineering evidence, but governance requires explicit approvals, risk acceptance, compliance mapping, and accountability. Those are governance outcomes, not just engineering steps (ISACA, 2019).

Finally, teams often confuse shipping with readiness. They treat deployment as the finish line, then discover that monitoring is incomplete, access controls are messy, incident runbooks are missing, or the operational owner is not prepared. ADDIS prevents this by making operational readiness and sustainment governance explicit, and by requiring evidence of readiness before approval (PMI, 2021).

Practical mapping guidance to reduce confusion

To keep the models aligned, use a few simple mapping rules. First, map ADDIS phases to SDLC activities. Analyze maps to discovery, requirements framing, and early prototyping. Design maps to architecture, control design, and test strategy. Develop maps to build, integrate, and validate. Acquire maps to due diligence, contract controls, onboarding, and integration testing. Implement maps to deployment, migration, and production validation. Sustain maps to monitoring, vulnerability management, patch governance, and continuous improvement.

Second, map gates to minimum evidence produced by SDLC and assurance practices. Gate evidence should include traceability from requirements to controls to tests to approvals. Secure SDLC practices are highly useful here because they formalize evidence production, such as secure requirements, design review, code review, automated checks, and test results that can be packaged into defensible bundles (NIST, 2022).

Third, map roles to decision rights. Engineering owns technical evidence. Security owns control expectations and assurance validation. Product owns outcomes and value measures. The PMO owns gate orchestration and decision record integrity. Governance boards own Go or No-Go decisions and residual risk acceptance. When this mapping is explicit, projects stop relying on informal influence and start operating as an accountable system.

Rules of thumb to keep governance and execution aligned

Use ADDIS to govern what matters, and use SDLC to deliver how it gets built. Lighten gate ceremonies for low-risk change, but never remove decision rights where risk is material. Require stronger evidence where exposure is higher, such as regulated data, critical infrastructure, sensitive integrations, material third-party dependency, or AI-enabled decisioning. If a team can show traceability, testing evidence, approval records, and residual risk disposition, gates become faster, not slower. Governance becomes a runway, not a roadblock.

When ADDIS and SDLC are aligned, confusion fades. The organization knows how to build, and it also knows how to prove readiness. It delivers with speed, and it also delivers with trust.

ADDIS control spine in action

A lifecycle model without decision control points becomes a narrative. People claim progress, yet readiness is unclear. The control spine becomes real through gates and evidence bundles. A gate is a decision point where leadership confirms readiness to proceed based on evidence. Evidence bundles are the structured packages of artifacts, approvals, test results, and risk decisions that support that gate decision. The goal is not to create heavy documentation. The goal is to create consistent proof.

In many organizations, gate reviews are treated as presentation events. Teams show slides, leaders ask a few questions, and the project proceeds. That model fails under pressure because it relies on confidence and storytelling. A mature gate is different. It requires evidence that can be reviewed independently. It requires a risk view that is current. It requires clear ownership of open issues. It produces a decision record that captures the outcome and any conditions. These behaviors align with a governance-centered approach to cybersecurity that emphasizes accountability, prioritization, and communication of risk posture across stakeholders (NIST, 2024b).

The gate outcomes should also be explicit and limited. Typically, there are four: Go, Conditional Go, Hold, and No-Go. Go means readiness is proven. Conditional Go means the project can proceed with clear conditions, owners, and timelines, and the conditions are not cosmetic. Hold means the project cannot proceed because evidence is insufficient or risk is unacceptable at this time. No-Go means the project should not proceed in its current form, and the organization must re-scope, redesign, or stop. These outcomes protect the organization from false momentum. They also protect the project team by creating a formal mechanism for raising readiness concerns without being viewed as obstructive.

Evidence bundles are the discipline that makes gates defensible. An evidence bundle is not a single document. It is a collection that can include scope definitions, requirements baselines, architecture decisions, risk register updates, testing results, security verification outputs, vendor assurance artifacts, operational readiness plans, and approvals. The exact contents vary by phase, yet the concept remains consistent. The evidence must show that the phase outcomes were achieved and that the next phase can begin without inheriting avoidable chaos. Secure development guidance reinforces the value of repeatable practices and verifiable outcomes, which is precisely what evidence bundles support (Souppaya et al., 2022).

In the ADDIS worldview, gates do not replace agile ceremonies or engineering workflows. They sit above them as governance decision points. A team can run sprints, deploy frequently, and iterate rapidly. Yet when the work crosses major thresholds, such as architecture commitment, external vendor onboarding, production deployment, or significant data flow changes, a gate ensures that leadership decisions are made with evidence. This is how ADDIS governs agile without strangling it.

Applying ADDIS across build, buy, and AI-enabled delivery

One reason ADDIS is practical is that it recognizes that modern technology delivery is not uniform. Some initiatives are pure engineering builds. Others are vendor acquisitions. Many are hybrid, where the organization acquires a platform and then builds integrations and extensions around it. ADDIS supports all of these because it is outcome-driven. It focuses on what must be true at each phase, not on the specific tools used to execute the work.

In a build scenario, the Develop portion emphasizes secure engineering and verification. Teams must demonstrate that secure coding practices exist, that dependency risks are managed, that builds are controlled, and that testing evidence is credible. In a buy scenario, the Acquire portion emphasizes vendor governance and shared responsibility clarity. Teams must demonstrate that the vendor's obligations are defined, that the organization's configuration responsibilities are understood, and that the deployed solution meets security and compliance expectations. In both scenarios, implementation and sustainment require operational proof. The system must be monitored, supported, and governed in production.

AI-enabled delivery introduces an additional overlay, not a separate lifecycle. The core phases remain, yet the evidence must expand. In Analyze, you validate data readiness, lawful use, and accountability. In Design, you define evaluation criteria, misuse cases, and guardrails. In Develop or Acquire, you validate AI-specific controls, such as prompt handling, access control to model interfaces, logging of sensitive events, and secure integration patterns. In Implement, you validate monitoring for behavior and misuse, and you confirm rollback and intervention mechanisms. In Sustain, you enforce drift monitoring, controlled updates, and periodic revalidation. The key is that AI risk management is integrated into the same governance structure, not treated as an optional ethics appendix. This integration is consistent with the broader principle that cybersecurity and digital trust must be governed as enterprise outcomes, and that governance must remain intact as technology evolves (NIST, 2024b).

ADDIS also supports a reality that mature organizations accept. Not all projects need the same level of rigor. What matters is proportionality. A low-risk internal tool does not need the same evidence bundle as a customer-facing platform that handles regulated data. Yet proportionality should be governed, not improvised. The PMO and governance boards should define tiers, such as low, medium, high, and critical, and then define the minimum evidence requirements for each tier. This keeps the organization efficient without becoming reckless. It also prevents the common failure where teams claim something is "low risk" simply to reduce governance friction.

The control spine concept becomes most valuable in this proportionality model. It ensures that the fundamentals remain consistent, even when the depth varies. Scope control remains mandatory. Risk ownership remains mandatory. Security requirements remain mandatory. Testing evidence remains mandatory. Operational readiness remains mandatory. What changes is how deep each element must go based on risk tier. This is how mature organizations scale discipline.

Why ADDIS matters now

ADDIS is not a new set of steps for teams to memorize. It is a disciplined way to connect leadership intent to delivery reality. It provides a lifecycle structure that forces early clarity, supports secure design, governs build and buy paths, validates readiness before production, and enforces sustainment accountability after release. The control spine concept is what prevents the method from becoming performative. It keeps governance consistent, it keeps evidence central, and it keeps risk acceptance explicit.

In the second edition, this matters more because delivery is faster and risk is broader. AI and emerging technologies can accelerate capability creation, yet they can also accelerate failure when accountability and evidence are weak. ADDIS gives organizations a way to move with speed while maintaining control. It gives leadership a way to fund innovation without funding hidden liability. It gives project teams a way to execute with clarity and defend decisions with proof. Most importantly, it makes secure technology project management an organizational habit, not a heroic effort.

In the next chapter, the book moves from the lifecycle overview to the mechanics of gate governance, decision outcomes, and evidence bundles. This transition is deliberate. ADDIS explains the journey. Gate governance explains how the organization proves it is safe to take the next step.

“Governance decides, delivery builds, evidence proves.”

Keep spine and engine distinct. ADDIS is the governance and decision spine, it sets direction, accountability, and gate decisions. SDLC and DevSecOps are the execution engine that turns intent into working increments.

Evidence is the bridge. The engine must continuously produce verifiable outputs, requirements traceability, design decisions, test results, and operational readiness artifacts, so gates are based on proof, not confidence.

Do not confuse motion with progress. Shipping code is activity. Progress is measured when risk is understood, controls are validated, and leaders can make defensible proceed or stop decisions.

Repeatability is the goal. When teams apply ADDIS consistently and run SDLC/DevSecOps inside it, delivery becomes predictable, audit-ready, and operationally trusted, not only “done.”

Treat ADDIS as the spine, treat SDLC as the engine, require evidence as the fuel that makes decisions credible.

Gates and Evidence Bundles

Technology projects rarely fail because teams did not work hard. They fail because the organization made critical decisions in fog. A project can look healthy on a dashboard while quietly accumulating exposure in identity design, vendor dependencies, data handling, testing depth, or operational readiness. The fog thickens near the end because delivery pressure rises, and nobody wants to be the person who slows momentum. So the organization does what humans often do when they are tired and invested, it substitutes confidence for proof. That is how a system ships with "temporary exceptions" that become permanent risk, and that is how a go live date becomes a gamble instead of an informed decision. This chapter is about removing the fog. Phase gates exist to ensure the organization does not confuse activity with readiness. Decision outcomes exist to make risk acceptance explicit rather than accidental. Evidence bundles exist to turn readiness into something that can be verified, audited, defended, and improved over time (NIST, 2024b).

Many delivery environments have some form of gate, even if they do not call it that. They have a kickoff approval, a design sign-off, a testing readiness review, or a production change meeting. The problem is that these checkpoints often drift into rituals. The project presents slides, leaders nod, and the team proceeds. The meeting ends, yet little has been decided and even less has been proven. The organization feels busy, which is comforting, but busyness is not assurance. Phase gates become powerful only when they are treated as decision points that require evidence. If the evidence is thin, the decision should be "not yet." If the evidence is strong, the decision can be "go forward" with confidence, not hope. That posture aligns with governance principles that emphasize guiding and monitoring technology use, clarifying accountability, and ensuring conformance is validated rather than assumed (ISO, 2015).

In the ADDIS methodology, gates are not a substitute for agile ceremonies, DevSecOps pipelines, or vendor implementation playbooks. Gates sit above execution methods as governance control points. They exist to protect the enterprise at moments when the cost of being wrong is high. A team can iterate rapidly, deploy frequently, and still need gates for architectural commitments, vendor onboarding, production releases, and major data flow changes. If a project is building or buying a capability that will hold sensitive data, touch critical operations, or introduce AI-enabled automation, the organization has a duty to ensure readiness is real. In this sense, gates are not bureaucracy. They are institutional memory and enterprise courage. They make it acceptable, even expected, to slow down at the exact moments when slowing down prevents a far larger failure later (NIST, 2024b).

A practical metaphor helps. Think of a project as a flight plan. The team can taxi quickly and still be unsafe if pre-flight checks are skipped. The goal of a gate is not to delay takeoff for fun. The goal is to confirm the aircraft is airworthy, the route is known, the weather is understood, and the crew is prepared. If those conditions are not met, the bravest decision is to hold. Not because progress is undesirable, but because catastrophic rework, regulatory impact, or reputational damage is worse than a disciplined delay. In secure delivery, the "weather" is the threat landscape, the compliance environment, and the dependency ecosystem. Those realities do not pause because the project is behind schedule. They continue to move, and gate governance is how you keep the project aligned with that moving reality.

A short dialogue illustrates the difference between a ritual and a real gate. A sponsor says, "Marketing announced the launch date. We cannot slip." The delivery lead replies, "We can make the date if we reduce testing and finish the security items after." A mature governance leader asks, "What conditions define safe release, and what evidence do we have today that those conditions are met?" That question changes the entire conversation. It moves from pressure to proof. It forces the organization to decide consciously what risk it is accepting, and it forces ownership to become visible. That is the spirit of phase gates in ADDIS, and it is consistent with modern governance-centered cybersecurity thinking that treats risk decisions as enterprise decisions, not team-level improvisation (NIST, 2024b).

Why phase gates matter

Phase gates exist because the lifecycle has natural points of commitment. After Analyze, the organization commits to a problem statement, a scope boundary, and a benefits hypothesis. After Design, it commits to architecture, trust boundaries, and control placement decisions that are expensive to reverse. Before production deployment, it commits to operational exposure, meaning the system will be reachable, used, and targeted. These are not ordinary milestones. They are commitment moments. Without gates, the organization tends to drift through commitment moments without noticing that the commitment has already been made. It signs a contract before vendor obligations are clarified. It finalizes architecture before threat modeling is completed. It deploys to production before monitoring is proven. Each drift event seems small in isolation, yet together they produce a system that is operationally fragile and hard to defend.

A gate is therefore a governance mechanism that forces timing. Timing is one of the most underappreciated forms of risk control. Many organizations can do the "right" security tasks, but they do them too late. They threat model after development when the architecture is already locked. They validate logging after go-live, when the first incident occurs. They clarify data classification after integrations spread sensitive data across multiple services. Secure delivery fails not only when the wrong tasks are performed, but also when the right tasks are performed at the wrong time. A gate aligns timing by requiring that certain truths be known before the organization moves forward.

A gate also forces ownership. Risk registers without owners are theater. Architecture decisions without accountable approvers are vulnerable to dispute later. Operational readiness claims without named operational owners are fragile promises. Gates convert these weak statements into accountable commitments. When a gate decision is recorded, it clarifies who decided, what they decided, what conditions exist, and who must close remaining gaps. This is governance made tangible, and it aligns with governance standards that emphasize accountability and the guiding and monitoring of IT use at the organizational level (ISO, 2015).

Gates further force consistency across the portfolio. Without gates, each team invents its own definition of "ready." One project may require penetration testing and a formal operational handover. Another may skip both and still be allowed into production. The inconsistency is not always visible until an incident occurs, at which point leaders ask why the organization tolerated lower standards for certain initiatives. A gate model creates a consistent minimum bar, then allows proportionality based on risk tier. The bar does not need to be heavy for every project. It needs to be real for every project. This is how you scale delivery without scaling chaos.

Finally, gates create learning. When evidence bundles are stored and decisions are recorded, the organization can compare predictions with outcomes. Did the risks identified in Design actually matter in production? Did the chosen controls prevent the expected failure modes? Did operational readiness assumptions hold? This feedback loop is often missing in organizations where projects "finish" and teams immediately move to the next initiative. A mature gate governance model makes learning a normal part of delivery. That learning improves templates, improves standards, and improves executive decision-making over time.

Gates should also be understood as a bridge between execution methods and governance expectations. An organization can use agile, hybrid, or vendor-led delivery approaches, yet still require the same governance truths. The truths are stable. The workflow is flexible. This is one reason secure development guidance is framed as practices that can be integrated into any SDLC rather than as a single rigid methodology. NIST's Secure Software Development Framework emphasizes integrated practices and verifiable outcomes that help organizations build and maintain secure software in a repeatable way, regardless of delivery style (Souppaya et al., 2022). Gates are one of the primary ways to ensure those practices are not optional, and that evidence of their execution is visible to decision-makers.

Decision outcomes that protect the enterprise

A gate is only as strong as the decisions it produces. If every gate ends in "Go" regardless of evidence, the gate is decorative. If the gate produces vague conditions that are never tracked, the gate becomes a disguised acceptance of risk. The discipline of decision outcomes is therefore central. In ADDIS gate governance, the most effective outcome set is limited and explicit: Go, Conditional Go, Hold, and No-Go. These outcomes are simple enough to be used consistently and meaningful enough to drive behavior.

"Go" means the evidence meets the criteria and risks are within acceptable thresholds. It does not mean perfection. It means readiness has been demonstrated and the organization can proceed with confidence. A real Go decision is supported by evidence that critical controls are designed and implemented for the phase, that testing evidence is credible for the phase, and that residual risk is understood. A Go decision should also include a clear statement of what readiness means at this stage, because readiness is phase-specific. Analyze readiness is not the same as production readiness.

Design readiness is not the same as sustainment readiness. A mature organization calibrates criteria accordingly.

"Conditional Go" means the organization can proceed, but only with explicit conditions that are tracked like commitments, not like suggestions. Conditional Go is useful because it allows progress while maintaining control, yet it is also dangerous if misused. The most common misuse is to attach conditions that are vague, such as "Complete security review soon," or "Improve monitoring later." Vague conditions are how risk becomes permanent. A responsible Conditional Go requires that each condition has an owner, a measurable completion definition, a deadline, and a verification step. It also requires clarity about what happens if the condition is not met. Does the project stop at the next gate? Does deployment pause? Does scope reduce? Conditional Go must be designed to create accountability, not to create cover.

"Hold" means the organization cannot proceed because readiness is not proven or risk is unacceptable at this point. Hold is not a punishment. It is governance doing its job. The best governance cultures treat Hold as a sign of maturity, because the organization is willing to protect itself against avoidable failure. Hold decisions should be accompanied by a clear remediation path, meaning what evidence is missing, what gaps must be closed, and what will be reviewed again to re-enter the gate. This prevents Hold from becoming a stall that drains morale. Instead, it becomes a disciplined reset that clarifies priorities.

"No-Go" means the initiative should not proceed in its current form. No-Go is rare, yet it is essential for governance credibility. Without No-Go, governance becomes a theater where the only acceptable outcome is progress, even when progress is unsafe or misaligned. No-Go does not always mean the idea is dead. It can mean the solution must be redesigned, re-scoped, re-sequenced, or re-funded. It can mean a vendor path should be abandoned because the shared responsibility model is unacceptable. It can mean the benefits case no longer justifies the exposure. No-Go is the outcome that proves governance is real.

The presence of these outcomes changes organizational behavior. Teams stop treating gates as slide presentations and start treating gates as readiness events. Sponsors stop assuming every promise can be kept and start seeing tradeoffs clearly. Security teams stop being isolated "blockers" and become part of the evidence-producing delivery system. The PMO stops being a reporting office and becomes an enabler of defensible decision-making. That is what a gate system is supposed to do. It creates a common language for decision-making across the enterprise.

Decision outcomes also require clearly defined decision authority. If the people in the room cannot accept risk on behalf of the organization, then risk acceptance will still happen, it will just happen informally. A mature gate model therefore defines who can approve which gate based on risk tier, data sensitivity, system criticality, and regulatory impact. It also clarifies that certain residual risks require executive acceptance, not team-level acceptance. For example, accepting a known weakness in privileged access controls or accepting incomplete monitoring for a customer-facing system should never be a silent project decision. It should be an explicit enterprise risk decision. This is consistent with governance principles that emphasize accountability and monitoring at the appropriate organizational level (ISO, 2015).

Decision outcomes should also produce a decision record that is brief but precise. It should capture what was reviewed, what was decided, what conditions exist, who owns them, and when the next verification will occur. This record is not only for audit. It is for operational clarity. It reduces re-litigation. It protects teams from shifting expectations. It also protects leaders by proving that risk decisions were conscious and that evidence supported the chosen path. In mature environments, decision records become a quiet form of institutional resilience.

Evidence bundles and how to run gates

Evidence bundles are the practical foundation of gate governance. They are the structured packages of proof that support a gate decision. In weak governance environments, evidence is replaced by narrative. A team says, “We tested.” A leader asks, “Are we secure?” The team says, “Yes.” Everyone moves on. That is not a decision. That is a story. Evidence bundles replace story with proof, and they do it without requiring excessive paperwork, if the organization designs them correctly.

The first principle of an evidence bundle is that it should contain outcomes, not opinions. It should include artifacts that can be inspected independently. It should include test results that can be traced to requirements. It should include risk registers that show ownership and current status. It should include approvals and decision logs that show authority. The bundle should also be phase-specific because the evidence required after Analyze differs from the

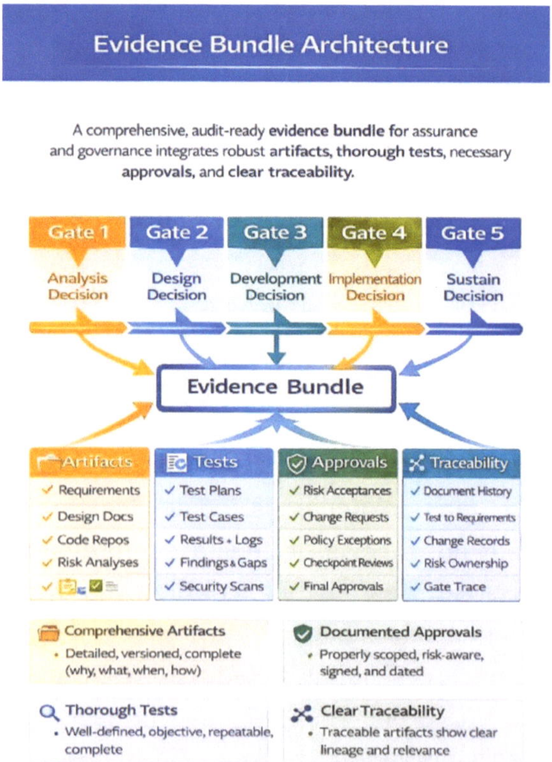

evidence required before production deployment. A well-designed evidence bundle is therefore a template that evolves by phase and scales by risk tier.

The second principle is that evidence should be produced as part of delivery, not as a last-minute gate exercise. If teams scramble to assemble artifacts one week before a gate, the artifacts are often incomplete and the evidence is often weak. Worse, the scramble encourages performative behavior. People produce documents because they must, not because the documents reflect real work. In mature environments, evidence is the natural exhaust of disciplined delivery. Requirements are managed, architecture decisions are recorded, testing is executed, and the results are stored. The gate is then a confirmation of ongoing discipline, not a sudden burst of documentation.

This is where secure development practices become crucial. SSDF emphasizes that organizations should integrate secure practices across the lifecycle and be able to demonstrate that those practices were performed (Souppaya et al., 2022). Evidence bundles operationalize that expectation. They make secure practices visible. They also help organizations avoid the false comfort of late-stage security reviews that cannot fix foundational design decisions. When evidence is produced earlier, decisions improve earlier, and the project becomes less fragile.

A practical evidence bundle structure can be understood as a consistent spine with phase-specific depth. The spine includes scope clarity, requirements clarity, architecture and control clarity, risk clarity, testing and assurance clarity, and operational readiness clarity. In the Analyze gate, evidence may include a defined problem statement, scope boundaries, a benefits hypothesis, a feasibility view, and an initial risk register with major dependencies and data classification assumptions. In the Design gate, evidence should include architecture diagrams that define trust boundaries, control placement decisions, threat modeling outputs with mitigations assigned, security requirements mapped to design elements, and a test strategy that includes security verification. In the pre-production gate, evidence should include functional and security test results, configuration validation results, operational readiness proof such as monitoring and incident response integration, a validated deployment plan, and a clear rollback capability. In sustainment readiness, evidence should include ownership assignments for patching, monitoring, vulnerability management, change control, and incident response operations. ISO/IEC 27001 reinforces this operational posture by emphasizing an information security management system that assigns responsibilities and maintains controls over time, not only at go-live (ISO, 2022).

Evidence bundles also require a clear view of open items. Mature governance does not demand that all issues be solved at every gate. It demands that open items be visible, owned, and acceptable relative to risk appetite. Visibility is the key. An open risk that is clearly documented, assigned, and tracked is manageable. An open risk that is hidden is dangerous. Evidence bundles make open items visible, which allows Conditional Go decisions to be meaningful and allows Hold decisions to be justified.

Running a gate meeting effectively is a skill. The best gate meetings are short because most review happens before the meeting. A quality function, often within the PMO or a quality review board, should validate that the evidence bundle is complete and coherent before governance time is consumed. This separation of quality validation from governance decision-making is one of the simplest ways to reduce gate friction. It prevents leaders from spending time on document hunting. It keeps the gate meeting focused on decisions, tradeoffs, and conditions.

The meeting itself should revolve around a small number of questions. Are the phase outcomes achieved? What risks remain, and who owns them? What evidence supports readiness? If the decision is

Conditional Go, what are the conditions, who owns them, and what is the verification plan? If the decision is Hold or No-Go, what is the remediation path? These questions sound basic, yet they are rarely answered cleanly in weak governance cultures because evidence is inconsistent and ownership is unclear. When evidence bundles are standardized, these questions become routine, and governance becomes faster, not slower.

Gate governance must also be compatible with modern delivery methods. In agile and DevSecOps environments, evidence is often produced continuously through backlogs, pipelines, and automated checks. That is an advantage, but only if the organization treats pipeline outputs as evidence and maintains traceability. DevSecOps can produce logs, scan results, test outcomes, and deployment records. Those records should flow into evidence bundles. Yet automation is not a replacement for decision authority. Pipelines can enforce many controls, but they cannot accept residual risk on behalf of the enterprise. Gates remain necessary for major releases, major architectural changes, vendor onboarding, and changes that introduce new high-risk data flows. Governance must remain intact as speed increases, otherwise the organization simply accelerates uncontrolled change into production (NIST, 2024b).

Acquisition and vendor implementation projects also require gate governance, sometimes even more than build projects. Organizations often assume that buying software reduces risk because the vendor is experienced. In reality, many failures in acquired systems come from configuration mistakes, unclear shared responsibility boundaries, weak integration design, and insufficient operational readiness. Evidence bundles for acquisition projects should therefore include vendor assurance artifacts, shared responsibility mapping, configuration standards, integration security validation, and operational readiness proof. The organization should be able to show what it required of the vendor, what it verified in the deployed environment, and what controls it owns going forward. Without this evidence, the organization is relying on assumptions, and assumptions are not controls.

AI-enabled initiatives introduce an additional evidence requirement because behavior risk can be subtle. A system can pass functional tests and still produce harmful outcomes if AI components behave unexpectedly under realistic use. For AI-enabled delivery, the evidence bundle should include a clear definition of intended use, clear boundaries for unacceptable outcomes, evaluation criteria and results, and monitoring readiness for misuse and drift. The goal is not to add heavy ethics paperwork. The goal is to ensure the organization can operate the capability responsibly after go-live. In the ADDIS model, AI does not create a separate lifecycle. It creates an assurance overlay that strengthens evidence expectations at the same gates.

Gate governance also fails when it is applied uniformly without proportionality. Not every change requires executive review. Not every internal tool requires heavy evidence. The solution is risk tiering. A mature PMO defines tiers, for example low, medium, high, critical, and maps each tier to minimum evidence requirements. The evidence bundle spine stays the same. The depth changes. A low-risk enhancement might require lighter artifacts and faster gate cycles. A critical customer-facing release might require deeper assurance evidence and executive risk acceptance. Proportionality is how you keep governance credible and sustainable.

There are common Pitfall that undermine gates, and they should be addressed explicitly because they recur in almost every organization. One Pitfall is the presentation gate, where narrative replaces evidence. The correction is pre-review of evidence bundles and a rule that the gate meeting is for decisions, not for reading. Another Pitfall is the checklist gate, where teams satisfy shallow requirements without meaningful assurance. The correction is outcome-based criteria, supported by evidence, with reviewers trained to ask “what proof exists" rather than "was a step performed." Another Pitfall is Conditional Go theater, where conditions are vague and never tracked. The correction is to treat conditions as deliverables, with owners, deadlines, and verification. Another Pitfall is governance bottleneck, where gates are so heavy that teams bypass them. The correction is risk

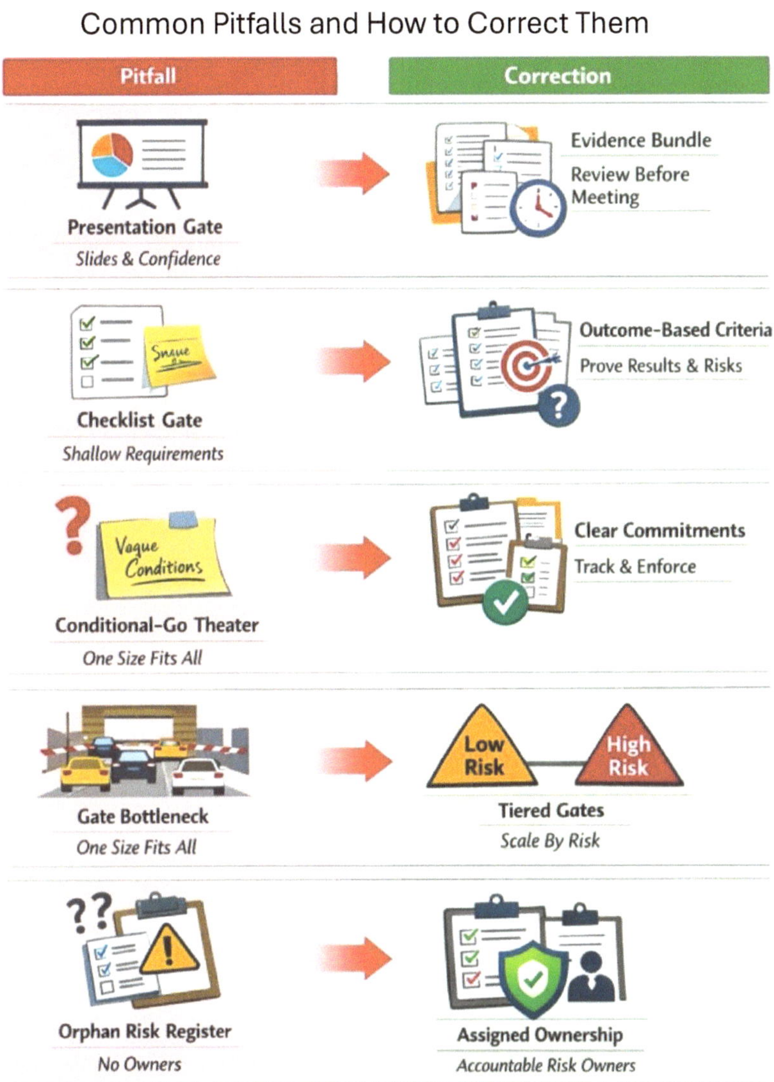

tiering and lean governance patterns for low-risk work. Another pitfall is orphan risk, where risks exist but have no owners. The correction is to make risk ownership a gate criterion. If a risk has no owner, it is not a managed risk. It is a future incident.

Implementing gates successfully requires cultural design, not just templates. Teams must believe gates are fair. Leaders must believe Hold and No-Go are legitimate outcomes. Security and compliance functions must act as partners in evidence creation, not as late-stage enforcers who appear only to stop delivery. The PMO must act as an enabler of discipline, helping teams understand what good evidence looks like and helping remove friction from the process. Over time, the organization should aim for a simple maturity outcome: gates become faster because evidence is continuously maintained. Decisions become easier because criteria are clear. The portfolio becomes safer because risk acceptance is explicit and recorded.

A phased rollout approach is often the most practical. Start with a small number of major gates, typically after Analyze, after Design, and before production release. Define clear outcomes and a simple decision record. Define evidence bundle templates that match those gates. Train project leaders and reviewers on how to produce and evaluate evidence. Use early pilots to adjust the templates and reduce unnecessary friction. As the organization matures, expand the gate model into sustainment governance, including periodic assurance checks and post-implementation reviews that capture lessons learned. This creates a feedback loop where governance improves delivery, and delivery evidence improves governance.

The value of this discipline shows up not only in avoiding incidents, but also in reducing wasted effort. Projects that are forced to clarify requirements and constraints early spend less time rebuilding later. Teams that are forced to define trust boundaries and control placement in design spend less time patching architectural gaps in implementation. Solutions that are forced to demonstrate operational readiness before go-live spend less time in production firefighting. In other words, gates protect time by preventing late truth. They protect trust by preventing uncontrolled exposure. They protect value by ensuring the organization delivers capabilities that can actually be sustained.

This chapter ties directly to the control spine concept introduced in the ADDIS overview. Phase gates are the points where the spine is tested. Decision outcomes are the moments where leadership demonstrates accountability. Evidence bundles are the artifacts that make readiness verifiable. When these elements work together, the organization moves with confidence grounded in proof. It can innovate without gambling. It can deliver faster without shipping blind. It can defend decisions when audits occur and when incidents demand explanation. Most importantly, it can build and preserve digital trust as a deliberate outcome of governance and execution, rather than as a fragile hope.

In the next chapters, this book will translate these concepts into phase-specific deliverables and playbooks. You will see what evidence bundles look like at each ADDIS phase. You will also see how security-by-design deliverables are integrated so teams do not rely on heroic effort to "remember security" under pressure. The goal is a repeatable system, where security and governance are embedded in the delivery flow, supported by clear decisions and credible proof. That is secure technology project management at scale (NIST, 2024b; Souppaya et al., 2022).

Evidence Makes the Gate Real.

"A gate is not a meeting. It is a decision backed by proof."

Evidence bundles turn governance into signal. They let leaders see what is true, what is uncertain, and what is still risky, without relying on slide confidence.

A good bundle is curated, not massive. Include only what proves outcomes: decisions, traceability, test results, remediation closure, and readiness artifacts.

Review happens before the meeting. The gate meeting is for resolving exceptions, confirming risk acceptance, and recording the decision, not for reading documents.

If proof is missing, the decision must change. "Conditional go" is valid only when conditions are specific, owned, time-bound, and verifiable.

When evidence is continuous, gates become faster and more credible.

Review Boards and Accountability

A technology project becomes difficult to govern the moment decisions are made without an accountable forum, without clear decision rights, and without evidence that can survive scrutiny. In many organizations, governance is treated as a calendar event, a monthly steering meeting, a slide deck review, a quick sign-off at the end of a phase. That approach fails under pressure because it depends on narrative confidence rather than verifiable readiness. When deadlines tighten, people interpret governance as an obstacle and they begin to route around it. Security work becomes negotiable. Quality becomes "we will fix it later." Operational readiness becomes an assumption. Then the organization discovers the true cost, rework, audit findings, production instability, incident response fatigue, and the slow erosion of trust that follows. The QRB/GRB model exists to prevent this failure pattern by turning governance into a disciplined operating mechanism, not a ceremonial checkpoint. It creates the forums where quality is validated early, where risk acceptance is explicit, and where accountability is assigned in a way that is defensible and repeatable (NIST, 2024b).

The heart of the QRB/GRB model is separation of concerns with tight coordination. A Quality Review Board, QRB, exists to protect integrity of delivery, meaning completeness, standards adherence, engineering discipline, test depth, and evidence quality. A Gate Review Board, GRB, exists to protect enterprise risk posture, meaning readiness to proceed across phases, acceptance of residual risks, alignment with policy and regulatory expectations, and accountability for the consequences of moving forward. When organizations combine these functions into a single meeting, they often get the worst of both worlds. Either the meeting becomes a document scavenger hunt, and leaders never reach the real decision, or it becomes a fast executive approval forum where evidence quality is not examined. The QRB/GRB model fixes that by creating two complementary layers. QRB validates the evidence and the quality story. GRB makes the phase decision using validated evidence and records the decision so it can be defended later.

This model aligns naturally with modern governance expectations. CSF 2.0 emphasizes that cybersecurity outcomes must be governed and communicated as part of enterprise risk management, rather than treated as isolated technical activities (NIST, 2024b). ISO/IEC 38500 similarly frames governance of IT as guiding and monitoring the organization's use of technology, with clear responsibilities and principles that support effective decision-making (ISO, 2015). In practical terms, QRB/GRB is a way to operationalize those ideas inside technology project execution. It provides a predictable routine for governance, a clear method for producing evidence, and a defined set of decision outcomes that reduce ambiguity and prevent accidental risk acceptance.

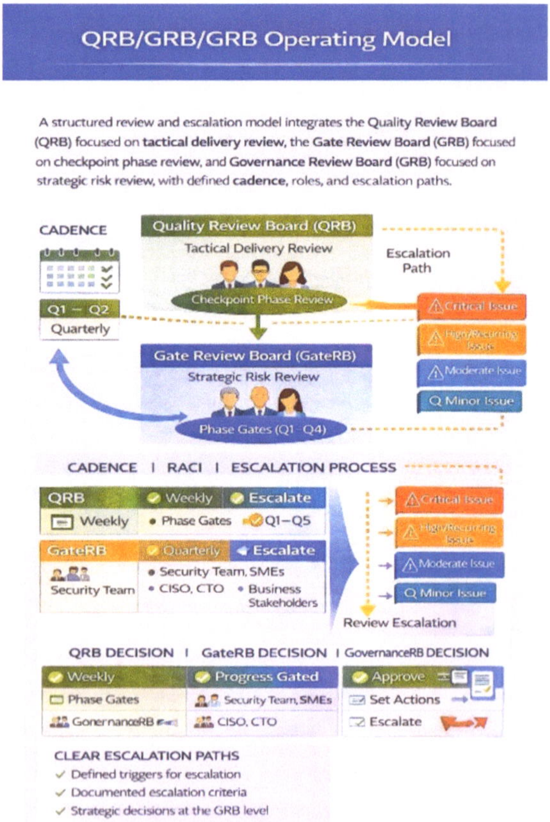

Separating Quality Review from Gate Decisions, QRB and GRB

A QRB is a quality assurance and readiness integrity forum. It is the place where deliverables and artifacts are examined for completeness, coherence, and alignment to standards. QRB asks questions that sound simple but are rarely answered cleanly when teams are rushing. Are requirements traceable to design decisions. Are security requirements treated like real requirements. Are architecture diagrams consistent with integration plans. Are test results credible, repeatable, and mapped to risk. Are third-party dependencies documented with ownership and controls. Are operational readiness elements present, such as monitoring, incident response integration, access controls, and rollback planning. QRB is less concerned with whether leadership wants to proceed and more concerned with whether the project has produced the proof that would justify proceeding. This evidence-first approach matches secure development guidance that stresses verifiable outcomes and repeatable practices across the lifecycle, rather than informal assurances (Souppaya et al., 2022).

A GRB is the decision authority forum. It is the gatekeeper of phase transitions, and it owns the final Go, Conditional Go, Hold, or No-Go decision. GRB does not exist to re-check every artifact at the same depth as QRB. It exists to make enterprise-level decisions using validated evidence, and to document those decisions, including residual risk acceptance when it occurs. GRB is where the organization answers, are we ready to proceed, are we willing to accept what remains open, and have we assigned owners to close gaps within a defined timeline. GRB is also where leaders confirm alignment with enterprise standards, policy, and strategic direction, including governance expectations for cybersecurity and resilience (NIST, 2024b).

The separation matters because it reduces governance friction while increasing governance rigor. QRB allows technical depth without executive time waste. GRB allows executive accountability without shallow evidence. Together, they create a system where project teams know what "good" looks like, and leaders know what they are approving. The model also reduces politics. Teams are not forced to defend quality concerns in an executive forum where schedule pressure dominates. Instead, quality concerns are surfaced and validated in QRB, then escalated to GRB as structured facts, not personal opinions. This is how governance becomes fair, and fairness is how governance becomes sustainable.

Board charters, membership, and decision rights

QRB and GRB must be chartered explicitly. Without a charter, boards drift into personality-driven behavior. With a charter, boards become institutional mechanisms that survive staff turnover and changing priorities. The charter should define purpose, scope, authority, membership, cadence, decision outcomes, escalation rules, and evidence expectations. It should also define what QRB can approve independently, what QRB can recommend, and what must be escalated to GRB.

Membership should be role-based, not person-based. QRB typically includes representation from solution architecture, engineering leadership, QA or testing leadership, security engineering or application security, cloud, or infrastructure engineering when relevant, data engineering when data is a major component, and operational readiness or SRE representation when production stability is a concern. Vendor management and procurement representation should be included when a third-party platform is part of the solution because configuration and shared responsibility risk must be validated, not assumed. QRB works best when members are practitioners who can evaluate evidence and spot gaps quickly.

GRB typically includes executive or senior leadership roles with authority to accept enterprise risk and allocate resources, such as CIO or delegate, CISO or delegate, head of architecture, head of operations, compliance, or risk representation for regulated environments, and PMO leadership to ensure portfolio consistency. GRB attendance should be stable enough to preserve decision continuity, yet flexible enough to invite specialists for high-risk topics, such as privacy counsel for personal data issues or AI governance representation for AI-enabled capabilities.

Decision rights must be explicit. QRB should have authority to determine whether evidence is sufficient for GRB review, and it should have authority to require remediation of evidence gaps before escalation. GRB should have authority to approve phase transitions and to accept residual risks, within defined limits and thresholds. Some risks should require a higher authority, such as enterprise risk committee or board-level oversight, especially when the risk involves regulated data exposure, material service disruption potential, or contractual commitments with significant liability. Defining these thresholds in advance prevents last-minute improvisation and aligns with governance principles that emphasize accountability and monitoring at the correct organizational level (ISO, 2015).

Evidence Bundles, Quality Checks, Gate Outcomes

The QRB/GRB model is only as strong as its evidence discipline. Evidence bundles are the structured packages that prove readiness. They should be standardized by phase and scaled by risk tier. Standardization is essential because it allows consistency across projects. Scaling is essential because not every project deserves the same level of ceremony. The organization should define risk tiers and map each tier to evidence depth requirements. This enables speed where risk is low and rigor where risk is high, without creating loopholes.

QRB typically operates using a quality checklist aligned to organizational standards. The checklist should include core categories such as scope and requirements integrity, design and architecture integrity, security-by-design control placement, secure development practices where applicable, testing completeness including security verification, third-party assurance, data governance and privacy considerations, and operational readiness. The checklist should be written as outcomes, not as vague activities. For example, "Threat model reviewed, mitigations assigned, and residual risks documented" is an outcome. "Security review performed" is not. The Secure Software Development Framework reinforces why outcomes matter because secure development must be demonstrated through repeatable practices and verifiable results, not by informal claims (Souppaya et al., 2022).

GRB decisions should use a limited set of outcomes to avoid ambiguity. Go means readiness is proven. Conditional Go means the project may proceed with explicit conditions, owners, deadlines, and verification steps. Hold means readiness is not proven or risk is unacceptable, and the project must remediate before proceeding. No-Go means the initiative should not proceed in its current form, and it must be re-scoped, re-designed, or terminated. These outcomes protect the organization from accidental risk acceptance. They also protect the project team by making the rules visible and consistent.

Decision records are a required artifact of GRB. They should capture what was reviewed, what was decided, what conditions exist, who owns conditions, when verification will occur, and what residual risks were accepted, by whom, and why. Decision records are not just for audit. They prevent re-litigation later and create organizational memory. In regulated environments, they also support conformance expectations under information security management system principles that emphasize defined responsibilities, control maintenance, and continual improvement (ISO, 2022).

Accountability is the silent failure point of most governance models. Projects often produce artifacts, yet ownership is unclear. When something breaks in production, people debate who was supposed to do what. QRB/GRB addresses this by institutionalizing accountability rules.

First, every major risk must have an owner. If a risk has no owner, it is not a managed risk. It is a future incident. Second, every gate condition must have an owner and a deadline, and the closure evidence must be specified. Third, every exception must have an explicit approver and an expiration. Exceptions without expiration become permanent vulnerabilities. Fourth, escalation paths must be defined. If a project cannot resolve a security control gap due to constraints, that gap must be escalated to GRB as a decision, not buried as a technical inconvenience.

RACI can be applied pragmatically. The goal is not to produce a complex matrix for its own sake. The goal is to eliminate ambiguity. For example, the business owner is accountable for business outcomes and for accepting business tradeoffs. The technology owner is accountable for architecture integrity and delivery quality. The security owner is accountable for defining control expectations and validating security evidence, yet not for accepting enterprise residual risk on behalf of business leaders. The operations owner is accountable for monitoring, incident response integration, and sustainment readiness. The PMO is accountable for governance process integrity, schedule realism, and evidence bundle consistency. When these accountabilities are clear, QRB reviews become sharper and GRB decisions become faster.

Escalation should be treated as a sign of maturity, not as a sign of conflict. When a team escalates a readiness concern, it is protecting the organization. A weak governance culture punishes escalation by labeling it obstruction. A mature governance culture rewards escalation because it prevents bigger failures. This is consistent with governance-centered thinking in cybersecurity frameworks, where communication, prioritization, and accountability are essential for managing risk effectively across stakeholders (NIST, 2024b).

QRB and GRB Across Delivery Models

QRB/GRB must work across delivery methods. In agile environments, QRB can align with sprint or increment boundaries, focusing on readiness for major thresholds rather than reviewing every sprint deliverable. QRB should be triggered by risk-based events, such as new integrations, new privileged access patterns, major architectural changes, and production release candidates. GRB should be triggered by phase transitions and high-impact releases. This keeps governance focused on what matters most.

DevSecOps can strengthen QRB/GRB by increasing evidence availability. Automated testing, static analysis, dependency scanning, infrastructure validation, and deployment logs can feed evidence bundles continuously. Yet automation does not eliminate the need for governance decisions. Automation can prove many controls, but it cannot accept residual risk. QRB should validate that pipeline evidence is meaningful, such as confirming scan coverage, verifying that risk thresholds are properly tuned, and ensuring exceptions are controlled. GRB should confirm that pipeline evidence supports readiness and that any residual risks are explicitly accepted by authorized leaders. This reinforces the SSDF expectation that secure practices be integrated and demonstrable across the lifecycle (Souppaya et al., 2022).

Vendor implementation projects require special attention because they often carry a false sense of safety. Organizations assume the vendor's product is secure, yet the biggest failures occur in configuration, integration, and shared responsibility misunderstandings. QRB should require evidence of shared responsibility mapping, configuration standards, access control design for administrative functions, logging integration, and secure integration patterns. GRB should require evidence that vendor risk is within acceptable thresholds and that exit considerations, support models, and contractual obligations are understood. Governance frameworks like COBIT emphasize structured governance and management objectives across enterprise information and technology, reinforcing that control cannot be assumed, it must be designed and monitored (ISACA, 2018).

AI-enabled delivery adds an additional assurance overlay that QRB/GRB must incorporate without creating a parallel governance system. QRB should validate that AI features have defined intended use, defined unacceptable outcomes, evaluation criteria, and monitoring requirements for misuse and drift. It should also validate that data used for training, tuning, or grounding is governed, classified, and permitted for use. GRB should confirm that accountability for model updates, prompt changes, and decision policies is assigned, and that residual behavior risks are explicitly accepted when necessary. The key is that AI does not remove the need for gates, it increases the need for evidence and accountable decisions because behavior risk can be subtle and operationally expensive if ignored.

Implementing the QRB/GRB model without creating bureaucracy

The biggest implementation risk is overbuilding the governance process. If boards become heavy, teams bypass them. If boards are too light, they become ceremonial. The solution is proportionality, standardization, and a clear operating routine .

Start by defining the minimal viable QRB and GRB. Minimal does not mean weak. It means focused. Define a small set of evidence bundle templates for key phases, such as Analyze gate readiness, Design gate readiness, and Production readiness. Define a risk tiering model and map evidence depth to tiers. Define QRB as the evidence integrity checkpoint, and require QRB completion before GRB scheduling for high-risk initiatives. This reduces executive time waste and increases decision quality.

Next, define cadence and triggers. QRB should not meet only on a calendar schedule. It should meet based on delivery triggers. For example, readiness for design gate, readiness for production deployment, readiness for onboarding a critical vendor, readiness for releasing AI-enabled capability that touches sensitive data. GRB can meet on a predictable cadence, but it should also support urgent sessions for high-impact releases, with strict evidence requirements to prevent "emergency governance" from becoming a loophole.

Then, operationalize condition tracking. Conditional Go decisions are only useful if conditions are tracked like deliverables. Conditions should live in the same tracking systems used for delivery, such as project plans or backlogs, with clear owners and verification steps. QRB should validate closure evidence. GRB should review condition closure status at subsequent gates. This prevents governance drift where conditions quietly expire without being addressed.

Finally, measure governance effectiveness. Metrics should not reward compliance theater. Metrics should reward improved outcomes. Examples include reduction in late-stage defects, reduction in emergency changes, improved audit readiness, reduction in high-severity findings at production gate, improved mean time to remediate critical vulnerabilities, and improved operational stability in the first 30 to 90 days after go-live. CSF 2.0's governance emphasis supports this orientation, because governance is meant to improve how organizations prioritize and communicate cybersecurity efforts, not merely document them (NIST, 2024b).

A practical scenario: how QRB/GRB prevents a high-cost failure

Consider a project implementing a vendor platform for customer onboarding, integrated with identity services, document upload, fraud checks, and analytics. The sponsor wants a fast release because competitors are moving. The team configures the platform, builds integrations, and runs functional tests. Everything looks fine in demos. Without QRB/GRB, the project reaches the final weeks and discovers several issues: privileged access roles are too broad, audit logging is incomplete, and document uploads are stored in a way that violates internal data retention policy. The schedule is now under stress, so leadership is asked to approve exceptions. The system goes live with weak controls, and within months an audit finding occurs, followed by a security event caused by misused administrative privileges.

With QRB/GRB, the story changes. During Design gate readiness, QRB requires explicit trust boundary documentation, role design evidence, logging integration evidence, and data retention alignment evidence. QRB flags the privileged access design gap early. The team corrects it before production readiness. During Production readiness, QRB validates that logs exist, alerts are configured, and incident response integration is ready. GRB reviews the evidence and makes a Go decision based on proof, not on demo confidence. The organization still moves fast, but it moves with control. The cost avoided is not theoretical. It is rework, incident response labor, audit remediation, and reputational harm. That is the practical value of governance boards when they are designed properly.

Takeaway: governance that produces trust on purpose

QRB and GRB are not extra meetings, they are the control system that makes secure delivery repeatable under real pressure. The Quality Review Board (QRB) exists to protect the integrity of evidence. It verifies that the required deliverables exist, that they are coherent, and that they are decision-grade. It also confirms that testing, validation, and traceability plans are strong enough to produce proof throughout execution, not only at the end. When QRB is done well, gate reviews stop being slide evaluations and become evidence evaluations. This directly supports modern expectations that cybersecurity outcomes must be governed through measurable oversight, not informal confidence (NIST, 2024b).

The Gate Review Board (GRB) exists to protect the organization's risk posture. It makes phase decisions explicit, records accountability, and ensures that residual risk is accepted consciously, not accidentally. GRB also scales governance by risk and criticality, so low-risk work is not buried by heavy process, and high-risk work is not waved through without proof. This aligns with management-system discipline that expects defined responsibilities, controlled operation of security controls, and continual improvement over time (ISO, 2022).

Together, QRB and GRB normalize a professional culture where "not yet" is a responsible outcome, not a political fight. They reduce late surprises by forcing clarity early. They remove ambiguity by assigning owners to risks and conditions. Most importantly, they make readiness a standard that can be proven, so delivery produces value without sacrificing trust.

መ

ADDIS PLAYBOOKS AND GATES

INTRODUCTION

Part መ is where the book becomes operational. Earlier parts established the "why" and the "what" of secure technology project delivery, including the reality that cyber risk, compliance pressure, supply chain dependency, and AI-enabled capabilities have changed what it means to deliver successfully. This part focuses on the "how," meaning how teams execute each ADDIS phase with clarity, how they prepare evidence that leadership can trust, and how they use gate decisions to prevent predictable failure patterns. In a modern enterprise, security and delivery are no longer separate conversations held at different times by different groups. They are inseparable, because technology delivery creates risk exposure at the same time it creates business value. That is why contemporary guidance places governance, accountability, and risk management at the center of cybersecurity outcomes, instead of treating them as afterthoughts or compliance side work (NIST, 2024b).

The practical goal of Part መ is simple to state and difficult to achieve without structure. You want to move fast without gambling trust. You want innovation without unmanaged exposure. You want speed that is sustainable, not speed that produces rework, outages, audit findings, and loss of confidence. Secure delivery becomes sustainable when an organization can answer a small set of hard questions at the right time. Is the work still aligned to business outcomes. Are risks understood and treated honestly. Are controls designed where they matter most. Is testing producing proof instead of optimism. Is the operating model ready for what you are about to release. Those questions are not asked once. They are asked repeatedly, at carefully chosen decision points, using evidence that is reviewed by people with the authority and expertise to make a real call.

That is the logic of the playbooks and gate reviews in this part. A phase playbook explains what "good" looks like during that phase, including major tasks, minimum deliverables, and the evidence that should exist by the time the phase closes. A gate review is the formal decision checkpoint at the end of the phase. It is where the organization decides whether the project has earned the right to proceed to the next phase based on predefined criteria and validated deliverables. The gate is not a meeting for status updates. It is a control checkpoint that evaluates readiness, quality, risk posture, and alignment with standards. In the ADDIS model, gates exist specifically to prevent projects from drifting forward on momentum while carrying unresolved risks, incomplete controls, and unclear operational ownership. This is consistent with secure development guidance that emphasizes integrating security throughout the lifecycle and producing demonstrable outcomes, rather than relying on late-stage fixes and informal assurance (Souppaya et al., 2022).

Part IV is organized to match the way real delivery unfolds. The Analyze phase frames the opportunity, confirms feasibility, clarifies requirements, and establishes early risk controls. The Design phase converts intent into secure architecture, control placement, and test strategy. Develop or Acquire executes the build track or buy track while generating test evidence and assurance closure. Implement moves the solution into production with validated migration, security checks, and operational readiness. Sustain governs the system after go-live through monitoring, patching, assurance, and continuous improvement. This sequence is not just procedural. It is a lifecycle of trust. Trust is framed early, built intentionally, validated before exposure, and preserved through disciplined operations.

This part is also built for proportionality. Not every project deserves the same depth of analysis, assurance, and documentation. Yet every project needs enough structure to remain governable. The solution is a consistent lifecycle with tiered depth. High-risk initiatives require deeper evidence bundles and stricter gate expectations. Lower-risk initiatives can use lighter bundles while still following the same logic and decision rights. This risk-based approach maps well to governance and information security management expectations, where controls and oversight are expected to be appropriate to the risk, the data sensitivity, and the criticality of the service (ISO, 2022).

Part [illegible] assumes a two-layer review system that keeps execution honest and keeps decision-making efficient. The first layer is the Quality Review, also referred to as the Quality Assurance review. This is a technical evaluation that focuses on deliverable completeness, compliance with standards, and the actual quality of the work produced in the phase. It is designed to find gaps early, while fixes are still affordable, and while the team still has room to correct course. In the ADDIS approach, the quality assessment is intended to be independent, and it can occur multiple times within a phase, but it must occur at least at the end of each phase before the gate review.

The second layer is the Gate Review. The gate review is a management review that occurs at the end of each phase, and it exists to decide whether the project is ready to progress. It assesses viability, phase deliverables, risk mitigation strategies, and adherence to standards, then it produces a decision outcome that authorizes forward movement, conditional movement, or a pause.

This sequencing matters. When quality reviews are done first, gate reviews become shorter, more decisive, and less political. The gate meeting stops being a debate about whether work is complete, and it becomes what it should be, a decision based on validated evidence.

This paired structure also reduces a common failure mode. In many organizations, “approval” is treated as a courtesy rather than a control. The team presents progress, leadership nods, and delivery advances. Later, defects and control gaps are discovered in testing, during deployment, or after go-live. That pattern is expensive, and it is not a mystery. It happens because the organization is making commitments without proof. Part σD is designed to replace courtesy approvals with evidence-based approvals.

The Quality Review Board

A Quality Review Board, abbreviated as QRB, is the cross-functional body responsible for validating quality and completeness of phase deliverables before they are presented for a gate decision. In the ADDIS model, the QRB is composed of process owners and technical representatives, commonly including a Quality Manager or designee, quality assurance personnel, project managers, cybersecurity experts, and infrastructure subject matter experts. The QRB focuses on monitoring adherence to standards and best practices, confirming that quality plans are in place and followed, and verifying that risks and defects are not being ignored.

The QRB’s role is not to manage the project. It is to protect the integrity of delivery by ensuring deliverables are real, complete, and consistent with expectations. In practical terms, the QRB reviews artifacts such as requirements sets, architecture documents, threat models, test plans, test results, defect trends, risk registers, control mapping, configuration baselines, and readiness checklists. It evaluates whether these artifacts are complete, coherent, and traceable, and whether they demonstrate that the work of the phase has been performed to an acceptable standard. This function is especially important for projects involving emerging technologies or complex vendor ecosystems because novelty and dependency can hide weak assumptions until the system is exposed to real conditions.

The QRB also plays a key decision-shaping role. While the gate decision itself is made at the governance level, the QRB determines whether the evidence bundle is mature enough to be put in front of the Gate Review Board. In the ADDIS context, the QRB maintains the technical and program focus, confirms completeness of required deliverables, validates work performed, and ensures adequate mitigation plans exist. When the QRB is functioning properly, it acts as a filter that prevents leadership from being asked to approve progress on the basis of incomplete or unverified work.

The Gate Review Board

A Gate Review Board, abbreviated as GRB, is the governing body that makes the formal decision at each gate. It evaluates project worthiness and approves the expenditure of resources to continue. It reviews status and risk, approves continued funding, and provides oversight on scope, schedule, and budget risks. In many organizations, the GRB is chaired by a C-suite officer or executive sponsor and includes senior leaders such as finance leadership and key IT leads, with a stable membership to ensure consistency and comparability across projects.

This board is where accountability becomes real. A GRB is not simply a steering committee that listens and advises. It is the body that must be willing to say "not yet" when evidence is weak. It must also be willing to approve forward movement quickly when evidence is strong. The GRB's strength is not in technical detail. It is in decision authority and enterprise alignment. That is why the GRB preserves a strategic and business focus, while the QRB preserves a technical and execution focus.

GRB membership should reflect the project's risk and impact. For a customer-facing platform, representation from cybersecurity, enterprise architecture, operations, and legal or compliance often becomes essential. For a regulated environment, risk management and internal audit may participate as observers or advisors to ensure evidence of quality and governance traceability. This is aligned with the broader governance principle that decision rights and oversight should be appropriate to risk, impact, and accountability expectations (ISO, 2015; NIST, 2024b).

Pass, fail, and decision outcomes that actually control risk

A gate is only meaningful if it produces outcomes that control behavior. In practice, organizations benefit from a clear decision set that is consistently used. The ADDIS gate review guidance highlights decision alternatives such as moving forward to the next phase, conditional progress with specific actions, or project suspension. This can be expressed in straightforward pass and fail terms that leadership understands and teams can execute.

A "Pass" decision means the project meets gate criteria and may proceed to the next phase. It does not mean risk is zero. It means risk is known, controls are on track, deliverables are complete enough to support the next phase, and the organization accepts the residual risk posture knowingly. A "Conditional Pass" means the project may proceed, but only with defined conditions, owners, and deadlines that must be completed to maintain the approval. This is useful when issues are real but manageable, and when delaying the entire project would create greater harm than proceeding under control. A "Fail" outcome typically maps to a hold, a phase rework decision, or in severe cases a project stop. The intention is not punishment. It is prevention. When evidence shows that controls are missing, risks are not mitigated, or readiness is not real, moving forward is an enterprise risk decision, not a project preference.

Pass and fail decisions should also be tied to evidence, not persuasion. That is why Part ɑɒ emphasizes evidence bundles. Evidence bundles make the gate decision defensible. They provide traceability for audits, post-incident learning, and executive accountability. They also reduce the temptation to treat gate reviews as ceremonial. This discipline is consistent with secure software delivery expectations that call for integrated practices and verifiable outcomes across the lifecycle (Souppaya et al., 2022), and it aligns with governance-centered cybersecurity frameworks that emphasize accountability and oversight as core components of cyber resilience (NIST, 2024b).

How the QRB and GRB work together across Part ɑɒ

Part ɑɒ assumes a workflow that is both practical and repeatable. During each phase, the project team produces deliverables and updates the evidence bundle continuously. The QRB performs quality reviews to validate that deliverables are complete, that testing and defect management are honest, and that risk mitigation plans are real. The QRB then determines whether the project is ready to present to the GRB for a gate decision, because in the ADDIS model the decision to advance to the GRB rests with the QRB, while the decision to advance to the next phase rests with the GRB. This sequencing prevents leadership from being forced into technical arguments during gate meetings, and it prevents teams from using executive urgency to bypass quality validation.

The gate meeting itself should be structured. The project compiles and organizes documentation, including plans, progress reports, risk assessments, and change logs. The GRB evaluates progress and alignment against predefined criteria and makes a decision. Outcomes are documented and communicated, and corrective actions are tracked when conditions or holds are issued. This structure turns governance into a delivery accelerator, because once teams know the rules and the evidence expectations, they stop being surprised by late objections.

This also aligns naturally with project governance concepts emphasized in project management practice. Projects require defined roles, decision rights, and governance structures that support consistent control, stakeholder engagement, and delivery assurance (PMI, 2021b). Part ꝏ essentially applies those governance expectations to the reality of modern secure delivery, where cyber controls, compliance obligations, and operational readiness must be validated as part of the definition of progress.

How to use the phase playbooks in this part

Each phase chapter in Part ꝏ is designed as an execution playbook. It answers four questions. What must be achieved in this phase. What must be produced. What must be reviewed and by whom. What must be true to pass the gate. The playbook approach is intentional, because many organizations treat phases as calendar periods rather than readiness states. Analyze ends because the schedule says it ends. Design ends because the team wants to start building. Implement ends because the system is live. Sustain begins because the project budget is exhausted. Those transitions are administrative. They do not prove readiness. Part ꝏ replaces administrative transitions with evidence-based transitions, where readiness is confirmed through quality reviews and gate decisions.

Part ꝏ also supports multiple execution styles. You can run agile delivery, DevSecOps, vendor-led implementations, or hybrid programs, and still use these playbooks. The difference is not the method of building. It is the method of proving. The playbooks define what you must be able to prove at each phase boundary. When teams embrace that approach, they stop seeing governance as interference and start seeing it as the mechanism that prevents rework and protects delivery credibility.

Part [illegible] is also designed to support scaling. If you are a PMO leader, you can standardize evidence bundle templates and gate criteria across projects and then tailor depth by risk tier. If you are a security leader, you can align security activities to phase milestones and require evidence that maps to secure development expectations. If you are an operations leader, you can require operational readiness evidence as a condition of deployment approval. If you are a sponsor, you can demand that decisions are supported by evidence rather than optimism. These are not separate agendas. They are the same agenda expressed through different responsibilities.

A phase-by-phase view of the gates and their evidence intent

In Analyze, the playbook emphasizes opportunity framing, feasibility, requirements clarity, and early risk controls. The objective is to prevent the organization from funding ambiguity. Gate 1 is where the GRB confirms that the initiative is viable, aligned, and bounded enough to justify deeper investment. In Design, the playbook emphasizes secure architecture, control placement, identity and access design, data protection design, and test strategy design. Gate 2 confirms architecture assurance and control validation readiness. It is where leaders confirm that the design is not building hidden risk into the foundation. In Develop or Acquire, the playbooks emphasize execution discipline that produces proof. For the build track, this includes secure engineering, security testing, and release readiness evidence. For the buy track, it includes vendor governance, contract controls, and third-party risk treatment. Gate 3 confirms build or buy readiness and assurance closure before deployment approval. In Implement, the playbook emphasizes deployment, migration validation, security validation, and operational readiness, because going live without operational readiness is a predictable failure. Gate 4 confirms production readiness and handover approval. In Sustain, the playbook emphasizes continuous monitoring, vulnerability and patch management, operational assurance, and continual improvement. Gate 5 confirms that operational governance is in place and that continuous assurance is functioning, not hypothetical.

Across all these phases, the QRB and GRB model provide the routine. QRB validates quality and completeness. GRB makes the governance decision to move forward, to move forward with conditions, or to hold. This routine is what turns ADDIS from a lifecycle diagram into a delivery control system.

Why this control system matters more emerging technology era

Emerging technologies raise uncertainty. AI-enabled features may behave differently across contexts, may require ongoing monitoring, and may introduce new misuse and abuse patterns. Cloud-based architectures increase speed and flexibility, yet they also increase misconfiguration risk and dependency on external services. Vendor ecosystems accelerate implementation, yet they also introduce third-party risk and contractual complexity. In this environment, the cost of being wrong grows. That is why governance must become more evidence-driven, not more bureaucratic. Cybersecurity frameworks increasingly emphasize governance and enterprise accountability because technical controls alone do not create resilience. The ability to make disciplined decisions, track risk acceptance, and validate outcomes is what makes resilience sustainable (NIST, 2024b).

Part σɒ prepares you to manage that reality. It provides the playbooks and gate mechanics that keep delivery honest under pressure. It also provides a structured path for truth-telling, where teams can surface risks and gaps early without being punished for transparency. That culture is a competitive advantage. Organizations that reward honesty build safer systems and deliver more predictably over time.

As you begin Part σɒ, keep one practical test in mind. If an executive asked you to defend the decision to proceed, what evidence would you present. If an auditor asked you to show how security requirements were met, what would you show. If an operations leader asked who will own incidents, monitoring, and changes after go-live, what would you answer. If those answers are unclear, the project may be active, but it is not ready. The phase playbooks and gate reviews in this part exist to ensure that readiness is not assumed, it is demonstrated.

A Phase-by-Phase View of the Gates and Their Evidence Intent

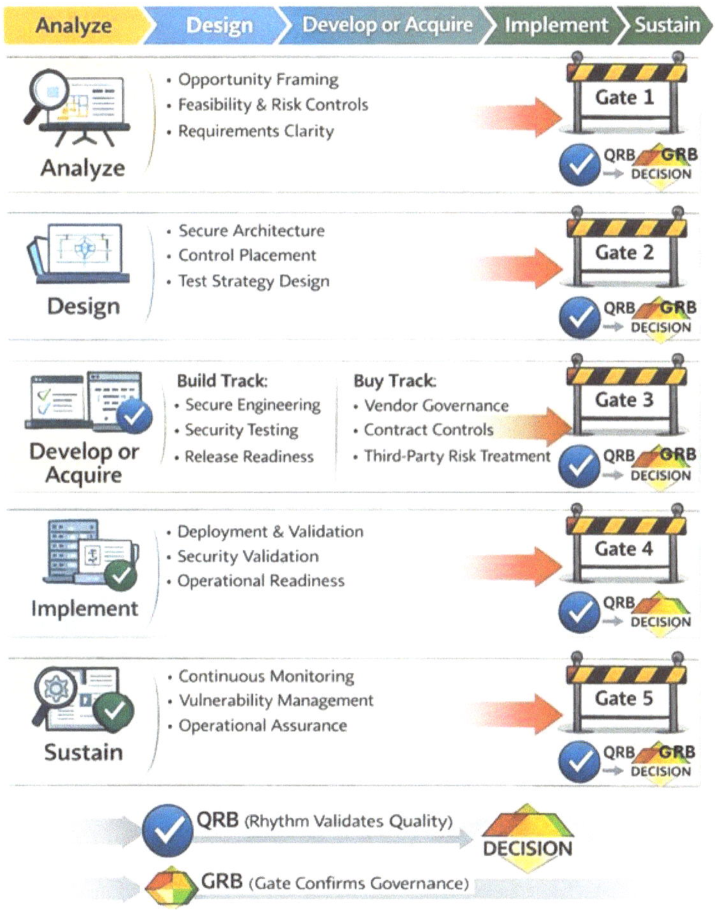

"The first deliverable of Analysis is not a document. It is clarity."

- **Do not fund ambiguity.** The purpose of the Analysis Phase is to turn a compelling idea into a bounded initiative with clear value, clear scope, and explicit assumptions.
- **Evidence comes before approval.** Gate 1 is not a confidence check. It is a viability decision that requires proof of feasibility, requirements clarity, and early risk controls.
- **If the problem is unclear, everything downstream becomes waste.** Design will optimize the wrong thing, build will produce the wrong solution, and implementation will harden the wrong risks into production.
- **Treat Analysis as a risk-reduction sprint.** The goal is to surface constraints early, align decision rights, and establish the minimum evidence bundle that makes the next investment defensible.

In governed delivery, the cheapest control is early clarity, and the most expensive failure is late discovery.

Analysis Phase

The Analyze phase is where a technology initiative earns the right to exist. That sentence may sound harsh, yet it reflects a reality that mature organizations quietly understand. Projects do not fail only because teams build poorly. They fail because organizations commit to the wrong problem, misunderstand constraints, underestimate risk, or assume operational readiness will "figure itself out later." Analyze is the phase that prevents those errors by turning a hopeful idea into a decision-grade business case, with explicit scope boundaries, measurable outcomes, feasibility evidence, and early risk controls that make Security by Design real before design work begins. In modern delivery environments, where dependencies are tangled, third parties are embedded, and AI-enabled features can amplify both speed and risk, Analyze is not a paperwork phase. It is the discipline that protects value, trust, and time (NIST, 2024b).

A useful metaphor is the foundation of a building. You can start framing a house quickly, and it will look like progress. Yet if the foundation is poured on weak ground, every floor you add increases the eventual collapse. Analyze is the foundation work. It stabilizes the initiative by forcing clarity on what the organization is solving, what success looks like, what constraints are non-negotiable, and what risks must be controlled early. This matters because cybersecurity and resilience are increasingly treated as governance outcomes, which means leaders are expected to make informed decisions about risk posture, not simply fund delivery and hope controls appear later (NIST, 2024b). Analyze is where those informed decisions begin.

The Analysis Phase is where the project earns the right to proceed. It converts an idea into a decision-ready plan by framing the opportunity, aligning stakeholders, clarifying requirements, and selecting a delivery path, while establishing the first security-by-design anchors that will govern the work through the remaining ADDIS phases. This phase also produces the early evidence needed for Gate 1, including the risk and threat baseline, compliance triggers, and the initial control expectations that shape architecture, vendor evaluation, and implementation readiness. The figure here summarizes the purpose, major activities, security-by-design anchors, and key outputs that together form the minimum defensible foundation for a Go or No-Go decision.

Cybersecurity risk assessment is not a one-time checklist, it is a governance loop that converts uncertainty into decision-ready evidence. The lifecycle begins by defining risk tolerance and scope, then moves through disciplined identification, analysis, prioritization, and treatment of risk across assets, vendors, cloud services, and AI-enabled misuse scenarios. The final step closes the loop by measuring outcomes and reassessing continuously, with ADDIS gates used as formal control points to confirm that risk decisions remain valid as the solution evolves. This figure summarizes the executive view of that lifecycle and highlights how assessment outputs become actionable inputs for governance, assurance, and accountable go/no-go decisions.

Analyze also creates a shared language. It aligns sponsors, product owners, architects, engineers, security leaders, compliance stakeholders, operations teams, and procurement. It turns informal assumptions into explicit statements that can be reviewed, challenged, validated, and owned. When teams skip this alignment, they still move fast at first. Then the same assumptions return like unpaid debt, with interest. The payment shows up as change requests, schedule slips, emergency exceptions, and a production launch that feels more like a leap than a step. Analyze reduces that debt by converting uncertainty into evidence and by documenting what remains uncertain so it can be resolved deliberately in Design.

Opportunity framing and problem definition

Opportunity framing starts with discipline around the problem statement. Many initiatives start with a solution statement. "We need a new platform," "We need to migrate to the cloud," "We need an AI chatbot," "We need a GRC tool." Solutions may be correct, yet they are not problems. Analyze forces a pivot from solutions to outcomes. What pain exists today, who experiences it, what is the measurable impact, and what improvement would define success. This is a governance question as much as it is a delivery question because governance exists to ensure technology decisions align to business objectives and are monitored for effectiveness (ISO, 2015).

A strong problem statement is specific, measurable, and bounded. It clarifies the current state, the target state, and the gap that matters. It also avoids two traps. The first trap is making the statement so broad that the project becomes a "boil the ocean" initiative. The second trap is making it so narrow that it solves a symptom while the root cause remains. The best problem statements are written in plain language and linked to measurable outcomes such as cycle time reduction, error rate reduction, improved customer completion rates, reduced operational cost, reduced incident frequency, improved audit outcomes, or improved service availability. This outcome orientation aligns with modern project management practice that emphasizes value delivery, stakeholder outcomes, and adaptive planning, rather than focusing only on schedule mechanics (PMI, 2021b).

Opportunity framing must also clarify who the user is and what journey the project affects. In many technology projects, the "user" includes internal staff, customers, vendors, partners, auditors, and operational teams. Each user group introduces different requirements and different risk surfaces. A customer-facing experience raises exposure, privacy expectations, and availability needs. An internal administrative experience raises privileged access risk. A partner API integration introduces third-party dependency risk. Analyze identifies these user groups and the trust boundaries implied by their access.

In the second edition context, opportunity framing must also account for AI-influenced expectations. Stakeholders may assume AI can automate decisions, improve service quality, or reduce cost quickly. Analyze should treat those expectations carefully. AI can accelerate capability, yet it can also create behavior uncertainty, data dependence, and monitoring burdens that are not obvious in early demos. Opportunity framing should therefore distinguish between "AI as a feature" and "AI as a risk-shaping dependency." If AI affects decision-making, customer communication, fraud detection, eligibility, security monitoring, or access control, the organization must treat it as a high-governance component, not as a cosmetic enhancement. This aligns with the governance emphasis in CSF 2.0 that encourages organizations to define roles, responsibilities, and oversight mechanisms for cybersecurity outcomes, especially as technology complexity increases (NIST, 2024b).

Opportunity framing ends with a clear value hypothesis. A value hypothesis states what value will be created, how it will be measured, and what assumptions must hold true. It also clarifies what could invalidate the initiative. If the value depends on clean data and the data is not clean, that is a critical feasibility risk. If the value depends on user adoption and the organization has not planned change management, that is a delivery risk. If the value depends on a vendor capability and the vendor cannot meet control requirements, that is a governance risk. Naming these assumptions early is not negativity. It is professionalism.

Feasibility, What Is Actually Possible

Feasibility is the part of Analyze that prevents magical thinking. It asks whether the organization can deliver and sustain the solution under real constraints. Feasibility must be multi-dimensional because projects rarely fail for only one reason. A solution can be technically feasible but operationally infeasible. It can be financially feasible but not compliant. It can be compliant on paper but infeasible due to vendor control gaps. Analyze forces these dimensions into view before the organization commits to architecture and build or buy decisions.

Technical feasibility asks whether the solution can be built or implemented using the organization's architecture standards, available skills, and integration capabilities. This includes whether the organization can support the required identity model, logging model, encryption requirements, network segmentation, and deployment patterns. If the project involves custom software development, technical feasibility must include secure development feasibility. Can teams produce secure code consistently, manage dependencies, and generate verification evidence through testing and pipeline controls. NIST's Secure Software Development Framework is relevant here because it outlines expected secure development practices such as preparing the organization, protecting the software supply chain, producing well-secured software, and responding to vulnerabilities, and it emphasizes integrating these practices into normal workflows (Souppaya et al., 2022). If the organization cannot perform these practices reliably, the risk profile of building increases, and acquisition or platform-based approaches may be safer.

Operational feasibility asks whether the organization can run the solution after go-live. This includes monitoring, incident response integration, patching and vulnerability remediation, access governance, backup and recovery, and staffing capacity. Operational feasibility also includes the support model. Who owns the platform day to day, who handles escalations, and who approves changes. Many projects fail here because operations is treated as a downstream concern. A system that cannot be operated cannot be secured sustainably, which aligns with ISO/IEC 27001's management-system orientation that emphasizes maintaining controls, responsibilities, and continuous improvement over time (ISO, 2022).

Financial feasibility asks whether the organization can fund not only delivery but also sustainment. Too many business cases budget for implementation and forget ongoing licensing, monitoring tools, staffing, incident response capabilities, training, and continuous assurance. Financial feasibility should include total cost of ownership thinking, even if numbers remain approximate in Analyze. The goal is not perfect accounting. The goal is to avoid funding a project that becomes an unfunded operational burden.

Regulatory and legal feasibility asks whether the initiative can comply with applicable regulations, contractual obligations, and internal policy constraints. This includes privacy obligations, data retention rules, cross-border data flow restrictions, and sector-specific regulatory requirements. Even when the project is not obviously regulated, internal policies often impose constraints, such as encryption requirements, vendor due diligence requirements, or minimum logging expectations. Analyze should identify which compliance domains apply and which stakeholders must validate obligations.

Data feasibility asks whether the data required for the solution is available, accurate, governed, and lawful to use. This is a rising cause of failure in AI-enabled and analytics-heavy projects. If the initiative depends on historical data for training or evaluation, Analyze must validate provenance, classification, and permissible use. If the initiative depends on real-time data integration, Analyze must validate integration feasibility, quality, and latency constraints. Data feasibility should also include privacy and security constraints because data classification determines what controls must be embedded early.

Vendor feasibility applies when a third-party is involved. It asks whether a vendor can meet control expectations, integrate properly, and support required service levels. It also asks whether the vendor's shared responsibility model is acceptable, whether the vendor's support model fits the organization's operations, and whether exit risks are manageable. Vendor feasibility is not only a procurement topic. It is a security and resilience topic because third-party dependency expands the organization's risk surface. Analyze should therefore treat vendor feasibility as part of early risk controls, not as a later checkbox.

A practical feasibility output is a feasibility narrative that explicitly distinguishes known facts, validated assumptions, and unresolved unknowns. Unknowns are not shameful. Hidden unknowns are dangerous. Analyze should list unknowns and propose how they will be resolved during Design, such as through proofs of concept, architecture spikes, vendor workshops, data profiling, or security requirement validation sessions. This transparency supports stronger gate decisions because leadership can see what the organization is committing to and what it is still learning.

Requirements baseline and scope boundaries

Analyze does not attempt to capture every requirement. It establishes a requirements baseline that defines what must be true for the initiative to be considered successful and governable. The baseline includes functional needs, non-functional requirements, and security and compliance requirements. It also includes scope boundaries that prevent uncontrolled expansion.

Functional requirements in Analyze should focus on outcomes rather than implementation detail. For example, "Enable customers to onboard digitally with identity verification and document submission" is a functional outcome. "Build three microservices with specific endpoints" is design detail and belongs later. The baseline should identify high-impact capabilities and define what is in scope and out of scope at a high level.

Non-functional requirements should be explicitly named because they often drive architecture and cost. Availability expectations, performance targets, scalability needs, latency constraints, and disaster recovery expectations are not "nice to have." They are design constraints. Security non-functional requirements such as audit logging, encryption, access control, and segmentation are equally critical. Treating these as constraints early is consistent with Security by Design because it ensures controls are placed intentionally rather than bolted on later.

Security requirements in Analyze should be expressed as minimum control expectations rather than detailed control designs. For example, identity requirements may include centralized authentication, least privilege role design, and privileged access governance. Data protection requirements may include encryption in transit and at rest for sensitive data. Logging requirements may include central log aggregation and alerting for security-relevant events. Vulnerability management requirements may include patch timelines and security testing expectations. These requirements should be aligned to the organization's baseline control framework where one exists, and where it does not, they should be aligned to recognized practices such as the governance and protection outcomes emphasized in CSF 2.0 and secure development practices emphasized in SSDF (NIST, 2024b; Souppaya et al., 2022).

Scope boundaries deserve special attention because scope drift is the silent killer of secure delivery. When scope expands, teams often sacrifice testing, documentation, and control validation to protect schedule. That trade is rarely explicit. It happens quietly. Analyze prevents this by making scope boundaries visible and by tying changes to governance. If scope changes materially, the business case and risk posture must be revisited. This is not bureaucracy. It is risk management. When you expand scope, you expand risk, and governance must respond accordingly (ISO, 2015).

Analyze should also document constraints as formal statements. Constraints may include technology standards, data residency constraints, internal policy requirements, budget limits, timeline pressures, or staffing constraints. The reason to document constraints is not to make excuses. It is to ensure design decisions later can be traced to realities that leadership accepted.

Early risk controls and Security by Design in Analyze

Early risk controls are the mechanism that makes Analyze a security-by-design phase rather than a business-only phase. These controls are not final security designs. They are the early actions that shape the project so security and governance are embedded from the start.

The first early risk control is risk tiering. Risk tiering classifies the initiative based on factors such as data sensitivity, system criticality, external exposure, third-party dependency, and regulatory impact. This classification determines how rigorous subsequent phases and gate evidence must be. Risk tiering is a governance mechanism because it ensures proportionality, meaning the organization applies heavier assurance where risk is higher and avoids unnecessary friction where risk is lower (NIST, 2024b). Without risk tiering, governance becomes inconsistent and teams either bypass controls or become buried under controls.

The second early risk control is data classification and data flow intent. Analyze should identify what data types are involved, what classification levels apply, and where data is expected to flow. Even a rough data flow intent statement is valuable because it prevents design surprises later. If the system will handle personal data, financial data, authentication data, or confidential business information, those classifications trigger different control expectations and different compliance obligations. This also influences vendor decisions because some vendors cannot support certain data handling constraints.

The third early risk control is an initial threat and misuse thinking exercise. At Analyze stage, this should be lightweight. The goal is not full threat modeling yet. The goal is to identify likely exposure points such as external APIs, privileged admin access, third-party integrations, data ingestion pipelines, and AI interfaces if relevant. This early thinking helps teams avoid the most common trap, building a solution that accidentally expands the trust boundary. It also helps determine what expertise must be involved in Design.

The fourth early risk control is third-party risk triage. If a vendor is likely, Analyze should identify whether the vendor will have access to sensitive data, whether the vendor will be a critical dependency, and whether the service model is compatible with the organization's security and operations requirements. This triage is not a full due diligence exercise yet. It is a gate to prevent the organization from committing to a vendor path that is already misaligned with policy constraints.

The fifth early risk control is establishing secure delivery expectations for build scenarios. If custom development is in scope, Analyze should confirm that secure development practices can be applied, such as secure coding standards, code review expectations, dependency management, and testing and scanning integration into the pipeline. SSDF provides a structured reference for these expectations, emphasizing that secure software outcomes require organizational preparation, protected development environments, verification practices, and vulnerability response processes (Souppaya et al., 2022). Analyze does not implement these controls, yet it confirms the organization can commit to them and resource them.

The sixth early risk control is defining governance touchpoints and decision rights. This includes identifying when QRB and GRB reviews will occur, which stakeholders must approve key decisions, and who can accept residual risk. It also includes defining how exceptions will be handled. Exceptions should be time-bound, approved, and tracked. Exceptions without expiration are simply hidden vulnerabilities. Formalizing this early prevents late-stage negotiation under pressure.

These early risk controls create a stable track for the project. They reduce the chance that security becomes a late-stage interruption. They also reduce the chance that operational readiness is treated as optional. In this sense, Analyze sets the tone of delivery culture. It tells the organization whether it will build trust on purpose or whether it will roll the dice.

Build versus buy decision framing

The build versus buy decision is one of the most impactful choices made in Analyze. It shapes delivery speed, cost, risk, and sustainment burden. Analyze should frame the decision with honesty rather than with preference. Many organizations default to buy to move faster, then discover integration, configuration, and vendor governance complexity. Others default to build for control, then discover sustainment burden and secure development maturity gaps. The correct decision depends on context, and Analyze provides that context.

For buy decisions, Analyze should evaluate whether the vendor meets baseline security and compliance expectations, whether the vendor's architecture fits integration standards, whether the vendor's service levels and support model fit operational needs, and whether the shared responsibility model is clear. It should also evaluate vendor lock-in risk and exit feasibility. This is not to create fear of vendors. It is to ensure vendor dependency is treated as an architectural and governance decision.

For build decisions, Analyze should evaluate whether the organization has the skills and tooling to deliver securely and sustainably. It should evaluate whether development teams can integrate secure practices into pipelines and produce testing evidence. It should evaluate whether operational ownership exists for the services built. It should also evaluate dependency risk because modern software is built from components, libraries, frameworks, and services. Secure development expectations from SSDF emphasize that software supply chain integrity and vulnerability response processes are not optional in modern delivery (Souppaya et al., 2022).

Hybrid decisions require the most discipline because they combine both risk surfaces. A platform may be acquired while significant custom integration and extension is built. In these scenarios, Analyze should identify which parts are vendor-owned, which parts are organization-owned, and where the control boundaries lie. It should also identify how testing evidence will be produced across both tracks. If that is unclear, Gate 1 should likely be conditional until the plan is clarified.

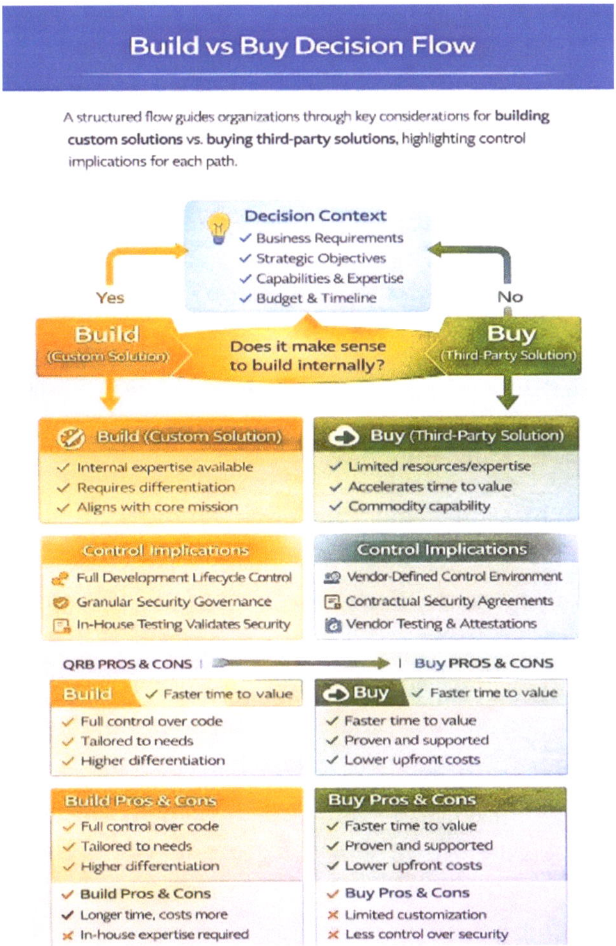

Outputs of Analyze and readiness for Gate 1

Chapter 11 will focus specifically on Gate 1, yet Chapter 10 must end with the practical outputs that prepare the initiative for that gate. Analyze should produce a set of artifacts that are lean but decision-grade. These typically include a problem statement and value hypothesis, a stakeholder and decision-rights map, scope boundaries and constraints, an options analysis with build-buy-hybrid considerations, an initial requirements baseline including security and compliance constraints, an initial risk register with owners, an initial data classification and data flow intent statement, and a high-level delivery approach including governance touchpoints and evidence expectations.

The most important output is not the document set. It is the readiness narrative that ties the artifacts together. The narrative explains what is known, what assumptions exist, what risks are visible, and what the organization is deciding now. It also clarifies what will be resolved in Design and how. This narrative is what allows leadership to make a defensible Gate 1 decision. It also aligns with governance principles that emphasize guiding and monitoring technology decisions with clear accountability and oversight (ISO, 2015). In other words, the artifacts provide proof, and the narrative provides meaning.

Analyze readiness also includes an honest view of resource feasibility. If critical roles are not available, such as security architecture support, data governance support, or operational ownership, the project should not pretend it can succeed without them. Gate decisions should reflect resourcing reality. A project that begins without essential expertise often accumulates hidden defects and then requests urgent help later, when it is least efficient to add it.

Finally, Analyze should set the expectation that evidence will be maintained throughout the lifecycle. Gate governance works only when evidence is produced continuously. If teams treat evidence as a last-minute assembly task, gate reviews become painful and political. A mature Analyze phase sets the rule early. Evidence is part of the work, not a separate reporting activity. This aligns with both CSF 2.0's governance emphasis and SSDF's practice-based orientation because both frameworks depend on repeatable execution and demonstrable outcomes (NIST, 2024b; Souppaya et al., 2022).

Summary and Next Steps

Analyze is where secure delivery begins in practice because it replaces optimism with discipline. It frames the opportunity in business terms, defines the problem in operational terms, and sets measurable outcomes that can later be verified. This early clarity matters because it prevents teams from confusing activity with progress. When success criteria are explicit, the project can be governed through evidence and decisions rather than slide confidence.

A disciplined Analysis Phase also surfaces constraints before the organization commits deeper funding. It evaluates feasibility across technical, operational, financial, regulatory, data, and vendor dimensions, so leadership does not fund ambiguity. In secure delivery, constraints are not inconveniences. They are the boundaries that protect schedule, scope, and risk posture. When constraints are recognized early, teams can design within them. When they are ignored, they reappear later as expensive rework, exceptions, or delayed go-live decisions.

Analyze establishes requirements baseline that includes security and compliance as real requirements, not optional enhancements. It brings forward early risk controls through risk tiering, data classification, lightweight threat thinking, third-party triage, and secure delivery feasibility checks. It also clarifies governance decision rights, including who can approve risk acceptance, exceptions, and compensating controls. This decision clarity prevents informal risk decisions from being made under pressure and later denied when problems surface.

Most importantly, Analyze produces decision-grade evidence. It gives leaders a defensible basis to approve the next step, because the initiative is viable, bounded, aligned, and understood well enough to justify deeper investment. When Analyze is done well, Design begins with clarity and a stable foundation. When Analyze is rushed or skipped, Design begins with assumptions, and assumptions quietly harden into architecture, contracts, data flows, and operational constraints that are difficult to reverse.

The next chapter, Gate 1, translates Analysis outputs into a formal evidence bundle and a Go or No-Go decision process. It ensures the organization proceeds only when readiness is proven, risk ownership is explicit, and accountability is recorded. This approach aligns with modern governance expectations that emphasize measurable outcomes, risk-informed oversight, and demonstrable control evidence (NIST, 2024b; ISO, 2022).

“Buying software does not outsource accountability.”

16

Gate 1: Analyze Review

Gate 1 is where the organization decides whether an idea becomes a committed initiative. It is not a meeting that exists to approve enthusiasm. It is a governance decision that confirms the initiative has produced decision-grade clarity and that the organization is willing to invest in Design with eyes open. When Gate 1 is weak, projects enter Design on momentum, not on proof. They carry unvalidated assumptions about data, constraints, vendor responsibilities, operational ownership, and security expectations. Those assumptions do not disappear. They grow teeth later, usually in the form of urgent changes, delayed releases, compliance surprises, or last-minute exceptions that become permanent exposure. When Gate 1 is strong, it becomes a stabilizer. It converts excitement into disciplined commitment, and it ensures the next phase begins with explicit constraints, accountable ownership, and a realistic view of risk posture (NIST, 2024b).

Gate 1 also serves a larger purpose in secure technology project management. It is the first formal point where cybersecurity and trust are treated as enterprise outcomes that leadership must govern. If Gate 1 only reviews scope and budget, security becomes an afterthought by default. If Gate 1 includes security-by-design constraints and early risk controls as non-negotiable evidence items, the project begins with trust embedded as part of feasibility, not as a late-stage negotiation. This aligns with CSF 2.0's governance emphasis, which frames cybersecurity as a managed enterprise capability, requiring defined roles, oversight, and decision-making tied to risk appetite and priorities (NIST, 2024b). Gate 1 is where those principles become operational.

A helpful metaphor is a bridge inspection before vehicles are allowed to cross. The organization can be eager to open the road, but opening the road without inspection is not speed, it is irresponsibility. Gate 1 is that first inspection. It confirms the ground is stable, the design work is warranted, and the risks are visible. It also confirms the project has a credible plan to produce evidence going forward. This is important because a gate system is only as strong as the evidence discipline behind it. If Gate 1 approves a project that cannot produce evidence later, the organization has already accepted a future governance failure.

The purpose and principles of Gate 1

Gate 1 exists to answer one decisive question. Has the initiative earned the right to proceed into Design. That question is answered through four proof categories: clarity, feasibility, risk posture, and accountability. Clarity means the problem is well-framed, the outcomes are measurable, and scope boundaries are explicit. Feasibility means the initiative is achievable under real constraints, including operational capacity and security expectations. Risk posture means the most important risks are identified, owned, and initially treated, including cybersecurity, privacy, compliance, and third-party dependency risks. Accountability means decision rights are clear, owners are assigned, and governance touchpoints are defined.

The first principle of Gate 1 is evidence over narrative. A project team can be talented and still be wrong. A sponsor can be confident and still be optimistic. Evidence is what protects the organization from confidence bias. Evidence should be concrete and reviewable. It should not rely on slide stories alone. This principle aligns with secure development thinking that emphasizes verifiable practices and outcomes, rather than informal assurance, especially when software and dependencies are complex and risk is distributed across the lifecycle (Souppaya et al., 2022).

The second principle is proportionality. Gate 1 is not meant to impose heavy bureaucracy on low-risk work. It is meant to enforce a consistent structure and scale depth based on risk tier. A low-risk internal automation can have a lighter evidence bundle. A customer-facing platform handling sensitive data should have deeper evidence. Proportionality is how governance remains sustainable and credible.

The third principle is early truth. Gate 1 does not require perfect knowledge. It requires honest knowledge. Unknowns are acceptable when they are visible and have a plan. Hidden unknowns are unacceptable because they create late shocks. Gate 1 is where unknowns are surfaced and turned into explicit Design-phase validation tasks.

The fourth principle is explicit risk acceptance. Risk acceptance will occur in complex initiatives, but Gate 1 ensures it is not accidental. If leadership decides to proceed while some risks remain unresolved, those risks must be documented, owned, time-bound, and governed through conditions. This approach is consistent with enterprise governance expectations that emphasize accountability and monitoring of technology decisions across the organization (ISO, 2015).

Gate 1 is only as strong as its inputs. The core input is the Analyze evidence bundle, which must be decision-grade and internally coherent. The evidence bundle should be concise enough to be reviewed and detailed enough to be trusted. In practice, the evidence bundle works best when it has a short executive summary and a set of supporting artifacts. The executive summary is the decision narrative. The artifacts are the proof.

The evidence bundle begins with a problem statement and opportunity framing brief. This artifact describes the current state pain, the impacted stakeholders, the measurable outcomes that define success, and the value hypothesis. It should also include success measures that reflect trust outcomes, not only business outcomes. Trust outcomes include reduced incident likelihood, improved audit posture, improved availability, reduced manual exception handling, and improved resilience. Treating trust as part of success is consistent with CSF 2.0's orientation toward governance and the integration of cybersecurity outcomes into enterprise decision-making (NIST, 2024b).

The scope and constraints statement is the next critical artifact. It defines what is in scope, what is out of scope, and what is explicitly deferred. It also identifies constraints such as architecture standards, data residency requirements, regulatory obligations, budget boundaries, timeline constraints, and operational limitations. Constraints are not excuses. They are realities that must shape design. When constraints are not documented, they emerge later as friction, and teams often respond by cutting assurance work to protect schedule, which increases risk.

The stakeholder and decision rights map is a foundational governance artifact. It identifies who must contribute, who must approve, and who can accept residual risk. It should include security, privacy, legal, compliance, architecture, operations, and procurement where relevant. It should also define the governance bodies involved, including the quality review function and the gate review function. Without this map, the project will later discover it needs approvals it did not schedule, and those late approvals create pressure and shortcuts.

The options analysis is the evidence that the organization did not fall in love with the first idea. It compares build, buy, and hybrid paths, and it provides decision rationale. If buy is likely, the analysis should include early third-party dependency implications and shared responsibility considerations. If build is likely, it should include secure development feasibility considerations. SSDF emphasizes that secure software outcomes depend on organizational preparation and repeatable secure practices, including protection of the development environment and software supply chain, and the ability to respond to vulnerabilities (Souppaya et al., 2022). Gate 1 should therefore ask a direct question when build is proposed. Can we realistically produce and maintain secure software under our current maturity and resourcing.

The requirements baseline must include functional outcomes, key non-functional requirements, and baseline security and compliance constraints. The baseline is not a detailed specification, but it must define the floor. For example, identity expectations, encryption expectations, logging expectations, and vulnerability management expectations must be visible early if the solution handles sensitive data or is externally exposed. ISO/IEC 27001 reinforces that information security must be managed systematically through defined controls and responsibilities, and that those controls must be maintained and improved over time (ISO, 2022). Gate 1 uses baseline requirements to ensure the project is not planning a path that ignores the control floor.

The initial data classification and data flow intent summary is an essential input. Data classification determines control intensity. Data flow intent determines integration risk. Even a rough view of what data types are involved, how sensitive they are, and where they will flow helps prevent later discovery that regulated or sensitive data is being moved into an unsuitable platform.

The initial risk register is another non-negotiable artifact. It should include the top risks across delivery, cyber, privacy, compliance, vendor dependency, operational readiness, and data quality. Each risk must have an owner, an initial treatment direction, and an escalation trigger. Risk without ownership is not risk management, it is anxiety documented.

Finally, the feasibility summary ties together technical, operational, financial, compliance, vendor, and data feasibility. This summary should explicitly list unknowns and define how those unknowns will be resolved during Design. Gate 1 does not punish unknowns. It punishes hidden unknowns.

Quality review before Gate 1

A strong Gate 1 process separates quality readiness from governance decision-making. Quality review occurs first. It validates that the evidence bundle is complete, coherent, and decision-ready. This quality review can be performed by a QRB function, a PMO quality practice, or a designated assurance team. The goal is not to slow delivery. The goal is to prevent the gate meeting from becoming a document scavenger hunt.

The quality review checks for completeness, internal consistency, and baseline compliance with governance expectations. It validates that the problem statement aligns with scope. It validates that scope aligns with feasibility. It validates that risks align with dependencies and constraints. It validates that ownership is assigned. It validates that baseline security and compliance constraints are explicitly captured, not implied. It also validates that the risk tier is defined and justified because risk tiering drives proportionality across future gates.

Quality review should produce a short outcome report with findings categorized by severity. Critical findings are blockers, meaning Gate 1 should not be scheduled until they are resolved. Major findings may be allowed into Gate 1 if they are documented as conditions and have owners. Minor findings can be corrected during Design, but they should still be tracked.

This quality-first model aligns with governance principles that emphasize guiding and monitoring technology use through structured accountability and oversight (ISO, 2015). It also aligns with secure lifecycle expectations because evidence integrity is a prerequisite for meaningful security assurance. When evidence is sloppy, security becomes a debate. When evidence is clean, security becomes a decision.

The Gate 1 review process

Gate 1 is the decision forum. It is typically a GRB meeting or a steering committee with explicit decision authority. The meeting should be short and decision-focused. That is only possible when the evidence bundle is distributed in advance and quality-validated.

Gate 1 begins with a decision narrative, not a presentation parade. The decision narrative should answer five questions. What problem are we solving, what success looks like, and why now. What solution paths were considered and why the preferred path is recommended. What constraints must be honored, including security and compliance constraints. What risks are visible and who owns them. What unknowns remain and how they will be resolved in Design. These questions force leadership to engage with readiness rather than with momentum.

The gate body then reviews the risk tier and confirms whether the proposed governance depth matches the tier. This is where leadership ensures proportionality. High-risk work should have deeper gate evidence requirements and likely higher decision authority. Low-risk work should not be strangled by heavy governance.

Gate 1 then reviews the top risks and their owners, focusing especially on risks that tend to cause late failure. These include unclear operational ownership, unclear data classification, unclear vendor responsibilities, unclear integration complexity, unrealistic schedule assumptions, and missing security baseline constraints. Gate 1 should explicitly ask whether any risk requires immediate escalation to enterprise risk management or legal counsel, particularly when sensitive data or regulated processes are involved.

The meeting then moves to a decision outcome. The decision outcomes should be limited and explicit: Go, Conditional Go, Hold, or No-Go. Go means the initiative is ready to proceed to Design with no critical gaps. Conditional Go means the initiative may proceed to Design with explicit conditions that are tracked, owned, and time-bound. Hold means the initiative cannot proceed because readiness is not proven. No-Go means the initiative should not proceed in its current form and must be reshaped or stopped.

The most important discipline in Gate 1 is how Conditional Go is managed. Conditional Go is valuable when it is used to allow design work while forcing early remediation of specific gaps. It becomes dangerous when conditions are vague or unenforced. Every condition must be written as an outcome, not an activity. Every condition must have an owner. Every condition must have a due date. Every condition must have a verification method. Every condition must have a consequence if unmet, such as Hold at the next checkpoint or an explicit risk acceptance escalation.

This decision discipline supports defensible governance because it ensures risk acceptance is authorized and recorded, rather than accidental. It also aligns with CSF 2.0's emphasis on governance and accountability for cybersecurity outcomes, which includes the expectation that organizations manage and communicate risk decisions through structured mechanisms (NIST, 2024b).

Gate 1 pass or fail criteria

Gate 1 must define what it means to pass or fail. Without clear pass or fail logic, the gate becomes subjective. Subjective gates produce inconsistent decisions, and inconsistency is where governance credibility collapses.

A project passes Gate 1 when it demonstrates clarity, feasibility, risk posture visibility, and accountability. Clarity means the problem statement is precise, outcomes are measurable, and scope boundaries are explicit. Feasibility means there is a credible path across technical, operational, financial, compliance, data, and vendor dimensions. Risk posture visibility means top risks are identified with owners and initial treatments, and the risk tier is defined and justified. Accountability means decision rights are clear, operational ownership is named, and governance touchpoints are scheduled.

A project fails Gate 1 when critical elements are missing or when the proposed solution conflicts with non-negotiable constraints. Failure can mean Hold, which is a pause for remediation, or No-Go, which is a reshape decision. Hold is appropriate when the initiative is valuable but not yet ready. No-Go is appropriate when the initiative is misaligned, infeasible, or ungovernable under current conditions.

There are also automatic fail triggers that should be treated as red lines for high-risk initiatives. If sensitive data classification is unknown, the project should not proceed. If no operational owner is willing to accept sustainment responsibility, the project should not proceed. If a vendor path is assumed without third-party risk triage and shared responsibility clarity, the project should not proceed. If baseline security constraints are not explicitly captured for an externally exposed or sensitive data system, the project should not proceed. These red lines are not rigid bureaucracy. They are common-sense guardrails based on patterns of failure.

Gate 1 Analysis and Decision Process

Gate 1 Readiness Pack

This Gate 1 Readiness Pack summarizes the Analysis Phase work and presents the evidence required for a Gate 1 decision. It is organized for fast review using a one-page cover sheet, an evidence bundle index, and decision rules that define minimum pass criteria and automatic hold triggers. The intent is to prevent the organization from funding ambiguity, and to ensure scope, constraints, feasibility, and risk ownership are explicit before Design begins. The gate decision should be based on the evidence referenced in this pack, not on presentation confidence.

A. Readiness workstreams

1. Purpose and outcomes: Finalize opportunity framing and measurable outcomes. Confirm the problem statement, stakeholder impacts, and success metrics, including trust metrics where applicable (NIST, 2024b).
2. Scope and constraints: Confirm scope boundaries and constraints. Define what is in scope, out of scope, and deferred. Document constraints across architecture, policy, regulation, budget, and operational capability (ISO, 2015).
3. Governance and accountability: Complete stakeholder mapping and decision rights. Identify required contributors and approvers, including who can accept residual risk and who owns post go-live operations.
4. Solution approach: Complete options analysis and recommended path. Evaluate build, buy, or hybrid options and document rationale and implications, including third-party dependency and secure development feasibility (Souppaya et al., 2022).
5. Requirements baseline: Establish baseline requirements. Define high-level functional outcomes, non-functional

requirements, and baseline security and compliance constraints as non-negotiable floors (ISO, 2022).

6. Early risk controls: Perform early risk controls. Complete risk classification, data classification assumptions, initial data flow intent, and third-party risk triage as applicable (NIST, 2024b).
7. Risk register and feasibility: Build the initial risk register. Identify top risks across cyber, delivery, privacy, compliance, vendor, data, and operations, then assign owners and initial treatments. Confirm feasibility across technical, operational, financial, compliance, data, and vendor dimensions. Document unknowns with a plan to resolve them in Design.
8. Decision narrative: Prepare the gate decision narrative. Summarize what is known, what is assumed, what remains uncertain, and what decision is requested.

B. Gate 1 evidence bundle index

1. Problem Statement and Opportunity Framing Brief
   Current state, target outcomes, measurable success metrics, and value hypothesis.
2. Scope and Constraints Statement
   In scope, out of scope, deferred items, and key constraints.
3. Stakeholder and Decision Rights Map
   Roles, approvers, governance bodies, and risk acceptance authority.
4. Options Analysis
   Build, buy, hybrid comparison and recommended path with rationale.
5. Requirements Baseline
   High-level functional needs plus key non-functional requirements and baseline security and compliance constraints.

6. Data Classification and Data Flow Intent Summary
   Data types, sensitivity assumptions, expected flows, storage, and access intent.
7. Initial Risk Register
   Top risks with owners, initial treatments, and escalation triggers.
8. Feasibility Summary
   Technical, operational, financial, compliance, data, and vendor feasibility, plus unresolved unknowns with a resolution plan.
9. Analyze Closure Summary
   Short synthesis for decision-makers, including risk classification and recommended Gate 1 outcome.

C. Review flow

Quality Review Board (QRB) process

- Submission: Project team submits the full evidence bundle and closure summary to the quality review function.
- Completeness check: Reviewers confirm all required deliverables exist and are readable and decision-grade.
- Consistency check: Reviewers validate alignment across problem statement, scope, constraints, requirements, feasibility, and risk register.
- Security and compliance baseline check: Reviewers confirm baseline security and compliance constraints are explicitly captured where risk classification demands it (ISO, 2022).
- Findings report: Reviewers issue findings categorized as critical, major, minor, each with owners and due dates.
- QRB outcome: Ready for Gate scheduling, or not ready until critical gaps are resolved.

Gate Review Board (GRB) process

- Pre-read distribution: Evidence bundle and QRB findings report distributed to gate decision-makers in advance.
- Decision narrative: Project leadership presents a short decision narrative focused on decision questions, not slide storytelling.
- Risk classification confirmation: Gate body confirms risk classification and proportional governance depth.
- Risk ownership and constraint validation: Gate body reviews top risks, owners, constraints, and non-negotiables.
- Decision outcome: Gate body issues Go, Conditional Go, Hold, or No-Go, recorded in a decision log.
- Condition management: If Conditional Go, conditions are documented with owners, deadlines, verification steps, and consequences for non-completion.

D. Decision rules

Outcomes

- Go: Evidence meets criteria, risks are within acceptable thresholds, and Design can proceed.
- Conditional Go: Design can proceed only with explicit conditions that are owned, time-bound, and verifiable.
- Hold: Design cannot proceed until specified gaps are resolved and evidence is resubmitted.
- No-Go: The initiative cannot proceed in its current form and must be re-scoped, redesigned, or terminated.

Minimum pass criteria

- Problem statement and success metrics are clear and measurable.
- Scope boundaries and constraints are explicit, including deferred items.

- Decision rights and accountable owners are defined, including operational ownership.
- Requirements baseline includes security and compliance constraints appropriate to risk classification (ISO, 2022).
- Risk classification is defined and justified.
- Initial risk register exists with owners and realistic treatment directions.
- Feasibility is credible across technical, operational, financial, compliance, data, and vendor dimensions.
- Unknowns are explicitly listed with a plan for Design-phase resolution.

Automatic Hold or No-Go triggers

- Data classification is unknown for sensitive or regulated data scenarios.
- No owner exists for high-impact risks, especially security and operational risks.
- Vendor dependency is assumed without third-party risk triage and shared responsibility clarity.
- Operational ownership and sustainment resourcing are undefined.
- Baseline security constraints are missing for externally exposed systems or sensitive-data systems.
- The initiative is misaligned with strategy or violates non-negotiable standards and constraints (ISO, 2015).

Common Gate 1 failure patterns and how to correct them

The first failure pattern is treating Gate 1 as a funding ceremony. When Gate 1 is only about budget approval, the organization pushes uncertainty into Design, then into Build, and then into production. The correction is to treat Gate 1 as readiness approval and to require evidence for constraints, risk tiering, and ownership. The second failure pattern is vague Conditional Go decisions. Vague conditions become invisible. The correction is to treat conditions like deliverables, with owners, deadlines, and verification. The third failure pattern is missing operational ownership. Without operational ownership, the project will go live and become an orphaned system. The correction is to require named operational owners and a sustainment assumption statement before Gate 1 passes. The fourth failure pattern is unclear data classification. Data classification drives security and compliance obligations. The correction is to require data classification assumptions and data flow intent as Gate 1 evidence items. The fifth failure pattern is unexamined vendor dependency. The correction is to require early third-party triage and shared responsibility mapping intent before moving into Design for buy or hybrid paths.

These corrections are not theoretical. They are the predictable adjustments that transform a gate from a ritual into a protective mechanism. They also reflect the broader governance concept that technology decisions must be guided and monitored with accountability, rather than made informally and justified later (ISO, 2015; NIST, 2024b).

Key Takeaways

Gate 1 is the first moment where secure technology project management becomes visible as governance practice. It confirms that the initiative has produced decision-grade clarity, that feasibility is credible, that risk posture is visible with owners and early treatments, and that accountability is assigned for both delivery and sustainment. It institutionalizes evidence discipline by requiring a structured Analyze evidence bundle, validated through quality review and decided through a formal gate forum. It provides clear pass or fail logic so the organization does not drift into Design on momentum alone. When Gate 1 is executed with discipline, Design begins with constraints and proof, not with assumptions and hope. That is how organizations deliver value while protecting trust, and that is how they avoid the costly failure patterns that repeat across portfolios when governance is informal (NIST, 2024b; ISO, 2022).

"No clarity, no commitment, Gate 1 is where optimism meets proof."

12

Design Phase

The Design phase is where a technology project either becomes defensible or becomes fragile. Analyze establishes what the organization is trying to achieve and why the initiative is worth pursuing. Design determines whether the organization can achieve it safely, reliably, and sustainably. This is the phase where assumptions harden into architecture choices, where trust boundaries are defined, where data flows become real, and where control responsibilities move from abstract policy statements into concrete control placement decisions. If Design is rushed, the project can still move quickly, yet it moves like a vehicle with loose bolts. It will run until the road becomes rough, and modern production environments are always rough. Attackers probe constantly, integrations evolve, cloud services change, vendors update components, and AI-enabled features behave differently under real usage than they do in demos. Design is where you prepare for that reality, not by attempting perfection, but by building a system that can be defended, monitored, and improved with discipline (NIST, 2024b).

Design is also the phase where Security by Design becomes measurable. Many teams say security is important. Some teams even have security requirements in a document. Yet if controls are not intentionally designed, they become late additions, and late additions are expensive and incomplete. Encryption can be bolted on, but if key management is unclear, the system is still weak. Logging can be added, but if logs lack context and do not trigger actions, monitoring becomes theater. Access controls can be configured, but if privilege boundaries are not designed, administrative functions become an incident waiting to happen. Design is the phase where these issues are prevented through intentional control architecture and test strategy decisions that produce evidence, not just intentions. Secure development guidance increasingly emphasizes integrated practices and verifiable outcomes across the lifecycle, and Design is where the organization decides how those outcomes will be achieved and proven later (Souppaya et al., 2022).

A disciplined Design phase produces three outcomes that matter to governance. First, it produces a secure architecture that clarifies trust boundaries, data flows, dependencies, and operational responsibilities. Second, it produces a controls design that maps policy expectations and risk realities into specific technical and procedural controls, with clear ownership and implementation approach. Third, it produces a test strategy that defines how the project will verify security, quality, and readiness, and how it will generate traceable evidence for Gate 2 and later gates. These outcomes are not academic. They are how leaders can approve build or acquisition execution with confidence that the project is not steering into avoidable risk (NIST, 2024b; ISO, 2022).

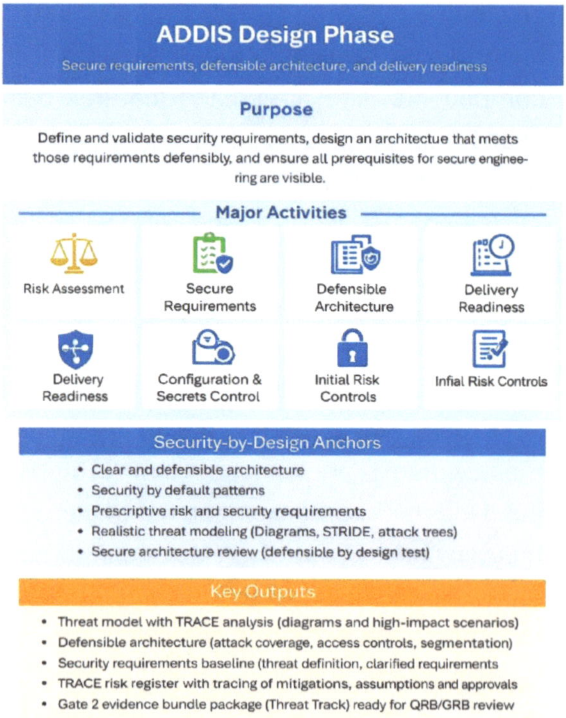

The Design Phase is where intent becomes structure. It translates business and security requirements into architecture decisions, control designs, and test strategies that will govern how the solution is built or acquired. This phase is also where teams prevent expensive rework by confirming trust boundaries, data flows, identity and access patterns, privacy requirements, and logging expectations before development accelerates. The figure below summarizes the purpose, major activities, security-by-design anchors, and key outputs that together form the design evidence needed to move confidently toward build or buy execution and to support the next gate decision.

Turning Requirements Into Design Requirements

Design begins by translating Analyze outputs into architecture constraints and design decisions. In the Analyze phase, the organization defines what success looks like and what constraints must be respected. In Design, those constraints become "must be true" statements that shape architecture. For example, if the solution will process sensitive data, it must be true that data is encrypted in transit and at rest, that access is governed through least privilege, and that logs provide auditability. If the solution is customer-facing, it must be true that authentication boundaries are clear, that session management is robust, and that the system can handle malicious traffic patterns. If the solution depends on a vendor platform, it must be true that shared responsibility boundaries are documented and that the organization controls the configuration and monitoring elements it is accountable for. These are not feature requests. They are the structural conditions of trust.

A strong design process anchors itself in architecture views that can be inspected. At minimum, the project should produce a logical architecture, a deployment architecture, and a data flow view. The logical architecture shows components and responsibilities, including identity services, application services, data stores, integration layers, and third-party services. The deployment architecture shows where those components run and what environments exist, including cloud accounts or subscriptions, network segments, runtime platforms, and boundary controls. The data flow view shows what data moves where, under what conditions, and through what interfaces. This view is essential because data flows are where security failures often happen, especially in complex integration ecosystems.

Trust boundaries should be made explicit in these views. A trust boundary is where the system transitions between zones of trust, such as between the internet and the application boundary, between application and database, between internal network and vendor network, or between a user context and an administrative context. When trust boundaries are implicit, teams unintentionally weaken them. When trust boundaries are explicit, teams can place controls deliberately and test them later. This is also where governance and risk management become practical. A governance-centered cybersecurity approach expects organizations to understand and manage risk through structured oversight, and trust boundary clarity is one of the earliest forms of risk visibility a project can offer (NIST, 2024b).

Identity is often the most critical boundary. In Design, identity architecture must answer practical questions. Who are the users and how are they authenticated. What is the authorization model and what roles exist. How are privileged functions separated from standard user functions. How is machine-to-machine identity handled for integrations. How are secrets stored and rotated. How are administrative access paths controlled and audited. Weak identity design is one of the most common reasons a system becomes indefensible, because compromised credentials remain the simplest path to high-impact outcomes. Design should therefore treat identity and access management as a core architectural pillar, not as a configuration detail.

Data protection must also be designed, not assumed. The project should define what data is stored, how it is classified, and what protection is required. Encryption choices should include key management approach and ownership. Tokenization or masking decisions should be explicit if data minimization is needed. Retention and deletion requirements should be incorporated so the system does not become a compliance liability. ISO/IEC 27001's management-system approach reinforces that information security controls must be defined, operated, and maintained, and that responsibilities must be clear, which implies design decisions must include operational ownership for controls like key management, logging, and access governance (ISO, 2022).

Logging and monitoring design is a frequent failure point because teams treat it as a final checklist item. In Design, the project should define what events are logged, what context is captured, how logs are protected, and how signals are turned into alerts. Monitoring should be tied to operational actions and incident response. A system that generates logs but cannot support detection and response is not ready for real exposure. Design should also define where monitoring responsibility sits. If a vendor platform is used, the shared responsibility model may place logging integration and alerting ownership on the buyer. That must be clear early.

Resilience must also be designed. Availability, recovery, and failure handling are security concerns as well as reliability concerns because service disruptions can become safety issues, financial issues, and reputational issues. Design should address backup strategy, recovery objectives where applicable, deployment rollback approach, and failure mode handling for critical integrations. It should also address dependency resilience, including vendor outages and third-party API failures. A secure system is not only hard to break into. It is also hard to knock over.

Controls design as an engineering activity

Controls design is where the project takes baseline expectations, risk register insights, and architecture decisions, then maps them into concrete controls and control ownership. This is the moment when

Security by Design becomes more than a slogan. Controls design should be traceable. It should show how each significant risk is mitigated, what control addresses it, where the control sits in the architecture, who owns it, and how it will be validated.

A practical approach is to group controls into control families that match how systems are defended. Identity and access controls cover authentication, authorization, privileged access, session handling, and secrets management. Data protection controls cover encryption, key management, data minimization, retention, and integrity. Platform and network controls cover segmentation, boundary protections, runtime hardening, and secure configuration. Application controls cover input validation, secure APIs, error handling, and protection against common exploit classes. Monitoring and response controls cover logging, alerting, incident response integration, and forensic readiness. Governance and change controls cover approval flows, segregation of duties, and release controls. This structure keeps control design understandable and reviewable.

Control ownership must be explicit. Many projects implicitly assume that security owns security controls. That is a misunderstanding. Security teams define expectations and validate evidence, yet controls are owned by the teams who operate them. Engineering may own application controls. Platform teams may own runtime hardening and network segmentation. Identity teams may own authentication services and privileged access tooling. Operations teams may own monitoring integration and incident response procedures. Security may own policy, standards, and independent assurance. This separation supports accountability and is consistent with governance principles that emphasize defining roles and responsibilities so technology decisions and outcomes can be guided and monitored effectively (ISO, 2015).

Controls design should also reflect proportionality. If the initiative is high risk, the project should design deeper controls and more rigorous validation. If the initiative is low risk, controls should still exist, but the depth and overhead should be lighter. Proportionality prevents governance fatigue while maintaining a consistent minimum bar.

Third-party and supply chain controls deserve explicit attention in modern environments. Many systems are assembled from dependencies, libraries, vendor services, and cloud features. Controls design should include how third-party risk is managed, including contract requirements, security assurance expectations, configuration responsibilities, and vulnerability response expectations. SSDF emphasizes that organizations should protect the software supply chain and be prepared to respond to vulnerabilities, and that these are integrated lifecycle practices rather than optional activities (Souppaya et al., 2022). Design is where you decide how those practices will be applied, including who will monitor vendor advisories, how patches and updates will be handled, and how component risk will be tracked.

If the project includes AI-enabled components, controls design must also include AI-specific control considerations without turning the design phase into an abstract ethics debate. AI changes data dependency, behavior uncertainty, and monitoring needs. Controls design should therefore define guardrails for data handling in prompts and outputs, define how access to AI interfaces is governed, define how output logging is handled safely, and define how misuse is detected. It should also define change control for AI components, meaning how model updates, prompt updates, and evaluation updates will be governed. These decisions can be lightweight at this stage, yet they must exist because they shape what evidence will be required at later gates (NIST, 2024b).

A control is not truly designed until the project defines how it will be validated. This is where controls design and test strategy connect. If you cannot test a control, you cannot prove it. If you cannot prove it, the control becomes a belief, not an assurance. Design should therefore include validation intent for significant controls, such as how access boundaries will be tested, how encryption will be verified, how logging and alerting will be validated, and how runtime hardening will be confirmed.

Using Threat Modeling to Improve Design Early

Threat modeling is sometimes feared because teams assume it will slow delivery. In mature environments, it accelerates delivery by preventing architectural rework and by clarifying what must be tested. Threat modeling in Design is not about creating fear. It is about creating focus. It asks what can go wrong, what the most likely attack paths are, where trust boundaries are weakest, and what mitigations should be built into the design rather than bolted on later.

A practical threat modeling approach in Design uses the architecture and data flow views as inputs. The team identifies assets such as identity tokens, customer data, financial transactions, administrative controls, and API keys. It identifies entry points such as web interfaces, APIs, integration endpoints, admin consoles, and data ingestion pipelines. It identifies trust boundaries such as internet to application, application to data store, internal to vendor, and user to admin. Then it identifies threat scenarios that matter. These scenarios drive mitigation decisions and test strategy decisions.

Misuse and abuse cases should be included, especially when AI is involved or when the system can be manipulated through user input. Misuse thinking asks how a system can be used in unintended ways, such as privilege escalation through admin workflows, data exfiltration through export functions, fraud through onboarding workflows, or prompt injection and data leakage through AI interfaces. This thinking is valuable because it anticipates real-world behavior rather than assuming users will behave as designed. When misuse cases are identified in Design, controls can be placed to prevent them and tests can be designed to detect them.

Threat modeling outputs should be practical. They should result in a short list of prioritized risks, mapped mitigations, and identified residual risks. Those outputs become part of the Design evidence bundle and part of the Gate 2 review. They also become part of the test strategy, because each high-priority threat should have corresponding validation activities. This aligns with the idea that secure development outcomes are achieved through integrated practices and verifiable results (Souppaya et al., 2022). Threat modeling is one of the practices that ensures security is designed and testable.

Test Strategy That Produces Proof

A test strategy in secure technology project management is not merely a plan to run tests near the end. It is the blueprint for how the project will generate evidence across the lifecycle. It defines what must be validated, when it will be validated, how it will be validated, and what artifacts will serve as proof at gates. This is why the test strategy belongs in Design. If you design the system without designing the proof, you will later scramble for evidence, and scrambling produces shallow assurance.

The test strategy should include multiple layers of validation. Functional testing validates that the system meets business needs. Integration testing validates that dependencies behave correctly and safely. Performance and resilience testing validates that the system holds under load and failure scenarios. Security testing validates that controls work and that common exploit paths are resisted. Configuration validation confirms that cloud and platform settings match security baselines. Operational readiness validation confirms that monitoring, alerting, incident response, and handover processes function.

Security testing should be designed as a layered approach. It should include code-level security checks where custom development exists, such as static analysis and dependency scanning, aligned to the organization's maturity. It should include dynamic testing for running applications, such as scanning and targeted security testing, especially for externally exposed surfaces. It should include API testing where APIs exist. It should include identity and authorization testing because broken access control remains one of the most common sources of high-impact vulnerabilities. It should include penetration testing or independent assessment for high-risk systems, timed so results can be remediated before production.

The test strategy should also define what constitutes "done" for security testing. Many teams run scans but do not define thresholds. Evidence becomes messy. A disciplined approach defines severity thresholds, remediation expectations, exception handling rules, and verification steps. Exceptions should be time-bound and approved. Otherwise, exceptions become permanent exposure.

Where DevSecOps pipelines exist, the test strategy should define how automated evidence will be captured. Pipeline logs, scan outputs, test reports, and approval records can serve as evidence artifacts if they are stored, traceable, and interpretable. The project should define where evidence is stored and how it will be packaged for gate reviews. SSDF's emphasis on integrating secure practices into the SDLC implies that organizations should be able to demonstrate that secure practices were performed and that results were addressed (Souppaya et al., 2022). A good test strategy turns that requirement into a practical evidence plan.

Test strategy should also include operational readiness tests. Can the team trigger alerts and see them in the right tools. Can incident response procedures be initiated. Can access be revoked quickly. Can the system be rolled back safely. Can backups be restored. Can monitoring dashboards show meaningful signals. These tests are often skipped because they feel operational, yet they are essential because a system that cannot be monitored and controlled cannot be governed effectively. ISO/IEC 27001's orientation toward ongoing control operation and improvement reinforces that operational controls are part of security, not separate from it (ISO, 2022).

If the project includes AI-enabled components, the test strategy must also include evaluation and monitoring validation elements. It should define what acceptable behavior means, what unacceptable outputs look like, how the system will be evaluated for those behaviors, and how monitoring will detect drift or misuse. Even if Part ϖ will later deepen this topic, Design must establish the test approach so the project does not treat AI behavior risk as a surprise near implementation.

A test strategy should also include traceability. Traceability is the link between requirements, risks, controls, and tests. It allows the project to show that security requirements were implemented and validated, and it allows governance bodies to see that high-impact risks were addressed systematically. Traceability reduces audit pain and reduces re-litigation during gate reviews. It is a practical form of evidence discipline.

Closing the Design phase and preparing for Gate 2

Design does not end when diagrams are drawn. It ends when the project has produced a coherent architecture, a mapped controls design, and a test strategy that can generate evidence. It ends when key design decisions are recorded, when ownership is assigned for control implementation, and when major uncertainties are identified with resolution plans. In other words, Design ends when the project can proceed to build or acquire execution without stepping into avoidable rework and avoidable risk.

The most important Design closure practice is ensuring that design decisions are not trapped in individual minds. Decisions must be recorded in a way that allows later reviewers, auditors, and operators to understand the rationale. Why was a control placed here and not there. Why was a vendor integration chosen. Why was a particular data flow permitted. Why were certain risks accepted. These records protect the organization later when questions arise, especially after incidents or audits.

Design closure must also confirm that stakeholders have reviewed and approved what they must own. Security should confirm that baseline control expectations are reflected in design. Architecture should confirm alignment with standards. Operations should confirm the design is operable. Procurement and vendor management should confirm that vendor plans align with due diligence expectations where applicable. The PMO should confirm that evidence bundles are forming and that Gate 2 readiness is on track. Governance is not only a final gate activity. It is an ongoing alignment mechanism.

This chapter intentionally points toward Gate 2. Gate 2 will review the architecture assurance posture and validate control design readiness. Yet Gate 2 can only be effective if Design produces evidence. The evidence should show trust boundaries, data flows, control mapping, threat modeling outputs, and test strategy plans. When that evidence is present, Gate 2 becomes a real decision, not a ritual. When evidence is absent, Gate 2 becomes a confidence exercise.

Design is where the project sets itself up to succeed under real conditions. It is where the organization acknowledges that secure delivery is not achieved by hope. It is achieved by intentional architecture, deliberate controls design, and a test strategy that produces proof. The next chapter will translate these Design outputs into the Gate 2 evidence bundle and the architecture assurance and control validation decision framework that determines whether the project may proceed into build or buy execution (NIST, 2024b; ISO, 2015).

Gate 2: Design Review

Gate 2 is the moment the organization decides whether the system is safe to build, safe to buy, and safe to operationalize. It is not a design presentation meeting. It is not a slide-driven checkpoint. It is the formal governance decision that confirms the Design phase has produced a coherent architecture, a defensible control model, and a test strategy that can generate evidence across build or acquisition execution. When Gate 2 is performed well, it becomes a stabilizing force. It prevents teams from entering execution with undefined trust boundaries, vague control ownership, brittle integrations, and untestable security assumptions. When Gate 2 is weak, projects move into development or vendor implementation with structural gaps. Those gaps appear later as rework, exceptions, audit findings, security incidents, or production instability. The cost is not only financial. The cost is trust, and trust is expensive to rebuild once damaged (NIST, 2024b).

In a modern environment, Gate 2 carries extra weight because the design surface is larger than it used to be. Systems now span cloud services, third-party platforms, managed identity providers, API gateways, data pipelines, and shared services that evolve continuously. Many projects also incorporate AI-enabled features, or they use AI-assisted tools that accelerate code changes, which can increase speed while also increasing the need for disciplined validation and governance. Gate 2 is where leadership ensures that speed is not purchased by quietly weakening assurance. Governance-centered frameworks increasingly emphasize that cybersecurity outcomes must be managed through oversight, decision rights, and accountable risk acceptance, rather than through informal assumptions and last-minute checks (NIST, 2024b). Gate 2 operationalizes that expectation for the Design phase.

A useful way to understand Gate 2 is to treat it as a "design-to-execution contract." Design produces the contract terms. Gate 2 approves those terms. The contract states what must be built or configured, where controls must exist, what evidence must be produced, and what risks remain. When the contract is clear, execution becomes smoother because teams are not negotiating architecture fundamentals while they are trying to deliver. When the contract is unclear, execution becomes chaotic because teams are forced to make architectural decisions under schedule pressure, and schedule pressure is where poor control decisions are made.

Gate 2 also protects the PMO and governance bodies from a familiar failure pattern. Many organizations run gates, yet they treat gates as schedule milestones rather than readiness decisions. If the organization treats Gate 2 as "we finished design documents," then the gate adds little value. Gate 2 is meant to test whether design outputs are decision-grade and whether the organization can defend moving into build or buy execution. That defensibility is crucial in environments that face audits, regulatory scrutiny, or heightened threat conditions. ISO/IEC 27001's management-system perspective reinforces that controls and responsibilities must be defined, implemented, and maintained systematically, which means design must be intentional and reviewable, not improvised (ISO, 2022).

The purpose and principles of Gate 2

Gate 2 exists to answer one decisive question. Is the Design phase complete enough, and the design coherent enough, that the organization can proceed into execution without stepping into avoidable risk. That single question breaks into four practical checks: architecture assurance, control validation readiness, evidence strategy readiness, and accountability readiness.

Architecture assurance means the architecture is complete at the level needed for execution. It does not need every micro-detail, yet it must clearly define the system components, interfaces, trust boundaries, data flows, deployment context, and dependency model. The architecture must also align with enterprise standards and constraints defined in earlier phases. If architecture is incomplete or inconsistent, teams will fill gaps during execution, and those late decisions are rarely governed properly.

Control validation readiness means the project has mapped risks and requirements to specific controls, placed those controls in the architecture, and assigned ownership for implementation and operation. It also means the project has defined how controls will be validated later. A control that cannot be tested is not a control. It is a hope. Secure lifecycle guidance emphasizes integrated, verifiable practices across the SDLC, which makes control validation planning an essential design output, not an optional later task (Souppaya et al., 2022).

Evidence strategy readiness means the project has a test strategy and evidence capture plan that will generate the artifacts required for future gates, particularly Gate 3 and Gate 4. Evidence strategy readiness includes traceability. Requirements must trace to design decisions, controls, and tests. Risks must trace to mitigations and validation. Without traceability, assurance becomes debate rather than proof.

Accountability readiness means ownership and decision rights are clear. Who owns the architecture decisions. Who owns each control. Who owns operational readiness. Who can approve exceptions. Who can accept residual risk. Governance principles emphasize that IT governance is fundamentally about responsibility and oversight, meaning decisions must be guided and monitored with clarity of roles, not left to informal drift (ISO, 2015). Gate 2 is where that clarity is tested.

Several principles make Gate 2 effective. The first is evidence over persuasion. A persuasive presenter can make an incomplete design sound complete. Evidence avoids that trap. The second is proportionality. Gate 2 depth must scale with risk tier. High-risk systems need deeper assurance and more formal validation planning. Low-risk systems still need structure, but lighter. The third is separation of quality readiness from governance decision. The Design gate works best when the evidence bundle is quality-reviewed before the gate meeting, so the gate meeting is a true decision forum rather than a document scavenger hunt. The fourth is explicit handling of unresolved items. Gate 2 does not demand perfection, yet it demands honesty. If items remain unresolved, they must become explicit conditions with owners, deadlines, and verification methods. Otherwise, “unresolved” becomes “forgotten,” and forgotten becomes “exposure.”

Gate 2 inputs and the Design evidence bundle

Gate 2 depends on a Design evidence bundle that is coherent, readable, and decision-grade. The bundle should be structured so that decision-makers can understand the design posture without drowning in detail, while technical reviewers can inspect the detail where needed. A good bundle uses a layered approach. It starts with a short decision narrative and then includes supporting artifacts.

The decision narrative is the executive-level design summary. It states what the architecture is, what the key decisions were, what tradeoffs were made, what the major risks are, what controls are designed to address them, and what validation plan will prove the controls. It also states what remains uncertain and how those uncertainties will be resolved during execution. This narrative is not marketing. It is a governance artifact. It allows leadership to approve design readiness based on facts and explicit tradeoffs.

The architecture artifacts are the first major component of the bundle. At minimum, the project should provide a logical architecture view, a deployment architecture view, and a data flow view. The logical view shows system components and responsibilities. The deployment view shows where those components run, including cloud accounts or subscriptions, network segments, runtime platforms, and boundary components such as gateways or load balancers. The data flow view shows what data moves where, under what conditions, and across what interfaces. These views are required because they make trust boundaries visible. Trust boundaries are the locations where the system transitions from one trust zone to another, and those are where controls must be placed deliberately.

Identity and access design should be explicitly represented, not buried in text. The design should clarify authentication flows, authorization model, role definitions, separation between standard and privileged access, and machine identity for integrations. Privileged access should be treated as its own boundary because administrative functions often become the highest-risk surface. When identity design is vague, access control becomes inconsistent during execution, and inconsistent access control is one of the most common root causes of serious security issues.

Data protection decisions must also be explicit. The design should state what data classes are in scope, where data will be stored, what encryption mechanisms will be used, and how key management ownership will work. It should also state retention and deletion requirements where they apply. When these decisions are postponed, teams often build storage patterns that later conflict with compliance expectations, forcing expensive redesign. ISO/IEC 27001 emphasizes systematic definition and operation of information security controls and responsibilities, which implies design must establish how control ownership and operation will work, not merely that controls "exist" (ISO, 2022).

Logging and monitoring design must be included in the architecture artifacts or in a dedicated monitoring design section. It should define what events will be logged, where logs will go, how alerts will be triggered, and who will respond. Monitoring is not just an operational concern. It is a security assurance concern because detection and response depend on it. If monitoring design is absent, the system may deploy without meaningful detection capability, and incident response becomes blind.

Controls design is the second major component of the bundle. Controls design should map requirements and risks to specific controls and should describe where each control sits in the architecture. It should also define ownership. Control ownership is where many projects fail. When ownership is unclear, controls become "everyone's job," and "everyone's job" becomes "nobody's job." Gate 2 should treat ownership ambiguity as a design defect.

Threat modeling outputs, or lightweight threat and misuse analysis outputs, should be included as part of the design evidence. The goal is not to create theoretical documents. The goal is to show that the project identified key threat scenarios and designed mitigations accordingly. Threat modeling also strengthens test strategy because it helps define what must be tested, particularly around trust boundaries and misuse paths.

The test strategy is the third major component of the bundle. Test strategy in Gate 2 is not a schedule. It is the proof blueprint. It should define validation layers, including functional tests, integration tests, performance tests, resilience tests, security tests, configuration validation, and operational readiness validation. It should also define evidence capture, thresholds, exception handling, and traceability. Secure software development guidance emphasizes that secure practices should be integrated into workflows and that organizations should be able to demonstrate those practices and outcomes, which makes the test strategy and evidence plan a core design deliverable (Souppaya et al., 2022).

If the system includes third-party services or vendor platforms, the evidence bundle must include a shared responsibility mapping and a plan for vendor controls validation. Many organizations assume vendor security equals system security. That assumption is false. The buyer often owns configuration, access governance, logging integration, monitoring, and incident response integration. Gate 2 should ensure those buyer responsibilities are explicitly designed and scheduled.

If the system includes AI-enabled components, the evidence bundle must include AI-specific design constraints and validation intent, at least at a baseline level. This can be lightweight in Part σɒ because Part ω expands the AI overlay, yet Design must still define what data can be used, how access to AI interfaces is controlled, how outputs are handled, and what monitoring is expected. AI behavior risk is not managed by hope. It is managed by guardrails, evaluation, and monitoring, which must be designed early to avoid late chaos.

Quality review before Gate 2

Gate 2 should not begin with a gate meeting. It should begin with a quality review of the Design evidence bundle. This quality review is typically handled by the Quality Review Board or by a designated assurance function. The purpose is to validate that the bundle is complete, consistent, and decision-ready. This creates two major benefits. It reduces executive time waste, and it reduces the political pressure that arises when technical reviewers raise issues in a high-pressure gate forum. Quality review makes technical gaps visible as facts, not as opinions.

The quality review examines the design for completeness and coherence. It checks whether the logical architecture matches the deployment view. It checks whether the data flows described align with the data classification assumptions. It checks whether identity boundaries are clear. It checks whether controls are mapped to risks and requirements, and whether control ownership is assigned. It checks whether the test strategy can actually validate the controls being proposed. It checks whether traceability exists at least at a baseline level. It also checks whether operational readiness elements such as logging and monitoring are designed, not postponed.

Quality review should also validate alignment with enterprise standards and constraints. If the organization has cloud landing zone standards, identity standards, encryption standards, logging standards, or secure configuration baselines, the design must align or explicitly request an exception. Exceptions must not be hidden. They must be documented with rationale and proposed mitigation. ISO/IEC 38500 emphasizes governance of IT through guiding and monitoring, which is undermined when exceptions become informal and invisible (ISO, 2015). Quality review prevents that invisibility.

Quality review outcomes should be structured. The evidence bundle is either cleared for Gate 2 scheduling or returned for remediation. Findings should be categorized as critical gaps, major gaps, and minor gaps. Critical gaps block Gate 2. Major gaps may be allowed into Gate 2 only if they are explicitly presented as conditions, with owners and deadlines. Minor gaps can be corrected during execution, but they should still be tracked. This structure reduces ambiguity and strengthens gate credibility.

The Gate 2 review process

The Gate 2 meeting is the formal decision forum. Its purpose is to decide whether the project may proceed into execution, meaning into build or vendor acquisition work. The meeting should be decision-focused. If the meeting becomes a document review session, that indicates the quality review step was skipped or ineffective.

Gate 2 begins with confirmation that the quality review has cleared the bundle or has documented remaining issues. The project team should then present a short decision narrative. The narrative should focus on the highest-impact design decisions and the readiness posture. It should highlight trust boundaries, data flows, integration dependencies, and control placement. It should also highlight what will be validated, when, and how evidence will be generated. A disciplined narrative is typically brief, yet dense with facts.

The gate body then reviews architecture assurance. The key question is whether the architecture is coherent, aligned, and sufficient for execution. This includes alignment with enterprise architecture standards, cloud standards, identity standards, and data governance constraints. It also includes confirming that the system's operating model is plausible. If the design requires operational capabilities that do not exist, the project is not ready to proceed.

Next, the gate body reviews control validation readiness. This includes confirming that controls are mapped to risks and requirements, that control ownership is assigned, and that validation methods are defined. It also includes confirming that high-risk controls such as identity boundaries, privileged access controls, encryption and key management, and logging and monitoring are not left vague. Where controls rely on vendor capabilities, Gate 2 must confirm that those capabilities are understood and that buyer responsibilities are explicit.

The gate body then reviews the test strategy and evidence plan. This includes confirming that security testing is layered, that thresholds and exception handling are defined, and that the plan supports traceability. It also includes confirming that operational readiness validation is part of the plan, not a final-week scramble. Secure lifecycle guidance emphasizes that integrated secure practices and evidence are central to assurance, which makes the test strategy a key governance artifact, not merely a QA artifact (Souppaya et al., 2022).

The gate body also reviews the risk posture. At Gate 2, risk posture includes design-level risks such as unresolved trust boundary decisions, unclear data flows, missing controls, unvalidated vendor responsibilities, or unrealistic operational assumptions. The gate body should also confirm whether any residual risks require explicit acceptance or escalation. This aligns with CSF 2.0's governance orientation, where cybersecurity is managed through oversight and risk decisions are tied to enterprise priorities and accountability (NIST, 2024b).

Finally, the gate body issues a decision outcome. The outcomes should remain consistent across the governance model: Go, Conditional Go, Hold, or No-Go. Go means design is complete enough and defensible enough to proceed. Conditional Go means the project may proceed with explicit conditions. Hold means the project cannot proceed because critical design gaps exist. No-Go means the project should not proceed in its current form, likely due to misalignment, infeasibility, or unacceptable risk without credible mitigation.

Conditional Go discipline is essential at Gate 2 because Design often contains unresolved items that can be legitimately resolved during execution. Conditional Go is a useful tool when conditions are narrow, time-bound, and measurable. It becomes dangerous when conditions are vague or numerous. If the gate issues Conditional Go, it must assign owners, deadlines, and verification methods for each condition, and it must define what happens if conditions are not met, such as an automatic Hold at Gate 3 readiness or an escalation to risk acceptance authority.

Pass or fail criteria for Gate 2

Gate 2 requires clear pass or fail logic because design readiness can otherwise become subjective. A project passes Gate 2 when architecture assurance is credible, controls design is mapped and owned, and the validation and evidence plan is strong enough to prove readiness later. It passes when the project has reduced uncertainty enough to justify execution investment.

A project fails Gate 2 when design is incomplete in ways that will create uncontrolled risk during execution. This includes unclear trust boundaries, unclear data flows, missing identity and access decisions, missing control ownership, missing monitoring design, or missing test strategy depth. It also includes misalignment with non-negotiable enterprise standards or compliance obligations. Hold is appropriate when the initiative remains valuable but must correct design gaps. No-Go is appropriate when the design direction is fundamentally misaligned or ungovernable.

Automatic fail triggers should exist for high-risk initiatives. If the design does not define data classification and protection approach for sensitive data, it should not proceed. If privileged access and identity boundaries are unclear, it should not proceed. If logging and monitoring design is absent, it should not proceed. If third-party responsibilities are unclear for a vendor-dependent system, it should not proceed. If the test strategy cannot produce evidence for key controls, it should not proceed. These triggers are practical because they reflect common failure patterns that lead to high-impact outcomes.

Distinct end-of-phase package for the Design phase and Gate 2

This section provides a complete, ready-to-use closure package for the Design phase and Gate 2, structured in the same practical format used for Gate 1. It is written to be operational, not descriptive, so teams can apply it directly when preparing for the Design closeout. The package includes the major tasks that must be completed, the required deliverables for the Gate 2 evidence bundle, and the steps for quality review and gate review. It also defines clear pass, conditional pass, hold, and no-go decision logic so Gate 2 outcomes are consistent, defensible, and evidence driven.

Gate 2 Readiness Pack

This Gate 2 Readiness Pack summarizes the Design Phase work and presents the evidence required for a Gate 2 decision. It is organized for fast review using a one-page cover sheet, an evidence bundle index, and decision rules that define minimum pass criteria and automatic hold triggers. The intent is to confirm that the design is coherent, secure by design, and testable, before the organization commits to build or acquire execution. The gate decision should be based on the evidence referenced in this pack, not on presentation confidence.

A. Readiness workstreams

1. Design views and trust boundaries: Finalize architecture views and trust boundaries. Produce coherent logical, deployment, and data flow views. Make trust boundaries explicit, including user boundary, admin boundary, integration boundary, and third-party boundary.
2. Identity and access design: Complete identity and access design. Define authentication flows, authorization model, role definitions, and privileged access boundaries. Define machine identity approach for integrations and services.
3. Data protection and lifecycle controls: Complete data protection design. Confirm data classes, storage locations, encryption approach, and key management ownership. Define retention and deletion requirements where applicable (ISO, 2022).
4. Logging, monitoring, and response design: Define logging and monitoring design. Identify security-relevant and operational events to log. Define log routing, alert triggers, and response ownership.

5. Controls mapping and ownership: Map risks and requirements to controls. Create control mapping from baseline requirements and top risks to specific controls and their locations in the design. Assign control owners and define implementation responsibility.
6. Threat and misuse analysis: Perform design-level threat and misuse analysis. Identify top threat scenarios and misuse paths based on design and data flows. Define mitigations and document residual risks.
7. Test strategy and evidence plan: Produce the test strategy and evidence plan. Define a layered validation approach, including security validation, configuration validation, and operational readiness validation. Define evidence capture, thresholds, exception handling, and traceability expectations (Souppaya et al., 2022).
8. Third-party responsibility model: Confirm third-party responsibility model if vendors are involved. Document shared responsibility boundaries and buyer-owned control areas. Identify vendor constraints that affect security, monitoring, or incident response.
9. Design closure narrative: Prepare the Design closure narrative. Summarize key design decisions, tradeoffs, risks, validation plan, and unresolved items with a resolution plan.

B. Gate 2 evidence bundle index

1. Design Phase Closure Summary
   A concise decision narrative, including readiness recommendation and requested Gate 2 outcome.
2. Design package
   Logical design diagram and component responsibilities.
   Deployment design including environments, network

boundaries, and runtime platforms. Data flow diagrams with data classification assumptions and trust boundaries.

3. Identity and Access Design
   Authentication and authorization model, role design, privileged access boundaries, and machine identity model for services and integrations.
4. Controls design and mapping
   Control matrix linking requirements and risks to controls, including placement, ownership, and validation intent.
5. Threat and misuse analysis
   Prioritized design-level threats and misuse cases, mapped mitigations, and residual risks.
6. Logging, Monitoring, and Incident Readiness Design
   Logging coverage intent, alerting design, monitoring responsibilities, and incident response integration intent.
7. Test Strategy and Evidence Plan
   Layered testing approach, security testing scope, thresholds, exception handling, and traceability approach (Souppaya et al., 2022).
8. Third-Party Shared Responsibility Summary
   Vendor responsibilities, buyer responsibilities, and validation plan for vendor-dependent controls.
9. Updated Risk Register
   Design-level risks, residual risks, owners, and any risks proposed for acceptance or escalation.

C. Review flow

Quality Review Board (QRB) process

- Submission: Project team submits the Gate 2 evidence bundle and Design closure summary to the quality review function.
- Completeness and coherence check: Reviewers confirm all required deliverables exist, are readable, and are internally consistent. Reviewers validate alignment between the design package, control mapping, and test strategy.
- Standards and constraint alignment check: Reviewers confirm the design aligns with enterprise standards and constraints. If exceptions exist, reviewers confirm they are documented with mitigation approach and approval path (ISO, 2015).
- Control testability check: Reviewers confirm each key control has a validation approach and evidence plan consistent with secure lifecycle expectations (Souppaya et al., 2022).
- Findings report: Reviewers' issue findings categorized as critical, major, minor, each with owners and due dates.
- QRB outcome: Ready for Gate scheduling, or not ready until critical gaps are resolved.

Gate Review Board (GRB) process

- Pre-read distribution: Evidence bundle and QRB findings report distributed to gate decision-makers in advance.
- Decision narrative: Project leadership presents a short readiness narrative focused on major design decisions, control placement, and the validation plan.
- Design assurance review: Gate body confirms trust boundaries, data flows, integration patterns, and alignment with standards and constraints.
- Control validation readiness review: Gate body confirms control mapping, ownership, and testability for high-impact controls.

- Test strategy and evidence review: Gate body confirms validation layers, security testing coverage, thresholds, exception handling, and traceability plan.
- Risk posture review: Gate body reviews design-level risks and residual risks, confirming owners and escalation needs (NIST, 2024b).
- Decision outcome: Gate body issues Go, Conditional Go, Hold, or No-Go, recorded in a decision log.
- Condition management: If Conditional Go, conditions are documented with owners, deadlines, verification steps, and consequences for non-completion.

D. Decision rules

Outcomes

- Go: Design evidence is complete and coherent, controls are testable, and execution can proceed with an acceptable risk posture.
- Conditional Go: Execution can proceed only with explicit conditions that are owned, time-bound, and verifiable.
- Hold: Execution cannot proceed until specified design gaps are resolved and evidence is resubmitted.
- No-Go: The initiative cannot proceed in its current form and must be re-scoped, redesigned, or terminated.

Minimum pass criteria

- Trust boundaries and data flows are explicit and consistent across design views.
- Identity model and privileged access boundaries are clearly defined.
- Data protection approach and key ownership are defined where sensitive data is in scope (ISO, 2022).

- Controls are mapped to risks and requirements with clear ownership.
- Logging and monitoring design exists with response ownership.
- Threat and misuse analysis has produced mitigations for top scenarios and documents residual risk.
- Test strategy can validate key controls and produce evidence and traceability (Souppaya et al., 2022).
- Third-party responsibilities are documented when vendors are involved.
- Design-level risks are visible, owned, and managed, including escalation and conditions where needed (NIST, 2024b).

Automatic Hold or No-Go triggers

- Sensitive data flows exist but data protection design is undefined.
- Privileged access and authorization boundaries are unclear.
- Logging and monitoring design is missing for an externally exposed or high-risk system.
- Controls mapping exists but ownership is unassigned.
- Test strategy cannot validate key controls, or lacks thresholds and exception handling.
- Vendor shared responsibility boundaries are unclear for a vendor-dependent solution.
- Design conflicts with non-negotiable enterprise standards without an approved exception process (ISO, 2015).

Common Gate 2 failure patterns and how to correct them

The first failure pattern is treating architecture as diagrams rather than as a decision system. Diagrams can look impressive while leaving critical questions unanswered, especially around trust boundaries and operational ownership. The correction is to require explicit boundary statements, data flow intent, and operating model assumptions as part of the evidence bundle.

The second failure pattern is controls that are listed but not placed. Teams may list encryption, logging, and access controls, yet they do not specify where those controls exist and who owns them. The correction is control mapping with placement, ownership, and validation method.

The third failure pattern is a test strategy that is a schedule rather than a proof blueprint. The correction is to require a layered validation plan with thresholds, exception handling, evidence capture, and traceability.

The fourth failure pattern is vendor dependence treated as a procurement concern. The correction is shared responsibility mapping and buyer-owned control validation intent in the design evidence.

The fifth failure pattern is Conditional Go conditions that are vague and unenforced. The correction is to treat conditions like deliverables, with owners, deadlines, verification, and consequences.

These patterns repeat because Design is the phase where teams feel pressure to “move on.” Gate 2 exists to ensure the organization moves on with the right structure, not with wishful thinking. This is consistent with governance-centered cybersecurity practice where decisions are made with oversight and accountability rather than on narrative confidence (NIST, 2024b).

Key Takeaway

Gate 2 is the first major assurance checkpoint where the organization proves that Security by Design is no longer an intention, it is a concrete design that can be built, acquired, tested, and defended. This gate confirms that the solution's trust boundaries and data flows are explicit, coherent, and agreed upon. It also verifies that the design makes security responsibilities clear. Controls must not only be defined, they must be placed in the right locations, assigned to accountable owners, and described in a way that makes them testable. Without this clarity, teams enter execution with assumptions, and assumptions become rework, exceptions, and hidden exposure.

Gate 2 focuses on evidence readiness as much as design completeness. It validates that the test strategy can produce proof throughout execution, not just at the end. That includes functional testing, integration testing, security validation, configuration validation, and operational readiness validation, scaled to the project's risk classification. It also requires traceability. Requirements and top risks must map to specific controls, and those controls must map to validation steps and evidence artifacts. When this chain is broken, the organization cannot demonstrate due diligence, and gate decisions become subjective.

The gate discipline matters because it separates two roles that are often confused. The quality review function checks whether the evidence bundle is complete, consistent, and decision-grade. The gate decision forum then focuses on the decision itself: whether the project can proceed into build or acquisition work, whether it can proceed with conditions, or whether it must pause. This structure prevents "meeting-driven approval" and replaces it with evidence-driven governance. It also makes unresolved items visible. Conditions are not vague promises. They must be specific, owned, time-bound, and verifiable. That keeps gaps from being buried and later normalized as operational debt.

When Gate 2 is executed with discipline, execution begins with shared understanding. Teams spend less time re-litigating design intent. Stakeholders collaborate around the same artifacts. Security and compliance requirements become buildable requirements instead of late-stage negotiation. This reduces rework, reduces exception pressure, and improves delivery predictability. It also strengthens audit readiness because the organization can show that design decisions were governed, reviewed, and validated in a repeatable way. That aligns with management system expectations for systematic security operation (ISO, 2022) and with secure lifecycle guidance that emphasizes integrated, verifiable practices (Souppaya et al., 2022). The next chapters build on this foundation by detailing the Build and Buy tracks and the Gate 3 readiness decision, where design intent must be implemented and validated before deployment planning can proceed.

Build with security.
Assume you are
defending what you design.

Good design has Security by Design at the center.

10 Develop - Build Phase

The Develop phase is where design intent becomes executable reality. In earlier phases, the organization clarified the opportunity, framed constraints, and approved a secure architecture and control model. In this phase, the team builds the solution, and just as importantly, it builds the proof that the solution is secure, reliable, and operable. If Analyze was the foundation and Design was the blueprint, Develop is the construction site where both craftsmanship and inspection discipline matter. The work is not finished when code compiles, features demo well, or sprint goals are met. In secure technology project management, the work is finished when controls are implemented as designed, tests prove they work, evidence is traceable, and the solution is ready for the rigor of deployment and sustained operations. Modern cybersecurity governance expects organizations to manage cybersecurity outcomes through accountability and evidence, not through informal confidence, and the Develop phase is where that evidence is produced at scale (NIST, 2024b).

Develop is also the phase where speed can become either a competitive advantage or a source of systemic risk. Teams often accelerate delivery using automation, reusable services, and AI-assisted engineering tools. Done well, those accelerators reduce defects and improve consistency. Done poorly, they amplify errors and spread insecure patterns quickly across environments. Secure engineering in the Develop phase is therefore not just about "writing secure code." It is about creating an execution system that produces secure outcomes repeatedly, even when delivery pressure rises. The NIST Secure Software Development Framework emphasizes integrating secure practices into the SDLC in a way that is repeatable and measurable, including protection of the development environment, verification of software, and a disciplined approach to vulnerability response (Souppaya et al., 2022). This chapter translates that expectation into a build track playbook: what to do, what to verify, what to capture as evidence, and how to define release readiness in a way that is defensible at Gate 3.

A common misunderstanding is that security belongs to the security team and quality belongs to QA. In modern delivery, those boundaries create gaps. Engineering owns engineering controls. Platform teams own runtime and infrastructure controls. Security defines expectations and validates evidence. Quality functions validate completeness and coherence of evidence bundles. Operations owns monitoring, incident response integration, and sustainment. Develop is where those ownership lines must become real through concrete tasks, traceable artifacts, and clear decision gates. ISO/IEC 27001 reinforces that information security controls and responsibilities must be systematically implemented and maintained, which implies the project must design control ownership into everyday work rather than treating it as a late documentation step (ISO, 2022).

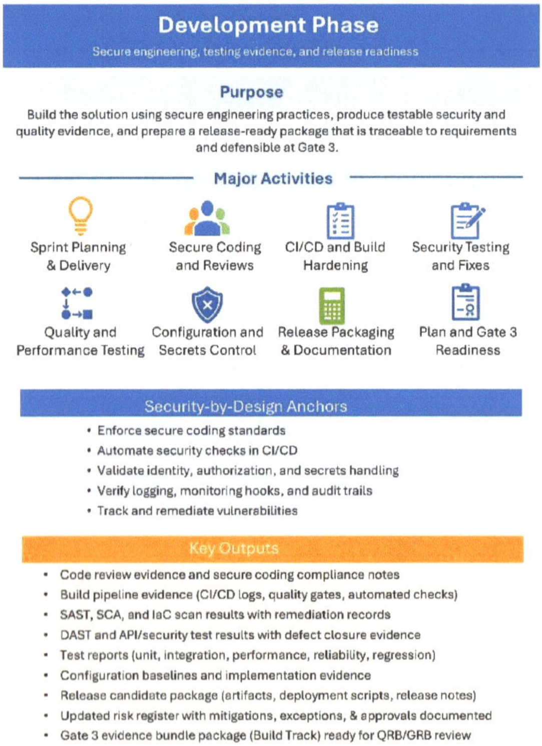

The Development Phase is where the solution is built with security engineered into the work, not added at the end. Teams convert design decisions into code, configuration, and deployment artifacts while generating proof that controls are implemented, tested, and traceable to requirements. This phase also creates the operational and assurance evidence needed for Gate 3, including secure build pipeline records, security test results, defect closure, configuration baselines, and release documentation. The figure below provides a compact view of the phase purpose, major activities, security-by-design anchors, and the key outputs that form the Gate 3 evidence bundle for quality and governance review.

Secure engineering as a delivery system

Secure engineering begins with engineering discipline, not with scanning tools. Tools help, yet tools cannot correct ambiguous requirements, inconsistent architecture decisions, unclear ownership, or chaotic configuration management. The Develop phase should therefore begin with a controlled execution environment and a clear plan for building in alignment with design decisions. The team should establish a working agreement that defines coding standards, branching and merge practices, review expectations, and how security and quality requirements will be treated in backlog prioritization. When teams treat security as optional backlog work, it gets postponed under pressure. When teams treat security as definition-of-done work, it becomes normal. This is one of the strongest cultural levers a project leader can pull, and it aligns with secure development guidance that emphasizes making secure practices part of standard workflows (Souppaya et al., 2022).

A build track solution is rarely "just code." It includes infrastructure as code, identity configurations, policies, secrets, integration workflows, and operational assets. Secure engineering therefore includes three parallel build surfaces: application code, infrastructure and platform configuration, and integration flows. Each surface must be governed. For application code, secure engineering includes secure API design, input validation, safe error handling, and protection of authorization boundaries. For infrastructure and platform configuration, secure engineering includes hardened baselines, segmentation design, secure configuration of managed services, and least privilege service roles. For integration flows, secure engineering includes secure authentication between services, protected secrets, safe data transformations, and resilient error handling.

One of the most important Develop phase decisions is how the team will manage identity and secrets. Identity is the control plane for nearly everything else. If service-to-service identity is weak, attackers and misconfigurations can move laterally. If privileged access is not governed, administrative actions become untraceable and hard to control. If secrets are stored in code or in shared files, the project has already created a long-term vulnerability. The project should implement centralized secrets management and define rotation and access patterns. It should also define how privileged administrative paths will be accessed and audited, which is often supported by a privileged access management approach or an equivalent governance mechanism in smaller environments. These decisions translate Design intent into enforceable reality, and they support the governance goal of measurable, accountable cybersecurity outcomes (NIST, 2024b).

Dependency management and software supply chain control are also central in Develop. Modern applications rely heavily on third-party libraries, frameworks, container images, and external services. A secure build track must treat dependencies as first-class risk objects. This means maintaining an inventory of critical dependencies, monitoring known vulnerability exposures, and defining a process for patching and updating. It also means controlling how dependencies are introduced. Ideally, the team uses approved repositories and validated sources, and it documents decisions when exceptions occur.

SSDF emphasizes supply chain protection and vulnerability response as core elements of secure development, not add-ons (Souppaya et al., 2022). In practice, this becomes a set of repeatable controls: dependency scanning, version control discipline, review gates for new components, and a clear approach to remediating critical findings.

Secure coding practices must be paired with peer review practices. Code review is not only about style. It is a control. It is where authorization logic is challenged, where risky patterns are caught early, and where misunderstandings are corrected. A disciplined code review process includes a security lens. Reviewers check for broken access control patterns, injection risks, insecure direct object references, weak logging around sensitive operations, and insecure use of secrets. The project does not need to turn every engineer into a security expert, yet it must define a minimum security review checklist appropriate to the system's risk tier. This is one of the most effective ways to reduce vulnerabilities without slowing delivery, because catching a flaw during review is far cheaper than fixing it during remediation sprints or after production.

Infrastructure as code deserves equal discipline. In many projects, the biggest security failures do not come from application code at all. They come from misconfigurations: overly permissive storage, exposed services, weak network segmentation, excessive roles, and missing logging. Infrastructure as code enables repeatability, yet it also enables repeatable mistakes. The Develop phase should implement baseline templates and policy checks that align with Design decisions. It should also define how changes to infrastructure code will be reviewed, tested, and promoted. This is where DevSecOps discipline becomes practical, but the goal is not to adopt fashionable tools. The goal is to create repeatable control enforcement.

The Develop phase should also establish an exception handling model. Exceptions are sometimes necessary. For example, a critical vulnerability may not be patchable immediately due to vendor dependencies or feature stability concerns. Yet exceptions must never be invisible. Each exception should be documented, approved by the right authority, time-bound, and tracked to closure. Exceptions that lack expiration are simply risk acceptance without accountability. A governance-centered delivery approach expects explicit risk decisions tied to accountability and oversight (NIST, 2024b). The exception model is how that expectation is operationalized during engineering execution.

Evidence-driven testing and assurance

Testing in the Develop phase is not a single event. It is a progressive validation process that generates evidence continuously. The key shift is mindset. Testing is not merely to find bugs. Testing is to prove controls and readiness. If the team waits until late phases to "run security," it will either delay release or ship with unresolved findings. If the team designs a layered test strategy and integrates it into the build pipeline, it creates predictable evidence and reduces late-stage shocks.

A layered testing model typically includes unit tests, integration tests, and system tests, plus a set of assurance checks that validate security and configuration. Unit tests validate small functional units and can also validate security logic such as authorization checks and input validation. Integration tests validate interactions between components, which is where many authorization and data-handling issues appear. System tests validate end-to-end workflows and user journeys. Beyond functional testing, the Develop phase should include security-specific verification, such as static analysis for code patterns, dependency analysis for known exposures, and dynamic testing against running services. The goal is not to run every tool possible. The goal is to choose the right layers for the system's risk tier and to ensure the output becomes usable evidence.

Evidence must be designed. It does not appear automatically. The project should define where test results will be stored, how they will be linked to builds and releases, and how they will be packaged for gate reviews. A practical approach is to define an evidence repository structure that ties each build to a set of artifacts: test reports, scan results, code review approvals, configuration validation results, and exception records. SSDF emphasizes repeatable secure development practices and the ability to demonstrate them, which means evidence must be captured in a way that is accessible and traceable (Souppaya et al., 2022). In governance terms, evidence is what allows leaders to approve progression without gambling.

Security testing should be tuned to what matters most. For externally exposed services, authorization testing, API abuse testing, and input validation testing are high priority. For systems handling sensitive data, data protection verification, logging verification, and access control verification are high priority. For systems with privileged administration, privileged path testing and auditability verification are high priority. For integration-heavy systems, service-to-service authentication and secrets handling validation are high priority. A disciplined project chooses test coverage based on threat-informed priorities rather than generic checklists.

Vulnerability management must be integrated into the Develop phase, not postponed to implementation. Vulnerabilities will be found. The question is whether the project handles them with discipline. A mature approach defines severity thresholds and response timelines. Critical findings must be fixed, or explicitly accepted with time-bound mitigation and documented authority. High findings must be fixed before release except when a documented exception is approved. Medium findings may be scheduled based on risk, yet still tracked. Low findings may be deferred, but not ignored. This approach aligns with the governance expectation of accountable risk decisions and ongoing monitoring of cybersecurity posture (NIST, 2024b). It also aligns with ISO/IEC 27001's orientation toward systematic control operation and continual improvement, where security is treated as managed, not ad hoc (ISO, 2022).

Testing evidence must also include configuration validation. In cloud and platform-heavy environments, configuration is often the primary control surface. The Develop phase should therefore verify baseline configurations, including network exposure settings, encryption settings, logging settings, and identity role policies. It should also verify that environments are separated appropriately, that production access is controlled, and that privileged actions are logged. This work is often considered "platform team work," yet from a governance standpoint, it is part of the project's evidence bundle because it affects production readiness.

One overlooked evidence category is negative testing and misuse testing. Many systems pass functional tests while failing under misuse conditions. For example, authorization may work for normal users but fail when identifiers are manipulated. Rate limiting may work for typical usage but fail under automation. Export controls may work in the UI but fail through the API. If AI interfaces exist, prompts can be used to attempt data exfiltration or to manipulate system behavior. The Develop phase should incorporate misuse cases into testing, at least for high-impact user journeys. This connects directly to the threat and misuse analysis performed in Design. Threat scenarios must lead to mitigations, and mitigations must lead to tests. This chain is how Security by Design becomes verifiable.

A strong project also treats test coverage as a governance question. What level of coverage is required for this risk tier. What types of testing are mandatory. Which tests must pass for promotion to staging. Which tests must pass for release candidate status. Which issues are release blockers. If these questions are not answered, release decisions become political and inconsistent. If they are answered, release decisions become disciplined and defensible.

Release Readiness Beyond the Build

Release readiness in the Develop phase is not the same as deployment readiness in the Implement phase. Develop phase release readiness is about confirming that what has been built is sufficiently complete, tested, and documented that it can proceed into the build or buy readiness gate with confidence. It is where the team confirms that the solution is not only functional, but also secure-by-design in implementation, and that the evidence exists to prove it.

Release readiness starts with readiness criteria. Criteria should include functional completeness for the agreed scope, control implementation completeness for baseline security requirements, and evidence completeness for testing and validation. It should also include basic operational readiness elements that must be implemented before deployment planning begins. These include logging instrumentation, monitoring hooks, alert definitions at least at baseline level, and operational runbook drafts. The reason to include operational assets early is simple. If you build without operational thinking, you will deploy a system that is hard to operate, and a system that is hard to operate is hard to secure. ISO/IEC 27001's perspective supports this because it treats security as a system of controls and responsibilities that must be maintained continuously, which is impossible when operational readiness is an afterthought (ISO, 2022).

Release readiness also requires change control discipline. Even in agile environments, there must be a structured release candidate process. This process defines when code is frozen, how release notes are generated, how known issues are documented, and how risk decisions are recorded. It also defines how configuration changes are managed across environments. This is where governance meets engineering reality. Governance does not mean slowing everything down. It means ensuring the organization can explain what changed, why it changed, and what evidence proves the change is safe.

Documentation during Develop should be purposeful and minimal, yet not absent. It should include architecture decision records for key choices, control implementation notes for major controls, operational runbook drafts for critical workflows, and support procedures for common incidents. It should also include user-facing documentation where required. Documentation is not a vanity activity. It is part of the evidence that the system can be sustained. A project that cannot explain itself becomes dependent on individual engineers, and that dependency is an operational risk.

Release readiness must also address training and readiness of support teams. If a system changes business workflows or introduces new operational patterns, support teams need training. If the system introduces new monitoring tools or alerting patterns, responders need training. If the system introduces new access roles, administrators need training. These readiness elements often feel “soft,” yet they are the difference between a stable go-live and a chaotic one.

For high-risk systems, independent assurance activities may be required before Gate 3. These can include penetration testing, independent code review, architecture assurance follow-up, or focused security testing by a separate team. The Develop phase must plan for these activities early because they can affect schedule. Independent assurance should not arrive as a surprise near release. It should be part of the evidence strategy approved at Gate 2.

One of the most important release readiness concepts is “release with known risk.” Sometimes, leadership decides to release while some issues remain. That can be acceptable when risks are low, mitigations exist, and acceptance is explicit and time-bound. It becomes dangerous when it is informal and habitual. The Develop phase should therefore treat risk acceptance as governance activity. Risk acceptance must be documented, owned, and linked to mitigation plans. This is consistent with a governance-centered cybersecurity posture that emphasizes accountability for risk decisions and monitoring of outcomes (NIST, 2024b).

Develop phase closure and readiness for Gate 3

At the end of Develop, the project should not simply declare "development complete." It should close the phase through an evidence-based readiness checkpoint that prepares the organization for Gate 3, which will decide whether build or buy work is sufficiently complete and assured to proceed toward deployment approval. For the build track, this closure includes verifying that the system is implemented according to design, controls are implemented and testable, and testing evidence is sufficient to justify progression.

The closure should be performed in two steps. First, a quality review validates that the evidence bundle is complete and coherent. Second, the governance review confirms readiness and issues a decision outcome. This separation mirrors the earlier gate discipline and reduces friction, because technical completeness is validated before executives and decision authorities convene.

A well-run Develop phase closure also supports portfolio learning. When evidence bundles are standardized and reviewed consistently, the organization can identify patterns. Perhaps many projects struggle with access control testing. Perhaps logging is often incomplete. Perhaps dependency vulnerabilities appear late due to poor update discipline. These patterns allow governance bodies and PMOs to invest in shared improvements rather than repeating the same lessons across projects.

The following closure package is intended to be used as the formal end-of-phase section for the Develop phase, and as the preparation baseline for the Build track contribution to Gate 3 readiness.

Major tasks in the Develop phase (Build Track)

The build team completes implementation and evidence work across code, infrastructure, controls, and readiness.

The team implements the designed architecture and control model, including identity boundaries, data protection mechanisms, logging instrumentation, and secure configuration baselines. The team establishes secure engineering workflows, including code review discipline, secure coding standards, and controlled branching and promotion practices. The team integrates dependency management and vulnerability handling into normal delivery, with defined thresholds and exception processes, supporting secure software lifecycle expectations that emphasize supply chain protection and vulnerability response (Souppaya et al., 2022). The team builds and executes a layered test approach, including functional, integration, security, and configuration validation. The team captures evidence continuously and maintains traceability from requirements and risks to controls and tests. The team drafts operational assets including runbooks, monitoring dashboards or alert definitions, and support procedures. The team prepares release readiness artifacts such as release notes, known issue logs, and risk acceptance records where applicable. Finally, the team prepares the Build track evidence bundle for quality review and Gate 3 readiness.

Key required deliverables for Develop phase completion

The bundle includes a build implementation summary that explains what was built, what changed from design assumptions, and how major controls were implemented. It includes testing evidence, including unit and integration test reports, system test results, and security testing outputs appropriate to risk tier. It includes dependency and vulnerability evidence, including vulnerability findings, remediation status, and approved time-bound exceptions where applicable. It includes configuration validation evidence for infrastructure as code and platform settings where those settings affect security posture. It includes access control evidence, such as role definitions and validation results for authorization boundaries. It includes logging and monitoring evidence at baseline level, demonstrating that the system generates meaningful events and that alerts and responses can be initiated. It includes operational readiness artifacts such as runbook drafts, support procedures, and escalation and ownership statements. It includes a release readiness summary that states readiness posture, residual risks, and what will be addressed in Implement, alongside explicit risk acceptance records when needed. These deliverables support governance expectations of evidence-based decision-making and systematic security management (NIST, 2024b; ISO, 2022).

Quality review process at the end of Develop

Before the gate forum considers readiness, a quality review validates completeness and coherence.

The project submits the Develop evidence bundle to the quality review function. Reviewers validate that required deliverables exist and are internally consistent with design intent. Reviewers validate that key controls are implemented and testable, that test outputs are interpretable, and that critical findings are resolved or formally managed through time-bound exceptions. Reviewers validate that evidence is traceable, meaning requirements and risks can be linked to controls and tests. Reviewers validate that operational readiness artifacts exist at least in draft form and that monitoring and logging evidence is sufficient to support later deployment validation. Reviewers document findings as critical, major, or minor, and assign owners and due dates. The quality review outcome is either pass to gate scheduling or fail to gate scheduling until critical gaps are resolved. This separation strengthens decision quality and preserves governance credibility because the gate meeting can focus on decisions rather than on evidence discovery (ISO, 2015).

Gate review process for end-of-Develop readiness (Gate 3)

The gate forum reviews readiness posture and decides whether the build output is sufficiently assured to proceed.

Decision-makers receive the evidence bundle and the quality findings report in advance. The project team presents a short readiness narrative focusing on what was built, what was validated, what risks remain, and what mitigation is planned. The forum reviews control implementation readiness, especially identity boundaries, data protection, logging and monitoring, and secure configuration. The forum reviews testing coverage and evidence quality, including security testing results and vulnerability management posture. The forum reviews operational readiness artifacts and ownership assumptions. The forum then issues a decision outcome consistent with the governance model: Go, Conditional Go, Hold, or No-Go, recorded in a decision log. If Conditional Go is selected, conditions are written as outcomes with owners, due dates, verification methods, and consequences if unmet.

Deliverable review pass or fail decision logic

Clear pass or fail logic prevents subjective readiness decisions.

A pass outcome is issued when the build implementation aligns with design intent, key controls are implemented and validated, test evidence is sufficient for the risk tier, critical vulnerabilities are remediated or formally managed, and operational readiness artifacts are credible for the next phase. A fail outcome is issued when critical controls are incomplete, evidence is insufficient, risk decisions are undocumented, or operational ownership is unclear.

Minimum pass criteria include implementation of baseline security controls appropriate to risk tier, completion of layered testing with usable evidence, documented remediation for critical findings, documented and time-bound exceptions where needed, and a credible operational readiness baseline including logging and monitoring instrumentation and draft runbooks (ISO, 2022; NIST, 2024b). Automatic fail triggers include unresolved critical vulnerabilities without approved exception authority, missing or unvalidated authorization boundaries, missing encryption or key management ownership for sensitive data, missing logging and monitoring evidence for high-risk systems, and lack of traceability between requirements, controls, and tests, because these gaps prevent defensible assurance and invite late-stage failure.

Key Takeaways

The Develop phase is where secure delivery becomes measurable. It turns architecture and control design into implemented controls, tested behaviors, and operational assets that can be sustained. It builds not only the system, but also the proof. It integrates secure engineering discipline into everyday workflows through code review, dependency management, configuration governance, and exception handling. It generates layered testing evidence that proves controls and readiness rather than merely producing output. It prepares release readiness by ensuring operational considerations are included early and that risk decisions are explicit and traceable. Most importantly, it sets the stage for Gate 3 by packaging evidence into a coherent bundle that can be quality-reviewed and governed. This evidence-first posture aligns with secure lifecycle guidance that emphasizes integrated, repeatable practices and demonstrable outcomes, and it supports enterprise governance expectations that cybersecurity and trust must be managed through accountability and oversight (Souppaya et al., 2022; NIST, 2024b).

“In secure delivery, ‘done’ means it works, it is safe, and it can be proven.”

Build is not only coding. It is the disciplined production of working increments plus the evidence that controls were implemented and verified.

Security debt is built the same way features are built. If you defer secure coding, dependency hygiene, and secrets handling, you will pay later in defects, exceptions, and incident response.

Every increment should ship with proof. Commit traceability, peer review evidence, test results, vulnerability findings, and remediation closure are part of the deliverable, not optional attachments.

Release readiness is a governance outcome. If you cannot explain what changed, what was tested, and what risk remains, you are not ready to move forward.

The Build Phase is successful when progress is measurable and defensible.

Acquire: Buy Phase

The Acquire phase exists because most modern technology solutions are not built from scratch. They are purchased, subscribed to, integrated, configured, and operated within an ecosystem of third parties. That ecosystem can accelerate delivery dramatically, yet it can also turn a project into a risk multiplier if vendor governance is weak. In a buy track, the organization is not only selecting functionality. It is selecting dependencies, service reliability assumptions, data handling practices, support models, and shared responsibility boundaries that will shape security posture for years. If the organization buys fast without governance, it often pays later through contract gaps, compliance surprises, limited audit rights, hidden data flows, weak incident response alignment, and operational fragility. The Acquire phase is where that future is negotiated and designed deliberately, with Security by Design principles applied to vendor choices and contractual commitments rather than only to code (NIST, 2024b).

Acquire is frequently misunderstood as a procurement step and a legal step, a stage that happens on the side while the project team waits. In secure technology project management, Acquire is a core engineering governance activity. It must produce the evidence that a vendor solution can meet security, compliance, operational, and resilience needs. It must also produce a contract structure that makes those needs enforceable. If controls are not contractually supported, they become optional vendor promises, and optional promises are the weakest form of risk control. ISO/IEC 27001 reinforces that an organization must manage information security through systematic controls and responsibilities, including controls related to supplier relationships and outsourced services, meaning vendor governance must be integrated into security management rather than treated as a separate business function (ISO, 2022).

The Acquire Phase governs how an organization selects, contracts, and onboards a third-party solution without inheriting unmanaged cyber and compliance risk. In this phase, security-by-design is enforced through due diligence, third-party risk management, privacy and security assessment, and contract terms that define controls, responsibilities, evidence expectations, and operational obligations. The ultimate goal is to produce a defensible Gate 3 evidence bundle for the Buy Track, including vendor selection rationale, risk assessment outputs, contract and Service Level Agreement (SLA) provisions, data protection commitments, integration planning, and a clear exit strategy. The figure below summarizes the phase purpose, the major activities, the security anchors that must be enforced contractually, and the key outputs required for governance review and Gate 3 readiness.

This chapter treats Acquire as a disciplined buy track playbook. It clarifies how to structure vendor governance, how to manage third-party risk controls, how to translate security requirements into contract language, and how to build an evidence bundle that can withstand Gate 3 scrutiny. The theme is simple. If a vendor will touch your data, enable your processes, or become part of your critical operations, then vendor governance is part of your security perimeter. That perimeter must be designed, tested, and governed.

Predictable Pitfalls in Vendor Delivery

Many acquisition failures repeat because teams confuse selection with assurance. They run demos, score features, negotiate pricing, and assume security will be handled through a standard questionnaire. Later, the team discovers the vendor cannot provide required logs, cannot integrate with identity standards, cannot support encryption ownership requirements, cannot meet data residency constraints, or cannot provide incident response collaboration. Those are not unusual surprises. They are predictable outcomes of weak acquisition governance.

Another failure pattern is the illusion of transfer. Teams believe buying a platform transfers security responsibility to the vendor. That is rarely true. In most cloud and software-as-a-service scenarios, the vendor owns the infrastructure and some platform controls, while the customer owns configuration, identity integration, access governance, data classification decisions, and monitoring integration. This shared responsibility model must be made explicit during Acquire because it determines what the organization must build, configure, and operate. If the organization does not understand what it owns, it cannot secure or govern the solution.

A third failure pattern is contract drift. Teams start with strong security requirements, then soften them to close the deal. They accept vague clauses, limited audit rights, and weak breach notification terms. The contract becomes a commercial document rather than a governance instrument. That is a strategic mistake because the contract is the mechanism that creates enforceability. Without enforceability, the organization cannot compel evidence, cannot compel remediation, and cannot compel transparency. In governance terms, the organization has accepted risk without a control lever.

A fourth failure pattern is ignoring exit. Vendor lock-in is not only a cost risk. It is a resilience risk. If the vendor fails, changes pricing drastically, suffers repeated outages, or becomes non-compliant, the organization needs a path to exit. If exit planning is not considered early, the organization becomes trapped. Acquire should therefore include exit feasibility as part of third-party risk thinking.

A final failure pattern is shallow operational alignment. Even if the vendor is secure, the solution can still fail if the support model does not align with the organization's operational needs. If escalation paths are unclear, if support hours do not match business needs, if patch timelines are incompatible, or if incident collaboration is weak, the system will become unstable and risky over time. Secure delivery is not only about controls. It is about sustainment.

These patterns matter because they show that acquisition governance is not optional overhead. It is risk prevention. It also aligns with CSF 2.0's governance emphasis, which frames cybersecurity as a managed enterprise capability requiring defined oversight, accountability, and risk-informed decision-making (NIST, 2024b).

Structuring the Acquire phase as a governance workflow

A disciplined Acquire phase follows a workflow that mirrors engineering thinking. It defines requirements, evaluates options, validates controls, negotiates enforceable commitments, and produces evidence for gate decisions. It is helpful to structure Acquire into four workstreams: vendor selection, third-party risk and assurance, contract and legal controls, and operational readiness integration.

Vendor selection includes functional fit, integration fit, architectural fit, and cost and value considerations. Third-party risk and assurance includes security posture assessment, compliance assessment, data handling validation, shared responsibility mapping, and evidence collection. Contract and legal controls include negotiating terms that enforce security, privacy, auditability, incident response collaboration, service levels, and exit rights. Operational readiness integration includes aligning monitoring, support, escalation, change management, and sustainment responsibilities.

These workstreams should run in parallel rather than sequentially because contract negotiation is shaped by risk findings, and risk findings are shaped by architectural integration questions. When teams separate these workstreams, they often negotiate contracts without understanding technical realities, or they design integrations without understanding contractual limits. Integrated acquisition governance prevents these disconnects.

The Acquire phase should also be risk-tiered. A low-risk internal tool with no sensitive data may require a lighter process. A customer-facing platform, a system handling regulated data, or a solution that becomes operationally critical should require deeper due diligence and stronger contractual controls. Proportionality keeps governance sustainable while ensuring high-risk acquisitions receive adequate scrutiny.

Defining Vendor Security Requirements

One of the most important tasks in Acquire is translating internal security expectations into vendor requirements that can be tested and contractually enforced. The requirements should be written in categories that match how vendors can respond and how the organization can validate.

Identity and access requirements should define whether the vendor supports centralized authentication, single sign-on, multi-factor authentication, role-based access control, and privileged access segregation. They should define how administrative access is controlled and audited. They should define whether the vendor supports integration with the organization's identity provider and whether the organization can enforce least privilege consistently.

Data protection requirements should define encryption expectations in transit and at rest, key management expectations where relevant, data residency constraints, data segregation requirements, and data retention and deletion expectations. If the system will handle sensitive or regulated data, requirements should include how data is stored, processed, backed up, and deleted. These requirements should also include how data access is logged and how the organization can obtain audit evidence.

Logging and monitoring requirements should define what logs the vendor can provide, what events are captured, how logs can be exported, and whether real-time integration with security monitoring tools is possible. Many vendor solutions provide limited logs. If the organization cannot detect abnormal behavior, it cannot govern the system. Logging is not a nice-to-have. It is an assurance mechanism.

Vulnerability and patch management requirements should define how the vendor manages vulnerabilities, how quickly patches are applied, how the organization is notified, and how emergency patching is handled. Requirements should include transparency about major vulnerabilities and a commitment to respond to critical issues promptly.

Incident response and breach notification requirements should define how incidents are detected, how customers are notified, what timeframes apply, and how collaboration will occur. They should define how forensic information will be shared. They should define what support is provided during incidents. These requirements become part of operational resilience.

Compliance and assurance requirements should define what independent assurance reports the vendor can provide, what certifications or attestations exist, and what audit rights the customer requires. Even when the organization accepts standard assurance reports, it should understand their scope and limitations. The goal is not to demand every report possible. The goal is to obtain sufficient evidence to justify the risk decision and to preserve auditability over time.

These requirement categories align with systematic information security management expectations and supplier controls orientation in ISO/IEC 27001, which emphasizes controlling risks related to external suppliers and ensuring security requirements are addressed in supplier relationships (ISO, 2022). They also align with governance expectations in CSF 2.0 that encourage organizations to manage cybersecurity through defined oversight and risk-informed decision-making (NIST, 2024b).

Third-party risk assessment

Third-party risk assessment in Acquire is not a questionnaire exercise. It is evidence generation. It should answer concrete questions about the vendor's security posture and about the customer's responsibilities. It should also identify what compensating controls the organization must implement if the vendor cannot meet certain requirements.

The assessment begins with scoping. What data will the vendor handle. What business processes will the vendor enable. What integration points will exist. What will the vendor host versus what will the organization host. What environments will exist. What administrative access will vendor personnel have. Without scoping, risk assessment becomes generic and often irrelevant.

Next, the assessment establishes the shared responsibility model. The project should document which controls are vendor-owned, which are customer-owned, and which are shared. This mapping should cover identity integration, access governance, logging integration, monitoring responsibilities, incident response responsibilities, data handling responsibilities, and configuration responsibilities. The shared responsibility model must be treated as part of the architecture evidence bundle because it shapes how the solution will operate.

Then, the assessment evaluates the vendor's ability to meet requirements. This includes reviewing vendor documentation, reviewing assurance reports where available, validating security capabilities through workshops, and asking for evidence such as configuration guides, logging samples, incident response procedures, and data handling statements. In some cases, proof of concept testing is useful, particularly for integrations and logging export capabilities. Evidence matters because vendor statements without proof can be misleading. In governance terms, evidence is how the organization makes a defensible decision.

Third-party risk assessment also includes evaluating vendor concentration and dependency risk. If the vendor becomes operationally critical, the organization must understand the vendor's resilience posture. This includes availability commitments, disaster recovery approach, data backup and recovery, and historical reliability indicators where available. It also includes support model details such as response times and escalation paths.

Finally, third-party risk assessment includes remediation planning. Not all gaps mean rejection. Some gaps can be mitigated through customer controls, contractual commitments, or design changes. For example, if vendor logs are limited, the organization may implement additional monitoring at integration points. If data residency is constrained, the organization may choose a different deployment region or adjust data flows. If encryption key ownership is not supported, the organization may reduce the sensitivity of data stored in the vendor platform or implement tokenization before data reaches the vendor. The key is that mitigation must be explicit and realistic.

Contracts as security control instruments

Contracts are where acquisition governance becomes enforceable. A contract is not merely a commercial agreement. It is the mechanism that defines obligations, evidence rights, incident responsibilities, and accountability boundaries. If the contract does not support security requirements, then the organization has little leverage after onboarding. That is why contract work must be treated as part of Security by Design.

Security and privacy clauses should define data ownership, permissible use of data, and limits on vendor use. They should define data confidentiality expectations. They should define subcontractor use and requirements for flow-down obligations. They should define data deletion obligations and verification. If the vendor uses data for analytics or model improvement, that must be explicitly governed. Even if the organization plans not to use AI features, many vendors incorporate AI in the background, and data usage terms can quietly expand. The Acquire phase should ensure data usage terms align with organizational risk appetite and compliance needs.

Audit and assurance clauses should define what evidence the vendor must provide, how often, and what rights the customer has to request additional evidence. Many vendors will not allow customer audits, yet they may provide third-party assurance reports. The organization must define whether those reports are sufficient and must define what happens if a report reveals significant issues. The contract should also define notification obligations for significant changes in security posture.

Incident response clauses should define breach notification timeframes, collaboration expectations, and support obligations. They should define how incident communication will occur and what information will be provided. They should define responsibility for costs and for remediation where appropriate. These clauses matter because during incidents, time is compressed and uncertainty is high. Clear contractual obligations reduce confusion.

Service level clauses should align with operational needs. Availability, performance, support response times, and maintenance windows should be specified. The contract should also define how service credits work, but more importantly, it should define escalation paths and repeated failure consequences. For mission-critical systems, the organization should consider additional resilience arrangements or redundancy planning.

Change management and feature change clauses should define how major changes are communicated, how deprecations are managed, and how customers are notified. Sudden vendor changes can break integrations and can create security gaps if new features are introduced without governance. These clauses support operational stability.

Exit and portability clauses are often overlooked. They should define data export mechanisms, formats, timelines, and assistance obligations. They should define deletion confirmation after exit. They should define what happens to configurations and integrations. Exit planning is a resilience control. Without it, the organization becomes dependent on a vendor without leverage.

Legal and compliance alignment must be integrated throughout contract negotiation. If the organization is subject to specific privacy regulations or sector obligations, the contract must reflect them. This is where legal counsel and compliance stakeholders must engage early rather than only at signature time.

Contracts should also align with the organization's internal governance model for exceptions. If the vendor cannot meet a requirement, that gap must be documented and approved through risk acceptance authority, ideally with contractual mitigation where possible. This ensures that deviations from baseline control expectations are not accidental.

This contract-as-control mindset aligns with systematic security management expectations and supplier relationship controls in ISO/IEC 27001 (ISO, 2022). It also supports governance expectations that technology risk decisions be explicit and accountable (NIST, 2024b).

Operational Alignment for Buy Solutions

Acquire is not complete when the contract is signed. The Acquire phase must also ensure the solution can be integrated and operated. Many vendor solutions fail not because the vendor is weak, but because integration and sustainment were underestimated. The buy track must therefore include integration planning and operational alignment as deliverables.

Integration planning begins with identity integration. How will users authenticate. What roles exist. How will provisioning and deprovisioning occur. How will privileged access be managed. How will service accounts be handled. Identity integration must be tested early because it shapes access governance.

Data integration planning is next. What data will flow to the vendor. How will data be transformed. What data will be stored in the vendor platform. What data must remain internal. How will data be synchronized and reconciled. How will data deletion work. These questions must be answered early to avoid building insecure or non-compliant data flows.

Logging and monitoring integration planning must also be addressed. How will logs be exported. How will they be correlated with internal monitoring. What alerts will be configured. Who will respond. If the vendor provides security notifications, how will those notifications integrate into incident response. These integration decisions are not optional. They are part of operational readiness.

Support model alignment must be made explicit. What are the vendor's support hours. What are response time commitments. How are escalations handled. Who is the customer's support lead. What is the internal escalation path. How are incidents triaged between vendor and customer. These details prevent chaos during outages and incidents.

Configuration governance is another common gap. Many vendor solutions are secure only when configured correctly. The organization must define configuration standards, review processes, and change control. It must define who can make configuration changes and how those changes are tested. It must define how configuration drift will be monitored. Without configuration governance, the organization can degrade the vendor solution over time.

Evidence bundles for buy track readiness and Gate 3 preparation

Acquire phase outputs must be packaged into a buy track evidence bundle that supports Gate 3 readiness. This bundle is the proof that the organization has selected a vendor responsibly and that the contract and operational alignment support secure deployment.

The evidence bundle should include a vendor selection summary and scoring rationale. It should include a third-party risk assessment summary and key findings. It should include the shared responsibility mapping. It should include security and compliance requirement mapping to vendor capabilities. It should include contract security clause summary and any negotiated deviations. It should include operational readiness integration plan for identity, logging, monitoring, incident response, and support. It should include an exit strategy outline. It should include an updated risk register capturing vendor-related risks and mitigations. Finally, it should include a recommendation narrative for Gate 3 readiness.

This evidence approach supports governance expectations for risk-informed decisions and accountability. It also supports audit readiness because the organization can show why it selected the vendor, how it validated security, how it enforced requirements contractually, and how it planned operational controls.

Acquire Phase Completion, QRB and Gate

Just like in other phases, Acquire should close with a quality review before the gate decision forum convenes. Quality review validates that the evidence bundle is complete and coherent. It checks whether requirements are mapped, whether shared responsibility is clear, whether contracts contain enforceable control clauses, and whether operational integration plans are credible. It also checks whether any deviations from baseline security expectations are documented and approved. If critical gaps exist, the evidence bundle is not ready for gate consideration.

Then, the governance forum reviews the buy track readiness as part of Gate 3, or as a pre-Gate 3 readiness checkpoint depending on the organization's model. The decision logic remains consistent: Go, Conditional Go, Hold, or No-Go. Conditional Go is common in Acquire because contract negotiations and vendor onboarding steps may be incomplete at the time of review. Yet conditions must be specific, owned, time-bound, and verifiable. Otherwise, they become invisible risk acceptance.

The following closure package is written as a distinct end-of-phase section. It incorporates major tasks, required deliverables, quality review process, gate review process, and deliverable review pass or fail logic. It is structured to mirror the disciplined style used in Chapter 11 and Chapter 13.

Major tasks in the Acquire phase (Buy Track)

The project confirms the vendor path and secures enforceable commitments that support security, compliance, and operational readiness.

The team finalizes vendor requirements covering identity integration, data protection, logging and monitoring capabilities, incident response collaboration, vulnerability handling, and service resilience. The team performs third-party risk assessment scoped to the actual data, integrations, and operational dependency model, and it documents shared responsibility boundaries. The team validates vendor capabilities through evidence review, workshops, and proof of concept testing where needed. The team negotiates contract terms that enforce security, privacy, auditability, breach notification, service levels, change communication, subcontractor controls, and exit and portability rights. The team aligns operational readiness by defining identity provisioning model, support and escalation model, logging and monitoring integration, and incident response coordination procedures. The team updates the risk register with vendor-related risks and compensating controls. Finally, the team prepares the buy track evidence bundle for quality review and gate readiness.

Key deliverables for Acquire phase completion

The deliverables should be concise yet enforceable and audit-friendly.

The evidence bundle includes a vendor selection decision summary and evaluation scoring rationale. It includes a supplier risk assessment summary scoped to the solution, data, and integrations. It includes shared responsibility mapping, identifying vendor-owned, customer-owned, and shared controls. It includes security requirement mapping to vendor capabilities and identified gaps, with compensating controls documented. It includes assurance evidence such as vendor certifications or independent reports where applicable, along with scope interpretation and limitations. It includes a contract security and privacy clause summary and a list of negotiated commitments, including breach notification, audit evidence rights, subcontractor requirements, and service level commitments. It includes an operational integration readiness plan covering identity and access integration, logging and monitoring integration, incident response collaboration, and support escalation procedures. It includes an exit and portability outline. It includes an updated risk register capturing vendor risks, mitigations, and any proposed risk acceptances. These deliverables support systematic security management and supplier relationship controls expectations (ISO, 2022) and provide evidence for governance decisions (NIST, 2024b).

Quality review process at the end of Acquire

Quality review confirms that the vendor path is defensible and contractually enforceable.

The project submits the buy track evidence bundle to the quality review function. Reviewers validate completeness, coherence, and enforceability. They check that shared responsibility boundaries are explicit, that security requirements are mapped to vendor capabilities, and that gaps have compensating controls or documented risk acceptance. They review whether contracts contain the necessary security, privacy, audit, incident response, and service level terms, and whether deviations are tracked. They verify that operational readiness plans exist for identity integration, logging integration, monitoring and alerting, incident coordination, and escalation paths. Findings are documented as critical, major, or minor with owners and due dates. The quality outcome is pass to gate consideration or fail until critical gaps are resolved.

Gate review process for end-of-Acquire readiness

The governance forum decides whether the vendor solution is ready to proceed toward deployment preparation.

Decision-makers receive the evidence bundle and quality findings report in advance. The project team provides a short readiness narrative focused on vendor fit, risk posture, shared responsibility clarity, contract enforceability, and operational alignment. The forum reviews whether the vendor solution can meet baseline security and compliance constraints and whether evidence supports that claim. The forum reviews contract commitments, especially auditability, breach notification, service levels, and exit rights. The forum reviews operational readiness plans and ownership. The forum issues a decision outcome: Go, Conditional Go, Hold, or No-Go, recorded in the decision log. Conditional Go conditions are documented with owners, deadlines, verification methods, and consequences.

Deliverable review pass or fail decision logic

Pass or fail logic keeps vendor selection disciplined and defensible.

A pass outcome is issued when the vendor is selected through a rational evaluation process, security and compliance requirements are mapped and supported by evidence, shared responsibility boundaries are explicit, contracts contain enforceable controls and obligations, operational integration plans are credible, and vendor-related risks are visible and owned. A fail outcome is issued when evidence is missing, contract terms do not support critical controls, shared responsibility is unclear, or operational alignment is inadequate.

Minimum pass criteria include explicit shared responsibility mapping, enforceable contract clauses for security, privacy, auditability, incident response, and service levels, and an operational plan for identity, logging, monitoring, and incident coordination (ISO, 2022). Automatic fail triggers include unclear data handling terms for sensitive data, lack of breach notification commitments, inability to obtain sufficient assurance evidence, inability to integrate with identity standards for high-risk systems, and absence of logging and monitoring integration capabilities for operationally critical systems, because these gaps prevent defensible governance and elevate long-term risk.

Key Takeaways

The Acquire phase is the Security by Design phase for vendor dependency because it determines whether the organization will gain capability without inheriting hidden exposure. Many acquisition efforts begin as feature comparisons and pricing negotiations. Secure delivery requires a different posture. Acquire reframes vendor selection as a governance decision that must be supported by evidence, enforceable obligations, and operational fit. It ensures the organization is not only buying a product, but also establishing the controls, assurance, and accountability needed to operate that product safely across its lifecycle.

A disciplined Acquire phase clarifies shared responsibility boundaries early. This is essential because most vendor solutions, especially cloud and managed services, shift risk rather than remove it. The supplier may secure the platform, but the customer still owns configuration, identity and access control, data handling, logging, monitoring, and incident response integration. Acquire forces the organization to name those responsibilities and confirm it can execute them. It also ensures operational alignment by validating integration requirements, support expectations, service ownership, and the runbook reality of day-to-day operations. Without this alignment, implementation becomes unstable and sustainment becomes reactive.

Acquire also translates security and resilience requirements into contract language that can be enforced over time. Security commitments that are not written, measurable, and auditable become optional in practice. For that reason, this phase emphasizes security clauses, evidence rights, breach notification terms, audit cooperation, data protection obligations, subcontractor controls, service-level resilience expectations, and clear remedies when obligations are not met. It also drives third-party risk treatment by requiring proof, not assurances, and by ensuring that exceptions are explicitly approved and tracked rather than silently absorbed.

By the end of Acquire, the organization should have a buy track evidence bundle that supports Gate 3 readiness. This bundle demonstrates that the vendor was selected through risk-informed criteria, that responsibilities are understood, that contract controls are in place, and that the solution is feasible to implement and operate securely. When Acquire is performed with discipline, the organization buys capability without buying unmanaged risk. It also positions implementation and sustainment for stability and continual assurance, consistent with systematic security management and governance expectations (ISO, 2022; NIST, 2024b).

"A vendor promise is not a control, evidence is."

12 Gate 3: Build/Buy Review

Gate 3 is where the organization makes a high-stakes choice with long shadows. It decides whether the solution, whether built internally or acquired from a vendor, is sufficiently assured to move from controlled engineering activity into controlled deployment activity. Gate 3 is not the first time the project should think about security or quality, yet it is the first time leadership must explicitly confirm that assurance is not still "in progress" in ways that would turn deployment into a gamble. In a secure delivery model, deployment approval is not granted because the team is tired or because the sprint plan says "release." It is granted because evidence shows that controls are implemented, risks are understood and owned, testing proves the controls work, and operational readiness is credible. This is the gate where confidence must be replaced with proof, and where the organization must decide whether the remaining uncertainty is manageable, or whether it is still unsafe to proceed (NIST, 2024b).

Gate 3 is also where the build track and buy track converge into a single readiness posture. In the build track, the question is whether engineering work has implemented the design intent and produced sufficient test evidence. In the buy track, the question is whether vendor onboarding is complete enough, contractual obligations and shared responsibility controls are enforceable and configured, and operational integration is ready. Many organizations treat these as separate worlds. That separation becomes a weakness because deployments rarely fail for one reason. They fail because small gaps stack together. A build solution may be strong, yet logging integration is missing. A vendor solution may be certified, yet identity governance is weak. A project may pass functional testing, yet release readiness is undermined by unresolved high-severity vulnerabilities or unclear rollback strategy. Gate 3 exists to stop the stack of small gaps from turning into a production incident, a compliance failure, or a long-term operational liability (ISO, 2015; NIST, 2024b).

A practical way to understand Gate 3 is to see it as the "assurance closure gate." Earlier phases designed what must be true. The Develop and Acquire phases built or procured the capability. Gate 3 confirms what is true, backed by evidence. It verifies that the security-by-design plan was executed, not merely written. It verifies that known issues are either resolved or explicitly accepted by the right authority with time-bound conditions. It verifies that the project is not about to move into production planning while still arguing about fundamentals such as identity boundaries, encryption ownership, logging coverage, or vendor responsibilities. This aligns with governance-centered cybersecurity expectations where accountability, risk decisions, and monitoring obligations are treated as executive responsibilities, not as technical afterthoughts (NIST, 2024b).

The purpose and principles of Gate 3

Gate 3 exists to answer one decisive question. Is the solution ready to be deployed responsibly. That single question breaks into four readiness pillars: assurance closure, risk closure, operational closure, and deployment control readiness.

Assurance closure means the project has completed the planned validation activities for the risk tier. It means key controls have been implemented, tested, and evidenced. It means critical security and quality defects are resolved or have been formally handled through an exception process. It means the project can demonstrate traceability from requirements and risks to implemented controls and test evidence, at least at the level appropriate for the system's risk tier. Secure software development guidance emphasizes integrating secure practices and being able to demonstrate them through evidence, which makes assurance closure an explicit gate goal, not an implied hope (Souppaya et al., 2022).

Risk closure means the project's risk register is current and realistic. Risks are not managed by listing them. Risks are managed through ownership, treatment, and decision. Gate 3 must confirm that high-impact residual risks are visible, assigned to owners, and either mitigated or explicitly accepted by the proper authority. This includes cyber risk, privacy risk, delivery risk, vendor risk, and operational risk. It also includes "risk created by delay," which sometimes matters when a system replaces an insecure legacy component. Risk closure is not the elimination of all risk. It is the elimination of unmanaged risk.

Operational closure means the system is operable. Operability is not a deployment detail. It is part of security because a system that cannot be monitored, controlled, and recovered cannot be defended. Gate 3 therefore validates that logging and monitoring are implemented at baseline level, that alerting and escalation paths exist, that runbooks are drafted, that support ownership is defined, and that incident response integration is planned and testable. ISO/IEC 27001's emphasis on systematic control operation and continual improvement reinforces that security is maintained through operational discipline, not just built through engineering activity (ISO, 2022).

Deployment control readiness means the organization can deploy without chaos. This includes change control, release candidate discipline, environment readiness, rollback capability, and migration readiness. It includes validating that deployment procedures are defined and that the project can produce evidence during deployment. Gate 3 does not require deployment execution. It requires that deployment execution will be controlled, observable, and reversible if needed.

Several principles make Gate 3 effective. The first is evidence first. The gate decision should rely on documented artifacts and test results, not on verbal assurance. The second is proportionality. A small low-risk internal change can pass with lighter evidence. A high-risk customer-facing system requires deeper evidence and may require independent assurance. The third is shared ownership. Gate 3 is not owned by security, and it is not owned by engineering alone. It is a governance decision that integrates engineering, security, operations, and business accountability. The fourth is disciplined exception handling. Gate 3 is often where exceptions are requested. Exceptions must be time-bound, approved, and tied to mitigation plans. Otherwise, the organization normalizes risk. The fifth is clarity of decision outcomes. Go, Conditional Go, Hold, and No-Go must remain consistent across gates to prevent confusion and to preserve governance credibility (ISO, 2015; NIST, 2024b).

Gate 3 inputs and the Build/Buy readiness evidence bundle

Gate 3 requires a combined evidence bundle that merges build track evidence and buy track evidence into one readiness package. The bundle should be organized so decision-makers can understand readiness quickly, while reviewers can inspect depth where needed. The evidence bundle typically begins with a Gate 3 readiness narrative. This narrative should be concise and decision-oriented. It should state what is being approved, what has been validated, what issues remain, and what decision is requested.

For the build track, the evidence bundle includes implementation and testing artifacts. It should show that the system was built according to the approved design, that controls were implemented as designed, and that testing results are sufficient for the risk tier. It should include security testing results, vulnerability remediation status, and any approved exceptions with explicit expiration dates and mitigation plans. It should include evidence of configuration validation where infrastructure and platform settings are critical to security posture. It should include evidence that identity and access control boundaries have been tested, especially for privileged functions and high-risk workflows. It should include evidence that logging and monitoring are implemented and that security-relevant events are captured.

For the buy track, the evidence bundle includes vendor onboarding and assurance artifacts. It should show that the contract and security commitments are executed and enforceable. It should include shared responsibility mapping that states what the vendor owns and what the customer owns. It should include evidence that customer-owned controls are configured, such as identity integration, role governance, logging exports, monitoring integrations, and administrative access governance. It should include evidence that incident response coordination is defined, that support and escalation paths are established, and that service-level expectations are clear. It should include a clear statement of any vendor-related risk gaps and compensating controls.

The combined evidence bundle should also include an updated risk register and a release readiness summary. The release readiness summary should state whether the solution meets the release criteria, whether unresolved issues remain, and whether those issues are acceptable. It should also state the deployment approach, including deployment sequencing, rollback strategy, and migration readiness. It should identify operational ownership and readiness assumptions.

The most important characteristic of a Gate 3 bundle is coherence. Coherence means the artifacts align. Risks listed in the register should have corresponding mitigations and test results. Controls claimed should have evidence. Exceptions noted should be documented and approved. Operational readiness statements should be supported by runbook drafts and monitoring configurations. When coherence is missing, gate decisions become arguments. When coherence is present, decisions become disciplined.

Assurance closure across build and buy tracks

Assurance closure is the heart of Gate 3. It is where the organization confirms that the planned assurance work is complete enough to proceed. In the build track, assurance closure includes confirming that secure engineering practices were followed, that testing results meet thresholds, and that vulnerability management is disciplined. It also includes confirming that evidence is traceable. Traceability does not require perfect tooling. It requires a credible link from requirements and risks to implemented controls and tests.

Secure software development guidance emphasizes the need to integrate secure practices into development and to verify that software meets security requirements, while also maintaining the ability to respond to vulnerabilities and manage supply chain risks (Souppaya et al., 2022). In practice, for Gate 3, this means the project should be able to show that code reviews occurred, that security testing was performed, that critical vulnerabilities were remediated, and that exceptions were approved and time-bound. It also means the project should show that dependencies were assessed and that supply chain risks are managed at least at baseline level, such as maintaining a current list of critical components and their vulnerability posture.

In the buy track, assurance closure includes confirming that vendor assurance claims are understood and that customer responsibilities are configured and validated. Vendor certifications or assurance reports can be useful, yet they do not guarantee that the customer's configuration is secure. Many major incidents in SaaS environments occur because of customer misconfiguration, weak identity governance, or insufficient logging and monitoring integration. Gate 3 therefore validates not only the vendor's posture, but also the customer's posture within the shared responsibility boundary.

Assurance closure must also address data protection realities. If the solution handles sensitive data, Gate 3 must confirm that data encryption is implemented, that key management ownership is defined, that data flows match what was approved in design, and that data retention and deletion logic is understood. This aligns with systematic security management expectations that emphasize defining and operating controls for protecting information assets (ISO, 2022).

A recurring challenge at Gate 3 is "partial closure," where teams claim assurance is mostly complete. Gate 3 does not forbid partial closure. It forbids unmanaged partial closure. If assurance work remains, the gate outcome must reflect it. That typically means Conditional Go with explicit conditions, or Hold if the remaining work is critical. The organization must avoid the pattern of approving deployment while critical security testing is still pending or while critical findings remain unresolved.

Operational closure and readiness to run what you deploy

Gate 3 is where operational reality arrives. A system can be brilliantly engineered and still fail in production because the organization cannot operate it. Operational closure therefore validates that the operational mechanisms are at least baseline ready. This includes monitoring and alerting, incident response integration, support ownership, and basic runbooks.

Monitoring should be designed to detect both security and stability signals. Security signals may include repeated failed authentication attempts, unusual administrative actions, unusual data exports, unexpected privilege escalations, and anomalous API usage. Stability signals may include error rates, latency spikes, resource saturation, and dependency failures. Gate 3 should validate that logging is not only turned on, but also usable. Logs must include context, must be protected from tampering, and must be accessible to responders. Monitoring must be tied to alerting, and alerting must be tied to response ownership. A system that cannot generate actionable alerts is not operationally ready.

Incident response integration is another critical element. The project should define how incidents are declared, how escalation occurs, and how communication will be managed during an incident.

For vendor solutions, this includes defining how vendor support participates. Operational closure does not mean performing a full incident simulation for every system. It means ensuring that the process exists and that the people responsible know what to do.

Runbooks should exist at least in draft form. A runbook is not a novel. It is a practical guide for responders. It should include how to check system health, how to restart services where relevant, how to roll back, how to manage access emergencies, and how to contact vendor support. Runbooks are also an assurance artifact because they show the organization can control the system under stress.

Operational ownership must be explicit. The project must define who owns the system after go-live, who owns security monitoring for it, who owns patch and change management responsibilities, and who owns user support. This is one of the most common causes of long-term failure. Projects deploy systems that become orphans. Orphan systems become insecure systems because no one maintains them with urgency.

ISO/IEC 27001 supports this operational focus by emphasizing ongoing management, monitoring, and continual improvement of security controls, which inherently requires clear ownership and the ability to operate controls continuously (ISO, 2022). Gate 3 is where operational readiness becomes a required condition of deployment approval rather than a hope.

Deployment control readiness and migration discipline

Gate 3 is the approval to proceed toward deployment. It therefore must validate that deployment will be controlled. Controlled deployment includes environment readiness, deployment procedures, rollback capability, and migration planning.

Environment readiness includes confirming that staging and production environments exist and are properly separated, that access to production is controlled, that logging and monitoring are connected, and that configurations match approved baselines. For vendor solutions, environment readiness includes confirming tenant configuration, identity integration, role definitions, and administrative boundaries.

Deployment procedures should be documented. This includes how the release will be promoted, how configuration changes will be applied, how validation will be performed post-deployment, and how rollback will occur if needed. Rollback is often treated as optional. In reality, rollback is a resilience control. If rollback is not possible, then the organization is accepting higher deployment risk, and that risk must be explicitly acknowledged.

Migration planning must also be validated. If the project includes data migration, Gate 3 must confirm that migration strategy is credible, that data mapping is understood, that validation steps exist, and that rollback or recovery is planned. Many production failures are not caused by application defects. They are caused by migration defects, such as incomplete data, corrupted data, or performance collapse during migration.

Gate 3 should also confirm that change control discipline exists. Change control does not mean rigid bureaucracy. It means the organization can explain what changed and why, and it can prove approvals occurred. This matters for auditability and for incident investigations. When changes are not controlled, post-incident analysis becomes guesswork.

Quality review before Gate 3

Gate 3 should not begin with an executive meeting. It should begin with a quality review that confirms the evidence bundle is complete, coherent, and decision-ready. The quality review function may be a QRB, a PMO assurance practice, or a combined quality and security readiness team depending on the organization.

The quality review checks the build track and buy track evidence for completeness. It verifies that required artifacts exist, that testing evidence is present and interpretable, that vulnerability remediation status is clear, and that exceptions are documented and approved. It verifies that shared responsibility controls for vendor solutions are configured and evidenced. It verifies that operational readiness artifacts exist, including monitoring integration and runbooks. It verifies that the risk register is current and that residual risks are owned. It also checks for consistency, meaning that if a document claims encryption is implemented, the evidence should show it. If a document claims logs are exported, the evidence should show it.

The quality review produces a findings report categorized by severity. Critical findings block the gate meeting. Major findings may proceed only if they are documented as gate conditions with owners and deadlines. Minor findings can be addressed during implementation planning, yet they must be tracked. This approach protects the gate forum from being forced to adjudicate technical completeness questions in real time.

This separation of quality readiness from governance decision aligns with IT governance principles that emphasize guiding and monitoring technology use through defined oversight mechanisms, which are undermined when decisions are made on incomplete or unclear evidence (ISO, 2015). It also supports the evidence orientation in secure software development guidance that stresses verifiable practices and outcomes (Souppaya et al., 2022).

Gate 3 review process and decision outcomes

The Gate 3 meeting is the formal governance decision forum. It confirms readiness to proceed toward deployment approval, meaning it authorizes entry into the Implement phase with deployment preparation and execution planning.

The meeting should begin with confirmation of quality review outcome. If critical findings remain, the gate should not proceed as a decision meeting. It should proceed as a remediation planning meeting, and the formal decision should be deferred.

If the bundle is ready, project leadership presents a short readiness narrative. The narrative should focus on assurance closure, operational readiness, deployment control readiness, and risk posture. It should highlight what evidence is strongest, what issues remain, and what conditions are proposed if Conditional Go is requested. For build track systems, it should summarize security testing results, vulnerability status, and release readiness posture. For buy track systems, it should summarize vendor onboarding status, control configuration status for customer-owned responsibilities, and contract enforceability.

The gate forum then reviews key decision areas. First, it reviews assurance closure. Are planned validations complete. Are critical findings resolved. Is evidence traceable. Second, it reviews risk posture. Are residual risks acceptable. Are risk owners assigned. Are risk acceptances documented. Third, it reviews operational closure. Are monitoring, logging, runbooks, and ownership ready. Fourth, it reviews deployment control readiness. Are environments ready. Is rollback planned. Is migration strategy credible.

The gate forum then issues a decision outcome. The standard outcomes should remain consistent: Go, Conditional Go, Hold, or No-Go.

Go means the solution is ready to proceed into Implement phase activities, including deployment planning and execution, with no critical gaps. Conditional Go means the solution may proceed, but only with explicit conditions that must be satisfied before deployment execution or before the next checkpoint. Hold means the solution cannot proceed because critical readiness gaps exist. No-Go means the solution should not proceed in its current form and requires rework or re-scoping.

Conditional Go must be managed with discipline. Conditions must be written as outcomes, not activities. Each condition must have an owner, a deadline, and a verification method. Each condition must have a consequence if not met, such as automatic Hold at the deployment execution checkpoint or escalation to risk acceptance authority. This discipline prevents conditions from becoming invisible.

Major tasks to complete for Gate 3 readiness

The project must complete tasks across build and buy tracks to create a unified readiness posture.

For the build track, the team completes implementation of the approved control model, including identity and access controls, data protection controls, logging and monitoring instrumentation, and secure configuration baselines. The team completes layered testing appropriate to risk tier, including functional, integration, security, and configuration validation. The team remediates critical and high-severity findings or obtains formal, time-bound exceptions with approved authority. The team finalizes release candidate packaging, including release notes, known issues log, and evidence repository completeness. The team confirms traceability from key requirements and risks to controls and tests, consistent with verifiable secure development practice expectations (Souppaya et al., 2022).

For the buy track, the team finalizes vendor onboarding and ensures contractual commitments are executed and understood. The team confirms shared responsibility mapping and implements customer-owned controls such as identity integration, role governance, logging export configuration, monitoring integration, and administrative access boundaries. The team validates incident response coordination and support escalation processes with the vendor. The team confirms data handling terms, data residency configuration where relevant, and data export and exit readiness posture.

Across both tracks, the project updates the risk register, validates operational ownership, drafts runbooks, ensures monitoring and alerting are connected, and prepares the combined Gate 3 evidence bundle and readiness narrative.

Key required deliverables for the Gate 3 evidence bundle

The evidence bundle should be concise, decision-grade, and coherent.

The bundle includes a Gate 3 readiness narrative summarizing what is being approved, what evidence supports readiness, what issues remain, and what decision is requested (NIST, 2024b). It includes an updated risk register with residual risks, owners, and proposed treatments or acceptances. It includes build track assurance artifacts such as security testing results, vulnerability remediation status, configuration validation evidence, and release candidate quality evidence. It includes buy track assurance artifacts such as vendor onboarding status, shared responsibility mapping, configured customer-owned controls evidence, and contract obligation summary. It includes operational readiness artifacts such as monitoring and alerting configuration summaries, logging export evidence where relevant, runbook drafts, and defined support ownership and escalation paths. It includes deployment readiness artifacts such as environment readiness confirmation, deployment approach summary, rollback strategy, and migration readiness plan where applicable.

For high-risk systems, the bundle should include independent assurance outputs if required by policy, such as penetration testing results or independent review findings, with remediation status.

Quality review process before the Gate 3 decision

The project submits the combined evidence bundle to the quality review function. Reviewers validate completeness, coherence, and traceability. They confirm that planned testing has been completed, that results meet thresholds, and that critical findings are resolved or formally managed through approved exceptions. They verify that vendor responsibilities and customer responsibilities are clearly separated and that customer-owned controls for vendor systems are configured and evidenced. They verify operational readiness, including monitoring and runbooks, and they verify the risk register reflects reality. Findings are categorized as critical, major, or minor, with owners and due dates. The quality outcome is either pass to gate scheduling or fail until critical gaps are resolved. This step protects governance credibility and aligns with principles of guided and monitored IT governance (ISO, 2015).

Gate 3 review process

Decision-makers receive the evidence bundle and the quality findings report in advance. The project leadership presents the readiness narrative, focusing on assurance closure, risk posture, operational closure, and deployment control readiness. The gate forum reviews the build track readiness, including testing evidence, vulnerability status, and release candidate discipline. The gate forum reviews the buy track readiness, including contract enforceability, shared responsibility control configuration, and operational integration. The gate forum reviews operational readiness, including monitoring and incident coordination, and it reviews deployment planning readiness, including rollback and migration readiness. The gate forum then issues a decision outcome, recorded in the decision log: Go, Conditional Go, Hold, or No-Go.

If Conditional Go is selected, conditions are documented as outcomes with owners, deadlines, verification methods, and consequences. Conditions should be limited in number and high in clarity.

Deliverable review pass or fail decision logic

Gate 3 pass or fail decision logic must be explicit because it is the point where organizations are most tempted to approve progress based on urgency instead of proof. Gate 3 is not about whether the solution "works." It is about whether assurance is closed to the level required by the risk classification, and whether the organization can proceed into implementation planning.

Gate 3 has two pass outcomes: **Go** and **Conditional Go**. **Go** is appropriate when assurance closure is complete for the risk classification and the evidence bundle demonstrates that high-impact risks are treated. Critical defects and critical security findings must be remediated, or formally managed through approved, time-bound exceptions with compensating controls and verification steps. Go also requires credible operational readiness. That includes functional logging and monitoring, working alert routing, assigned responders, and runbooks that match the production environment and permissions. In addition, deployment controls must be defined and feasible. Environment readiness, change control, access restrictions, rollback capability, and migration readiness, when migration is in scope, should be evidenced and traceable to the release candidate or onboarding milestone.

Conditional Go is appropriate when limited gaps remain, but those gaps do not prevent safe progression into implementation planning. Conditional Go must be disciplined. Conditions should be written as measurable outcomes rather than vague promises. Each condition must have an owner, a due date, a verification method, and a consequence if it is not met. Conditions should also be linked to specific artifacts in the evidence bundle, so closure can be verified.

Gate 3 also has two fail outcomes: **Hold** and **No-Go**. **Hold** is appropriate when critical readiness gaps exist that make forward movement unsafe. Typical Hold situations include missing security testing evidence for a high-risk system, unresolved critical vulnerabilities without approved exceptions, unvalidated identity and privileged access boundaries, missing logging and monitoring readiness for an externally exposed system, or unclear operational ownership. Hold is not a delay for its own sake. It is a control that forces closure of gaps before they become production exposure.

No-Go is appropriate when the solution is fundamentally not ready or cannot meet non-negotiable standards and risk appetite. It applies when the design or implementation approach cannot satisfy core security and compliance requirements, or when vendor constraints prevent required monitoring, auditability, or control ownership. No-Go signals that the initiative must be re-scoped, redesigned, changed in approach, or terminated, rather than pushed forward with hope.

Minimum pass criteria should be defined up front and applied consistently. At a minimum, the project should show completion of planned assurance activities appropriate to the risk classification, remediation or formal handling of critical findings, evidence that identity and access boundaries are implemented and tested, evidence that data protection controls exist when sensitive data is involved, and evidence that logging and monitoring produce usable signals with assigned owners. The risk register must be current and coherent, with residual risk decisions explicit. Finally, deployment control readiness must be credible, including rollback and migration plans when relevant (ISO, 2022; NIST, 2024b).

Automatic Hold or No-Go triggers should include unresolved critical vulnerabilities without time-bound approval authority, absence of required security testing evidence for high-risk systems, unclear shared responsibility boundaries for vendor solutions, inability to obtain necessary logs for detection and response, lack of named operational ownership, and absence of rollback planning for high-impact deployments. These gaps break verifiability, accountability, and recoverability, which are the minimum foundations for defensible deployment approval.

Gate 3 Readiness Pack

This Gate 3 Readiness Pack summarizes the Develop or Acquire Phase work and presents the evidence required for a Gate 3 decision. It is organized for fast review using a one-page cover sheet, an evidence bundle index, and decision rules that define minimum pass criteria and automatic hold triggers. The intent is to confirm that build and buy workstreams have produced closure-quality proof, that operational readiness is credible, and that deployment controls are defined before the organization approves movement into Implement planning.

A. Readiness workstreams

1. Unified readiness posture: Consolidate build and buy readiness into one posture. Produce a single readiness narrative and a combined evidence bundle that aligns build track proof with buy track proof.
2. Build track control implementation alignment: Confirm implementation aligns to design intent. Verify key controls are implemented as designed, including identity and access boundaries, data protection, logging and monitoring, and secure configuration baselines.
3. Build track layered testing and assurance completion: Complete layered testing and assurance appropriate to the risk classification. Execute functional, integration, security, and configuration validation testing, and capture interpretable evidence.
4. Build track findings remediation and exception discipline: Remediate critical and high-severity issues. If exceptions are required, obtain approved, time-bound exceptions with mitigations, verification steps, and expiration dates.

5. Build track release candidate discipline: Finalize release candidate readiness. Freeze scope for the release candidate, finalize release notes and known issues log, and ensure evidence is traceable to the release candidate identifier.
6. Buy track onboarding and enforceability: Finalize vendor onboarding and enforceability. Confirm contracts and security obligations are executed. Ensure auditability, incident obligations, and service-level terms are active and understood.
7. Buy track customer-owned controls implementation: Implement and validate customer-owned controls within the shared responsibility model. Configure and validate identity integration, role governance, administrative boundaries, logging exports, and monitoring integration.
8. Buy track incident and support integration: Confirm incident and support integration. Validate escalation paths, incident collaboration steps, communication channels, and responsibilities between vendor and customer teams.
9. Operational readiness baseline: Confirm operational readiness baseline. Ensure logging produces usable events, monitoring and alerting exist, runbooks are drafted, and operational ownership is documented.
10. Deployment control readiness: Confirm deployment control readiness. Validate environment readiness, change control approach, rollback capability, and migration readiness plan when migration is in scope.
11. Risk register reconciliation: Update and reconcile the risk register. Ensure residual risks are current, owners are assigned, mitigations are documented, and any risk acceptance requests are explicit.

B. Gate 3 evidence bundle index

1. Gate 3 Readiness Narrative: Concise decision summary stating what is being approved, what evidence supports readiness, what remains open, and the requested outcome.
2. Combined Build/Buy Readiness Summary: Single view of readiness across build assurance, buy assurance, operational readiness, and deployment controls.
3. Updated Risk Register: Current risks and residual risks with owners, treatment status, and proposed acceptances.
4. Build Track Assurance Evidence: Testing results summary and detailed reports (functional, integration, security, configuration validation) appropriate to risk classification. Vulnerability remediation status with proof of fixes and verification. Approved exception log with expiration dates, approvers, mitigations, and verification plan. Configuration validation evidence for critical infrastructure and platform settings. Access control and privileged boundary validation for high-risk workflows.
5. Buy Track Assurance Evidence: Shared responsibility mapping and control ownership boundaries. Contract security obligations summary including audit evidence rights, breach notification, service levels, and subcontractor controls. Evidence of configured customer-owned controls, identity integration, roles, admin boundaries, logging export, and monitoring integration. Vendor onboarding status and remaining onboarding conditions.
6. Operational Readiness Artifacts: Logging and monitoring configuration summary, alert definitions, and ownership assignments. Incident response and escalation integration summary including vendor participation. Runbook drafts and support procedures for critical workflows and failure scenarios.

7. Deployment Readiness Artifacts: Environment readiness confirmation and access restrictions. Deployment approach summary with release candidate identifiers and validation steps. Rollback strategy and rollback test intent or evidence where applicable. Migration plan and migration validation steps when migration is in scope.
8. Independent Assurance Outputs: Penetration testing or independent review results when required, including remediation status and closures.

C. Review flow

Quality Review Board (QRB) process

- Submission and intake: Project team submits the combined Gate 3 evidence bundle and readiness narrative to the quality review function.
- Completeness and coherence check: Reviewers verify all required artifacts exist, align with each other, and support the readiness claims.
- Assurance closure validation: Reviewers confirm planned testing is completed for the risk classification, results meet defined thresholds, and critical findings are resolved or formally managed.
- Buy track responsibility validation: Reviewers confirm shared responsibility boundaries are explicit and customer-owned controls are configured and evidenced.
- Operational readiness validation: Reviewers confirm monitoring, alerting, logging usability, runbook drafts, and ownership assignments exist.
- Risk posture validation: Reviewers confirm the risk register is current, residual risks have owners, and proposed acceptances are documented.

- Findings report: Reviewers produce findings categorized as critical, major, minor, each with an owner, due date, verification method, and closure evidence.
- QRB outcome: Ready for Gate scheduling, or not ready until critical gaps are resolved.

Gate Review Board (GRB) process

- Pre-read distribution: Evidence bundle and QRB findings report distributed to decision-makers in advance.
- Readiness narrative: Project leadership presents a short readiness summary focused on assurance closure, risk posture, operational readiness, and deployment control readiness.
- Build track readiness review: Gate body reviews testing evidence, vulnerability status, exception discipline, and release candidate readiness.
- Buy track readiness review: Gate body reviews contractual enforceability, shared responsibility mapping, and evidence of configured customer-owned controls.
- Operational readiness review: Gate body reviews monitoring and logging readiness, incident response integration, runbooks, and operational ownership.
- Deployment control readiness review: Gate body reviews environment readiness, change control approach, rollback strategy, and migration readiness if applicable.
- Decision outcome: Gate body issues Go, Conditional Go, Hold, or No-Go, recorded in a decision log, including conditions if applicable.
- Condition management: If Conditional Go, conditions are documented with owners, deadlines, verification methods, and consequences if not met.

D. Decision rules

Outcomes

- Go: Evidence confirms assurance closure for the risk classification, critical issues are resolved or formally managed, operational readiness baseline is credible, and deployment controls are defined and feasible.
- Conditional Go: Evidence is broadly sufficient, but limited and specific gaps remain. Conditions are owned, time-bound, and verifiable, and gaps do not prevent safe progression into Implement planning.
- Hold: Critical readiness gaps exist that prevent safe progression. Remediation is required before moving forward.
- No-Go: The solution cannot proceed in its current form due to fundamental misalignment, unacceptable risk, or inability to meet non-negotiable requirements.

Minimum pass criteria

- Planned assurance activities are complete for the risk classification and evidenced.
- Critical and high-severity issues are remediated, or formally accepted through approved, time-bound exceptions.
- Identity and access boundaries, including privileged access paths, are implemented and validated.
- Data protection controls are implemented and evidenced where sensitive data is involved.
- Logging and monitoring produce usable signals, alerting exists, and owners are assigned.
- Operational readiness artifacts exist, including runbook drafts and incident escalation integration.

- Shared responsibility boundaries are explicit for vendor solutions, and customer-owned controls are configured and evidenced.
- Risk register is current, residual risks are owned, and acceptance requests are documented.
- Deployment approach includes change control, rollback strategy, and migration plan when migration is in scope.

Automatic Hold or No-Go triggers

- Unresolved critical vulnerabilities without approved exception authority and expiration.
- Missing security testing evidence for a high-risk or externally exposed system.
- Unvalidated authorization boundaries, or unclear privileged access controls.
- Missing encryption or unclear key ownership for sensitive data flows.
- Logging and monitoring readiness absent for systems requiring detection and response capability.
- Vendor shared responsibility unclear, or customer-owned controls not configured for a vendor-dependent solution.
- No operational owner assigned, or no credible runbook and escalation baseline exists.
- No rollback strategy for high-impact deployments, or no migration validation plan when migration is in scope.

Common Gate 3 Issues

One common issue is treating Gate 3 as a schedule checkpoint rather than an assurance checkpoint. The correction is to require evidence and to separate quality review from the gate decision so incomplete bundles do not reach decision-makers.

Another one is weak exception discipline. Teams request exceptions without expiration dates or without mitigation. The correction is to enforce time-bound, owned exceptions with verification and consequences, and to treat repeated exceptions as a governance signal that design or platform practices must improve.

A third issue is incomplete operational readiness. Teams assume operations will “figure it out” during deployment. The correction is to require baseline runbooks, monitoring integration, and ownership before approval to proceed toward deployment.

A fourth issue is vendor control ambiguity. Teams assume the vendor “handles security.” The correction is to require shared responsibility mapping and evidence of configured customer-owned controls, especially identity, logging, and monitoring integration.

A fifth issue is migration underestimation. Teams treat migration as a technical detail, not as a risk event. The correction is to require migration strategy, validation plan, and rollback approach as Gate 3 artifacts when migration is in scope.

These corrections preserve the purpose of Gate 3. The gate exists to prevent unmanaged risk from entering production disguised as progress.

Summary and Next Steps

Gate 3 is where secure technology project management proves it is more than process. It is where the organization confirms that assurance work is complete enough to deploy responsibly, that risk is visible and owned, that operations are ready to run and defend what will be deployed, and that deployment itself will be controlled, observable, and reversible when needed. It merges the build track and buy track into a single readiness posture and demands coherence across evidence, contracts, controls, and operational plans. It uses a quality review to validate evidence readiness and a gate decision forum to authorize progression into deployment preparation with explicit decision outcomes and accountable conditions.

When Gate 3 is executed with discipline, deployment becomes a managed event rather than a leap of faith. The organization can explain why it is deploying, what proof supports readiness, what risks remain, and who owns those risks. This aligns with governance principles that emphasize guiding and monitoring technology use through accountability (ISO, 2015) and with cybersecurity governance expectations that place evidence and oversight at the center of risk management (NIST, 2024b). It also aligns with secure software development guidance that expects secure practices and verification to be integrated and demonstrable (Souppaya et al., 2022). The next phase, Implement, will take this approval, and translate it into controlled deployment, migration, stabilization, and operational handover, where the organization must preserve assurance while moving from planned readiness to real-world performance.

G3 Gate 3: Build / Buy Readiness Gate

Decision to Deploy

PURPOSE: *Prove readiness to move into controlled* implementation and release

BUILD

- **Secure engineering evidence** (coding standards, peer review evidence)
- **CI/CD security controls** evidence (SAST/SCA/secret scanning/IaC scanning as applicable)
- **Security test results** + remediation status (critical issues closed or governed)
- **Release readiness package** (versioned release candidate + configuration baseline)

BUY

- **Third-party due diligence summary** (security posture, obligations, risks)
- **Contract control map** (security, privacy, audit, SLAs, right-to-test, *exit)*
- **Proof-of-concept results** (security + integration + data handling validation
- **Onboarding and integration** controls (IAM, logging, monitoring, data protection)

SHARED

- **Updated risk register** + explicit residual risk acceptance approvals
- **G3 Decision record** (including conditions and deadlines

BUILD

- **Secure engineering evidence** (coding standards, peer review evidence)
- **CI/CD security controls evidence** (SAST/SCA/secret scanning/IaC scanning as applicable)

SHARED

- **Updated risk register** + explicit residual risk acceptance approvals
- **G3 Decision record** (including conditions and deadlines

12 Implementation Phase

The Implement phase is the moment a project stops being a controlled construction effort and becomes a live organizational change event. In Develop and Acquire, the work happens in environments designed to absorb mistakes, testing is repeatable, rollback is easier, and exposure is limited. Implementation changes that physics. Once the solution moves into production, users behave in unpredictable ways, integrations face real-world traffic and failure patterns, data inconsistencies surface, and adversaries can observe and probe. The Implement phase is therefore not "just deploying." It is the disciplined transition from a proven release candidate into a dependable operational capability, with security, compliance, resilience, and accountability carried forward rather than lost in the excitement of go live. If earlier phases established governance and assurance as the spine of delivery, Implement proves whether that spine can carry the weight of reality (NIST, 2024b).

This is also the phase where the organization's culture reveals itself. In mature environments, teams treat go live like a controlled flight, with checklists, rehearsals, communication protocols, and contingency plans. In immature environments, teams treat go live like a leap, hoping the parachute opens. The difference is not a project management preference. It is a security outcome. Systems fail most visibly during implementation because pressure compresses decision time, and compressed decision time can produce risky shortcuts, especially in access controls, configuration hardening, monitoring readiness, and rollback discipline. The Implement phase is where project leadership must guard against the temptation to treat stability and security as "post go live enhancements." Post go live enhancements often become permanent exposure.

Implementation must also reflect how technology has changed. Cloud deployment models, API ecosystems, and vendor platforms increase dependency complexity. AI-enabled features and AI-assisted workflows add behavior variability, new data handling risks, and new monitoring requirements. None of these realities can be managed through a simple release checklist. They require controlled deployment processes, evidence-driven validation, and operational readiness that includes detection and response capability. A governance-centered cybersecurity approach expects organizations to manage these risks through accountable decisions and ongoing oversight, rather than by assuming that security ends when testing ends (NIST, 2024b). Implement is where that expectation becomes operational practice.

A practical way to understand Implement is to divide it into four intertwined tracks: deployment execution, migration and cutover, security validation in production context, and operational readiness and handover. These tracks should not be treated as separate workstreams that occasionally meet. They must be synchronized because each one affects the other. A migration plan affects monitoring requirements. A rollback plan affects how you validate security controls. A vendor dependency affects cutover sequencing. A privileged access design affects who can execute deployment steps and how those actions are audited. Implementation succeeds when these tracks align and when decisions are based on evidence rather than urgency.

The Implementation Phase is where plans become production reality, and where weak controls, unclear ownership, or incomplete readiness evidence can turn a launch into an incident. This phase governs controlled deployment, data migration and cutover, integration validation, security validation in the live environment, and the operational handover needed to sustain the solution safely. The objective is not simply to go live, it is to go live with verified controls, measurable observability, and accountable operational readiness. The figure below summarizes the phase purpose, the major activities that drive production readiness, the security-by-design anchors that must be verified in production, and the key outputs required to support Gate 4 approval and handover.

Implement as a controlled transition

The first discipline of Implement is to treat deployment as a controlled transition rather than a single event. Teams often plan for one big day and forget the weeks around it. Yet implementation begins long before deployment day and continues after it through stabilization and operational acceptance. A mature implementation plan includes pre-deployment readiness work, rehearsal cycles, go live execution, immediate post go live validation, stabilization, and formal handover. Each stage has entry criteria, tasks, evidence, and decision points.

Pre-deployment readiness is where teams confirm that environments are prepared and that access boundaries are enforceable. For a build solution, this includes confirming production environment configuration baselines, verifying that secrets and keys are managed correctly, and verifying that production access is restricted and auditable. For a vendor solution, this includes confirming tenant configuration, identity integration, administrative role boundaries, logging exports, and monitoring integration. Implementation should never be the first time the team attempts these configurations. They should be rehearsed and documented so the final move is execution, not discovery.

Rehearsal cycles are the second discipline. The project should rehearse deployment steps, migration scripts, cutover sequencing, and rollback procedures in environments that mimic production as closely as feasible. Rehearsals are where you discover hidden dependencies and timing assumptions. They also build muscle memory, which matters because deployment day is stressful, and stress degrades judgment. Rehearsals also produce evidence. If you cannot demonstrate that rollback works, then rollback is a theory. If you cannot demonstrate that monitoring triggers alerts during a rehearsal, then monitoring readiness is unproven. Implement is where you convert theories into tested capabilities.

Go live execution is the visible moment, yet it should be the least surprising moment. Teams should have a runbook that lists steps, owners, dependencies, time windows, and validation checks. Communications should be planned, including the language used for status updates, escalation triggers, and decision authority for halting or rolling back. This communication discipline is not bureaucracy. It is safety. It prevents conflicting actions and reduces the risk that someone makes an uncoordinated change under pressure.

Post go live validation follows immediately. It confirms that core business workflows work, that integrations behave, that performance is acceptable, that monitoring signals are present, and that security boundaries remain intact. Many teams validate functionality, then move on. Secure delivery also validates access control, logging, alerting, and privileged activity auditability. If security validation is postponed, the system may operate with silent exposure. The goal is not to run every security test in production. The goal is to validate the controls that must remain true for the system to be defensible.

Hypercare stabilization is where teams monitor closely, respond quickly, and reduce risk through active observation and fast remediation. Hypercare should not become an excuse for sloppy go live. It should be a planned stabilization period with defined duration, staffing, metrics, and exit criteria. Exit criteria should include stable error rates, stable performance, resolved high-priority defects, and confirmed operational ownership.

Finally, formal handover transfers responsibility to the operational owner in a controlled way. Handover is not an email. It is an acceptance process that confirms runbooks exist, support teams are trained, monitoring and escalation paths are active, and maintenance responsibilities are understood. ISO/IEC 27001 reinforces that security controls must be operated and maintained systematically, which depends on clear responsibilities and operational capability, not just design and implementation completion (ISO, 2022). Handover is how the project ensures the system will be sustained, not merely launched.

Deployment Execution, Access, and Change Control

Deployment execution has two invisible components that determine whether the process is secure: who can do what, and how changes are controlled and audited. Projects sometimes treat these as separate from deployment. They are deployment. If privileged deployment actions can be performed by too many people, or performed without logging, then the system's first production actions may already violate governance expectations. If changes are deployed without traceable approvals, the organization loses its ability to explain what changed and why, which undermines incident investigation and auditability.

The Implement phase should enforce a deployment access model aligned to least privilege. Only designated roles should have the ability to execute production deployment steps, change configurations, or run migration scripts. Those roles should be time-bound where possible, monitored, and auditable. Separation of duties should be applied when risk tier requires it, especially for high-impact systems. For example, the person who prepares a release candidate may not be the person who approves production release. The person who approves may not be the person who executes. These boundaries reduce insider risk and reduce accidental changes.

Change governance during Implement should focus on clarity rather than friction. Teams need an authoritative release identifier, a release note summary, and a formal approval record. Even in agile environments, production changes should be traceable. This is consistent with governance principles that emphasize guiding and monitoring the use of IT in the organization, ensuring accountability and transparency in decisions and outcomes (ISO, 2015). Traceability is also practical. When something breaks, you need to know exactly what changed.

Deployment discipline also requires environment integrity checks. Before deployment, teams should verify that environment configurations match approved baselines, including network exposure settings, encryption settings, logging settings, and identity integrations. For cloud environments, this includes verifying that production accounts or subscriptions are separated, that access is restricted, and that monitoring pipelines are functional. For vendor environments, this includes verifying tenant configurations, role boundaries, and logging exports.

Release promotion practices matter. If the organization uses CI/CD pipelines, the pipeline should be configured so that release promotion requires approvals, and so that evidence is captured automatically. If the organization uses manual deployment, the runbook should specify approvals and recording steps. The objective is the same: a controlled path from release candidate to production with recorded evidence.

A final deployment discipline is readiness to halt. Many failed implementations continue because teams are reluctant to stop. A good implementation plan defines halt triggers, such as unexpected performance degradation, failed critical workflow tests, missing monitoring signals, or anomalies in privileged access behavior. Halt triggers support safety. They also support governance because they make the decision to stop explicit and acceptable rather than embarrassing.

Migration and cutover

Migration and cutover are often more dangerous than deployment itself because data is unforgiving. If you move the wrong data, users lose trust immediately. If you move incomplete data, business processes fail subtly. If you move corrupted data, you create long-term errors that are expensive to fix. Migration failures are also security failures because they can expose data through misrouted transfers, create access control drift, or leave sensitive data in unprotected staging locations.

Implementation should begin migration planning early, even if migration execution occurs later. Migration planning includes data mapping, data cleansing, data validation, and reconciliation approaches. It also includes security requirements for migration, such as encryption during transfer, access restrictions on migration tooling, and secure disposal of temporary migration files. Data should not be copied into spreadsheets, personal folders, or unmanaged storage during migration because this creates uncontrolled exposure.

A strong migration plan defines cutover strategies. A "big bang" cutover replaces everything at once. It can be efficient but risky. A phased cutover moves segments over time, which can reduce risk but increases complexity. A parallel run keeps both systems active for a period, allowing validation, but can increase operational workload and synchronization complexity. The choice should be based on risk tier, operational tolerance, and dependency patterns.

Cutover sequencing should include dependency readiness. Many systems depend on upstream and downstream integrations. Cutover can fail if a dependency is not ready or if interfaces change unexpectedly. The implementation plan should therefore include integration validation steps during cutover and contingency steps if an integration fails. This is where rehearsals matter. Integration rehearsals reveal hidden assumptions such as timeouts, rate limits, and data format constraints.

Migration validation should include both technical and business checks. Technical checks confirm record counts, integrity constraints, and system performance. Business checks confirm that critical workflows produce expected outcomes. Reconciliation checks confirm that the new system reflects the reality of the old system where expected. This validation should be documented because it becomes part of go live evidence. Without documented validation, the organization cannot demonstrate that it moved responsibly, which matters for audit and for incident analysis.

Rollback planning for migration must be realistic. Some migrations are reversible. Others are not. If rollback is not feasible, then the implementation plan must include stronger pre-cutover validation and stronger contingency measures. It should also include a recovery plan that describes how to restore service if cutover fails, even if rollback is limited. This plan is essential for critical systems and aligns with operational resilience expectations embedded in systematic security management.

Migration also intersects with identity and access controls. When users are migrated, access roles must be migrated correctly. Role mapping errors can create excessive access or deny critical access. Implementation should therefore include role migration validation. It should verify that privileged roles remain restricted and that default roles do not accidentally include administrative privileges. These errors are common in vendor platforms where role models differ from internal systems.

For AI-enabled components, migration can include additional complexities such as migrating training datasets, feature stores, vector indexes, or prompt templates and policy configurations. Even if Part ω covers AI governance more deeply, Implement must still treat these artifacts as part of operational reality. They must be versioned, validated, and monitored because changes can cause behavior drift and unexpected outputs.

Security validation in production context

Security validation during Implement is not a repeat of the entire security test suite. It is a targeted set of checks that confirm the production environment has not undermined the security posture established during Design and Develop or Acquire. The key idea is control continuity. Controls that were proven in staging must remain true in production. Implementation is where continuity can break because production configurations differ, access controls are broader, and monitoring pipelines are different.

Security validation should begin with identity and access checks. The team should validate authentication flows, multi-factor requirements where applicable, and authorization boundaries for critical workflows. It should validate that privileged access is restricted, audited, and time-bound if that is part of the operating model. It should validate that service accounts and integration credentials are stored and rotated correctly. It should also validate that emergency access procedures exist and are controlled.

Next, security validation should confirm encryption and key management behavior. It should verify that sensitive data is encrypted in transit and at rest where required, and that key ownership and access to keys align with governance expectations. For vendor solutions, this includes confirming that customer-controlled key options are configured when required, or that compensating controls are in place if key control is not supported.

Logging and monitoring validation is one of the most critical steps. In many implementations, logging breaks silently. Logs may not be forwarded correctly, alerts may not trigger, or the security operations team may not have access. Implementation should validate that security-relevant events appear in monitoring systems and that alerting works. It should also validate that logs include the context needed for investigations, such as user identifiers, source IP or equivalent context, request identifiers, and administrative actions. Evidence of monitoring readiness supports the organization's ability to detect and respond, which is central to governance-centered cybersecurity practice (NIST, 2024b).

Configuration validation should also be performed in production, especially for cloud resources and externally exposed services. Misconfiguration is a frequent cause of exposure. Implementation should confirm network exposure settings, firewall rules, API gateway configurations, and storage permissions. It should confirm that default accounts are disabled, that sample credentials are removed, and that administrative endpoints are protected. These checks do not need to be exhaustive, yet they must cover the highest-risk surfaces.

Vulnerability validation during Implement should focus on what changed. If the release candidate included remediation, confirm that remediation is present in production. If exceptions were approved, confirm that compensating controls are active and that monitoring for exception-related risks is in place. This is how exceptions remain governed rather than ignored.

Security validation should also include abuse and misuse checks for high-risk workflows. For example, verify that authorization boundaries hold when identifiers are manipulated. Verify that rate limiting works for critical APIs if applicable. Verify that export features require appropriate permissions. For AI-enabled interfaces, perform lightweight checks to confirm that sensitive data is not inadvertently exposed through prompts and that output filtering or policy controls behave as expected in production context. These checks are not meant to solve all AI risk, yet they confirm that baseline guardrails are not missing.

This evidence-driven approach aligns with secure development guidance that emphasizes integrated practices and verification, including producing evidence that secure practices were performed and outcomes were achieved (Souppaya et al., 2022). It also aligns with ISO/IEC 27001's emphasis on operating and maintaining controls, which requires validating that controls are functioning in the real environment, not only in a test environment (ISO, 2022).

Operational readiness, stabilization, and handover

Operational readiness is where implementation becomes sustainable. Many projects deploy successfully and then quietly fail because the operational capability is weak. Tickets pile up, alerts are ignored, patching becomes inconsistent, and ownership becomes unclear. A secure delivery model treats operational readiness as part of implementation, not a separate operations problem.

Operational readiness begins with role clarity. The project must confirm who owns the system post go live, who owns security monitoring, who owns configuration change control, who owns vendor relationship management, and who owns incident response leadership. These owners must have authority, not just responsibility. They must have access, tools, and time.

Next, operational readiness requires runbooks. Runbooks should cover health checks, common failure patterns, restart or recovery steps, rollback triggers, access emergency procedures, and escalation paths. They should also include vendor escalation information where applicable. Runbooks should be realistic. They should reflect what operators can actually do, not what a perfect world would allow.

Monitoring readiness must be validated, not assumed. Dashboards should exist for critical metrics. Alerts should exist for critical conditions. Alert routing should be tested, at least once, so responders know where alerts go and how they will act. Incident response integration should include communication templates, decision authority, and escalation steps. Even a lightweight tabletop rehearsal for critical systems can reveal confusion and reduce risk.

Stabilization requires planned staffing and an explicit timeline. Hypercare should define coverage hours, roles, escalation paths, and triage rules. It should define what qualifies as a release blocker versus a post-go-live issue. It should also define how changes will be managed during stabilization. Frequent changes can destabilize systems, yet sometimes changes are necessary. Hypercare governance balances speed and stability.

User training and adoption support should also be part of operational readiness. A secure system can be undermined by confused users and improvised workflows. If users cannot complete tasks easily, they will seek workarounds that bypass controls. Training reduces that risk. Support materials, quick reference guides, and clear support channels reduce frustration and reduce unsafe behavior.

For vendor solutions, operational readiness includes vendor governance continuity. Who monitors vendor advisories. Who manages renewal decisions and contract obligations. Who manages access reviews. Who reviews vendor audit reports or assurance updates. This is where vendor governance becomes continuous rather than a one-time acquisition activity.

Handover closes the loop. It should include a formal acceptance that operational teams have the necessary artifacts and that responsibilities are transferred. It should also include a backlog of post go live improvements, including technical debt, deferred enhancements, and planned remediation for time-bound exceptions. Those items should not disappear. They should become part of sustainment governance.

Key Takeaways

The Implement phase is where secure delivery meets reality. It is the disciplined transition from validated release candidate to operational capability, executed through controlled deployment, careful migration and cutover, targeted production-context security validation, and credible operational readiness. The phase demands rehearsal, checklists, communication discipline, and the courage to halt or roll back when evidence indicates risk. It also demands that monitoring and incident response readiness are not treated as optional, because detection and response are part of security in production. Implementation succeeds when controls remain continuous across environments, when residual risks are explicit and owned, and when operational teams are prepared to sustain and improve the system.

This phase directly supports governance expectations that cybersecurity is managed through oversight and accountability, and that systems are operated with an ongoing ability to monitor and respond to risk (NIST, 2024b). It also supports the systematic control and responsibility approach of ISO/IEC 27001, which treats security as a managed system requiring operational capability and continuous maintenance (ISO, 2022). Finally, it reflects secure development principles that emphasize integrating verification and evidence into delivery rather than relying on last-minute confidence (Souppaya et al., 2022). The next chapter, Gate 4, will formalize implementation readiness by evaluating production readiness evidence, handover approval conditions, and the decision logic for confirming the organization is ready to transition from post-go-live into sustained operations.

“Go-live is not the finish line,

it is day one of accountability.”

Gate 4: Implementation Review

Gate 4 is the point where the organization stops asking, "Can we deploy?" and starts answering a more consequential question, "Are we ready to operate, defend, and sustain what we deployed?" Gate 3 approved readiness to proceed toward controlled deployment. Chapter 17 described the disciplined execution of deployment, migration, production-context validation, stabilization, and operational readiness. Gate 4 is the governance decision that confirms implementation outcomes are real, risks are managed, and the operational organization is prepared to own the solution without the project team acting as a permanent crutch. It is not a celebration meeting, and it is not an administrative checkpoint. It is the formal approval to transition from project-led stabilization into business-as-usual operations, with clear accountability, measurable readiness evidence, and explicit acceptance of any residual risks (NIST, 2024b).

Gate 4 exists because production environments are unforgiving. A system can be successfully deployed and still be operationally unsafe. It can appear stable while silent monitoring gaps exist, while runbooks are incomplete, while access governance is weak, or while the incident response path is untested. That is how organizations end up with "working systems" that produce outages, security incidents, compliance failures, and reputational harm months later. Gate 4 protects the enterprise from that slow-motion failure. It demands evidence that the system is not only running, but also governable. Governable means it can be monitored, patched, changed, recovered, audited, and defended under stress. This concept aligns with governance principles that emphasize guiding and monitoring technology use through accountability and oversight, rather than relying on informal heroics (ISO, 2015).

A useful way to frame Gate 4 is as the handover gate. The handover is not a document transfer. It is a responsibility transfer. Once handover is approved, operational owners become accountable for system performance, security posture, and continuous compliance. The project team may still support a limited stabilization window, yet the operating model must be clear and enforceable. ISO/IEC 27001 reinforces that security is a managed system of controls and responsibilities that must be sustained, which depends on explicit ownership, operational procedures, and continuous monitoring, not on the presence of the original delivery team (ISO, 2022). Gate 4 is where the organization proves it can sustain those responsibilities.

Gate 4 is also where the organization confronts the reality of residual risk. Residual risk always exists. The question is whether residual risk is known, owned, and monitored, or whether it is hidden and normalized. Gate 4 provides a structured moment to confirm which issues were resolved, which issues remain, and which issues are accepted temporarily under time-bound conditions. This approach supports the CSF 2.0 emphasis on governance and risk-informed decision-making, where cybersecurity outcomes are managed through accountable decisions and continuous oversight (NIST, 2024b).

What Gate 4 decides and why it is different from Gate 3

Gate 3 is readiness to proceed into implementation, including controlled deployment planning and execution. Gate 4 is readiness to stay in production safely, meaning the system can be operated without extraordinary measures. Gate 3 is about assurance closure and deployment approval. Gate 4 is about production readiness and handover approval. The difference matters because implementation can look successful while operational readiness is incomplete. Many organizations have experienced this pattern. The system goes live, the project declares victory, and within weeks the operational team is overwhelmed by alerts they do not understand, users report confusing access issues, patch cycles stall, and the vendor escalation path is unclear. Nothing "broke" during deployment, yet the system becomes fragile over time.

Gate 4 therefore focuses on outcomes rather than intentions. It verifies that monitoring is not just configured, but actionable. It verifies that incident response is not just written, but integrated. It verifies that access governance is not just planned, but enforced. It verifies that operational teams are trained and equipped. It verifies that the backlog of post go live remediation is visible, prioritized, and governed. It also verifies that the organization can handle the next change safely. A system is not truly production-ready if the first patch or configuration update becomes a crisis.

Gate 4 also introduces a stronger accountability shift. In Gate 3 and during early implementation, the project leadership is typically accountable for readiness. In Gate 4, operational leadership must accept ownership, including service management responsibility, security monitoring responsibility, and compliance responsibility. That acceptance must be explicit. It must be recorded. It must include named owners. If ownership is ambiguous, the organization has not achieved handover readiness, even if the system is technically stable.

What Gate 4 Must Confirm Before Production

Gate 4 works best when production readiness is evaluated across a small set of dimensions that cover both security and operations. The goal is not to create bureaucracy. The goal is to ensure the organization does not miss the basics that later become painful incidents.

Operational stability readiness is one dimension. It includes evidence that the system is stable under normal load, that error rates are within acceptable ranges, that performance meets minimum expectations, and that major defects discovered during the post go-live stabilization period have been resolved or mitigated. It also includes evidence that the system's dependencies are stable, and that integration points have acceptable failure behavior. This dimension is not only about user experience. It is about resilience. Unstable systems create operational noise, and operational noise weakens detection because teams learn to ignore alerts.

Security readiness is another dimension. It includes confirmation that access controls are enforced as deployed, that privileged access is restricted and auditable, that secrets and keys are managed properly, and that production configuration hardening is in place. It includes confirmation that the security monitoring pipeline works, including log forwarding, alert routing, and response procedures. It also includes confirmation that any deployment-time exceptions have been resolved or are governed through time-bound risk acceptance. This aligns with the CSF 2.0 focus on governance and continuous management of cybersecurity outcomes, rather than treating security as a pre-deployment activity only (NIST, 2024b).

Operational monitoring and incident readiness is a third dimension. This includes dashboards, alert thresholds, on-call procedures, escalation paths, and incident communications. It includes validation that the operational team can triage events, distinguish normal behavior from abnormal behavior, and collaborate with security teams and vendors when needed. Incident readiness should not rely on personal knowledge. It should rely on documented procedures and tested alert routing. ISO/IEC 27001 emphasizes ongoing operation of controls, which requires monitoring, responsibilities, and repeatable processes (ISO, 2022).

Service management readiness is another dimension, especially for systems that will be maintained and changed frequently. This includes change control practices, patching cadence, release management procedures, configuration management, and asset inventory updates. It includes confirmation that the system is integrated into the organization's operational governance practices, including ticketing and support workflows. IT service management guidance emphasizes that stable operations depend on defined practices for incidents, problems, changes, and continual improvement, which are central to sustained production readiness even when the project team is no longer present (Axelos, 2019).

Compliance and audit readiness is a fifth dimension. Even if the system is not regulated, auditability matters. Gate 4 should confirm that evidence required for audits can be produced, including access logs, administrative activity logs, change records, and vendor assurance evidence where applicable. For regulated environments, Gate 4 should confirm that compliance obligations are met, or that any deferred obligations are documented with acceptable remediation timelines. This aligns with ISO/IEC 27001's emphasis on maintaining an information security management system that can demonstrate control operation and continuous improvement (ISO, 2022).

Business readiness is a sixth dimension, and it is often underestimated. It includes user training, updated procedures, support readiness, and adoption readiness. A technically stable system can fail if users are not prepared. Users will create workarounds, and workarounds can bypass controls. Gate 4 should confirm that user-facing support materials exist, that training has occurred where needed, and that business owners accept the new process model.

Finally, continuity readiness is the dimension that separates mature organizations from fragile ones. Continuity readiness includes backup and recovery verification, disaster recovery readiness where required, and the ability to restore service after a disruption. Gate 4 should confirm that backups are working and that restoration procedures are documented and feasible. It should also confirm that recovery responsibilities are defined and that recovery objectives are understood. Without continuity readiness, the organization is not truly production-ready, even if the system is running today.

Gate 4 Decisions with Governance Discipline

Gate 4 must produce clear, consistent decision outcomes. The standard outcomes should remain consistent with the broader gate governance model: Go, Conditional Go, Hold, or No-Go.

Go means production readiness is demonstrated, operational ownership is accepted, and handover can be approved. Conditional Go means the system can remain in production and handover can proceed, but specific conditions must be met within defined time windows to reduce residual risk and close readiness gaps. Hold means handover cannot proceed because critical readiness gaps exist, and the project must remain accountable until those gaps are resolved. No-Go means the organization must not proceed with the current operational posture, and may require rollback, re-scoping, or significant remediation due to unacceptable risk.

Conditional Go is common at Gate 4 because real-world stabilization can reveal issues that are not catastrophic, yet still important. Conditional Go can be a mature decision when conditions are narrow, owned, time-bound, and verifiable. It becomes dangerous when Conditional Go is used to approve handover while critical monitoring, access governance, or incident readiness gaps remain. Gate 4 should treat certain gaps as non-negotiable because they eliminate the organization's ability to defend the system.

Gate 4 should also formalize the post go-live stabilization exit. Post go-live stabilization is not a permanent operating model. Gate 4 can approve the transition from post go-live stabilization into normal operations by verifying exit criteria, including stabilized service metrics, manageable ticket volumes, resolved priority defects, and confirmed on-call readiness. If these exit criteria are not met, the organization should treat the system as not fully handed over, even if it remains in production.

The evidence-first approach to Gate 4

Gate 4 depends on evidence. Evidence should be simple, decision-grade, and aligned to readiness dimensions. The best Gate 4 evidence bundles tell a coherent story. They show what changed, what was validated, what was learned during stabilization, what risks remain, and how operations will sustain the system. They also show that operational owners are ready, trained, and accountable.

Evidence should include operational metrics from the stabilization period. It should include performance and error rate trends. It should include incident and defect summaries, including what was resolved and what remains. It should include security validation evidence, including confirmation that key access boundaries, logging pipelines, and alert routing work. It should include confirmation of production configuration baselines and any approved deviations. It should include evidence that change control and patching procedures are defined and owned. It should include runbooks and support procedures. It should include training and handover acceptance evidence.

Evidence should also include the post go live remediation backlog and risk register updates. Gate 4 must confirm that deferred items are visible, prioritized, and governed. Otherwise, deferred items become forgotten items, and forgotten items become permanent exposure. This is one of the most common governance failures after go live.

Gate 4 Readiness Pack

This Gate 4 Readiness Pack summarizes the Implement Phase outcomes and presents the evidence required for a Gate 4 decision. It is organized for fast review using a one-page cover sheet, an evidence bundle index, and decision rules that define minimum pass criteria and automatic hold triggers. The intent is to confirm that production is stable, security and monitoring are functioning in the production context, and operational ownership is ready to accept the service. The gate decision should be based on evidence and acceptance records, not on deployment completion.

A. Readiness workstreams

1. Production stabilization and service health: Stabilize production performance and service health. Confirm error rates, latency, availability, and capacity are within agreed thresholds. Ensure high-priority defects and incidents discovered during post-go-live stabilization are resolved or mitigated with documented plans.
2. Production-context security validation: Complete production-context security validation. Validate identity and access boundaries, privileged access controls, secrets and key handling, and configuration hardening in production (NIST, 2024b).
3. Monitoring, logging, and alert routing: Validate monitoring, logging, and alert routing. Confirm security-relevant logs and operational telemetry are flowing, alerts trigger correctly, and responders can access evidence needed for triage and investigation (ISO, 2022).
4. Incident response and escalation integration: Confirm incident response and escalation integration. Ensure escalation paths,

communications procedures, and vendor participation steps are defined and operational.

5. Runbooks and operational procedures: Finalize runbooks and operational procedures. Complete runbooks for health checks, recovery steps, rollback actions, access emergencies, and common failure scenarios. Align runbooks with operational tooling, permissions, and on-call practices (Axelos, 2019).
6. Operational ownership and support readiness: Confirm operational ownership acceptance and support readiness. Establish named service owners, security monitoring owners, change owners, and vendor managers. Confirm staffing, access, and on-call coverage expectations.
7. Change, patch, and configuration management readiness: Confirm change, patch, and configuration management readiness. Validate patch cadence, change approval workflow, configuration baseline management, and asset inventory updates (Axelos, 2019).
8. Business readiness and training completion: Confirm business readiness and training completion. Ensure user training and support materials exist, support channels are prepared, and business owners accept new workflows.
9. Continuity and recovery readiness: Validate continuity readiness. Confirm backups, restoration steps, recovery responsibilities, and disaster recovery readiness where required. Document recovery expectations aligned to criticality.
10. Findings and exception closure discipline: Close or govern all open findings and exceptions. Resolve critical issues, document residual risks, and secure time-bound approvals for exceptions with owners and verification steps (ISO, 2015; NIST, 2024b).

11. Gate 4 bundle packaging and acceptance artifacts: Prepare the Gate 4 evidence bundle and acceptance artifacts. Package stabilization metrics, validation results, operational artifacts, risk posture, and handover acceptance records into a decision-grade bundle.

B. Gate 4 evidence bundle index

1. Gate 4 Production Readiness Narrative
   Concise summary of production outcomes, stabilization status, key risks, and the requested Gate 4 decision.

2. Stabilization Metrics and Service Health Evidence
   Availability, error rate, latency, capacity indicators, plus summary of major production issues and resolutions.

3. Post Go-Live Defect and Incident Summary
   Structured list of incidents and high-priority defects, actions taken, remaining items, and prevention steps.

4. Security Readiness Evidence
   Access control validation results, privileged access auditability confirmation, secrets and key management confirmation, and production hardening validation (ISO, 2022; NIST, 2024b).

5. Monitoring and Logging Readiness Evidence
   Log forwarding confirmation, alert routing test evidence, dashboard summaries, and responder access validation.

6. Incident Response and Escalation Package
   Escalation paths, roles, communication templates, vendor engagement steps, and on-call procedures.

7. Runbooks and Operational Procedures
   Operational runbooks, recovery procedures, rollback procedures, access emergency procedures, and

troubleshooting steps for common failure scenarios (Axelos, 2019).

8. Service Management Readiness Artifacts
   Change management workflow, patch management approach, configuration baseline management, and service catalog or ownership record as applicable (Axelos, 2019).

9. Training and Business Readiness Artifacts
   Training completion evidence, user support materials, updated business procedures, and support readiness confirmation.

10. Continuity and Recovery Artifacts
   Backup and restore evidence, recovery procedures, and disaster recovery readiness evidence where required.

11. Updated Risk Register and Exception Log
   Residual risks with owners, approved exceptions with expiration dates, mitigation steps, and verification plan (ISO, 2015).

12. Handover Acceptance Record
   Formal acceptance from operational owners confirming responsibilities, access, tooling readiness, and ongoing governance commitments.

C. Review flow

Quality Review Board (QRB) process

- Submission and intake: Project team submits the Gate 4 evidence bundle, readiness narrative, and handover acceptance artifacts to the quality review function.
- Completeness and coherence check: Reviewers validate required artifacts exist, align with each other, and support readiness claims.

- Production stability validation: Reviewers confirm stabilization metrics meet thresholds, high-priority defects are addressed, and known issues are documented with mitigation.
- Security and monitoring validation: Reviewers confirm access boundaries, privileged access governance, logging pipelines, and alert routing tests are functioning and evidenced (ISO, 2022; NIST, 2024b).
- Operational readiness validation: Reviewers confirm runbooks, on-call readiness, escalation paths, and operational ownership are explicit and feasible (Axelos, 2019).
- Risk and exception validation: Reviewers confirm residual risks are current, owners are assigned, and exceptions are approved, time-bound, and verifiable (ISO, 2015).
- Findings report: Reviewers produce findings categorized as critical, major, minor, each with an owner, due date, verification method, and closure evidence.
- QRB outcome: Ready for Gate scheduling, or not ready until critical gaps are resolved.

Gate Review Board (GRB) process

- Pre-read distribution: Evidence bundle and QRB findings report distributed to decision-makers and operational owners in advance.
- Readiness narrative: Project leadership presents a brief readiness summary focused on stabilization outcomes, operational readiness, security readiness, and handover posture.
- Production readiness review: Gate body reviews service health metrics, defect, and incident outcomes, and whether post go-live stabilization exit criteria are met.
- Security readiness and monitoring review: Gate body reviews access governance, privileged activity auditability, logging

coverage, alert routing tests, and response readiness (NIST, 2024b).

- Operational ownership and service management review: Gate body reviews runbooks, staffing and on-call coverage, change and patch governance, and ongoing ownership commitments (Axelos, 2019).
- Risk posture review: Gate body reviews residual risks, exception discipline, remediation backlog governance, and decision authority for risk acceptance (ISO, 2015; ISO, 2022).
- Decision outcome: Gate body issues Go, Conditional Go, Hold, or No-Go, recorded in a decision log, including conditions and owners if applicable.
- Condition management: If Conditional Go, conditions are documented with owners, deadlines, verification method, and consequences if unmet.

D. Decision rules

Outcomes

- Go: Production stability is demonstrated, security and monitoring readiness are evidenced, operational ownership is accepted, and handover can proceed.
- Conditional Go: Production is stable enough to proceed with handover, but limited gaps remain. Conditions are specific, owned, time-bound, and verifiable.
- Hold: Critical readiness gaps exist. Handover cannot proceed, and the project remains accountable until remediation is verified.
- No-Go: Operational posture is unacceptable. The organization must not proceed as planned. Rollback, major remediation, or re-implementation may be required.

Minimum pass criteria

- Stabilization metrics meet thresholds. Major issues are resolved or mitigated with documented plans.
- Access control and privileged governance are validated in production, and administrative actions are auditable.
- Logging and monitoring pipelines are functional, alerts route correctly, and responders can access evidence.
- Incident response and escalation procedures exist, and responsibilities are understood.
- Runbooks and operational procedures are complete enough for common scenarios and failure modes (Axelos, 2019).
- Operational owners are named and prepared, including on-call coverage and change governance.
- Residual risks are visible, owned, and governed. Exceptions are approved and time-bound (ISO, 2015).
- Continuity and recovery readiness are confirmed at the level required for system criticality.

Automatic Hold or No-Go triggers

- Missing or non-functional logging and monitoring for a high-risk or externally exposed system because detection and response cannot be performed (NIST, 2024b).
- Uncontrolled privileged access or inability to audit because accountability cannot be enforced (ISO, 2015).
- Unresolved critical security issues without approved time-bound exceptions because risk is unmanaged.
- No named operational owner or no credible runbook and on-call readiness because sustainment is not feasible (Axelos, 2019).
- Inability to restore service through defined recovery procedures for critical systems because continuity readiness is absent.
- Uncontrolled remediation backlog with no ownership or timeline because residual risk will be normalized.

Common Gate 4 failure issues and how to correct them

A frequent Gate 4 failure issue is confusing "the system is running" with "the system is ready." Running is simply an observation. Readiness is a proven capability to operate safely under real conditions. The correction is to require operational readiness evidence, not uptime claims or successful deployment screenshots. Gate 4 should confirm that support structures exist, that responsibilities are clear, and that the organization can sustain the service after the project team steps back.

Another common failure issue is weak monitoring integration. Teams assume monitoring is in place because dashboards were created, yet alert routing has not been tested, logs are incomplete, or responders do not have the access and runbooks needed to act quickly. The correction is to make monitoring verification an explicit gate requirement. Test alert routing end to end. Validate log completeness for critical events. Confirm that responders can access systems, investigate incidents, and escalate issues without delays.

A third failure issue is informal handover. Projects transfer responsibility by sending documents, while operational teams lack training, authority, or confidence. The correction is formal operational acceptance with named service owners, on-call readiness, and clear change governance. Gate 4 should verify that the operating model is real, not assumed.

A fourth failure issue is residual risk that is promised to be fixed later without a credible plan. The correction is disciplined exception handling and a governed remediation backlog with owners, timelines, and verification steps.

Finally, some releases depend heavily on the project team to remain stable. If the builders must stay involved to keep production working, handover has not occurred. The correction is progressive transition during stabilization and clear exit criteria that must be met before the organization declares readiness.

Key Takeaways

Gate 4 represents the organization's commitment to sustainable production, not simply a successful deployment event. It is the point where leadership confirms that the solution can operate safely and predictably under real conditions, including routine change and unexpected stress. A clean cutover proves that the system can be started. Gate 4 proves that the system can be run, defended, and supported as a reliable service.

At this gate, the organization verifies stability through observable service health, such as error rates, latency, availability, and capacity trends, along with evidence that high-priority defects and incidents discovered during the post go-live stabilization period have been resolved or mitigated with clear plans. Gate 4 also validates the security posture in production context. That means identity and access boundaries function as designed, privileged actions are controlled and auditable, secrets and keys are handled correctly, and configuration hardening is enforced. Just as important, monitoring must be real. Logs must flow, alerts must route to the right responders, and responders must have access and procedures to investigate and contain issues.

Gate 4 is also where operational ownership becomes explicit. It confirms that named service owners, security monitoring owners, change owners, and vendor managers have accepted responsibility, and that on-call coverage and escalation paths are functional. Runbooks must exist for common failures, recoveries, and emergency access scenarios. Change control and patch routines must be defined in a way that protects stability without freezing progress. Finally, Gate 4 ensures residual risks are visible and governed. Exceptions must be time-bound, owned, and verifiable, with clear consequences if they remain open.

This evidence-first, accountability-first approach aligns with governance principles that emphasize guiding and monitoring technology use through responsible decision-making (ISO, 2015). It also aligns with ISO/IEC 27001's expectation that security controls and responsibilities are systematically operated and maintained over time (ISO, 2022). In addition, it reflects CSF 2.0's governance focus on oversight, risk-informed decisions, and continuous monitoring rather than one-time assurance (NIST, 2024b). After Gate 4, Sustain becomes the long game, where governance shifts from project routine to operational routine, and trust is protected every day, not only at go-live.

Before you run in production,

be sure you are ready to operate.

Production-ready means operationally ready.

“Go-live is not the finish line. It is the moment the organization becomes accountable at scale.”

Gate 4 protects trust. A successful deployment is not proof of readiness. Readiness means the system can be operated safely, monitored continuously, and supported under stress.

Evidence beats confidence. Gate 4 should rely on proof, migration validation, security validation, defect and risk status, and operational handover readiness, not slide assurance.

Operational readiness is a security control. Monitoring, alert thresholds, incident playbooks, rollback capability, and access governance determine whether the organization can contain failures quickly.

Risk acceptance must be explicit. If residual risks remain, document the owner, scope, time window, and verification plan. If the risk cannot be owned, the release is not ready.

Gate 4 is the point where delivery becomes an operational obligation.

Sustainment Phase

The Sustain phase begins when the applause fades and the system becomes part of the organization's daily heartbeat. Gate 4 confirmed production readiness and approved handover, yet handover is only the start of the long game. In Sustain, the organization proves it can keep the system secure, stable, compliant, and valuable as threats evolve, dependencies change, users adapt, and the business demands new capabilities. This is where secure technology project management stops looking like a project discipline and starts looking like an operating discipline. If the earlier phases established security by design and evidence-based governance, Sustain is where those commitments are tested continuously, not on a schedule the project team controls, but on a schedule the world controls (NIST, 2024b).

Sustain is where most organizations quietly win or quietly lose. Many systems fail not because they were built poorly, but because they are maintained poorly. Monitoring degrades, alerts become noise, patch cycles slip, access reviews become ceremonial, vendor relationships become passive, and configuration drift spreads across environments. Over time, the system becomes a liability, and the organization treats that liability as normal. Sustain is designed to prevent normalization of risk. It turns "secure at launch" into "secure in motion." It also turns "stable at go live" into "stable under change." ISO/IEC 27001 reinforces that security must be managed as a system, which includes ongoing operation, monitoring, and continual improvement of controls, not only initial implementation (ISO, 2022). Sustain is where that standard becomes practical reality.

The Sustain phase is often misunderstood as operations, separate from governance, and separate from delivery. In the ADDIS model, Sustain is an explicit phase because governance must not stop when the project plan stops. Cybersecurity governance, quality governance, and operational governance converge in Sustain into a single accountability framework. The organization must be able to demonstrate that controls remain effective, that changes are managed, that incidents are handled and learned from, and that risks are continually reassessed. This aligns with CSF 2.0's focus on governance and continuous management of cybersecurity outcomes, where security is treated as an enterprise capability that requires ongoing oversight, not a one-time checklist (NIST, 2024b).

A practical way to navigate Sustain is to think in four loops that run continuously. The first loop is the detection loop, which covers monitoring, alerting, and response. The second loop is the maintenance loop, which covers patching, vulnerability remediation, configuration management, and change control. The third loop is the assurance loop, which covers audits, evidence retention, control testing, compliance checks, and vendor assurance updates. The fourth loop is the improvement loop, which covers problem management, technical debt reduction, resilience improvements, automation, and governance maturity. These loops are not separate workstreams. They overlap. A vulnerability may trigger maintenance work, which triggers a change control event, which triggers evidence updates, which triggers an improvement investment to prevent recurrence. Sustain succeeds when these loops reinforce each other and remain visible to governance.

The Sustain Phase is where delivery success is proven over time, not on go-live day. Once a solution is in production, governance must continuously verify that controls remain effective, risks stay within tolerance, vulnerabilities are managed, changes are disciplined, and operational teams can detect, respond, and recover with confidence. Sustain therefore turns security-by-design into security-by-operations through monitoring, patching, incident learning, assurance reporting, and lifecycle improvement. The figure below summarizes the Sustain

Phase purpose, the major activities that keep the solution secure and reliable, the security-by-design anchors that must remain continuously enforced, and the key outputs required to demonstrate ongoing compliance, resilience, and readiness for Gate 5 operational assurance.

Sustain as an operating model of accountability

Sustain begins with accountability clarity. A system must have a named operational owner, a security monitoring owner, a change and release owner, and a vendor relationship owner when vendors are involved. These owners must have authority, not only responsibility. They need access to logs, tools, dashboards, and the ability to prioritize remediation and operational work. When ownership is fragmented and unclear, issues linger. Issues that linger become incidents. ISO/IEC 38500 emphasizes that governance of IT requires clear responsibilities and oversight mechanisms, which are undermined when accountability is ambiguous (ISO, 2015). Sustain institutionalizes accountability by

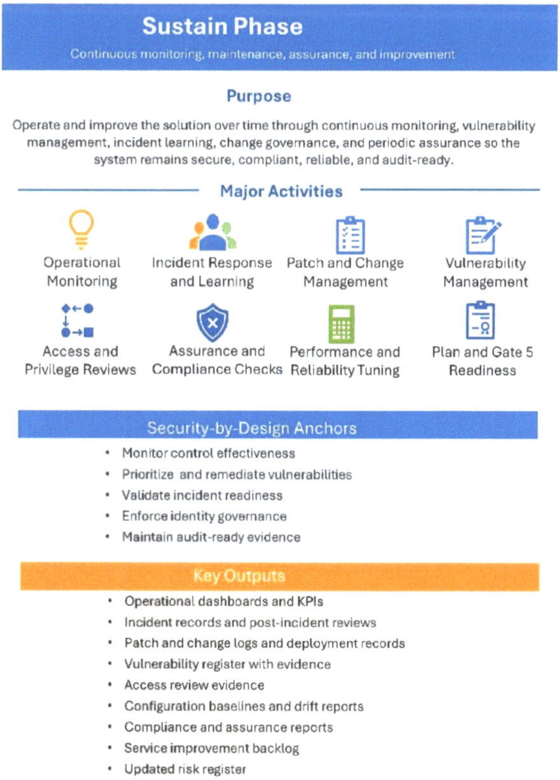

tying it to recurring operational governance routines, including review cadences, metrics, and escalation paths.

A second element of Sustain operating model is the service definition. The organization should define what service levels matter, what availability and performance expectations exist, what data protection expectations exist, and what "normal" looks like in terms of operational signals. Without a defined service baseline, teams cannot detect drift because they do not know what drift is. Baselines do not need to be perfect or complex. They need to be explicit enough to support decisions. Baselines also allow governance boards and management to understand whether performance and security are improving or degrading.

The third element is the control boundary definition. The organization must clearly define what parts of the system are in scope for monitoring, patching, and change control. Modern systems include cloud services, managed platforms, APIs, integration pipelines, and third-party components. Sustain must maintain an accurate inventory of those components and their ownership. When inventory is incomplete, patching and monitoring become incomplete by default. System inventory is not an administrative chore. It is the foundation for risk management and continuous assurance, and it supports the systematic control operation expected in ISO/IEC 27001 (ISO, 2022).

Finally, Sustain requires a disciplined decision and escalation model. Not every operational issue should reach executive governance. Yet some issues must, such as repeated incidents, persistent critical vulnerabilities, unacceptable vendor performance, compliance failures, or major architectural risks. Sustain should define thresholds that trigger escalation to governance review boards. This keeps governance meaningful, focused on decisions and trends rather than on noise. It also preserves accountability, because when thresholds are explicit, teams cannot hide chronic problems behind optimistic updates.

Continuous Monitoring and Detection as Core Defense

Monitoring in Sustain is not a dashboard collection. It is a detection and response capability. A secure system is not one that never fails. It is one that fails in observable ways, where detection is fast, containment is possible, and learning is systematic. CSF 2.0 frames cybersecurity outcomes as managed and monitored, emphasizing the need to maintain visibility and oversight into security posture and risk (NIST, 2024b). Sustain implements that expectation through continuous monitoring practices.

Continuous monitoring begins with telemetry integrity. Logs must flow reliably. They must include security-relevant context. They must be protected from tampering. They must be retained according to policy and regulatory requirements. If log pipelines break, the system becomes blind. Blind systems are not defendable systems. Sustain should therefore treat logging health as a first-order operational metric, not as a background concern. It should include periodic validation that logs are present, complete, and accessible to responders, and it should include alerting when telemetry degrades.

Alerting must also be tuned. Many organizations suffer from alert fatigue. When alert fatigue sets in, teams ignore alerts, and attackers benefit from the noise. Sustain should include a deliberate alert management practice that categorizes alerts by severity, defines response expectations, and periodically reviews alert quality. High-severity alerts should be rare and meaningful. Medium alerts should be actionable with clear triage paths. Low alerts may be aggregated for trend analysis. Alert governance is not glamorous, yet it is one of the most powerful Sustain controls because it determines whether the organization can respond when risk emerges.

Detection in Sustain should include both security and reliability signals. Security signals include repeated authentication failures, anomalous privilege use, unusual data exports, unusual administrative actions, suspicious API usage patterns, and changes in access or configuration that were not approved. Reliability signals include error rate spikes, latency increases, dependency failures, and resource saturation. The boundary between reliability and security often disappears in production. A stability failure can become a security failure when teams bypass controls during outages. Sustained monitoring that integrates both domains is therefore essential.

Incident response integration is the next step. Sustain should ensure that alerts trigger an incident workflow when thresholds are met. This workflow includes triage, containment, communication, and remediation. It includes evidence preservation for investigations. It includes escalation to leadership when impact thresholds are met. ISO/IEC 27001 expects that organizations define and maintain incident management processes as part of systematic security operations (ISO, 2022). Sustain is where those processes must be practiced, not just documented.

A mature Sustain practice also includes detection coverage reviews. Over time, systems change. New features are deployed. New integrations are added. Vendors update platforms. If monitoring does not evolve, coverage gaps emerge. Sustain should therefore include a recurring review of monitoring coverage against architecture changes and risk changes. This keeps detection aligned to reality rather than to the original design.

If the system includes AI-enabled components, Sustain must also consider behavioral monitoring. AI features can drift, data distributions can shift, and model outputs can change as inputs change. Even when the organization does not retrain models frequently, behavior can change due to upstream data changes or vendor updates. Sustain should therefore include monitoring of AI-specific operational indicators such as output error rates, policy violations, data quality indicators, and abuse patterns. This does not replace the deeper AI governance overlay in Part ω, yet it ensures that AI-related operational risks do not remain invisible in production. This aligns with the broader governance expectation that emerging technology risks must be continuously observed and managed rather than assumed stable.

Maintenance, vulnerability management, and controlled change

Maintenance is the backbone of Sustain. Patching, vulnerability remediation, configuration management, and controlled change are what keep systems from decaying into risk. The most dangerous pattern in Sustain is maintenance debt, where patching slips and vulnerabilities accumulate because operational work is undervalued compared to new features. Sustain must treat maintenance as a value activity because maintenance preserves trust, uptime, and compliance.

Vulnerability management in Sustain starts with clarity. What assets are in scope. How are vulnerabilities discovered. How are they

prioritized. How quickly must critical vulnerabilities be remediated. Who owns remediation. How are exceptions managed. These are governance decisions because they define risk appetite in operational terms. Secure software development guidance emphasizes vulnerability response as a core lifecycle activity, meaning vulnerability handling must continue after release and must be integrated into normal operations (Souppaya et al., 2022). Sustain operationalizes that by creating a repeatable vulnerability workflow, including triage, remediation, verification, and closure.

Remediation should be risk-tiered and time-bound. Critical vulnerabilities should have short remediation windows and should trigger escalation if remediation is delayed. High vulnerabilities should also be time-bound with clear owners. Medium vulnerabilities may be scheduled, but should not disappear. Low vulnerabilities may be addressed opportunistically, yet they should still be tracked. This discipline prevents the slow accumulation of exposure.

Exception handling remains important in Sustain. Sometimes remediation is not immediate due to vendor constraints, compatibility issues, or operational risk of patching. Exceptions can be legitimate, yet they must never become permanent. Exceptions must have expiration dates, mitigation steps, monitoring requirements, and explicit approval authority. They must be reviewed periodically. This keeps risk acceptance visible and accountable, consistent with governance principles and CSF 2.0's emphasis on risk-informed decisions and accountability (ISO, 2015; NIST, 2024b).

Configuration management is another sustainment control often overlooked. Configuration drift is a common root cause of security exposure, especially in cloud environments and vendor platforms. Sustain should treat configuration baselines as controlled artifacts. Changes to critical configurations should require approvals, should be recorded, and should be validated. Infrastructure as code helps, yet drift can still occur through manual changes and vendor updates.

Sustain should therefore include periodic configuration compliance checks and reconciliation routines.

Change control is not about slowing change. It is about controlling it. Sustain should define change categories, such as standard changes, normal changes, and emergency changes. Emergency changes will happen during incidents and outages. The question is whether emergency changes are documented and reviewed afterward. Post-incident review should confirm that emergency changes did not create new exposure. IT service management principles emphasize structured change and incident practices to preserve stability and enable continual improvement (Axelos, 2019). Sustain benefits from this discipline because it reduces the chance that operational pressure will produce uncontrolled risk.

Release management should also exist in Sustain. Even small changes can break systems. Sustain should define release cadences, testing expectations, and rollback procedures. Rollback capability remains important beyond implementation. Many organizations discover too late that rollback only existed during go live, and after that it became too complex. Sustain should maintain rollback readiness, at least for critical components.

Vendor management is part of maintenance when vendor solutions are involved. Vendor platforms update regularly, sometimes with security implications and behavior changes. Sustain should include routines for reviewing vendor advisories, reviewing vendor release notes, and assessing whether vendor changes require customer configuration changes or new monitoring. Vendor governance should not disappear after contract signature. It should become a continuous relationship with accountability, evidence, and escalation paths, consistent with supplier relationship controls orientation in ISO/IEC 27001 (ISO, 2022).

Continuous Assurance, Compliance, and Audit Readiness

Assurance in Sustain is about proving that controls continue to work, not merely believing they do. Many organizations treat audit preparation as a periodic scramble. A mature Sustain practice treats audit readiness as continuous. This reduces disruption and increases confidence. It also supports the idea of evidence bundles across gates, because evidence should not stop being collected after the final implementation gate. In Sustain, evidence becomes operational evidence rather than project evidence, yet it serves the same purpose, to support governance decisions and external accountability.

Assurance begins with control testing routines. These routines can include periodic access reviews, privileged access reviews, logging and monitoring validation, backup restoration tests, and configuration compliance checks. The frequency should be risk-tiered. Critical systems require more frequent assurance. Lower-risk systems require lighter assurance. The goal is proportionality without negligence.

Access governance is a core sustainment control. Over time, users change roles, teams reorganize, vendors rotate staff, and service accounts proliferate. Sustain should include periodic reviews of user access, privileged access, and service account access. It should also include reviews of administrative actions and emergency access usage. Access governance supports accountability and reduces insider and misuse risk. It also supports audit readiness because access controls are central in many compliance contexts (ISO, 2022).

Evidence retention and evidence quality are often underestimated. Sustain should define what evidence must be retained, where it is stored, and how it can be retrieved. This includes change records, incident records, vulnerability remediation records, access review records, and vendor assurance updates. Evidence must be retrievable quickly when needed, especially during audits and investigations. ISO/IEC 27001's systematic approach implies that organizations can demonstrate control operation, which requires reliable evidence management (ISO, 2022).

Assurance also includes measuring and reporting. Sustain should produce meaningful metrics that reflect security and operational posture. Metrics can include patch compliance rates, vulnerability backlog age, mean time to detect and respond, incident counts and severity trends, change failure rates, uptime and performance metrics, and alert quality metrics. Metrics should be used for decisions, not for decoration. When metrics are used for decisions, they improve behavior. When metrics are used for optics, they become manipulated and untrustworthy.

Continuous Improvement, Resilience, and Learning Discipline

Sustain is where improvement becomes either a habit or a myth. Organizations often hold post-incident reviews, yet fail to implement improvements. Sustain must create a closed learning loop where incidents and near misses become inputs to system improvements, process improvements, and training improvements. This is how resilience grows over time.

Problem management is one improvement mechanism. When incidents recur, the organization should treat recurrence as a signal of systemic weakness rather than as bad luck. Root cause analysis should focus on contributing factors such as missing monitoring, weak configuration discipline, unclear ownership, or untested recovery procedures. The outcome should be concrete improvements with owners and deadlines. This aligns with IT service management principles that emphasize continual improvement and learning from incidents to reduce future impact (Axelos, 2019).

Technical debt management is another improvement mechanism. Many security and operational risks are technical debt in disguise. Outdated libraries, brittle integrations, hard-coded configurations, and manual operational steps create risk. Sustain should maintain a technical debt register and integrate it into governance routines. Technical debt should be prioritized based on risk and operational burden, not only based on convenience. This helps prevent the long-term decay that makes systems expensive and unsafe.

Automation is a practical improvement lever in Sustain. Automation can reduce human error, improve consistency, and shorten response time. Automation can include automated patching for certain components, automated configuration compliance checks, automated log validation, automated access review workflows, and automated evidence packaging for audits. Automation should be governed, because poorly designed automation can amplify mistakes. Yet when designed well, it becomes a resilience multiplier. Secure lifecycle guidance supports the idea that repeatable, verifiable practices reduce risk and increase consistency, which is often enabled by automation (Souppaya et al., 2022).

Resilience improvements should also be deliberate. Sustain should assess whether single points of failure exist, whether backup restoration procedures are feasible, whether disaster recovery readiness meets business needs, and whether vendor dependencies are manageable. Resilience is not only about hardware. It is about people, process, and decision clarity during stress. Sustain should therefore include periodic continuity tests appropriate to the system's criticality.

If AI-enabled capabilities exist, improvement includes monitoring and adjusting guardrails. Prompt patterns evolve. Abuse patterns evolve. Policy configurations may need tuning. Output evaluation may require periodic review. Sustain should treat AI-related guardrails as living controls, not as fixed settings. Even when AI governance is handled more deeply in the AI overlay chapters, operational improvement still matters because AI systems can drift and degrade quietly.

Preparing for Gate 5, Sustainment and Continuous Assurance

Sustain does not mean endless operations without review. It includes formal governance checkpoints. Gate 5 exists to evaluate sustainment governance, operational effectiveness, and continuous assurance readiness. Chapter 20 will define the gate decision mechanics, yet in Chapter 19 the Sustain phase should already set up the evidence and routines needed for that review.

Preparing for Gate 5 means establishing a sustainment evidence bundle that includes operational metrics trends, incident and problem summaries, vulnerability and patch compliance trends, access review evidence, monitoring health evidence, vendor assurance updates, and continuous improvement outcomes. It also means demonstrating that the system is being managed as a service with clear ownership and disciplined change control. In other words, Sustain prepares an operational proof package that shows the organization is not merely keeping the lights on, it is governing the system responsibly.

This preparation reinforces the ADDIS concept of evidence bundles across gates. Gates are not paperwork. They are structured decision moments supported by evidence. Sustain makes sure evidence collection and accountability do not stop after project completion. It also makes sure the organization can demonstrate continuous governance, which is central to both IT governance and cybersecurity governance expectations (ISO, 2015; NIST, 2024b).

Key Takeaways

The Sustain phase is where secure delivery becomes durable. It transforms a successfully implemented system into a governable service that can withstand threats, changes, and operational stress. Sustain maintains continuous monitoring and detection capability so the organization can see what is happening and respond quickly. It maintains maintenance discipline through patching, vulnerability remediation, configuration governance, and controlled change. It maintains assurance and audit readiness by testing controls, managing evidence, and measuring outcomes. It builds resilience and improvement through learning loops, technical debt reduction, and automation. It also maintains vendor governance and shared responsibility boundaries so third-party dependencies remain managed rather than assumed. This work aligns with ISO/IEC 27001's expectation of systematic control operation and continual improvement (ISO, 2022), with IT governance principles that emphasize accountability and oversight (ISO, 2015), and with CSF 2.0's governance-centered framing of cybersecurity as a continuously managed enterprise outcome (NIST, 2024b). By the time the organization reaches Gate 5, sustainment should not be a story told in slides. It should be a reality proven through evidence, metrics, and accountable routines.

"Security that cannot be sustained is security that never existed."

Gate 5: Sustain Review

Gate 5 is the moment the organization proves it can govern a system beyond the project lifecycle. Earlier gates protected the enterprise from building the wrong thing, building it insecurely, or deploying it without evidence. Gate 5 protects the enterprise from the slow decay that turns a successful implementation into a long-term exposure. It is the governance decision that confirms operational ownership is real, continuous monitoring is effective, maintenance discipline is sustained, assurance evidence is credible, and improvement is not optional. Gate 5 is therefore not a ceremonial wrap-up. It is the formal verification that the system has transitioned from "delivered" to "managed," and that the organization can maintain digital trust through ongoing accountability and continuous assurance (NIST, 2024b).

In many organizations, security and quality are strongest during projects because attention is concentrated and funding is visible. After go live, attention disperses. Budget shifts. Teams rotate. Vendors release updates. New priorities push the system into maintenance mode, and maintenance mode quietly becomes neglect mode. That is where risk grows. Logs break. Patches slip. Access reviews become a checkbox. Exceptions become permanent. The system keeps running, yet it becomes less governable every month. Gate 5 exists to prevent this pattern by requiring evidence that sustainment governance is functioning and that the organization is operating controls as a living system, consistent with the expectations of an information security management system approach (ISO, 2022).

Gate 5 also formalizes the enterprise concept of continuous assurance. Assurance is not only an audit activity. It is an operational capability that proves controls remain effective and that risk decisions remain visible and accountable. Continuous assurance uses metrics, evidence retention, periodic control testing, and governance routines to maintain defensible posture. This aligns with CSF 2.0's emphasis on governance and the continuous management of cybersecurity outcomes, where organizations are expected to maintain oversight, accountability, and monitoring rather than treating cybersecurity as a one-time project deliverable (NIST, 2024b). Gate 5 is where the organization demonstrates that this philosophy is not a statement of intent, but a practiced routine.

A useful way to see Gate 5 is as a health check on the operating model. Gate 4 approved production readiness and handover. Gate 5 confirms that the operating model is stable and repeatable. It validates that operational responsibilities are owned, that controls are functioning, that evidence is being produced and retained, and that improvements are being implemented. It also validates that the system has been integrated into enterprise governance routines, including change governance, incident governance, vendor governance, and compliance oversight. Gate 5 is therefore the capstone gate for the ADDIS lifecycle, but it is also the doorway into long-term governance.

What Gate 5 decides and why it matters

Gate 5 answers a practical question with strategic implications. Is the system being operated in a way that preserves security, resilience, compliance, and business value over time. This question is more subtle than earlier gate questions because sustainment issues often hide behind normal operations. A system can meet uptime targets and still have weak monitoring. It can meet performance targets and still have uncontrolled privileged access. It can have few incidents and still have a growing vulnerability backlog. Gate 5 looks beneath surface performance and examines whether the governance mechanisms that protect digital trust are functioning.

Gate 5 is also where leadership confirms accountability is not diluted. A project has a natural accountability structure. It has a sponsor, a project manager, and a delivery team with defined milestones. Sustainment does not have that natural structure unless it is intentionally designed. Gate 5 verifies that sustainment accountability exists through named owners, clear escalation thresholds, and governance routines. This aligns with IT governance principles that emphasize responsibility and oversight for the use of technology, ensuring that IT continues to support business objectives while risks are managed (ISO, 2015).

The outcomes of Gate 5 are similar to other gates: Go, Conditional Go, Hold, or No-Go. Yet the meaning of these outcomes is slightly different. Go means sustainment governance is functioning and continuous assurance is credible. Conditional Go means sustainment governance is functioning but requires specific improvements within defined time windows, often related to alert hygiene, patch compliance, access reviews, or evidence management. Hold means sustainment governance is not functioning sufficiently, and corrective actions must be implemented before the system can be considered sustainably governed. No-Go is rare but necessary when the system's sustainment posture is unacceptable, such as when monitoring is absent, privileged access is uncontrolled, or compliance failures are persistent. In extreme cases, No-Go can trigger re-implementation, platform replacement, or operational restructuring.

Gate 5 is also a forcing function for maturity. Some organizations treat sustainment as a cost center and improve only after incidents. Gate 5 is the counterweight. It demands proactive improvement based on evidence and trends, not only based on crisis. This is how organizations prevent minor cracks from becoming structural failures.

Gate 5, Operational Governance and Continuous Assurance

Gate 5 should be evaluated across a small set of pillars to prevent it from becoming unfocused. The pillars should reflect what makes a system governable over time. A practical set of pillars includes operational ownership and service governance, continuous monitoring and response readiness, maintenance and vulnerability discipline, access governance and privileged control, assurance and audit readiness, vendor governance where applicable, and continual improvement.

Operational ownership and service governance means the system has clear owners and defined service expectations. Owners include a service owner, a technical owner, a security monitoring owner, and a change owner. Service expectations include availability targets, performance baselines, and support expectations. Gate 5 validates that these owners are active, not nominal. It verifies that they attend governance reviews, manage backlogs, and respond to issues. This pillar matters because accountability drives behavior. Without ownership, sustainment becomes reactive and fragmented.

Continuous monitoring and response readiness means the system is observable and defendable. It includes confirmation that logging pipelines are healthy, that alerts are meaningful, that the on-call and escalation model is functioning, and that incident response integration is operational. It also includes confirmation that monitoring coverage evolves with system changes. This pillar reflects the reality that detection is not a static setup. It must be maintained and tuned. CSF 2.0 emphasizes the need for continuous monitoring and governance structures that support cybersecurity outcomes, which makes monitoring readiness a core Gate 5 concern (NIST, 2024b).

Maintenance and vulnerability discipline means patching and remediation workflows are consistent and time-bound. It includes vulnerability discovery, triage, remediation, verification, and closure. It includes exception handling discipline with expiration dates and compensating controls. It includes configuration drift management. Secure software lifecycle guidance emphasizes that vulnerability response and secure maintenance must continue beyond release, which supports treating maintenance discipline as a long-term governance obligation (Souppaya et al., 2022).

Access governance and privileged control means access reviews occur, privileged access is controlled and audited, service accounts are managed, and emergency access is governed. Access governance is one of the highest-return sustainment controls because it reduces both insider risk and misuse risk. It also supports audit readiness and accountability.

Assurance and audit readiness means evidence is retained, control testing occurs periodically, and compliance obligations are tracked and met. ISO/IEC 27001's systematic approach expects ongoing monitoring, internal audits, and continual improvement, meaning assurance is not episodic but integrated into operations (ISO, 2022). Gate 5 therefore validates that assurance routines exist, such as access review evidence, backup restore tests, monitoring health checks, and audit evidence packaging.

Vendor governance, when vendors are involved, means vendor performance is monitored, vendor advisories are reviewed, contract obligations are tracked, shared responsibility controls remain configured, and exit readiness is not forgotten. Vendor risk is not eliminated by buying a platform. It is managed through continuous governance.

Continual improvement means the organization learns from incidents, reduces technical debt, improves automation, and invests in resilience. Gate 5 verifies that improvement is not rhetorical. It verifies that improvements are tracked, owned, and delivered, and that recurring issues trigger deeper fixes rather than repeated firefighting.

Evidence bundle design for Gate 5

Gate 5 must be evidence-first. Yet evidence should be organized and decision-grade. The objective is not to overwhelm reviewers. It is to prove sustainment governance is functioning. A strong Gate 5 evidence bundle includes a sustainment governance narrative, operational metrics trends, incident and problem summaries, vulnerability and patch compliance trends, access review evidence, monitoring health evidence, change governance metrics, vendor governance evidence where applicable, and assurance artifacts such as audit logs and control testing results.

The sustainment governance narrative should state how the system is being operated, what the service model is, what has changed since Gate 4, what incidents occurred and what was learned, and what improvements are underway. It should also state the current risk posture and whether any exceptions exist, including their status and expiration. This narrative should be concise and should point to evidence sections.

Operational metrics trends should include availability, performance, error rates, and capacity signals where relevant. Trends matter more than snapshots. A snapshot can be manipulated by timing. Trends show whether the system is improving or decaying. Incident and problem summaries should include incident counts, severity, mean time to detect and respond, and recurring causes. They should also include evidence of post-incident reviews and improvement actions.

Vulnerability and patch compliance trends should show the vulnerability backlog by severity, age of unresolved vulnerabilities, patch compliance rates, and exception inventory. Gate 5 should focus on critical and high vulnerabilities and on the discipline of remediation rather than on raw counts. Raw counts can mislead. Discipline does not.

Access review evidence should include periodic user access reviews, privileged access reviews, and service account reviews. It should show that access is removed when no longer needed and that privileged access is monitored. Monitoring health evidence should include log pipeline health, alert tuning outcomes, and proof that alert routing works. Change governance evidence should include release cadence, change failure rate, rollback frequency, and change approval traceability. These metrics support operational governance by showing whether changes are controlled and safe.

Vendor governance evidence should include vendor advisories review routine, vendor performance metrics, SLA adherence, and any vendor incidents or major changes. It should also include evidence that shared responsibility controls remain configured, especially identity integration, logging export, and administrative boundaries.

Assurance artifacts should include evidence of periodic control testing such as backup restoration tests, monitoring validation tests, and configuration compliance checks. It should also include audit readiness artifacts that show evidence can be retrieved and that compliance obligations are monitored. This supports ISO/IEC 27001's emphasis on ongoing auditing and continual improvement (ISO, 2022).

Quality review before Gate 5, keeping governance honest

As with other gates, Gate 5 should not begin with a governance forum meeting. It should begin with a quality review that validates the evidence bundle is complete and coherent. Quality review checks whether metrics are credible, whether trends are supported by data, whether incident reviews exist, whether remediation actions are tracked, and whether evidence is retrievable. It also checks whether exceptions are truly time-bound and whether the organization is meeting its own sustainment standards.

Quality review also evaluates whether the sustainment operating model is functioning. Do named owners exist. Are on-call rotations staffed. Are governance meetings occurring. Are changes controlled. Are access reviews completed. These are structural indicators. When structural indicators are weak, outcomes degrade eventually. Quality review should surface these weaknesses before the gate forum is asked to make a decision.

Gate 5 Readiness Pack

This Gate 5 Readiness Pack summarizes Sustain Phase governance and presents the evidence required for a Gate 5 decision. It is organized for fast review using a one-page cover sheet, an evidence bundle index, and decision rules that define minimum pass criteria and automatic hold triggers. The intent is to confirm that operational governance is active, continuous monitoring and maintenance are functioning, and assurance evidence is retrievable. Gate 5 confirms the system is being operated as a managed service, not simply kept running.

A. Readiness workstreams

1. Sustainment ownership and service governance
   Confirm sustainment ownership and service governance is active. Validate named service owners, technical owners, security monitoring owners, and change owners. Confirm governance cadence and escalation thresholds are defined and functioning (ISO, 2015).
2. Continuous monitoring and response readiness
   Validate continuous monitoring and response readiness. Confirm log pipeline health, alert routing functionality, on-call readiness, and incident triage capability. Document monitoring coverage updates and gaps (NIST, 2024b).
3. Maintenance and vulnerability discipline
   Demonstrate maintenance and vulnerability discipline. Provide evidence of vulnerability triage, remediation timelines, patch compliance, verification practices, and exception governance with expirations (Souppaya et al., 2022).
4. Access governance and privileged control
   Demonstrate access governance and privileged control. Complete periodic user access reviews, privileged access

reviews, and service account reviews. Document removals, corrections, and auditability.

5. Change and configuration governance
   Validate change and configuration governance. Confirm release management, change approval traceability, rollback discipline, and configuration drift detection and remediation.
6. Assurance routines and audit readiness
   Demonstrate assurance routines and audit readiness. Execute periodic control tests such as monitoring validation, backup restore tests, and configuration compliance checks. Confirm evidence is retrievable and stored in a consistent location (ISO, 2022).
7. Vendor governance where applicable
   Validate vendor governance where applicable. Confirm vendor advisory review routine, SLA monitoring, shared responsibility control configuration, and escalation paths.
8. Continuous improvement execution
   Document continuous improvement execution. Present completed improvement actions from incidents and problems, technical debt reduction steps, automation improvements, and resilience enhancements.
9. Sustainment risk posture reconciliation
   Update and reconcile the sustainment risk posture. Refresh the risk register and exception inventory, confirm owners, and ensure mitigation and monitoring plans exist for residual risks.
10. Gate 5 evidence bundle packaging
    Prepare the Gate 5 sustainment evidence bundle. Package metrics, evidence, findings, and governance outputs into a coherent decision-grade bundle.

B. Gate 5 evidence bundle index

1. Gate 5 Sustainment Governance Narrative
   Summary of how the system is governed in operations, what changed, key risks, and the requested decision outcome.
2. Operational Performance and Stability Trends
   Availability, latency, error rates, capacity indicators, and service health trend analysis.
3. Incident and Problem Management Summary
   Incident count and severity trends, response time trends, root cause themes, post-incident reviews, and prevention actions.
4. Monitoring and Detection Evidence
   Log pipeline health evidence, alert routing test evidence, alert tuning outcomes, dashboard coverage summary, and responder access proof (NIST, 2024b).
5. Vulnerability and Patch Compliance Evidence
   Vulnerability backlog by severity and age, remediation performance, patch compliance rates, verification evidence, and exception inventory with expirations (Souppaya et al., 2022).
6. Access Governance Evidence
   User access review records, privileged access review records, service account inventory and review, and audit logs supporting accountability (ISO, 2022).
7. Change and Configuration Governance Evidence
   Change approval traceability samples, change success and failure trends, rollback records, and configuration drift checks.
8. Assurance and Audit Readiness Artifacts
   Control testing evidence, internal audit outputs where applicable, evidence retention and retrieval proof, and compliance obligations status (ISO, 2022).
9. Vendor Governance Evidence
   Vendor performance and SLA tracking, advisory review records,

shared responsibility control verification, and escalation contact procedures.

10. Continuous Improvement Backlog and Completion Evidence
    Improvement roadmap, completed actions, technical debt highlights, and automation improvements.
11. Updated Risk Register and Exception Log
    Residual risks with owners and treatment status, approved exceptions with compensating controls, expiration dates, and verification plan (ISO, 2015).

C. Review flow

Quality Review Board (QRB) process

- Submission and intake: Operations and service owners submit the Gate 5 evidence bundle and sustainment narrative to the quality review function.
- Completeness and coherence check: Reviewers verify required evidence exists, aligns, and supports sustainment readiness claims.
- Monitoring and response validation: Reviewers confirm telemetry health, alert routing proof, on-call readiness evidence, and signal quality (NIST, 2024b).
- Maintenance and vulnerability validation: Reviewers confirm patch compliance discipline, remediation timelines, verification evidence, and exception governance integrity (Souppaya et al., 2022).
- Access and change governance validation: Reviewers confirm access review completion, privileged access controls, change traceability, and configuration drift management (ISO, 2022).
- Assurance and evidence management validation: Reviewers confirm periodic control testing exists, evidence is retrievable, and compliance tracking is credible (ISO, 2022).

- Findings report: Reviewers document findings as critical, major, minor with owners, due dates, and verification method.
- QRB outcome: Ready for Gate scheduling, or not ready until critical gaps are resolved.

Gate Review Board (GRB) process

- Pre-read distribution: Evidence bundle and QRB findings report distributed to governance decision-makers and operational owners.
- Sustainment narrative: Operational leadership presents the sustainment model, metrics trends, risk posture, and improvement outcomes.
- Operational governance review: Gate body reviews service ownership, governance cadence, escalation model, and whether service expectations are being met.
- Continuous monitoring and response review: Gate body reviews telemetry health, alert quality, response readiness, and incident performance trends (NIST, 2024b).
- Maintenance and vulnerability review: Gate body reviews vulnerability backlog trends, patch compliance, exception discipline, and remediation performance.
- Assurance and audit readiness review: Gate body reviews control testing outputs, evidence retention and retrieval readiness, compliance status, and audit findings if applicable (ISO, 2022).
- Vendor governance review: Gate body reviews vendor performance and advisory handling, shared responsibility control verification, and vendor risk posture.
- Continuous improvement review: Gate body reviews improvement completion rate, technical debt actions, automation progress, and resilience enhancements.

- Decision outcome: Gate body issues Go, Conditional Go, Hold, or No-Go, recorded in a decision log, including conditions and owners if applicable.
- Condition management: If Conditional Go, conditions are documented with owners, deadlines, verification method, and consequences if unmet.

D. Decision rules

Outcomes

- Go: Sustainment governance is functioning, monitoring and maintenance discipline is credible, assurance evidence is retrievable, and continuous improvement is active.
- Conditional Go: Sustainment governance is functioning, but specific gaps remain. Conditions are narrow, owned, time-bound, and verifiable.
- Hold: Critical sustainment gaps exist. Corrective actions are required before Gate 5 can pass, especially for monitoring, access control, and critical vulnerability posture.
- No-Go: Sustainment posture is unacceptable. Governance is ineffective, and operational restructuring or major remediation is required to prevent ongoing exposure.

Minimum pass criteria

- Named owners and governance cadence exist and are active (ISO, 2015).
- Telemetry is healthy, alert routing works, and response capability is demonstrable (NIST, 2024b).
- Patch and vulnerability management shows consistent remediation performance and time-bound exceptions (Souppaya et al., 2022).

- Access governance reviews are completed. Privileged access is controlled and auditable (ISO, 2022).
- Change governance is traceable and configuration drift is managed.
- Assurance routines exist, evidence is retrievable, and compliance obligations are tracked (ISO, 2022).
- Vendor governance is active where applicable and shared responsibility controls remain configured.
- Improvement actions from incidents and problems are tracked and delivered.
- Risk register and exception log are current, owned, and governed.

Automatic Hold or No-Go triggers

- Non-functional monitoring and logging pipelines for a system requiring detection and response because the system cannot be defended (NIST, 2024b).
- Uncontrolled privileged access or inability to audit administrative actions because accountability cannot be enforced (ISO, 2015).
- Persistent unresolved critical vulnerabilities without time-bound, approved exceptions and compensating controls because risk is unmanaged.
- No active service owner or no viable on-call and escalation model because sustainment is not feasible.
- Evidence is not retrievable for audits or investigations, because continuous assurance is not credible (ISO, 2022).
- Vendor risk is unmanaged where vendors are critical dependencies, including lack of advisory review routine and unclear escalation paths.

Closing Summary

Gate 5 is the governance proof point that sustainment is real. It confirms that the organization can operate the solution as a service, not as a project that ended at go live. At this gate, leadership verifies that ownership is explicit and active, including service ownership, security monitoring ownership, change ownership, and vendor management where applicable. It also confirms that monitoring and response readiness are functioning in practice. Logs must be available and usable, alerts must route correctly, and responders must have the access, runbooks, and escalation paths needed to contain issues quickly.

Gate 5 validates maintenance discipline as a routine capability. Vulnerability management must show measurable performance, including triage speed, remediation timelines, exception handling with expirations, and verification of fixes. Patch and configuration compliance must be visible by criticality so leaders can see whether the system is drifting toward exposure. Access governance is also confirmed through periodic access reviews, privileged access controls, and auditability for administrative actions. Finally, the gate tests whether assurance is continuous. Control checks, backup and recovery tests, and compliance tracking must produce evidence that is retrievable for audits and investigations.

Gate 5 also confirms that learning is active. Post-incident lessons must be tracked, improvements must be delivered, and recurring issues must lead to design and process changes. This prevents the slow drift that turns early success into long-term liability and protects digital trust over time. These practices align with accountability and monitoring principles in IT governance (ISO, 2015), continual improvement expectations in ISO/IEC 27001 (ISO, 2022), and CSF 2.0's emphasis on ongoing governance and monitoring of cybersecurity outcomes (NIST, 2024b).

G5 Gate 5: Sustain Review

Continuous Assurance Decision

PURPOSE: Prove ***control effectiveness*** in operation and continuous *improvement* discipline.

Minimum evidence:

- **Operational governance cadence** (reviews, owners, metrics, escalation path)
- **Vulnerability management cycle evidence** (KPis, backlog, SLAs, exceptions)
- **Patch and configuration compliance evidence** (by criticality and tier)
- **Access review attestations** (privileged + critical roles, cadence, evidence)
- **Incident readiness evidence** (runbooks, exercises, lessons learned tracking)
- **Continuous monitoring evidence** (log coverage, alerts, response performance)
- **G5 Decision record** + improvement backlog governance.

Evidence Bundle → QRB check → GRB decision → *Owned actions*

w

AI GOVERNANCE OVERLAY

INTRODUCTION

If Part *ap* is the control spine of delivery, Part *w* is the nervous system that detects when the solution is behaving differently than planned, when risk has shifted, and when accountability must become sharper. Traditional technology projects already carry uncertainty, yet they tend to be uncertainty we can bound. We can usually define requirements, test for correctness, measure performance, and lock down configuration. AI disrupts that comfort. AI behaves less like a static tool and more like a dynamic participant in the system. It learns patterns, amplifies data realities, and sometimes produces outcomes that are technically valid yet operationally unsafe. That shift does not invalidate secure SDLC or Security by Design, it raises the bar. It forces project leaders to govern not only the build, but also the behavior, the data, the outputs, and the ongoing drift. The overlay in this part exists because the organization cannot "project-manage" AI risk into submission. It must govern it into defensibility, using the same evidence-based gate discipline you applied across ADDIS, now expanded for AI-specific hazards and obligations (NIST, 2023).

AI governance is often described as ethics, policy, or compliance. That is only a slice. In delivery terms, AI governance is operational control. It is the ability to prove that accountability is assigned, that risks are identified and treated, that model behavior is evaluated against agreed criteria, that security and privacy are protected across the AI lifecycle, and that change is controlled once the system is in production. The most expensive AI failures are rarely caused by a single bad decision. They are caused by a chain of small decisions, each made under time pressure, each made without sufficient evidence, and each assumed to be "someone else's responsibility." Part ω is designed to break that chain by making responsibilities explicit, by embedding AI controls into each gate, and by defining what evidence looks like when the system includes models, data pipelines, and probabilistic outputs.

A practical way to frame the AI overlay is to ask a blunt question: when the system makes a decision or produces an output, can you explain why, defend its safety, and show who is accountable. If the answer depends on guesswork or tribal knowledge, governance is weak. If the answer depends on logs, evaluation results, documented assumptions, and clear sign-offs, governance is becoming real. That is the standard the modern enterprise is moving toward, not only because regulators and auditors demand it, but because business leaders need it to protect trust. The OECD AI Principles

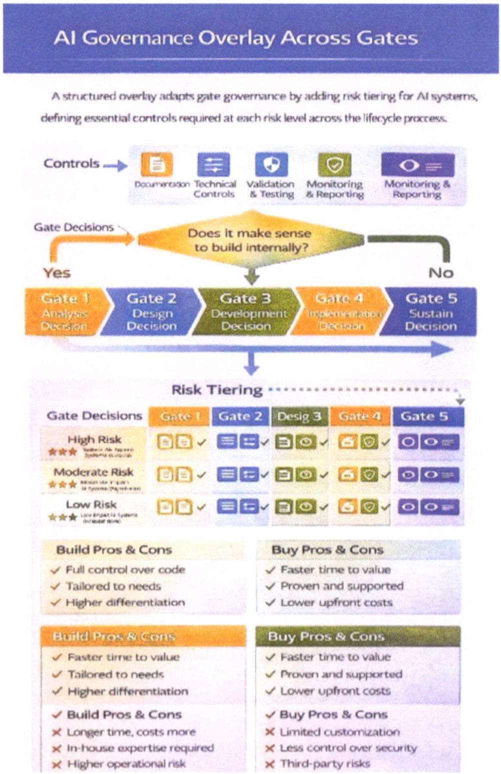

emphasize trustworthy AI and responsible stewardship, including respect for human rights, transparency, robustness, and accountability, which are not abstract ideals in project delivery, they translate into concrete controls and verifiable practices (OECD, 2019). The question is not whether you support these principles. The question is whether you can operationalize them under deadlines.

This overlay is especially necessary because AI changes the nature of "requirements." In traditional delivery, requirements define what the system must do. In AI-enabled delivery, requirements also define what the system must not do, what it must do consistently, and what it must do safely under edge cases. Those "must not" requirements are governance requirements. They include constraints such as avoiding exposure of sensitive data, avoiding discriminatory outcomes in high-impact decisions, resisting manipulation and prompt abuse in generative interfaces, maintaining model performance under data drift, and ensuring outputs can be traced to inputs and configurations. Each of those constraints has a security angle and a project governance angle. If you treat them as afterthoughts, the system may pass functional tests and still fail the enterprise.

AI also changes what "testing" means. Traditional testing checks correctness, integration, and performance. AI testing must also validate behavior under distribution shifts, adversarial inputs, biased data, and misuse. It must evaluate how the model performs across slices of data that matter for safety and fairness, and it must validate whether guardrails work when users behave creatively. In a project environment, the danger is that teams run a few benchmark tests, declare success, and move on. Governance requires deeper discipline. NIST's AI Risk Management Framework frames trustworthy AI through characteristics such as validity and reliability, safety, security and resilience, accountability and transparency, privacy, and fairness, and it emphasizes that risk management must be continuous and lifecycle-based, not a one-time hurdle (NIST, 2023). That lifecycle framing fits naturally with ADDIS. It is also the reason Part w is structured as an overlay rather than a separate "AI chapter" bolted onto the end.

Another reason Part w matters is regulatory gravity. The EU AI Act is now a comprehensive legal framework that classifies AI uses by risk and imposes requirements, especially for high-risk systems, including obligations related to risk management, documentation, transparency, human oversight, and post-market monitoring (European Union, 2024). Even if your organization is not headquartered in the EU, global supply chains and customer expectations are pulling governance upward. A vendor may demand AI assurance evidence. A bank may require model risk governance. A regulator may ask for traceability. Your board may ask the simplest question that is also the hardest: "Are we exposed?" AI governance becomes the language you use to answer that question responsibly.

The overlay also exists because the AI policy landscape is volatile. A program built around one set of expectations can change quickly as administrations shift priorities and as new guidance emerges. For example, the U.S. Executive Order 14110 that drove many federal AI safety efforts was rescinded in January 2025, illustrating how quickly the policy anchor can move (NIST, 2025). When policy anchors move, organizations that rely on ad hoc compliance panic. Organizations that rely on structured governance adapt. Part w is designed to help you build the structured governance muscle so you are not thrown off balance every time the environment changes.

What Sets AI Projects Apart

The most important difference is that AI systems are not only engineered, they are trained and tuned. Training introduces a dependency on data quality, data lineage, and labeling decisions. Tuning introduces a dependency on human feedback, prompt patterns, and evaluation choices. In other words, a portion of system behavior is produced through statistical learning rather than deterministic code.

That creates new failure modes. A bug is often reproducible. A model failure can be probabilistic, context-dependent, and sensitive to subtle changes. This makes evidence more important, not less.

A second difference is that AI introduces new assets that must be governed. Code is an asset. Data is an asset. Models are assets. Prompts and system instructions can become assets. Evaluation datasets become assets. Feature stores, vector databases, and embeddings become assets. Each asset can leak, be poisoned, be misconfigured, or be manipulated. Each asset also has lifecycle requirements, versioning, retention, and access control needs. When these assets are unmanaged, the system becomes hard to audit and hard to defend. ISO/IEC 42001 addresses this reality by framing AI governance as a management system with policies, objectives, lifecycle processes, and continual improvement, designed for organizations that develop, provide, or use AI systems (ISO, 2023a). Part ϖ uses this management-system mindset because it scales. It avoids heroics. It builds repeatability.

A third difference is that AI expands the threat landscape. Traditional systems face threats such as credential theft, injection attacks, misconfiguration, and data exfiltration. AI systems face all of those plus additional threats such as data poisoning, model inversion, prompt injection, training data extraction, and misuse at scale. Generative AI adds unique risks around harmful content generation, hallucinations that appear plausible, and leakage of sensitive information through conversational interfaces. NIST's Generative AI profile extends AI RMF thinking into these risks and provides actions organizations can use to manage generative AI risk in alignment with their goals and priorities (NIST, 2024b). That matters for project leaders because it turns "we should be careful" into "here is what we must verify."

A fourth difference is the accountability problem. In AI-enabled systems, decision-making can be distributed across a vendor model, a platform, your data pipeline, your prompt layer, and your application code. When something goes wrong, blame can bounce between teams. Governance prevents this by defining accountability up front. Who is the model owner. Who is the data steward. Who is responsible for evaluation. Who approves deployment. Who monitors drift. Who can roll back. This is why Part ω treats accountability as an engineering requirement, not an organizational preference.

To make this concrete, imagine a quick exchange in a project meeting.

- A product owner says, “The model is good enough, users love it.”
- A security lead asks, “Good enough for what risk tier, and what happens when someone tries to manipulate it?”
- A project manager adds, “What evidence do we need before Gate approval?”
- A governance chair concludes, “If we cannot answer with evidence, we are not ready.”

This is the posture Part ω institutionalizes. It converts vague optimism into measurable readiness.

How Part ω integrates with ADDIS gates

Part ω is not a standalone “AI compliance” section. It is an overlay that plugs into the same gate logic you used in Parts III and IV. The central move is simple: every gate has an AI extension. If the solution includes AI, each gate must evaluate AI-specific risks and AI-specific evidence. If the solution does not include AI, the extension collapses gracefully and the gates remain as-is. This design keeps your governance model consistent and prevents AI from becoming a special-case loophole.

In the Analyze phase, the AI overlay forces clarity about whether AI is actually needed, what impact domain you are in, what data you will rely on, and what harm scenarios must be controlled. It also forces early risk tiering. The EU AI Act's risk-based approach is a good conceptual example of why early classification matters, because obligations intensify for higher-risk AI use cases (European Union, 2024). Even outside the EU context, risk tiering helps allocate the right level of evaluation, oversight, and assurance.

In the Design phase, the AI overlay turns architecture into accountable design. It requires explicit choices about model sourcing, data governance, evaluation design, guardrails, human oversight, and logging. It also requires defining what "acceptable performance" means, including accuracy thresholds, reliability expectations, safety constraints, and fairness criteria where relevant. This is where AI begins to resemble safety engineering. You are not only designing features, you are designing constraints.

In the Develop or Acquire phase, the overlay requires build-track evidence such as training data lineage, model versioning, evaluation reports, security testing specific to AI components, and guardrail validation. On the buy track, it requires shared responsibility clarity, vendor documentation, model and data assurances, and configuration evidence for customer-controlled controls. The goal is not to demand perfection from vendors. The goal is to avoid blind trust.

In the Implement phase, the overlay extends production readiness. It requires validation that monitoring covers AI signals, that guardrails function in production context, and that drift and abuse monitoring are in place. It also requires rollback paths, because model behavior may degrade after deployment even when the code does not change.

In the Sustain phase, the overlay becomes continuous assurance. It requires periodic evaluation, drift monitoring, incident handling for AI failures, and governance routines that revisit risk tiering and control effectiveness. This fits naturally with ISO management system thinking and with ISO/IEC 23894 guidance on integrating AI risk management into organizational processes and functions (ISO, 2023b). Sustain is where the organization proves it can maintain AI controls, not only design them.

Across all phases, the concept of the evidence bundle remains central. You are not building documents for their own sake. You are building proof. Proof that the system is trustworthy in the ways that matter, and that decisions were made responsibly with accountable sign-offs. This is consistent with AI RMF's framing that risk management should be practical, flexible, and continuous, supporting both innovation and trustworthiness (NIST, 2023).

The governance outcomes Part 𝓌

Part 𝓌 is designed to produce a small set of outcomes that matter across industries.

First, it produces accountability that holds under stress. When an incident happens, the organization should not debate who owns the problem. Ownership should be explicit. Responsibilities should be documented. Escalation should be clear.

Second, it produces traceability that survives scrutiny. If a regulator, auditor, or board asks why a model behaved a certain way, the organization should be able to show model version, training data sources, evaluation results, configuration settings, and change history. This is not about explaining every parameter. It is about providing a defensible chain of evidence.

Third, it produces risk-tiered rigor. Not every AI use case requires the same level of governance. A chatbot that answers public marketing questions is different from an AI system that influences credit decisions, employment screening, medical prioritization, or identity verification. A mature governance model scales effort to risk. It does not treat every model as a crisis, and it does not treat high-impact AI as a toy. The risk-based orientation in the EU AI Act reflects this scaling logic, even if your organization applies it through internal policy rather than through EU legal obligation (European Union, 2024).

Fourth, it produces security by design for AI assets. It ensures that data, models, evaluation artifacts, and prompt layers are protected through access control, logging, and secure configuration. It also ensures that AI-specific threats are considered and tested, rather than assumed away.

Fifth, it produces continuous assurance, meaning the organization maintains confidence in AI behavior over time. Drift happens. Threats evolve. Vendors update platforms. The only sustainable answer is continuous monitoring, periodic evaluation, and governance routines that adapt. AI RMF emphasizes ongoing management and the need to incorporate trustworthiness considerations throughout design, development, deployment, and use (NIST, 2023). ISO/IEC 42001 reinforces continual improvement as a management system expectation for AI governance (ISO, 2023a). Those are not academic statements. They are sustainment realities.

How to use Part 𝓌 during delivery

Part 𝓌 is structured for project leaders, product leaders, PMOs, security leaders, and governance boards. It assumes you already understand the ADDIS spine and the gate mechanics from earlier parts of the book. It then adds the AI overlay in a way that can be executed under real delivery pressure.

Chapter 21 focuses on AI governance for project leaders. It addresses accountability, risk tiering, and oversight structures. It will help you establish who owns what, how oversight should be designed, and how to scale governance based on risk. It treats governance as part of delivery, not as an external compliance layer.

Chapter 22 focuses on AI system lifecycle delivery controls, with emphasis on data governance, model risk, evaluation, and monitoring. This chapter turns AI risk into concrete lifecycle controls. It builds bridges between secure SDLC, data governance, and model evaluation practices. It also addresses how to manage the "model supply chain," meaning the dependencies and assurances involved when you acquire models, use APIs, or adopt vendor platforms.

Chapter 23 focuses on AI assurance, metrics, evidence, and audit readiness across the gates. This chapter is the proof chapter. It defines what evidence looks like in each phase, how to measure readiness, and how to package proof in a way that governance boards can evaluate quickly. It also defines how to prepare for audits and regulatory questions without drowning the project in documentation.

There is also a deeper philosophy embedded here. AI governance is not about stopping innovation. It is about enabling innovation without gambling the enterprise. When governance is strong, teams move faster because they spend less time debating what is acceptable and more time executing toward clear criteria. When governance is weak, teams move fast until they hit the wall, and then they move slowly while they investigate, remediate, and rebuild trust. This part is designed to keep you on the first path.

In the next chapter, we begin with the leadership layer. We define risk tiering for AI use cases, clarify accountability roles, and establish oversight structures that match the risk. That is where AI governance becomes a delivery system rather than a policy statement.

AI Governance and Oversight

AI changes the way project leaders carry responsibility. In a traditional technology project, success is often defined by delivering scope on time, within budget, and with acceptable quality. Security by Design expands that definition by insisting that confidentiality, integrity, availability, and resilience are non-negotiable outcomes, validated through evidence across the SDLC. AI adds another layer: behavior that can shift under real-world conditions, decisions that may be difficult to explain in plain language, and risks that can scale faster than your change-control calendar. When AI is part of the solution, project leadership becomes less like managing a construction site and more like managing a living system, where governance is the fence, the alarm system, and the operating manual combined. NIST's AI Risk Management Framework frames this reality clearly, AI risk must be managed across the lifecycle, with accountability, transparency, safety, security, and resilience treated as properties to be continuously improved rather than declared once and forgotten (NIST, 2023).

Many organizations treat AI governance as an "ethics initiative" parked somewhere near legal or compliance. That approach underestimates delivery reality. AI governance is not merely about what is acceptable, it is about what is controllable. It is the discipline of ensuring that the organization can consistently answer five questions with evidence. Who is accountable. What risks are being managed. What controls are in place. What monitoring is running in production. What happens when the system behaves badly. These questions align naturally with management-system thinking, which is why ISO/IEC 42001 positions AI governance as a management system with policies, objectives, lifecycle processes, and continual improvement (ISO, 2023a).

Project leaders sit at the center of this. They are the translators between aspiration and execution. They turn board-level intent into delivery constraints. They turn security requirements into acceptance criteria. They turn "responsible AI" into concrete tasks, owners, timelines, and evidence. If they do not do this translation early, the organization pays later, usually at the worst time, when the product is almost ready, when budgets are tight, and when reputational risk is highest.

A simple conversation illustrates the problem. The product lead says, "Users love the AI assistant, can we launch next month?" The security lead replies, "What is our plan for prompt injection, data leakage, and abuse at scale?" Legal asks, "Are we in a regulated use case, and what documentation can we produce if challenged?" The project manager looks at the plan and realizes none of these questions have owners or deliverables. That is the moment where governance either becomes a late-stage blockage or becomes a structured path forward. This chapter is about choosing the structured path.

Accountability That Works When It Matters

Accountability in AI projects fails in predictable ways. First, responsibility is assigned without authority. Someone is told they "own model risk," yet they cannot access the evaluation data, cannot influence vendor configuration, and cannot stop the release. Second, responsibility is spread so widely that nobody feels it. Many people are "involved," yet no one is accountable for outcomes. Third, responsibility is assigned too late, after technical decisions have locked in risk. A strong AI governance overlay prevents these failures by making accountability explicit, role-based, and tied to gate approvals.

Project leaders should start with a named accountable executive for the AI-enabled outcome, not only for the project. This is typically the business sponsor, product executive, or service owner. Their accountability is not to tune parameters, it is to accept and fund the controls required for trust. Under IT governance principles, governing bodies evaluate, direct, and monitor the use of technology, and accountability must sit with leaders who can make tradeoffs visible and enforceable.

Next, define the "AI accountable owner," a role that is distinct from a project manager and distinct from a data scientist. This owner is accountable for the AI system's behavior in production, including risk tiering decisions, evaluation sign-off, monitoring expectations, and post-deployment reassessment. In smaller organizations, this may be the product owner or engineering owner. In larger organizations, it may be an AI product owner working alongside model risk and security leadership. The key is that this owner can say "no" when evidence is insufficient, and can require remediation before gate approval.

Then define the supporting owners that make accountability executable. At minimum, most AI-enabled projects require a data owner or steward accountable for data sourcing, quality, lineage, and access controls, a model owner accountable for model selection, training or tuning decisions, and version control, a security owner accountable for threat modeling and security controls across the AI pipeline, and a compliance or risk owner accountable for regulatory alignment, documentation completeness, and assurance readiness. ISO/IEC 23894 emphasizes integrating AI risk management into organizational functions and activities, which in practice means these owners must be integrated into delivery, not consulted at the end.

One practical way to make this real is to build an "AI accountability map" as part of your project charter. The map should not be an abstract org chart. It should link roles to decisions. Who approves the risk tier. Who approves training data sources. Who approves model selection. Who approves evaluation thresholds. Who approves deployment. Who approves changes after deployment. Who can trigger rollback. A governance model works when decisions have owners, and owners have evidence requirements and escalation pathways.

Project leaders should also define accountability for third-party AI. Many AI capabilities arrive through APIs, managed services, and vendor platforms. Organizations sometimes pretend that vendor AI is the vendor's responsibility. That is an illusion. The vendor may own certain controls, but you still own the decision to use the system, the configuration choices, the data you feed it, the context in which outputs are used, and the monitoring you deploy around it. This shared-responsibility reality is why governance must include vendor management and supplier assurance, and why project leaders must insist on evidence, not marketing language.

Accountability also requires human oversight design. A common governance mistake is to say "humans are in the loop" without defining what that means. Who is the human. What do they review. How often. Under what thresholds. With what training. With what authority to override. The EU AI Act's risk-based approach underscores that higher-risk uses require stronger controls and governance, including obligations that push organizations toward clear oversight mechanisms and documentation.

Finally, project leaders should treat accountability as a security control. When accountability is unclear, incidents expand. Response slows. Evidence becomes fragmented. Decisions become defensive. Clear accountability tightens the loop between detection, action, and learning. That is why accountability is not "soft governance." It is a hard control that protects digital trust.

Risk Rating Aligned to Gates

Risk tiering is the hinge point of AI governance. Without risk tiering, teams either over-control everything, which kills delivery momentum, or under-control high-impact AI, which invites failure. The goal is proportionality. You want a tiering model that is simple enough to use during Analyze, yet strong enough to withstand audit and board scrutiny later.

A strong tiering model uses multiple factors because AI risk is multidimensional. The first factor is business impact, meaning the harm that could occur if the AI fails, behaves unpredictably, or is misused. Harm can be financial, operational, safety-related, privacy-related, or reputational. The second factor is decision influence, meaning whether AI outputs are informational, advisory, or determinative. Informational outputs guide humans. Determinative outputs directly trigger actions like denial of service, blocking transactions, or ranking applicants. The third factor is reversibility, meaning how easily a harmful output can be corrected before impact occurs. The fourth factor is data sensitivity, meaning whether the system processes confidential, personal, regulated, or proprietary data. The fifth factor is exposure and scale, meaning how widely the AI is deployed, how many users interact with it, and how quickly a failure could propagate. These factors align with the risk-based regulatory direction globally, including the EU AI Act's classification logic that differentiates unacceptable risk, high-risk, and lower-risk uses.

Project leaders can implement tiering as a four-level model. Tier 1 can represent low-risk AI, where outputs are informational, data is non-sensitive, and the harm of error is minor. Tier 2 can represent moderate-risk AI, where outputs influence decisions, data may be sensitive, and errors can cause meaningful harm, but strong human oversight and reversibility exist. Tier 3 can represent high-risk AI, where outputs materially affect people, finances, safety, or compliance, where data is sensitive, and where errors are hard to reverse. Tier 4 can represent critical-risk AI, where misuse or failure could trigger severe harm, systemic disruption, or legal exposure, and where the system must meet the highest governance rigor.

The point is not the labels, the point is what tiers trigger. Tiers should trigger gate requirements. At Tier 1, you may require baseline documentation, baseline security controls, and basic evaluation evidence. At Tier 2, you add stronger evaluation requirements, stronger monitoring requirements, and explicit human oversight design. At Tier 3 and Tier 4, you require formal model risk review, independent evaluation or red teaming for abuse scenarios, stronger documentation, stronger audit evidence, and tighter change control with post-deployment monitoring and periodic reassessment. NIST AI RMF provides a useful structure for this because it frames risk management across governance, mapping, measuring, and managing functions, encouraging organizations to scale actions to context and risk (NIST, 2023).

Risk tiering should be decided early, ideally during Analyze and confirmed at Gate 1. Waiting until Design to tier risk is too late because architecture choices will already constrain what controls are feasible. Risk tiering should also be revisited at each gate because risk can change. A system that starts as advisory can become determinative when the business sees efficiency gains. A dataset that starts as non-sensitive can become sensitive when combined with other sources. A generative AI assistant can become a compliance risk when deployed to customer-facing channels. Continuous reassessment is not bureaucracy, it is risk realism.

Project leaders should also distinguish between AI capability risk and AI usage risk. The same model can be safe in one context and unsafe in another. A language model used to draft internal emails has one risk profile. The same model used to generate customer advice in a regulated industry has another risk profile. Governance must therefore tier the use case, not the model brand.

Generative AI deserves special attention because it introduces unique threats such as prompt injection, data leakage through conversational interaction, and misleading outputs that appear plausible. NIST's Generative AI profile provides actions that help organizations manage these risks in alignment with AI RMF. This matters for project leaders because it reinforces that generative AI governance requires both security controls and behavior evaluation controls, not just traditional application testing.

Risk tiering should also connect to your enterprise risk taxonomy. If the organization already categorizes risks under cyber, privacy, operational resilience, compliance, and reputational risk, then AI risks should map into that taxonomy. This helps governance boards understand AI risk using familiar language. It also prevents AI from becoming a parallel risk universe. ISO/IEC 42001's management system approach supports this integration mindset, because it expects organizations to establish policies and objectives and maintain continual improvement, which naturally aligns to enterprise governance and risk systems.

Finally, risk tiering must be documented as an evidence artifact. A tiering decision without documented rationale is not governance, it is opinion. The documentation should state the use case, decision influence, data sensitivity, exposure, reversibility, and the resulting tier. It should also state what controls are required at that tier. This becomes a living artifact across gates.

Structures That Support Fast, Safe Delivery

Oversight is where governance becomes operational. Many organizations either create too many committees or too few. Too many committees create gridlock. Too few committees create blind spots. The right oversight model is layered, risk-based, and aligned to the ADDIS gates so decisions happen at the right time, with the right evidence, by the right people.

At the core, project leaders need an AI governance forum that can make cross-functional decisions. This can be an AI Governance Council, an extension of the QRB or GRB model, or a specialized review board that is triggered for Tier 3 and Tier 4 AI use cases. The forum should include product leadership, engineering leadership, security leadership, risk or compliance leadership, data governance leadership, and legal representation. Its job is not to manage daily tasks. Its job is to approve risk tiering, approve control plans, approve deployment readiness, and monitor post-deployment performance and incidents. This aligns with the idea that governance bodies evaluate, direct, and monitor, while execution teams build and operate.

Project leaders should also define independent challenge mechanisms. AI systems are vulnerable to confirmation bias, teams fall in love with early demos, especially when the AI looks impressive. Independent challenge can come from security red teams, independent evaluation teams, model risk management groups, or internal audit involvement depending on tier. The OECD recommendation on AI emphasizes trustworthy AI and responsible stewardship, which implies organizations must not rely solely on the enthusiasm of builders when risks affect people and trust.

Oversight also requires decision cadence. A practical cadence is to review AI governance at each gate, and then to establish a post-deployment cadence that matches risk tier. Tier 1 may require quarterly checks. Tier 2 may require monthly checks. Tier 3 and Tier 4 may require continuous monitoring dashboards with formal monthly reviews and immediate escalation for defined triggers. The cadence should be part of the operating model, not negotiated each time an issue occurs.

A key oversight deliverable is the “AI control plan.” This plan lists required controls across data, model, application, security, and operations. It specifies owners, acceptance criteria, and evidence required. It is essentially a Security by Design control matrix expanded for AI. For generative AI, the control plan should explicitly include guardrails, misuse detection, prompt-injection defenses, data leakage prevention, output filtering where appropriate, and monitoring for abuse patterns, aligned to recognized risk guidance such as NIST’s GenAI profile.

Oversight should also include escalation triggers. These triggers are pre-defined conditions that force review or rollback. Examples include detection of sensitive data leakage, evidence of prompt injection leading to policy violations, drift beyond defined thresholds, systematic degradation of evaluation metrics, significant changes in model behavior after vendor updates, or repeated incidents of misuse. Triggers should be designed as operational controls. When triggers are explicit, teams are not trapped debating whether action is needed during an incident. They act, then review.

Project leaders should ensure oversight includes evidence management. AI governance becomes fragile when evidence is scattered across notebooks, emails, and informal chats. Oversight forums should require evidence to be stored in a structured repository aligned to the gate evidence bundle concept. This supports audit readiness and supports learning. ISO management system standards emphasize maintaining documented information and continual improvement, which reinforces that evidence must be retrievable and maintained as part of governance, not treated as a temporary project artifact.

Executing with Discipline from Day One

The fastest way to improve AI governance is to change what happens in the first two weeks of the project. Many teams wait until design reviews to discuss AI risks. That is like installing seatbelts after the crash test. Project leaders should begin with an AI governance kickoff, which is distinct from the general project kickoff. The AI governance kickoff establishes accountability roles, confirms the initial risk tier, defines what evidence will be required at each gate, and identifies early risk assumptions that must be tested quickly. It also confirms whether the project is building, buying, or blending AI capabilities, because control responsibilities differ by track.

In that kickoff, the project leader should insist on an explicit statement of AI purpose and boundaries. What decision or workflow is the AI augmenting. What it will not do. What humans remain responsible for. What data it will access. What outputs will be considered unacceptable. This statement becomes a governance anchor. It becomes a test reference. It becomes a communication artifact for stakeholders. It also prevents scope drift into riskier territory without conscious approval.

Next, build the AI risk register early. Do not wait for "later risk analysis." AI risk must be treated like cyber risk, it compounds if ignored. The risk register should include risks such as data quality and lineage gaps, privacy exposure, security threats specific to AI, vendor dependency risk, model drift risk, explainability gaps, fairness concerns where relevant, and operational misuse. ISO/IEC 23894 is designed to help organizations integrate AI risk management into their activities and functions, which in project terms means AI risks belong in the same governance machinery as other delivery risks, including owners and treatment plans.

Project leaders should also require an evaluation strategy early. Teams often treat evaluation as something done near the end. For AI, evaluation design begins early because it influences what data you collect, how you label, what ground truth you accept, and what thresholds you set. Evaluation should include functional performance, but also safety, security, and resilience behaviors where applicable. For generative AI, evaluation must include adversarial testing and misuse testing, because production users will do what your testers do not imagine. NIST's AI RMF and GenAI profile both emphasize the need to measure and manage trustworthiness characteristics through lifecycle-based actions.

Security by Design must be extended to AI assets. Project leaders should ensure the threat model explicitly includes AI threats, not only application threats. Threat modeling must cover training data poisoning where training occurs, prompt injection where generative interfaces exist, model inversion or extraction risks where exposure exists, and data leakage risks across logging and conversation histories. Even when the model is vendor-hosted, the application context and data flows remain yours, and governance must treat them as in-scope.

Another early control is change control for models and prompts. Organizations often have strong change control for code, but weak change control for model configuration and prompt engineering. Yet prompts and system instructions can materially change behavior. Project leaders should require versioning, review, and approval for prompt changes in higher tiers, just as they would for code changes. This becomes even more important when vendor models update automatically, because the organization must detect behavior changes and respond quickly.

Project leaders should also manage the human side. AI changes roles. It changes expectations. It changes workflows. Governance must ensure training and guidance exist for users who rely on AI outputs. Human oversight is not only a design choice, it is a training commitment. Users must understand limitations and escalation paths. When organizations fail to train users, they get the worst of both worlds, the AI is blamed for errors, and humans over-trust it anyway.

Finally, project leaders must manage “governance friction” carefully. The goal is not to slow delivery. The goal is to remove uncertainty. When risk tiering and evidence requirements are clear, teams move faster because they know what done means. When requirements are vague, teams build in the dark and discover constraints at the end. Good governance feels like guardrails, not like shackles.

Key Takeaways

AI governance for project leaders is a discipline of accountable delivery. It starts with explicit accountability that maps roles to decisions and ties those decisions to evidence. It continues with practical risk tiering that scales rigor to impact, aligns to gates, and is revisited as the solution evolves. It is sustained through oversight structures that enable cross-functional decisions, independent challenge, clear cadence, and strong evidence management. This approach aligns with NIST AI RMF's lifecycle-based risk management framing and with NIST's guidance specific to generative AI risks. It also aligns with ISO/IEC 42001's management system approach for AI governance and ISO/IEC 23894's guidance on integrating AI risk management into organizational functions. It aligns with the OECD's focus on trustworthy AI stewardship and with the risk-based regulatory direction embodied in the EU AI Act.

Most importantly, this chapter reframes the project leader's job. You are not merely delivering an AI-enabled feature. You are delivering a capability that must remain trustworthy under pressure. That requires structure. It requires evidence. It requires the courage to say "not yet" when the organization has not earned "yes." In the next chapter, we move deeper into lifecycle controls, data governance, model risk, evaluation, and monitoring, where governance becomes measurable and where "trustworthy" becomes something you can prove.

"AI amplifies intent,
including flawed intent."

AI Lifecycle Controls

AI-enabled delivery succeeds or fails on a simple truth: you do not control the model, you control the system around the model. The model may be trained elsewhere, tuned by a vendor, updated by a platform, or shaped by data you did not fully anticipate. Yet the organization still owns the outcome, the harm, the regulatory exposure, and the loss of trust when things go wrong. That is why this chapter treats AI governance as lifecycle delivery control. It is not a policy conversation that lives outside the project. It is a practical set of controls that project leaders, security teams, and governance boards can execute, verify, and approve through evidence bundles across the gates. NIST's AI Risk Management Framework (AI RMF) makes this lifecycle posture explicit by framing risk management as a continuous set of activities that map, measure, and manage AI risks, supported by governance structures that keep accountability and decision-making clear across design, development, deployment, and use (NIST, 2023).

The goal is not to turn every AI project into a research program. The goal is to prevent AI from becoming an unmanaged variable inside an otherwise disciplined secure SDLC. When organizations struggle with AI initiatives, the root cause is rarely "the model was bad." More often, the data was poorly governed, the evaluation was thin, the change control was weak, monitoring was incomplete, and oversight lacked clear thresholds for escalation. Those weaknesses are predictable. They are also fixable. Fixing them requires a delivery-grade control set that integrates cybersecurity, privacy, quality engineering, and operational readiness into a single spine. ISO/IEC 42001, as an AI management system standard, reinforces this direction by emphasizing structured governance and continuous improvement through an organizational management system approach, rather than relying on ad hoc decisions per model or per team (ISO, 2023a).

The chapter is organized around four practical control domains that follow the AI system lifecycle. First is data governance, because data is the oxygen of AI and the fastest path to unintended harm. Second is model risk management, including build, buy, and hybrid choices, model supply chain concerns, and the security threats that target models and pipelines. Third is evaluation, because what you do not measure you cannot govern. Fourth is monitoring and continuous assurance, because AI systems do not stay stable simply because you declare them stable. Together, these controls turn AI delivery into something you can defend, not merely something you can demo.

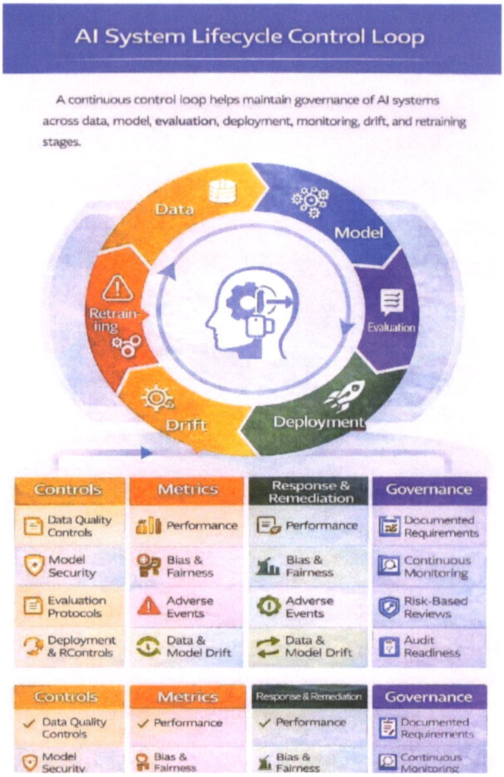

Lifecycle controls as delivery controls

To integrate AI into secure technology project management, you need to treat AI lifecycle controls as first-class deliverables, just like requirements, architecture, test plans, and deployment runbooks. In the ADDIS gate model, each gate can carry an AI extension that is proportional to risk tier. The extension is not additional paperwork for its own sake. It is a set of evidence expectations that confirm the system is governable at that stage. That approach aligns naturally to AI RMF because the framework is designed to be flexible and context-aware, encouraging organizations to scale actions based on impact, environment, and intended use while still maintaining a consistent risk management structure (NIST, 2023).

A practical way to think about AI lifecycle controls is to treat them like "control gates for uncertainty." Traditional SDLC assumes that once code is tested and released, behavior is mostly predictable. AI breaks that assumption. Behavior can change as data changes. Behavior can degrade as users attempt misuse. Behavior can shift when a vendor updates a hosted model. Therefore, your delivery controls must be designed to manage uncertainty, not to eliminate it. That means you will define acceptable behavior boundaries, test those boundaries, deploy guardrails, monitor drift, and continuously reassess. When this is done well, AI becomes an asset that strengthens decision-making. When it is done poorly, AI becomes a hidden dependency that weakens governance.

The lifecycle view also forces clarity about what "AI system" means. In modern delivery, the AI system is rarely just a model. It includes data ingestion, preprocessing, feature engineering, storage, training or fine-tuning pipelines, inference endpoints, retrieval systems such as vector databases, prompt templates, guardrails, and user interfaces. Each component introduces its own risks and control needs. NIST's Generative AI profile was created specifically because generative AI introduces risks that are novel or intensified, and those risks are expressed through system design choices like retrieval augmentation, prompt routing, and output handling (NIST, 2024a).

This chapter therefore focuses on controls that can be applied consistently regardless of whether you build or buy. If you build, you must control training pipelines and model artifacts. If you buy, you must control vendor integration, configuration, and usage boundaries. If you blend, you must do both. Either way, the organization must be able to show that risks are identified, controls exist, and evidence proves those controls are operating.

Data governance controls that prevent failure

Data governance is the part of AI delivery that teams want to postpone and leaders cannot afford to postpone. Data problems do not announce themselves early. They surface late, often after deployment, when bias claims appear, when privacy exposure is discovered, when the model makes "confidently wrong" outputs, or when operational outcomes diverge from expectation. AI risk guidance underscores this by highlighting the need to integrate risk management into AI-related activities and functions, including how data is sourced, used, and governed (ISO, 2023b).

A disciplined data governance control set begins with data inventory and classification. The project must document what data sources will be used, who owns them, what sensitivity categories apply, and what constraints exist around usage. This includes training data, evaluation data, and production inference data. It also includes derived data such as embeddings, vector representations, and feature stores. A common delivery failure is treating embeddings as "not the original data." In many cases, embeddings can still reveal sensitive patterns, and they remain security-relevant assets. If you do not classify and protect them, you leave a gap in your security posture.

Next is lineage and provenance. For every significant data source, the project should capture where it came from, how it was collected, what transformations were applied, what filtering or labeling decisions were made, and what quality controls were performed. Lineage is not only for compliance. Lineage is your ability to debug. When the model behaves unexpectedly, lineage helps you determine whether the problem is data drift, data corruption, labeling bias, or pipeline failure. ISO/IEC 23894 emphasizes integrating risk management into AI activities and functions, and data lineage is one of the clearest ways to make that integration real in day-to-day delivery (ISO, 2023b).

Data quality controls must also be explicit. AI systems amplify data realities. If the data is incomplete, the model learns incompleteness. If the data is biased, the model learns bias. If the data is outdated, the model learns outdated patterns. Quality controls therefore include completeness checks, duplicate detection, outlier analysis, sampling reviews, label consistency checks, and coverage analysis across meaningful slices. These controls should be scaled to risk tier. A low-risk internal assistant may require lighter controls. A high-impact system influencing financial, employment, healthcare, or access decisions requires deeper quality work, because error and bias can create real harm.

Privacy controls should be treated as design constraints, not post-deployment patches. Data minimization should be enforced so the system only processes what is necessary. Access controls should be designed so that training pipelines, evaluation data, and prompt logs are not accessible to broad groups. Retention controls should be explicit, including how long prompt logs are stored, how access is audited, and how deletion is handled. These controls should align with the organization's information security management approach, and they should be integrated into evidence bundles as proofs, not promises (ISO, 2023a; NIST, 2023).

Generative AI adds specific data governance hazards. Prompt logs can unintentionally capture sensitive data. Retrieval augmentation can expose sensitive documents if access boundaries are weak. Conversation memory features can persist information longer than intended. "Helpful" debug logging can become a data leak. NIST's Generative AI profile emphasizes actions around documenting how models are adapted, how data is used, and how risks are mitigated throughout the generative AI lifecycle, reinforcing that data governance for GenAI is not optional engineering hygiene, it is a risk control (NIST, 2024a).

Data governance also extends to external data, including licensed datasets, public web sources, and vendor-provided training sets. For project leaders, the governance question is not simply "Is it legal?" The question is "Is it defensible?" Can you demonstrate that you have permission to use the data. Can you demonstrate that you can remove data if required. Can you demonstrate that you can answer questions about provenance if challenged. This is especially important in regulated contexts and in high-impact AI uses, where documentation and traceability expectations intensify.

Finally, data governance must include misuse and poisoning considerations. Training data poisoning is a known risk, and it can occur not only in model training, but also in retrieval pipelines when external content is ingested without strong controls. OWASP's Top 10 for LLM applications explicitly lists training data poisoning and supply chain vulnerabilities as key risk categories, which is a reminder that AI data pipelines are attack surfaces, not just engineering pipelines (OWASP, 2023).

AI Model Risk Controls and Evaluation Discipline

Model risk management starts with an uncomfortable reality: models are not neutral components. They embody assumptions, training choices, and tradeoffs that affect safety, security, and fairness. Whether you build or buy, you need a model risk process that is clear enough to execute and strong enough to defend. NIST AI RMF supports this by emphasizing trustworthiness characteristics such as validity and reliability, safety, security and resilience, accountability, transparency, privacy, and fairness, and by encouraging organizations to map and measure these characteristics in ways that fit their context (NIST, 2023).

A practical model risk control set begins with model selection and justification. The project should document why a particular model family was chosen, what alternatives were considered, and what constraints drove the choice, such as latency, cost, explainability needs, or regulatory requirements. If you acquire AI, this justification includes vendor selection, vendor assurances, and shared responsibility boundaries. If you build, it includes architecture choices and training strategy. This documentation is not bureaucracy. It is decision traceability, and traceability is governance.

Model artifact management is next. Models should be treated like software releases. They need versioning, configuration documentation, deployment approvals, rollback plans, and access controls. Many organizations have strong change control for code but weak change control for models and prompt layers. This gap becomes dangerous when model updates change behavior. A disciplined governance approach treats model releases and prompt changes as controlled changes, with review and evidence requirements that scale to risk tier.

Security by Design for AI requires explicit threat modeling for AI-specific threats. Threat modeling should cover model theft or extraction risks, model inversion risks, data leakage through inference, prompt injection, insecure output handling, and misuse of plugins or tools connected to models. OWASP's LLM Top 10 provides a practical taxonomy for these risks and is helpful for project teams because it translates abstract AI security concerns into recognizable vulnerability categories (OWASP, 2023).

MITRE ATLAS expands this idea by mapping adversarial threats and tactics targeting AI systems, providing a way for defenders to structure threat modeling, and testing around real attack patterns across the AI lifecycle (MITRE, 2025). This is particularly valuable in higher-risk contexts because it keeps security teams from relying on generic checklists. Instead, it encourages scenario-based testing, such as testing whether an attacker can poison a dataset, manipulate a retrieval system, or exfiltrate sensitive information through carefully crafted prompts.

Model risk management must also address the reality of overreliance. AI outputs can appear confident even when wrong. Teams can become dependent on “smart” systems and reduce human skepticism. OWASP highlights overreliance as a risk category because it is not a technical bug, it is an operational failure mode that increases harm when AI is used as an authority rather than as an assistant (OWASP, 2023). Project leaders should treat overreliance as something that can be controlled through UI design, training, workflow design, and clear escalation paths. This is an example of how governance crosses into product design. If the UI encourages blind trust, governance will fail even if the model is strong.

Evaluation is where model risk management becomes measurable. A project cannot claim readiness without evaluation that reflects real-world use. Evaluation must be designed early because it affects data collection, labeling, and acceptance thresholds. Evaluation should include baseline functional metrics, but it must also include safety and misuse evaluations when the use case demands it. NIST AI RMF emphasizes measurement and management of trustworthiness characteristics, and the GenAI profile provides more targeted actions for evaluating and mitigating generative AI risks (NIST, 2023; NIST, 2024a).

A practical evaluation approach includes several layers. First is in-domain performance evaluation. Does the model achieve acceptable results on representative tasks. Second is robustness evaluation. Does the model degrade gracefully under noisy inputs, partial data, or unexpected phrasing. Third is slice evaluation. Does performance differ across meaningful groups or contexts, and is that difference acceptable. Fourth is safety evaluation. Does the system produce prohibited outputs, expose sensitive data, or violate policy boundaries. Fifth is adversarial evaluation. Can users manipulate the system through prompt injection, jailbreak attempts, or tool misuse. These layers should be tailored to risk tier. Low-risk AI may need only the first two layers. High-risk AI needs all layers with deeper rigor.

Evaluation must also be tied to clear acceptance criteria. A common governance failure is running evaluation but not defining what success means. Project leaders should require threshold statements, for example, "The system must meet X accuracy on dataset Y, must not expose sensitive data under defined red-team prompts, must demonstrate prompt injection defenses across defined attack patterns, and must meet drift monitoring readiness requirements." These become gate acceptance criteria and reduce ambiguity.

If the solution is generative AI, evaluation must include prompt injection and output handling tests as first-class requirements. OWASP lists prompt injection and insecure output handling as top vulnerabilities, and they are relevant because they connect directly to how an AI system can be manipulated into leaking information, taking unintended actions, or generating harmful content (OWASP, 2023). NIST's GenAI profile similarly emphasizes managing risks unique to generative AI and proposes actions that support governance and lifecycle control (NIST, 2024a).

Evaluation results must be stored as evidence artifacts, not as informal notes. Evidence should include evaluation datasets used, the time period of data, the model version, prompt version where applicable, configuration parameters, and test environment details. Without these, evaluation cannot be reproduced, and non-reproducible evaluation is weak evidence. This is where AI governance becomes similar to quality engineering. Repeatability is not optional. Repeatability is proof.

Continuous Monitoring from Gates to Sustainment

A system that cannot be monitored cannot be governed. Monitoring is therefore a delivery control, not only an operations activity. AI monitoring must include both security signals and behavior signals. Security signals include suspicious prompt patterns, unusual data access, repeated failed authentication attempts, anomalous API usage, and evidence of prompt injection attempts. Behavior signals include performance drift, data drift, changes in output distributions, increases in policy violations, and changes in user feedback patterns.

NIST AI RMF frames risk management as continuous, and the GenAI profile reinforces the need to manage generative AI risk as a lifecycle practice, including documenting changes and applying continuous improvement techniques to mitigate risks (NIST, 2023; NIST, 2024a). ISO/IEC 42001 reinforces continual improvement within an AI management system, which implies that monitoring and feedback loops are part of governance, not optional enhancements (ISO, 2023a).

Monitoring must be designed during Design and Implement, not left to Sustain. The project should define what will be logged, how logs will be protected, how long logs will be retained, and who will have access. It should also define alert thresholds and escalation triggers. These triggers should align with the governance board's oversight model. For example, a Tier 3 or Tier 4 system might require immediate escalation if a sensitive data leakage pattern is detected, if prompt injection attempts succeed beyond a defined threshold, or if drift crosses agreed limits.

Post-deployment monitoring also has regulatory relevance. The EU AI Act includes obligations related to post-market monitoring for high-risk AI systems, reinforcing that deployment is not the end of responsibility, it is the beginning of ongoing oversight (European Union, 2024). Even when your organization is not directly regulated under EU law, this direction reflects a broader governance expectation: high-impact AI should not be deployed and forgotten.

Monitoring must also be connected to incident response. AI incidents can look different from traditional security incidents. They can include a model producing harmful outputs at scale, an AI assistant leaking sensitive information through conversation logs, or an attacker manipulating a prompt chain to force unauthorized actions. Your incident response procedures must therefore include AI-specific scenarios, including evidence capture needs like prompt traces, model versions, configuration settings, retrieval sources accessed, and tool calls executed. This is where integration with security monitoring and operational readiness becomes essential.

An effective continuous assurance model also includes periodic re-evaluation. Monitoring tells you what is happening. Re-evaluation confirms whether the system still meets thresholds and whether controls still work. Re-evaluation can be scheduled, such as monthly or quarterly depending on tier, and it can be triggered, such as after major model updates, vendor platform updates, data pipeline changes, or security incidents. Re-evaluation is where governance proves it can adapt, rather than merely react.

If the system uses third-party AI models, monitoring must include vendor change awareness. Vendor platforms can update models and change behavior. Even if your code does not change, your outputs can. Therefore, continuous assurance must include methods to detect behavior changes, such as canary tests, regression evaluation suites, and output distribution monitoring. These methods allow you to detect "silent drift," which is drift that appears as a change in user satisfaction or risk signals before it appears as a measurable performance regression.

Finally, monitoring must support learning and improvement. Governance is not only about controlling risk, it is about reducing risk over time. When monitoring reveals recurring issues, such as repeated prompt injection attempts, repeated user misunderstandings, or recurring drift patterns, the organization should implement improvements. Improvements can include stronger guardrails, better access controls, better user training, better retrieval filtering, or better evaluation coverage. This is continuous improvement in action, and it aligns to management-system thinking and lifecycle risk management guidance (ISO, 2023a; NIST, 2023).

Summary and Next Steps

This chapter reframed AI delivery controls as governable lifecycle practices. Data governance controls prevent invisible failures by enforcing inventory, lineage, quality discipline, privacy boundaries, and protection of AI-adjacent assets like embeddings and prompt logs. Model risk controls treat models, prompts, and configurations as managed artifacts with versioning, change control, and threat modeling, supported by practical security taxonomies such as OWASP's LLM Top 10 and threat perspectives such as MITRE ATLAS (OWASP, 2023). Evaluation controls convert trust into evidence through layered testing that includes performance, robustness, slice evaluation, safety, and adversarial misuse testing, aligned with AI RMF and the GenAI profile (NIST, 2023; NIST, 2024a). Monitoring and continuous assurance controls keep systems governable after deployment through logging, alerting, escalation triggers, re-evaluation routines, and post-deployment oversight expectations that reflect modern regulatory direction (European Union, 2024).

In the next chapter, we turn these controls into an assurance model that is explicitly aligned to gates. We define what evidence is required, how to package it, how to measure readiness, and how to make audit and board scrutiny survivable without drowning delivery teams in unnecessary documentation. That is the point where AI governance becomes not only a set of controls, but a repeatable, evidence-driven decision system.

AI Assurance and Audit Readiness

AI programs do not fail only because the model underperforms. They fail because the organization cannot prove the system is safe enough, secure enough, and controlled enough to deserve trust at scale. Assurance is the discipline that makes that proof possible. It is the difference between a confident demo and a defensible release. It is also the difference between a one-time launch and a sustainable operating capability, especially when AI behavior can drift, user interactions can be adversarial, and vendor model updates can change outcomes without warning. NIST positions AI risk management as a lifecycle activity that requires governance, measurement, and management, and that framing is the foundation for assurance in secure technology project delivery (NIST, 2023).

In the context of AI-enabled systems, evidence must be treated as a governance asset, not as an after-the-fact compliance artifact. Effective assurance depends on the deliberate generation, validation, and preservation of evidence across the system lifecycle, including design decisions, data handling practices, model evaluations, operational monitoring, and corrective actions. When evidence is structured, traceable, and decision-aligned, it enables accountability, supports risk-based oversight, and allows organizations to demonstrate due diligence to executives, auditors, and regulators. The following figure illustrates how AI assurance evidence is produced, connected, and consumed across technical, operational, and governance domains to support informed gate decisions and continuous assurance.

In secure SDLC and Security by Design, assurance is not merely testing. Testing is one method of generating evidence, but assurance is the larger system of controls, metrics, reviews, and accountability decisions that determine whether evidence is sufficient for the risk tier.

Assurance answers questions that testing alone cannot. Are we using the right data, and can we prove its provenance. Are we controlling the model and prompt changes like we control code changes. Have we evaluated misuse scenarios, not just normal use. Can we detect and respond when the system behaves badly in production. Do we have an evidence trail that can survive audit, legal scrutiny, and board-level challenge. This is why ISO/IEC 42001 approaches AI governance as a management system with defined processes and continual improvement, because assurance must be repeatable and not dependent on heroics (ISO, 2023a).

Assurance also has a practical purpose: it keeps gate governance from becoming subjective. Without explicit evidence expectations, gate reviews turn into debates. One leader feels confident, another feels uneasy, and the decision becomes political. With assurance, gate reviews become evidence based. The question is not "Do we believe it is ready." The question becomes "Did the system meet the defined readiness criteria, and can we show proof." This is consistent with the risk-based direction seen in major regulatory regimes such as the EU AI Act, which intensifies obligations for higher-risk AI uses and pushes organizations toward documented risk

management, oversight, and post-deployment monitoring (European Union, 2024).

This chapter turns assurance into an executable approach aligned to the ADDIS gates and the evidence bundle concept established earlier in the book. It defines what "AI assurance" means in delivery terms, which metrics matter and why, how to build evidence bundles that are lean but strong, and how to make audit readiness a natural byproduct of disciplined governance rather than an emergency drill.

Assurance as a delivery discipline

AI assurance is the practice of demonstrating, with structured evidence, that the AI-enabled system meets defined trustworthiness requirements for its risk tier, across its lifecycle. It includes governance decisions, technical controls, evaluation results, security testing, operational monitoring, and documented accountability. NIST's AI RMF organizes risk management through functions that emphasize governance, mapping context, measuring performance and risk, and managing risk responses, which is a practical blueprint for structuring assurance activities across gates (NIST, 2023).

A helpful mental model is to treat assurance as a three-part contract between the delivery team, the governance board, and the business sponsor.

First, the delivery team commits to produce evidence, not just features. The evidence is scoped to risk tier and to the gate decision being made.

Second, the governance board commits to evaluate readiness using clear criteria, not intuition. That evaluation may include independent challenge, especially at higher tiers.

Third, the sponsor commits to fund the controls required to sustain trust, including monitoring and periodic revalidation. Sponsors often fund building, but they underfund assurance. AI governance fails when assurance is treated as overhead rather than as value protection.

In practice, assurance fails for predictable reasons. Evidence is scattered, inconsistent, or not reproducible. Evaluation focuses on "average performance" and ignores edge cases and misuse. Security testing covers the web application but ignores AI-specific threats. Monitoring is planned but not implemented. Roles are named but accountability is unclear when incidents occur. ISO/IEC 23894 emphasizes integrating AI risk management into organizational activities and functions, which implies that assurance must be embedded into delivery workflows and not tacked on after engineering is complete (ISO, 2023a).

Metrics that make trust measurable

Metrics are the language of assurance, but only if you choose metrics that reflect real risk. Many teams select metrics because they are easy to compute. Assurance metrics must be chosen because they are decision-relevant. They must help a governance board decide whether the system is ready for the next stage and whether residual risk is acceptable.

A useful way to structure AI assurance metrics is in five families.

The first family is data and provenance metrics. These measure whether the data is fit for purpose and governable. Examples include completeness and coverage, label consistency, drift indicators between training and production distributions, percentage of data with verified lineage, and access control adherence for sensitive datasets. These metrics directly support traceability and help prove that the system's behavior is not grounded in unknown or unmanaged data. They also support post-incident analysis, because data lineage is often the fastest way to isolate root causes.

The second family is model performance and reliability metrics. These include accuracy, precision and recall, calibration, error rates by critical slices, stability across repeated runs, and robustness under noisy or adversarial inputs. For generative AI, performance metrics may include task success rates, factuality checks where feasible, refusal correctness for policy constraints, and consistency of behavior under prompt variations. NIST's GenAI profile emphasizes identifying and managing risks unique to generative AI and proposes lifecycle actions that include evaluation and measurement aligned to organizational goals (NIST, 2024b).

The third family is security and abuse-resistance metrics. These measure whether the system can withstand adversarial behavior and whether controls are effective. Examples include prompt injection success rates under red-team tests, sensitive data leakage rates under defined attack prompts, unauthorized tool execution attempts blocked, and model or pipeline attack detection performance. OWASP's Top 10 for LLM applications provides a practical taxonomy for AI security risks such as prompt injection, insecure output handling, training data poisoning, supply chain vulnerabilities, and excessive agency, and that taxonomy can be translated into measurable security test outcomes (OWASP, 2023).

The fourth family is governance and oversight metrics. These measure whether controls are operating, not merely documented. Examples include percentage of model and prompt changes that followed approval workflow, evidence bundle completeness rates at each gate, time-to-close for assurance findings, and number of waived controls with documented risk acceptance. These metrics prevent governance from becoming ceremonial.

The fifth family is operational and continuous assurance metrics. These measure whether the system remains trustworthy after deployment. Examples include output policy violation rates in production, drift detection triggers, mean time to detect and respond to AI-related incidents, rate of user escalations, and periodic revalidation pass rates. This family is essential because AI risk is rarely static. Continuous monitoring and feedback loops are core expectations in management-system thinking and in lifecycle risk guidance (ISO, 2023a).

A critical principle is that metrics must be tied to thresholds and actions. A metric without a threshold is trivia. A threshold without an escalation path is theater. In assurance, every key metric should map to one of three outcomes: acceptable, needs remediation, or triggers governance escalation. This is how metrics become decision tools rather than dashboard decoration.

Another principle is independence where needed. For higher-risk systems, some evaluation and testing should be performed by a party that is not the builder. This can be an internal assurance team, a security red team, a model risk function, or an external assessor depending on organizational maturity. MITRE ATLAS offers a structured way to think about adversary tactics and techniques targeting AI systems, which can strengthen independent testing by anchoring scenarios to real attack patterns rather than hypothetical fears (MITRE, 2025).

Evidence bundles that are lean but strong

Evidence is not documentation volume. Evidence is documentation quality and relevance. A strong evidence bundle is the minimum set of artifacts required to prove readiness for the gate decision. It should be designed to be auditable, reproducible, and traceable.

To keep evidence bundles lean, project leaders should enforce a simple rule: every artifact must answer a specific gate question. If it does not, it belongs in working notes, not in the evidence bundle. This prevents the common failure of dumping everything into a repository and calling it "evidence."

An effective evidence bundle typically includes five layers.

The first layer is intent and context. This includes the use case definition, risk tiering rationale, scope boundaries, and accountability map. This layer answers "What are we building, why, and who owns the risks."

The second layer is design and control intent. This includes architecture and data flow diagrams, control mapping, threat modeling outputs, and the AI control plan that lists required controls, owners, and acceptance criteria. This layer answers "How is the system designed to be safe and secure."

The third layer is build or acquisition evidence. For build, this includes model versioning, training or fine-tuning configuration, data lineage documentation, secure development practices, and security testing results. For buy, this includes vendor assurances, configuration baselines, shared responsibility statements, and third-party risk evidence. NIST SP 800-218A is useful here because it augments secure software development practices with AI-specific considerations, supporting a structured way to show that AI model development and integration followed secure development practices (NIST, 2024a).

The fourth layer is evaluation and verification evidence. This includes evaluation plans, test datasets, results, robustness testing, misuse testing, and pass-fail criteria. For generative AI, it should include red-team prompt suites and results, plus output handling validations aligned to major risk categories (NIST, 2024b; OWASP, 2023).

The fifth layer is operational readiness and continuous assurance evidence. This includes monitoring plans, logging design, alert thresholds, incident response playbook updates, rollback plans, and sustainment revalidation schedules. This layer answers "What happens when reality is messier than the test environment."

A governance board should be able to review the evidence bundle in two passes. The first pass is executive, focusing on risk tier, residual risk summary, and readiness statement. The second pass is technical and assurance-focused, sampling evidence for sufficiency and consistency. If the bundle cannot support both passes, it is not ready.

Gate-by-gate AI assurance across ADDIS

Assurance becomes powerful when it is aligned to the gates, because gates are where the organization makes irreversible commitments. Each gate is a decision about resource allocation, risk acceptance, and operational exposure. AI assurance adds clarity to those decisions.

For Gate 1, the Analyze Gate, the assurance goal is to prove that the organization understands what it is building and why AI is appropriate. This is where weak programs begin. If the problem statement is vague, the model selection will be arbitrary. If the data sources are unknown, every later control will be fragile. Evidence at this gate should therefore include the AI use case definition, risk tiering rationale, initial data inventory and classification, early threat and misuse scenarios, and a preliminary evaluation strategy. NIST AI RMF's mapping function is highly relevant here because it emphasizes understanding context, stakeholders, and intended use, and building a risk picture early rather than after design choices are fixed (NIST, 2023).

The pass-fail logic for Gate 1 should be strict. Pass means the use case is clearly defined, AI necessity is justified, risk tier is assigned with rationale, key data sources are identified with ownership, and an evaluation strategy exists with measurable success criteria. Fail means the project cannot explain its AI purpose, cannot identify data sources, cannot assign accountability, or cannot articulate how it will measure harm and misuse. A conditional pass may be allowed for lower tiers if missing items are minor and time-bounded, but for high tiers a conditional pass should be rare because it often becomes permanent debt.

For Gate 2, the Design Gate, the assurance goal is to prove that the architecture is governable. This includes data governance design, security controls, human oversight design, and monitoring design. Evidence should include architecture and data flow diagrams, control mapping, threat modeling for AI-specific threats, defined guardrails for generative systems, evaluation plans with datasets and thresholds, and a defined approach for change control of model versions and prompt templates. ISO/IEC 42001 reinforces that lifecycle management and continual improvement are core management system expectations, which implies that design must include governance routines and not only technical components (ISO, 2023a).

The pass-fail logic for Gate 2 centers on completeness and feasibility. Pass means the design includes controls that match risk tier, owners are assigned, acceptance criteria are defined, and monitoring and incident response integration are designed. Fail means the design does not address AI-specific threats, treats data governance as an afterthought, lacks evaluation thresholds, or relies on vague statements such as "we will monitor later."

For Gate 3, Build or Buy Readiness, the assurance goal is to prove that the system has been built or acquired in a way that produces verifiable trust. This is where evidence volume can explode if not controlled. The key is to focus on proof of secure and responsible build, plus proof of evaluation depth. Evidence should include model and prompt version control records, data lineage and quality checks, security test results tied to threat scenarios, red-team results for misuse, and remediation closure for high-severity findings. For vendor acquisitions, evidence should include vendor assurance artifacts, configuration baselines, third-party risk controls, and proof that shared responsibility is understood and operationalized. NIST SP 800-218A supports this gate by providing AI-focused secure development tasks and considerations that can be used to structure build evidence and show disciplined development practices for AI models and systems (NIST, 2024a).

Pass-fail logic at Gate 3 should be anchored to risk tier and critical findings. Pass means critical controls are implemented, evaluation meets thresholds, high-severity security issues are remediated or formally accepted with risk rationale, and operational readiness items are on track. Fail means evaluation is incomplete, red-team findings are unresolved, model and prompt changes are uncontrolled, or key vendor assurances are missing.

For Gate 4, the Implementation Gate, the assurance goal is to prove production readiness and the ability to sustain trust on day one of go-live. This gate often fails when teams focus on deployment mechanics and neglect AI monitoring and guardrail enforcement in production context. Evidence should include production monitoring dashboards, alert thresholds, logging and retention controls, rollback plans for model or configuration changes, incident response playbook updates for AI scenarios, and final validation that guardrails work in the production environment. For generative AI, this includes validating that prompt injection defenses and output handling controls remain effective when connected to real systems and real data. OWASP's risk categories provide a practical checklist for what must be validated in production, including prompt injection and insecure output handling, because these risks often manifest through integration choices rather than model training choices (OWASP, 2023).

Pass-fail logic at Gate 4 should emphasize operational readiness and containment. Pass means the system can be monitored, incidents can be responded to, rollbacks can be executed, and governance oversight cadence is in place. Fail means monitoring is not implemented, logging is unsafe or uncontrolled, escalation triggers are undefined, or the team cannot prove it can detect and contain misuse.

For Gate 5, the Sustain Gate, the assurance goal is to prove continuous assurance. This is where AI governance either becomes real or fades into "we will handle it later." Evidence should include drift monitoring results, periodic revalidation outcomes, incident reports, and lessons learned, ongoing vendor update impacts where relevant, and governance review minutes that show oversight is active. ISO/IEC 23894 explicitly emphasizes integrating AI risk management into AI-related activities and functions and describes processes for effective implementation and integration, which aligns with sustainment routines such as periodic reviews, continuous monitoring, and corrective actions (ISO, 2023a).

Pass-fail logic at Gate 5 is about demonstrating that controls remain operating and that governance is learning. Pass means drift is monitored, revalidation is scheduled and executed, incidents are handled with evidence, and changes follow controlled workflows. Fail means the system is running without meaningful monitoring, evaluation is not repeated, and governance cannot demonstrate improvement over time.

Audit Ready by Design

Audit readiness becomes manageable when you treat evidence bundles as structured, consistent, and versioned across gates. Auditors, regulators, and boards rarely ask for your entire data lake. They ask for proof that you know what you are doing, that you can trace decisions to evidence, and that you can demonstrate controls are operating. If your gate evidence bundles are well-designed, you can answer most audit questions quickly.

The core audit-ready package for AI systems typically includes a documented use case and risk tier, an accountability map, a control plan, data lineage and governance documentation, evaluation reports with reproducible details, security testing and misuse testing results, change control records, monitoring and incident response documentation, and post-deployment review evidence. This package aligns closely with management-system thinking in ISO/IEC 42001, which emphasizes governance structures, documented processes, and continual improvement, and it aligns with lifecycle risk management guidance in ISO/IEC 23894 (ISO, 2023a).

Audit readiness also benefits from control mapping. Control mapping is not a massive spreadsheet exercise if done pragmatically. The project should map key controls to one or two frameworks used as anchors, then reference others as needed. A practical pairing is NIST AI RMF for AI trustworthiness and risk framing, plus a management-system anchor such as ISO/IEC 42001 for governance process maturity. For generative AI systems, the NIST GenAI profile can be used as a targeted overlay for GenAI-specific risk actions (NIST, 2023; NIST, 2024b).

Security auditors will also ask how you managed AI-specific threats. This is where using recognized taxonomies helps. OWASP's LLM Top 10 provides a common language for major vulnerabilities, and MITRE ATLAS provides a scenario-driven perspective grounded in adversary tactics and techniques (OWASP, 2023). If your threat model and tests reference these categories, audit conversations move from vague anxiety to structured evidence.

Another audit readiness principle is reproducibility. If you cannot rerun critical evaluations, your evidence is fragile. Reproducibility does not require you to reproduce training for every audit. It requires you to preserve evaluation datasets, preserve configuration details, preserve model, and prompt versions, and preserve test scripts or prompt suites, so you can show that the reported results correspond to a specific system state.

Finally, audit readiness requires disciplined exception handling. In real delivery, there are waivers and risk acceptances. The governance failure is not that waivers exist. The failure is that waivers are undocumented, unowned, or permanent. A mature approach requires waivers to have a documented rationale, an expiration date, and a remediation plan. This is how governance avoids turning "temporary compromise" into "normal operating mode."

Key Takeaways

AI assurance is the method by which secure technology project management keeps trust intact while innovation accelerates. Metrics convert trustworthiness goals into measurable thresholds. Evidence bundles convert scattered artifacts into gate-ready proof. Gate-by-gate assurance integrates AI governance into the same disciplined decision system used across ADDIS, preventing AI from becoming a special-case loophole. Audit readiness becomes natural when evidence is structured, reproducible, and tied to accountable decisions. This approach aligns with NIST AI RMF's lifecycle risk management framing, the targeted guidance of NIST's GenAI profile, and the management-system discipline of ISO/IEC 42001, supported by AI risk management guidance in ISO/IEC 23894 (NIST, 2023; NIST, 2024b).

Most importantly, this chapter reinforces a challenge that separates mature organizations from fragile ones. If a system cannot be explained, monitored, and governed, it should not be deployed into environments where trust matters. Assurance is how you prove governability. It is how you keep gates meaningful. It is how you prevent AI from turning your delivery engine into a trust liability. The next part of the book will return to broader best practices and execution patterns, but the assurance spine established here should remain in force wherever AI is involved, because trust is earned through evidence, and evidence is earned through disciplined delivery.

“In AI delivery, trust is not claimed. It is measured, recorded, and defended.”

Make trust measurable. Define a small set of thresholds that signal readiness, such as performance floors, safety constraints, and stability indicators. When thresholds are clear, assurance becomes repeatable instead of subjective.

Turn artifacts into proof. Treat the evidence bundle as the working package that connects metrics, evaluations, approvals, and monitoring outputs into gate-ready documentation. If evidence is scattered, governance becomes guesswork.

Keep AI inside the same discipline. AI does not require a special exemption path. It requires stronger evidence and tighter accountability within the same gate routine , so exceptions do not become loopholes.

Deploy only what you can govern. If you cannot explain behavior, monitor drift and misuse, and show accountable decisions, you do not have an operational system. You have an unmanaged risk.

Assurance keeps gates meaningful by making governability visible and provable.

ζ

CASE STUDIES & PRACTICAL EXECUTION

Introduction

If Parts I through V are the blueprint and the control spine, Part ζ is where the method meets the work. It is where secure technology project management stops sounding like a philosophy and starts behaving like an operating system. The intent is not to bury you in process. The intent is to make secure delivery repeatable. Repeatable means the work survives staff turnover, vendor pressure, shifting deadlines, and the uncomfortable reality that emerging technology changes faster than policies do.

Most organizations do not struggle because they lack frameworks. They struggle because frameworks do not translate cleanly into daily decisions. A project manager needs to know what to ask on Tuesday morning when a vendor claims an integration is "standard." A product owner needs to know how to write requirements that make security testable, not merely aspirational. A CISO needs to know how to turn "high risk" into clear gate criteria and evidence expectations. A governance board needs to know how to review without becoming a bottleneck. Part ζ is written for those moments, the moments when the project is moving, the risks are real, and the organization needs clarity more than it needs slogans.

This part also responds to a modern truth that has become impossible to ignore. Technology projects are no longer only about delivering features. They are about delivering trust. Trust is not abstract, it is the measurable confidence that the system will behave within acceptable bounds, even when it is under stress, attacked, misused, or changed over time. That is why practical execution is anchored in outcomes and evidence. Frameworks like the NIST Cybersecurity Framework 2.0 are useful not because they add paperwork, but because they give a common taxonomy of cybersecurity outcomes that teams can use to communicate, prioritize, and demonstrate progress without prescribing a single method for every environment (NIST, 2024b).

Part ∠ is also where the ADDIS gate governance model becomes operational muscle memory. Gate governance is only as strong as the artifacts and behaviors that feed it. When evidence is inconsistent, boards become subjective. When evidence is weak, decisions become political. When roles are unclear, risk acceptance becomes accidental. The practical guidance and the case studies in this part help prevent that drift. They create standard review routines, standard language for readiness, and a consistent approach to demonstrating assurance.

There is another reason this part matters, especially now. AI and other emerging technologies create a new class of delivery friction. They increase attack surface, increase uncertainty, and increase the speed at which system behavior can change. Traditional delivery habits that were “good enough” for conventional applications become fragile under AI workloads. That is why this part treats AI as a practical overlay, not as a separate universe. The NIST AI Risk Management Framework (AI RMF) emphasizes that AI risk management is lifecycle-based, that governance is foundational, and that organizations must map context, measure risks, and manage them through controls and accountability

(NIST, 2023). The practical implication is simple. You do not govern AI by intention. You govern AI by instrumentation, evaluation, evidence, and change control.

To keep this part usable, the content is organized around three themes: execution patterns that make secure delivery repeatable, case studies that make governance behaviors memorable, and practical guidance that helps you run secure delivery without turning governance into a brake pedal.

The first objective is speed with discipline. Many leaders hear "security" and assume it means delay. That assumption is often caused by poor integration, not by security itself. When security controls are built into delivery workflows, they reduce rework and prevent surprise failures. A disciplined secure SDLC approach, supported by the Secure Software Development Framework (SSDF), provides a core set of secure development practices that can be integrated into any SDLC model so teams are not forced to reinvent security for each project (Souppaya et al., 2022).

The second objective is evidence-based gate governance. Gate reviews should not be theatrical. They should be decision points supported by concise evidence bundles. Evidence bundles are how delivery teams prove that risks are identified, controls are designed, controls are implemented, and controls are validated. This aligns with management system discipline in standards like ISO/IEC 27001, which emphasizes structured risk management and continuous improvement rather than one-time compliance activity (ISO, 2022). A stable evidence approach makes internal and external assurance easier because it creates traceability.

The third objective is alignment across roles and operating models. Delivery is now multi-model. Some initiatives are Agile, some are hybrid, some are waterfall, some are vendor-led, and many are a blend. This part does not assume one method. It assumes that governance and controls must travel across methods. It also assumes that accountability must survive organizational complexity. Frameworks like COBIT 2019 are often used by governance leaders because they connect enterprise governance and management objectives to accountability, risk, and value, which helps keep oversight coherent even when delivery models vary (ISACA, 2019).

The fourth objective is operational readiness and sustainment realism. Many project failures occur after "success." A system goes live, and the organization discovers it cannot monitor, patch, or govern it reliably. Secure delivery is incomplete if the system cannot be sustained. For AI-enabled systems, this matters even more. You must monitor drift, misuse, and changes in behavior, and you must be able to prove what version of the model or configuration was active when an incident occurred (NIST, 2023).

Finally, this part is designed to reduce noise. Practical guidance can become a trap when teams collect artifacts like souvenirs and then ignore them. The approach here is intentionally bounded. Use fewer artifacts, make them higher quality, keep them consistent, and make them defensible.

How to use this guidance without creating bureaucracy

Practical guidance only works when it reduces effort rather than adding it. The most common failure pattern is turning "good practice" into mandatory paperwork. That leads to checkbox behavior, shallow content, and resistance from delivery teams. The correct approach is to treat structured guidance as an accelerator. It provides defaults. It standardizes language. It reduces decision fatigue. It creates evidence in a format governance can review quickly.

Start by selecting a small set of "always-on" artifacts. These are the artifacts that every project should produce because they are foundational to Security by Design and defensible governance. For most organizations, the always-on set includes a problem statement and scope definition, a requirements baseline with security requirements embedded, an architecture and data flow view, a threat model or structured risk analysis, a test strategy with security testing included, and an operational readiness baseline. SSDF supports this approach because it outlines secure development practices that naturally map to these deliverables across planning, design, implementation, and release (Souppaya et al., 2022).

Next, scale depth based on risk tier. This is where governance becomes intelligent rather than heavy. A Tier 1 internal automation may not require deep red-team testing, but it still needs identity controls, change control, and basic monitoring. A Tier 4 system affecting financial decisions, customer access, or critical operations needs stronger evidence and stronger review. NIST CSF 2.0 is useful here because it supports outcome-based prioritization, letting organizations scale their cybersecurity risk governance and management practices based on context and maturity (NIST, 2024b).

For AI-enabled projects, add the AI overlay evidence when AI is a material component of decisioning, automation, or user interaction. The overlay is not extra paperwork. It is the minimal set of additional controls required to govern uncertainty. This includes data inventory and lineage documentation, evaluation and misuse testing evidence, model, and configuration versioning records, monitoring signals for drift and abuse, and incident response extensions for AI scenarios (NIST, 2023). For generative AI applications, the OWASP Top 10 for LLM applications provides a practical list of common vulnerability categories, such as prompt injection and insecure output handling, which can be translated directly into test cases and control checks (OWASP, 2023).

Then, tailor the artifacts to your operating model. If your teams use Agile, embed evidence into backlog workflows. Convert requirements into user stories with security acceptance criteria. Convert control requirements into Definition of Done checks. Use structured prompts as starting points, then keep them light. If your teams use waterfall or hybrid, align evidence to phases and gate readiness. The goal is not to force one delivery style. The goal is to ensure that security and governance outcomes are achieved regardless of style.

Finally, treat your evidence approach as a living system. ISO/IEC 27001 emphasizes ongoing improvement of the security management system, which implies that artifacts and controls should evolve based on incidents, audit findings, and delivery lessons (ISO, 2022). Each time a project experiences rework due to missing evidence, you refine what "minimum defensible" means. Each time a gate review gets stuck due to ambiguity, you clarify the pass or fail criteria. Each time an incident reveals missing monitoring signals, you improve operational readiness.

A small behavioral pattern separates mature organizations from struggling ones. Mature teams treat structured prompts as conversation starters, not as documents. You should be able to sit in a workshop and use the guidance to drive discussion.

Project lead: "If we ship in six weeks, what is the fastest way we can still be defensible?"

Security lead: "Show me the data lineage, show me the threat model for this workflow, show me the test evidence for the top abuse paths, and show me the monitoring plan. If we cannot show those, we are shipping hope."

Governance chair: "Hope is not an approval strategy. Bring the evidence bundle."

That exchange is not harsh. It is healthy. It is what keeps the organization from mistaking speed for readiness.

How the case studies are structured

Case studies exist because people remember stories longer than they remember rules. A well-designed case study compresses years of lessons into a narrative you can replay when you face a similar situation. In Part ℒ, the case studies are not written to be dramatic. They are written to be diagnostic. Each case highlights a pattern, the decisions that shaped the outcome, the control gaps that mattered, and the governance behaviors that either prevented failure or enabled it.

The cases are intentionally contrasted. You will see examples of traditional technology projects alongside AI-enabled projects because the comparison reveals where AI changes the risk profile and where it does not. Many controls remain stable across both. Identity, access control, secure configuration, and patch management still matter. Evidence bundles still matter. Gate governance still matters. What changes is the uncertainty and the abuse surface. Generative AI introduces new pathways for manipulation, such as prompt injection, tool misuse, or sensitive information exposure through conversational interfaces (OWASP, 2023). That is why the case studies emphasize how teams discovered, tested, and contained those pathways.

Each case study uses a consistent structure so you can learn quickly. It begins with context, including business drivers and constraints. It then describes the delivery model and governance model. It highlights the most important risks and threat scenarios. It identifies the gate decisions and the evidence that supported those decisions. It captures what went wrong, if something went wrong, and what the organization changed as a result. This approach aligns with lifecycle risk thinking in the NIST AI RMF, which emphasizes understanding context, measuring, and managing risk, and integrating governance into the lifecycle (NIST, 2023).

Case studies also highlight a reality that practitioners often avoid saying out loud. Technology risk is rarely purely technical. It is usually organizational. Projects fail when accountability is unclear, when decision rights are ambiguous, when incentives reward speed without responsibility, and when evidence is treated as a last-minute chore. That is why governance frameworks remain relevant. They provide structure for who decides, who approves, and who owns residual risk. COBIT is useful as a reference point because it frames governance and management objectives in a way that supports accountability and alignment with stakeholder value, even when technology is complex (ISACA, 2019).

Practical Execution Guidance

Part ζ also provides practical execution guidance because many leaders know what they want, but they struggle to make it happen in real time. The difference between an elegant framework and an effective delivery system is routine. A routine is the repeating cycle of planning, building, validating, and proving readiness.

A secure delivery routine starts with early alignment. In the first weeks of a project, leaders must lock down scope boundaries, classify data, define the risk tier, and assign accountability. This is where the project stops being an idea and becomes a governed initiative.

Next comes a design routine that treats controls as architecture, not as patches. Threat modeling, control mapping, and test strategy should happen while architecture is still flexible. If you wait until build, your options narrow and your costs rise. SSDF supports embedding security early in the SDLC, including ensuring requirements and architecture decisions support secure outcomes and reduce vulnerabilities downstream (Souppaya et al., 2022).

Then comes an execution routine where evidence is produced continuously. In secure delivery, every sprint should produce not only features but also proofs. Security testing results, dependency checks, configuration baseline evidence, and remediation closure become part of normal progress. This is also where supply chain considerations become real. Modern systems rely on third-party components, and secure delivery requires knowing what you are shipping and where it came from. That is why artifact discipline, versioning, and provenance are recurring themes.

For AI projects, the routine includes continuous evaluation and monitoring readiness. AI is not a static artifact. It behaves differently depending on inputs, context, and changes in data distributions. Risk management therefore requires measurement and management throughout the lifecycle, not only at build time (NIST, 2023). Practical execution includes maintaining evaluation suites, running regression tests when configurations change, and validating that monitoring signals can detect drift and misuse. It also includes testing for common vulnerability paths in generative AI, such as prompt injection and insecure output handling, because these are routine failure modes when systems are integrated without guardrails (OWASP, 2023).

Gate readiness becomes a natural output of this routine . Instead of preparing for gates with panic, teams prepare with accumulation. Evidence bundles are built over time, and quality reviews sample evidence to confirm readiness. This is where governance becomes an accelerator. Boards can approve quickly when evidence is consistent and when pass or fail criteria are clear.

Finally, practical execution includes sustainment as part of delivery. Too many projects treat sustainment as somebody else's problem. Mature teams treat sustainment as a requirement. Monitoring, incident response, patching workflows, access reviews, and continuous assurance routines must be operational at go-live, not planned after go-live. ISO management system thinking reinforces this by emphasizing continual improvement and structured maintenance of security practices (ISO, 2022).

This is also where project management principles matter. The best secure delivery systems are not driven by fear. They are driven by value delivery and disciplined execution. Project management standards emphasize principles of value, adaptability, and accountability, and those principles align well with Security by Design when security is treated as part of value protection rather than as an obstacle (PMI, 2021b).

Closing perspective for the reader

Part ረ is written to be used, not admired. Approach it like a field manual. Use case studies as pattern recognition exercises. Ask your team, “Where are we in this story, and what would prevent us from becoming the cautionary version of it?”

If you are a project manager, treat this part as your guide for asking the right questions early and for building evidence that protects your schedule later. If you are a security leader, treat it as a way to standardize expectations without turning every project into a custom negotiation. If you are a PMO leader, treat it as a mechanism for scaling governance across portfolios. If you are a board member or executive, treat it as your method for ensuring that approval decisions are defensible and repeatable.

Above all, treat secure delivery as a habit. Habits are built through repetition, not through intention. Case studies build memory. Practical execution guidance builds routine . When these are combined with the ADDIS gate governance model, secure SDLC practices, and AI-aware assurance, the organization builds something rare and valuable: the ability to deliver modern technology at speed while keeping trust intact (NIST, 2024b; Souppaya et al., 2022).

This is the promise of Part ረ. It is not perfection. It is governability. It is the ability to say, with confidence and proof, that the organization is not merely building technology, it is building technology that deserves to be relied upon.

20

Secure Delivery Playbook

Secure delivery is not a department. It is a way of working. When it works, it looks almost boring from the outside: decisions are made early, risks are named plainly, controls are designed into the system, and evidence is produced as the work progresses. When it fails, it fails loudly and expensively. The organization pays in outages, breaches, audit findings, rework, and reputational damage. In the age of AI and emerging technology, the cost of "almost secure" is rising because the attack surface expands and the behavior of systems can shift over time. That is why modern project leaders must treat security as a delivery outcome, not as a compliance task. The NIST Cybersecurity Framework 2.0 reinforces this by framing cybersecurity as risk management and governance, not merely technical controls, and by emphasizing outcomes that organizations can adapt to their context and maturity (NIST, 2024b).

This chapter focuses on what experienced teams do differently. It presents best practices that scale across traditional technology projects and AI-enabled systems, highlights failure patterns that repeat across industries, and explains execution patterns that make secure delivery repeatable. The purpose is practical. You should be able to take the guidance here and translate it directly into how you run intake, requirements, architecture, build, testing, deployment, sustainment, and gate reviews. It is also intentionally honest. Many "best practice" lists are aspirational. This chapter emphasizes what actually survives real constraints, tight deadlines, vendor pressure, and competing priorities.

Best practices that scale across projects

The first best practice is to anchor delivery in governance outcomes, not activity volume. Many organizations measure security by counting tasks: number of scans, number of policies, number of trainings. Mature organizations measure security by outcomes: reduction in critical vulnerabilities, improved time to patch, improved detection and response, fewer access exceptions, fewer incidents, and stronger audit readiness. CSF 2.0 is useful because it gives a stable vocabulary of outcomes that can be used to align executives, delivery leaders, and security teams, even when the technology changes (NIST, 2024b).

The second-best practice is to build security into the SDLC using defined practices rather than relying on individual expertise. When security depends on heroics, it will eventually collapse. The Secure Software Development Framework (SSDF) is a practical reference because it defines a core set of secure development practices that can be integrated into any SDLC model, including planning, design, implementation, testing, and release activities (Souppaya et al., 2022). In secure technology project management, SSDF functions as a baseline. Your organization can add more controls, but it should not fall below this minimum without conscious risk acceptance.

The third best practice is to treat identity as the control plane. Teams often focus on perimeter defenses while attackers focus on identity, access, and privilege. Secure delivery improves dramatically when identity and access management is treated as a first-class architecture component, with strong authentication, least privilege, and role-based access boundaries that match the delivery operating model. This becomes even more important in AI-enabled systems because prompts, logs, embeddings, retrieval sources, and model endpoints become new data surfaces. If identity controls are weak, these surfaces become open doors.

The fourth best practice is to design for evidence, not for promises. If you want gate reviews to be efficient and defensible, you must generate evidence as you work. Evidence is not a late-stage report. Evidence is the system of artifacts that prove controls were designed, implemented, and validated. In practice, this means your requirements include security requirements, your architecture includes control mappings, your sprints produce test results, and your release readiness includes verified security conditions. This is why SSDF is valuable. It is structured around practices that naturally produce evidence, which makes audit readiness easier to achieve without last-minute scrambling (Souppaya et al., 2022).

The fifth best practice is to align secure delivery to a management system mindset. A management system does not mean bureaucracy. It means consistency, accountability, and continuous improvement. ISO/IEC 27001 is widely used because it defines requirements for an information security management system, including risk treatment and continual improvement, which supports governance discipline beyond single projects (ISO, 2022). When organizations connect secure delivery practices to an Information Security Management System (ISMS), they reduce the “reinvent everything each project” problem. They also make controls easier to audit because governance structures are stable.

The sixth best practice is to embed supply chain integrity into delivery by default. Modern systems depend on open-source libraries, third-party services, cloud components, and vendor integrations. If you do not secure the supply chain, you do not secure the product. SLSA helps here because it provides a structured, incremental way to improve software supply chain integrity and to reduce tampering risks across the pipeline, from source to build to release (OpenSSF, n.d.). In delivery terms, supply chain best practices include dependency governance, secure build pipelines, artifact signing where feasible, provenance tracking, and strict control over who can publish production artifacts.

The seventh best practice is to operationalize “shift left and shift right.” Shift left means addressing security early, in requirements and design, and continuously in CI pipelines. Shift right means instrumenting systems in production, monitoring them, and learning from real behavior. Secure delivery fails when teams do only one of these. If you only shift left, you still get drift and operational surprises. If you only shift right, you accept avoidable design flaws. Mature programs do both, and they treat learning as part of governance.

The eighth best practice is to treat AI systems as systems, not models. AI changes secure delivery because the model is only one component in a broader pipeline that includes data, prompts, retrieval, tools, and interfaces. NIST’s AI RMF emphasizes lifecycle risk management and encourages organizations to map context, measure risks, and manage controls in ways that support trustworthy and responsible AI (NIST, 2023). For generative AI, OWASP’s Top 10 for LLM applications provides a practical risk taxonomy, including prompt injection and insecure output handling, which helps delivery teams translate abstract AI risks into testable control requirements (OWASP, 2023).

The ninth best practice is to define accountability that survives stress. Under pressure, organizations revert to informal power. If accountability is unclear, security decisions become inconsistent, and incidents become political. This is why governance frameworks like COBIT are often used because they emphasize enterprise governance and management objectives that connect stakeholder value, risk, and control responsibilities (ISACA, 2019). In practical terms, accountability must be defined as decision rights: who can approve exceptions, who can accept residual risk, who can block a release, and who owns controls in sustainment.

The tenth best practice is to treat secure delivery as a product of culture and process, not only technology. Tools matter, but they do not compensate for weak governance. If the culture rewards speed without accountability, security becomes a cost that teams try to avoid. If the culture rewards defensible outcomes, security becomes an asset that protects value.

Recurring Failures and Common Pitfalls

Pitfalls are valuable because they are predictable. If you can name them early, you can design around them.

A common pitfall is confusing activity with control. A team runs a vulnerability scan and assumes the system is secure. A team performs a pen test and assumes risks are addressed. A team writes a policy and assumes it is followed. These are comforting illusions. Secure delivery depends on control effectiveness, not activity completion. This is why outcome-based frameworks are useful. They force you to ask whether the organization can actually achieve and sustain desired outcomes, not merely whether it can produce artifacts (NIST, 2024b).

Another pitfall is pushing security "downstream." Teams delay threat modeling until after build, delay access reviews until after integration, delay logging until after deployment, and delay incident playbooks until after the first incident. Downstream security is expensive security. It creates rework, delays, and friction between teams. Secure delivery requires early alignment, especially around high-impact controls such as identity boundaries, network segmentation, data handling, and audit logging.

A third pitfall is building systems that cannot be monitored. Monitoring is often treated as a "nice to have" because it does not show up in demos. Yet monitoring is what makes systems governable after release. If you cannot detect misuse, drift, or anomalous access, you cannot manage risk in real time. For AI systems, this pitfall is amplified. If you do not log prompt activity safely, track model versions, and monitor output quality and policy violations, you will not know when the system becomes unsafe. You will learn through harm.

A fourth pitfall is uncontrolled change. Mature teams control changes to code, infrastructure, and configuration. Immature teams treat changes as "quick fixes." AI introduces a subtle version of this pitfall because changes can occur through prompts, retrieval content, training data, and vendor model updates. If change control is weak, the system becomes a moving target. NIST AI RMF emphasizes lifecycle thinking and ongoing evaluation, which implies that organizations must manage change as a risk factor, not as an afterthought (NIST, 2023).

A fifth pitfall is tool sprawl without integration. Organizations buy scanning tools, posture tools, and dashboards, but they do not connect them into delivery workflows. Engineers treat them as noise. Security teams treat them as "coverage." Executives treat them as "assurance." Nobody trusts the signals. Secure delivery requires integration into CI pipelines, ticketing, code review, release approvals, and operational monitoring. Tools should reduce cognitive load, not increase it.

A sixth pitfall is vendor and third-party blind trust. Organizations often outsource capability and inadvertently outsource accountability. In reality, regulators and customers hold the organization accountable for the outcome, even if a vendor caused the failure. Secure delivery requires third-party risk controls that are contractually enforceable, technically verifiable, and operationally monitored.

A seventh pitfall is treating compliance as the finish line. Compliance can be helpful because it forces baseline discipline. Yet compliance alone does not guarantee security, and it often lags the threat environment. Management system standards and risk frameworks are more effective when they are used as scaffolding for continuous improvement rather than as checklists to satisfy once (ISO, 2022).

An eighth pitfall is misunderstanding AI risk as purely "bias and ethics." Those risks matter, but AI security risks are also concrete engineering risks. Prompt injection, insecure output handling, training data poisoning, model theft, and excessive agency are risks that can be tested and mitigated like other security threats (OWASP, 2023). Teams fail when they treat AI risk as abstract, and they succeed when they translate AI risk into requirements, tests, and operational controls.

A ninth pitfall is the "one big gate" mentality. Some organizations treat gate reviews as a single approval moment before production. This creates panic and incentivizes superficial compliance. In disciplined delivery, gates are not surprises. Evidence is built progressively, and quality reviews happen continuously. Gate reviews confirm readiness, they do not discover readiness.

A tenth pitfall is underfunding sustainment. Many programs spend heavily on build and underinvest in monitoring, patching, and continuous assurance. That strategy is fragile even for traditional systems. For AI-enabled systems, it is dangerous. AI systems must be continuously monitored, evaluated, and updated. If you do not fund that, you are deploying a system that will degrade, and you will be surprised when it does.

Execution patterns that make secure delivery repeatable

Best practices become useful when they are packaged into repeatable patterns. Patterns are "how we do it here" methods that survive team changes and scaling.

One execution pattern is the control spine pattern. The control spine is the minimum set of controls and evidence artifacts that every project must produce, regardless of delivery method. It usually includes security requirements, architecture control mapping, threat modeling, secure build pipeline controls, security testing evidence, release readiness checks, and monitoring readiness. The spine is stable. Projects add additional controls based on risk tier. This approach aligns well with the SSDF mindset because SSDF practices can serve as a baseline spine that teams can implement consistently across SDLC models (Souppaya et al., 2022).

A second execution pattern is the “golden path” for secure pipelines. A golden path is the simplest, supported way to build and deploy systems securely. Teams are allowed to diverge, but divergence requires justification and additional controls. Golden paths reduce friction because developers do not need to invent security each project. They also reduce audit burden because evidence is produced consistently. Supply chain frameworks like SLSA are useful references for designing golden paths that improve artifact integrity and reduce tampering risk through stronger provenance and pipeline controls (OpenSSF, n.d.).

A third execution pattern is “two-speed assurance.” Not every risk is equal, so assurance should be proportional. Lower-risk systems use lighter review, automation, and sampling. Higher-risk systems require deeper evaluation, independent challenge, and stricter pass-fail thresholds. This is not leniency. It is risk economics. You spend assurance effort where the potential harm is greatest. CSF 2.0 supports this principle by encouraging organizations to use the framework outcomes to prioritize risk management actions based on context and maturity (NIST, 2024b).

A fourth execution pattern is evidence bundle engineering. Instead of treating evidence as an end product, teams design evidence bundles as part of project planning. They decide early what artifacts will exist, who owns them, where they live, and what acceptance criteria apply. This reduces late-stage friction and helps boards make faster decisions. It also prevents the “document dump” problem because evidence bundles have defined scope.

A fifth execution pattern is the “security story” integration pattern. In Agile and hybrid delivery, security is often lost because it is not broken into backlog items. Mature teams convert security requirements and controls into user stories, technical stories, and acceptance tests. They integrate security testing into Definition of Done. They treat vulnerabilities as defects with SLAs. They track remediation work as part of the delivery plan.

A sixth execution pattern is continuous threat modeling. Many teams treat threat modeling as a one-time workshop. Better teams treat it as a living artifact. As the architecture changes, as new integrations are added, as user behavior becomes clearer, the threat model is updated. For AI-enabled systems, threat modeling must include AI-specific threats like prompt injection and data poisoning, and it must map to real controls and tests, which OWASP's LLM Top 10 helps operationalize (OWASP, 2023).

A seventh execution pattern is AI control overlay by risk tier. The AI overlay is a small set of additional controls that activate when AI is involved, scaled by tier. These controls typically include data governance evidence, model and prompt version control, evaluation suites for normal and adversarial use, safety, and misuse testing, monitoring for drift and abuse, and incident response playbook updates for AI events. NIST AI RMF is a useful anchor because it treats these actions as lifecycle risk management activities rather than as one-time compliance tasks (NIST, 2023).

An eighth execution pattern is a clear exception management system. Exceptions will happen. The secure delivery question is whether exceptions are controlled. Mature organizations require exceptions to have a documented rationale, a risk owner, an expiration date, and compensating controls. This prevents exception creep, where temporary shortcuts become permanent risk.

A ninth execution pattern is "release readiness as a checklist plus proof." Release readiness should not be a meeting where people say they are ready. It should be a structured review of key conditions, each backed by evidence. SSDF supports this pattern because its practices naturally translate into checkable release conditions, including verifying that code changes are reviewed, vulnerabilities are addressed, and secure configuration is enforced (Souppaya et al., 2022).

A tenth execution pattern is the "operational handshake." In many failures, engineering delivers a system and operations inherits risk without understanding. The operational handshake is a formal, evidence-backed transfer that confirms monitoring, alerting, access controls, runbooks, and incident procedures are ready, and that ownership is clear. This is especially important for AI-enabled systems because operational teams must understand model behavior, versioning, monitoring signals, and rollback strategies. If operations cannot operate the system, the system is not truly delivered.

Practical rules for real-world decision making

Even with established patterns, project leaders need clear rules to make fast decisions. Secure delivery is often a sequence of tradeoffs, and tradeoffs become dangerous when they are made implicitly.

One rule is simple: when a decision increases the blast radius, demand stronger evidence. If a new integration expands access to sensitive data, require stronger access controls and better logging. If a new feature increases automation of actions, require stronger authorization and tighter monitoring. If AI adds tool-calling capability, set strict boundaries and test those boundaries, because too much system agency can turn helpful automation into harmful actions (OWASP, 2023).

Another rule is to treat uncertainty as risk. When teams say "We are not sure how users will use it," that is not a neutral statement. It is a signal that monitoring and guardrails must be stronger. When teams say "The vendor will handle that," that is a signal that shared responsibility must be clarified and verified. When teams say "We will fix it after launch," that is a signal that the system may not be governable under real conditions.

A third rule is that every gate decision should be tied to a clear risk acceptance statement. If you ship with known high-severity vulnerabilities, someone must accept that risk explicitly. If you deploy AI without monitoring for drift and misuse, someone must accept that risk explicitly. This is accountability. Without it, risk becomes nobody's responsibility.

A fourth rule is to privilege repeatability over brilliance. Teams often celebrate clever architecture. Secure delivery celebrates repeatable execution. That means standard pipelines, standard logging, standard access controls, standard evidence bundle structures, and consistent quality reviews. Repeatability reduces surprises and makes assurance scalable.

A fifth rule is to "measure what you will be judged by." If the board will ask about incidents, measure detection, and response time. If auditors ask about control operation, measure control adherence. If customers ask about privacy, measure data minimization, and access reviews. If AI is involved, measure policy violations, injection resistance, and drift, because those are the indicators that most directly predict trust failure (NIST, 2023; OWASP, 2023).

A sixth rule is to keep references and frameworks disciplined. Too many frameworks create confusion and bloat. A practical approach is to anchor on a small set that covers your needs. CSF 2.0 for cybersecurity risk outcomes, SSDF for secure development practices, ISO/IEC 27001 for management system discipline, and for AI systems, NIST AI RMF plus OWASP LLM Top 10 for practical security risk translation. This keeps governance clear and reduces the temptation to over-document.

Key Takeaways

Secure technology project management becomes reliable when secure delivery is treated as an operating model, not as a late-stage test. Best practices that scale include outcome-based governance, SSDF-aligned SDLC integration, identity-first architecture, evidence-driven gates, management system discipline, supply chain integrity, and continuous monitoring. Failure patterns repeat because organizations confuse activity with control, push security downstream, underinvest in monitoring, allow uncontrolled change, trust vendors without verification, and treat compliance as the finish line. AI amplifies these risks by increasing attack surface and introducing behavioral drift, which is why AI assurance and AI security practices must be embedded into the same delivery spine used for all technology projects (NIST, 2024b; Souppaya et al., 2022).

Execution patterns make the difference between aspiration and reality. The control spine pattern, golden paths, proportional assurance, evidence bundle engineering, continuous threat modeling, and an AI control overlay by risk tier create a delivery system that can scale across teams and technologies. When these patterns are institutionalized, secure delivery stops being a recurring crisis and becomes a dependable capability. That is the real objective of this chapter. Not perfect security, but governable security, proven through evidence, maintained through monitoring, and strengthened through continuous improvement.

Case Studies and Lessons

Case studies are the bridge between a method and a habit. A method can look strong on paper, yet fail in the hallway conversation where deadlines, vendor pressure, and executive urgency collide. In those moments, teams do not need more theory. They need a repeatable way to decide, to document, and to move forward without gambling the organization's trust. That is why this chapter is built around three practical stories. Each one is anchored in the ADDIS lifecycle, tested through Gate Governance, and judged by evidence rather than assurances. The goal is not to present perfect projects. The goal is to make secure delivery recognizable and repeatable in environments where uncertainty is normal and tradeoffs are unavoidable (NIST, 2024b; Souppaya et al., 2022).

Across all three cases, the same principle holds. Secure SDLC is not a checklist, it is an operating discipline. Teams build trust when security activities are planned, executed, and evidenced as part of delivery, not treated as a late inspection step. The NIST Secure Software Development Framework is useful because it defines core practices that can be integrated into any SDLC style, whether a team works in agile sprints, a hybrid program, or a vendor-led implementation (Souppaya et al., 2022). NIST CSF 2.0 is equally helpful because it provides a common language for cybersecurity outcomes and puts governance at the center through its "Govern" function. That emphasis helps leaders translate cybersecurity intent into accountable oversight, decision rights, and measurable expectations (NIST, 2024b).

To keep these cases practical, each one follows a consistent pattern. First, the business context and delivery constraints are stated clearly so the reader can see what drove urgency, scope boundaries, and resourcing. Second, the threat and risk realities are made explicit. This includes what data is involved, where trust boundaries sit, what integrations expand exposure, and what operational constraints limit control options. Third, the Gate evidence bundle is described, not as paperwork, but as decision support. Readers see what artifacts were required, what proof was reviewed, what questions were answered, and how conditions were documented when readiness was incomplete. Finally, each case ends with lessons that would have been expensive if learned later, such as unclear ownership, weak monitoring integration, contract controls that were not enforceable, or risks that were accepted implicitly instead of governed.

The three stories are deliberately varied to reflect common delivery realities. One centers on in-house development where speed, architectural choices, and testing discipline determine whether the build produces proof or produces exposure. Another focuses on vendor acquisition, where the most common failure is mistaking vendor confidence for customer-ready security. It shows why shared responsibility must be explicit, why contract terms must translate into enforceable controls, and why onboarding must include identity, logging, monitoring, and operational integration. The third case reflects AI-enabled delivery, where intended use, unacceptable use, data provenance, evaluation thresholds, and misuse testing become essential evidence, not optional enhancements. In all three, the ADDIS gates create disciplined decision points. They help teams stop, prove readiness, and move forward with accountable ownership and defensible evidence.

Taken together, these case studies show how secure technology project management becomes repeatable. They demonstrate that governance does not slow delivery when it is evidence-driven. It reduces rework, prevents surprise risk, and builds confidence that the organization can deliver value without accumulating hidden liability (NIST, 2024b; Souppaya et al., 2022).

CASE STUDY 1

In-House Development Using ADDIS Gates

A mid-sized financial services organization, here called HarborBridge Credit, decided to modernize its customer onboarding and account-servicing platform. The legacy system was brittle, slow to change, and expensive to maintain. Business leaders wanted faster onboarding, fewer abandoned applications, and better digital self-service. The technical team wanted a clean break from a monolith. Security leaders wanted fewer compensating controls and fewer exceptions. Everyone wanted the launch before the next product season, which meant the schedule was not merely a plan, it was a political commitment.

The project was scoped as an in-house build: a web and mobile experience backed by API-driven services, hosted in a hybrid cloud architecture. The system would touch personally identifiable information, regulated financial data, identity verification workflows, and third-party data sources. That combination creates a predictable risk landscape: account takeover, API abuse, data leakage, fraud-driven automation, and supply chain vulnerabilities. The organization had seen smaller incidents before, credential stuffing, bot abuse, and one painful data exposure due to misconfigured access controls. The sponsor's instructions were clear: "Move fast, but do not make us famous for the wrong reason."

Analyze phase and Gate 1, when speed tries to outrun clarity

The Analyze phase started with a common failure pattern, a strong solution vision and a weak problem boundary. Marketing wanted a "frictionless experience." Operations wanted fewer calls. Risk wanted better fraud checks. Security wanted stronger identity proofing and centralized logging. The first intervention was governance, not technology. The PMO and the Gate Review Board required a single-page scope boundary statement that answered three blunt questions: What data classes are in scope, what integrations are in scope, and what will not be delivered in this release. The team also tiered the project as high impact because it affected customer access and regulated data. That tier decision was not cosmetic. It triggered deeper evidence requirements for design, testing, and operational readiness.

At Gate 1, the pass or fail hinge was the evidence set. The Gate Review Board required: a problem statement, scope boundary, initial data classification, a preliminary threat model, and a security requirements baseline embedded into functional requirements. This is where SSDF thinking paid off early. Instead of treating security as a late-stage test, the team integrated secure requirements into the same backlog that drove functional delivery, aligning with SSDF's emphasis on integrating secure practices into SDLC implementations (Souppaya et al., 2022).

The threat model was intentionally pragmatic. It focused on top abuse paths: credential stuffing, session hijacking, API authorization bypass, improper rate limiting, insecure direct object references, and log tampering. Security did not bring fear, it brought a map. The team's dialogue shifted:

- Product lead: "Can we just build, we know the features."
- Security architect: "We can build, but first we decide what 'safe enough' means. If we do not define it now, we will argue about it at the end, and the deadline will win."
- Sponsor: "Define it now. Show me what proof I will need to approve."

Gate 1 passed because the project was no longer an idea. It was a governed initiative with defined decision rights, explicit risk tiering, and a minimum defensible evidence baseline, aligned to governance principles emphasized in modern cybersecurity frameworks (NIST, 2024).

Design Phase and Gate 2, Turning Security into Blueprint

The Design phase produced two artifacts that changed outcomes. First, a data flow view that highlighted trust boundaries and identity flows, not just components. Second, a control map that linked threats to controls and linked controls to testable requirements. This prevented a common design failure, controls described in words, but not expressed in architecture.

Three design decisions were especially important.

1. Identity and authorization were treated as product features, with a centralized policy model for APIs, not scattered authorization checks across services.
2. Logging was designed as a control system, including event schemas, correlation IDs, and retention requirements, rather than "we will log what we can."
3. Secrets management and encryption boundaries were designed upfront, so keys and tokens were not handled casually in app configuration.

At Gate 2, the Quality Review Board inspected evidence rather than opinions. They sampled the requirements, checked whether security acceptance criteria existed, and verified traceability from threats to controls to tests. The Design Gate decision was not "the architecture looks good." It was, "the architecture is testable, the controls are explicit, and the evidence plan is realistic."

This is the moment many organizations rush. HarborBridge did not rush. They treated Gate 2 like pouring a foundation. A foundation is invisible later, which is exactly why it must be strong now.

Gate 3, Proving Readiness Beyond Working

In the Develop phase, the team used CI/CD pipelines with embedded security checks. They did not call it "DevSecOps" as a slogan. They treated it as evidence generation. Static analysis, dependency checks, secrets scanning, and container image scanning produced audit-ready logs. The team also built a lightweight "release evidence bundle" that accumulated sprint by sprint. This eliminated the end-of-phase "paper sprint" that produces shallow evidence.

The most consequential governance decision came mid-build. A critical third-party library vulnerability surfaced in a common component. Engineering wanted to patch later because integration testing was underway. Security insisted on immediate remediation. The PMO forced a time-boxed decision: patch now, re-test now, or formally accept residual risk with compensating controls and an expiry date. The sponsor asked one question: "How long will we carry the risk, and how will we know if it is exploited?" That question, simple and uncomfortable, changed the default behavior. The team patched, re-tested, and moved on.

Gate 3 required clear evidence categories: security testing results focused on the highest-risk workflows, remediation status showing critical findings were closed or formally governed, and an exception log with named owners, compensating controls, and expiry dates. It also required configuration baseline proof for each environment so the release candidate could be defended and reproduced. The gate passed because the team treated evidence as a continuous output throughout build and onboarding, not as a last-minute scramble. Readiness was demonstrated through traceable proof, not confident claims.

Implement and Gate 4, Proving Readiness Under Stress

In the Implement phase, the team ran a controlled rollout. They validated monitoring coverage, ensured alerts reached real responders, tested rollback paths, and executed an incident simulation focused on account takeover. Operational readiness was treated as a control, not a checklist.

Gate 4 was nearly delayed because monitoring gaps were discovered. This is the moment when weak governance would have approved anyway. Strong governance did not. The Gate Review Board required completion of three items: finalized alert thresholds for fraud patterns, confirmation of log completeness for key transactions, and validated on-call escalation paths. The delay was three days. The avoided outage, reputational damage, and rework were worth far more than three days.

Sustain and Gate 5, From Project to Operational Promise

Gate 5 focused on continuous assurance. Vulnerability management cadence, access reviews, control monitoring, and a quarterly re-validation plan were documented and funded. Ownership was transferred cleanly. The system did not "go live and disappear." It became governable.

Case Study 1 lessons

The strongest lesson was not technical. It was behavioral: the team treated Gate Governance as a method for accelerating clarity. They learned that every time they delayed evidence, they increased negotiation later. They also learned that the most expensive defects are the ones you deploy into production with confidence.

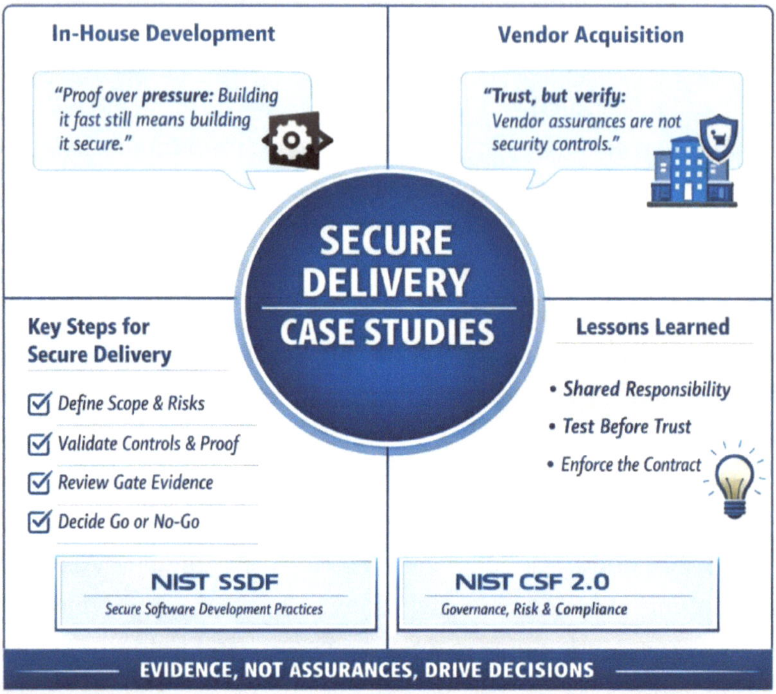

"In every case study, the lesson is the same: evidence turns urgency into safe progress."

CASE STUDY 2

Vendor Acquisition and Third-Party Risk

The second case is a different animal. LumenCare Health Network needed a customer engagement platform for patient communications and appointment workflows. Leadership decided to acquire a SaaS solution rather than build. The reasoning was sound: faster time to value, vendor expertise, and predictable operating costs. The risk, however, was also predictable: shared responsibility confusion, integration complexity, data privacy exposure, contract gaps, and fragile reliance on vendor assurances.

This case demonstrates a truth that many organizations learn painfully. When you acquire technology, you are not outsourcing accountability. You are importing risk into your ecosystem. That is why governance must treat vendor delivery as a secure SDLC variant, not as a shortcut.

Analyze phase and Gate 1, defining "what we are buying"

The first governance move was to define the solution boundary. SaaS platforms often become "the new core" without leadership noticing. LumenCare required a formal statement of what data would flow into the vendor, what data would remain internal, and what integrations were required. The project was classified as high risk because it touched health data and operational processes.

Gate 1 evidence requirements were expanded for vendor acquisition. In addition to the business case and scope, the Gate Review Board required: an initial vendor risk posture assessment, security requirements embedded in procurement criteria, and an integration risk analysis. The board explicitly rejected marketing brochures as evidence.

This aligns with CSF 2.0's emphasis that cybersecurity outcomes are governance-driven and must be integrated into organizational decisions, including supplier relationships and risk prioritization (NIST, 2024).

Design Phase and Gate 2, Contract Control, and Integration Risk

The Design phase in vendor acquisition is often neglected because "the product already exists." That is a dangerous belief. The most important design work is not building features, it is defining the shared responsibility model and hardening the integration boundary.

At Gate 2, LumenCare required three categories of evidence.

1. Shared responsibility mapping: what the vendor controls, what the organization controls, and what is jointly controlled.
2. Security architecture of integration: authentication methods, authorization logic, token handling, failure modes, and audit trails.
3. Contractual control clauses: incident notification timelines, security testing rights, audit report availability, breach support obligations, data deletion and return, subcontractor transparency, and exit planning.

This is where regulatory pressure becomes practical. Even if the organization is not directly under EU DORA, DORA provides a useful model for demanding operational resilience and disciplined oversight of ICT risk in financial contexts, including strong expectations for managing ICT disruptions and resilience (European Parliament and Council, 2022). NIS2 also reinforces cybersecurity obligations across covered entities and increases governance expectations, which raises the reputational cost of weak vendor oversight (European Parliament and Council, 2022).

The Gate Review Board asked a question that became a refrain: "If the vendor fails at 2 a.m., what exactly happens here, and what can we do without them?" That question forced a real exit and resilience plan, not a theoretical one.

Develop phase and Gate 3, validating what the vendor claims

Gate 3 in a vendor scenario is the point where the organization validates security controls in its own context. Vendor compliance reports may help, but they do not validate your configuration or your integration.

LumenCare's Gate 3 evidence set included: configuration hardening proof, identity and access control validation, integration security testing results, and incident response coordination testing with the vendor. They also required evidence that the vendor's incident notification obligations were operational, not just contractual.

A common point of friction emerged. The vendor initially resisted certain security test requests. The procurement team wanted to compromise to preserve the relationship. Security and governance leaders refused to sign off. They used a simple rule: no right to validate, no right to trust. The final contract included test rights and clear timelines.

This case also illustrates why SEC governance expectations matter even beyond public companies. The SEC's cybersecurity rules require disclosures about cybersecurity risk management, strategy, and governance, and they heighten board-level visibility into cyber risk (SEC, 2023). When governance becomes disclosable, vendors can no longer be treated as "somebody else's problem."

Implement and Gate 4, Third-Party Operational Handover

LumenCare's Gate 4 was focused on operational readiness for a shared environment. That meant validated logging access, tested escalation paths with vendor support, clear RACI for incident handling, and rehearsal of data restoration and service continuity steps. A vendor ticketing portal is not an incident response plan. A contract is not an escalation path. Gate 4 forced these to be real.

The go-live succeeded, but the first month revealed a subtle weakness. Audit logs were available, but not in a timely way. The security operations team could not easily correlate events. The organization updated the integration to stream events into its own monitoring platform, improving detection and response capability. This is a practical example of "control ownership." You can buy software, but you still own security outcomes.

Sustain phase and Gate 5, vendor oversight becomes routine

Gate 5 required a governance routine: quarterly vendor review, annual contract control review, continuous risk scoring, and a planned re-validation schedule after major vendor releases. The organization also required transparency on vendor subcontractors for critical functions. This sustained discipline aligns with the continuous improvement expectations typical of management system standards like ISO/IEC 27001, which emphasizes maintaining and continually improving an information security management system (ISO, 2022).

Case Study 2 lessons

The clearest lesson was that vendor acquisition can compress build time, but it expands governance demand. LumenCare learned that the most dangerous assumption in buy-track delivery is, "the vendor handles that." It sounds efficient, yet it often hides shared responsibility gaps, weak configurations, and missing visibility for monitoring and response. The safer posture is simple and repeatable: "show me the evidence and show me the boundary." Evidence proves what is implemented and testable. Boundaries clarify what the vendor owns, what the customer must configure, and who is accountable when something fails.

CASE STUDY 3

AI-Enabled Solution with an AI Governance Overlay

The third case involves a modern pressure point. NorthPeak Insurance wanted to deploy a generative AI assistant to improve customer service and claims processing. The plan was to use a retrieval-augmented generation approach to answer policy questions, summarize claim notes, and draft customer communications. Leadership saw a clear ROI: fewer calls, faster responses, improved consistency. The technical team saw manageable integration. Security saw a new category of risk, not merely a new feature.

AI projects introduce uncertainty that traditional systems do not. The same prompt can yield different outputs. Small changes in input can yield large changes in response. The system can be manipulated through crafted inputs, and model outputs can become a control bypass if downstream systems trust them. That is why the NIST AI RMF emphasizes lifecycle risk management and governance to promote trustworthy AI systems (NIST, 2023).

Analyze Phase and Gate 1, Use Boundaries

NorthPeak began with a deceptively simple question: "What exactly will the AI assistant be allowed to do?" If the answer is vague, governance will fail later. The Gate Review Board required: intended use, unacceptable use, user groups, data access boundaries, and accountability for outcomes. They also required a risk tier classification that reflected the system's potential to influence customer decisions and claims processing outcomes.

The team created a structured misuse scenario list. It included prompt injection attempts, data exfiltration through the conversation layer, customer impersonation, unauthorized access to claim records, and overreliance risks where staff blindly trust generated content. These categories map closely to OWASP's LLM risk list, which highlights prompt injection and insecure output handling among the top risks for LLM applications (OWASP, 2023).

Gate 1 passed only after the organization defined a conservative initial scope: the assistant would answer policy FAQs and draft internal summaries, but it would not autonomously approve claims, execute transactions, or trigger downstream actions without human confirmation.

Design phase and Gate 2, controlling data, prompts, and outputs

In AI-enabled systems, the design boundary is the control boundary. NorthPeak made four design decisions that shaped risk.

1. Data minimization and segmentation: the assistant could access curated knowledge sources and role-based claim summaries, not raw sensitive repositories.
2. Output handling controls: generated responses were treated as untrusted until validated, especially when used in customer communications. This directly addresses OWASP's warning that insecure output handling occurs when downstream components blindly accept LLM output (OWASP, 2023).
3. Human-in-the-loop governance: staff reviewed drafts, and the system logged edits and approvals, creating traceability.
4. Evaluation-by-design: the team built an evaluation suite covering hallucination patterns, sensitive data leakage tests, prompt injection resilience, and policy compliance checks.

The AI governance overlay was framed using NIST AI RMF concepts. The governance team required clarity on risk tolerance, evaluation metrics, and monitoring signals, consistent with AI RMF's emphasis on governance and measurable risk management through the lifecycle (NIST, 2023).

At Gate 2, the Quality Review Board demanded evidence that the assistant's guardrails were not aspirational. They required proof of:

data lineage for knowledge sources, access controls, prompt management, output validation methods, and incident response extensions for AI misuse scenarios.

The organization also aligned its AI governance approach with ISO/IEC 42001, which provides requirements and guidance for establishing and maintaining an AI management system and emphasizes managing AI risks and opportunities through structured governance (ISO/IEC, 2023).

Develop or Acquire and Gate 3, Deployment Safety Proof

NorthPeak chose a hybrid approach: an external model API combined with internal retrieval, orchestration, and monitoring. This is a common pattern, and it creates a layered supply chain. Gate 3 therefore required evidence from both sides: vendor assurances plus internal validation.

The security team insisted on a rule that felt strict at first: the model output can never execute actions. If the assistant suggested a workflow, the system could propose, but a separate deterministic service would validate and execute, only after human confirmation. This is a direct defense against excessive agency and insecure output handling patterns common in LLM systems.

Testing was structured like an adversarial exercise. The team ran prompt injection tests, attempted to extract sensitive claim data through conversational manipulation, and validated that the assistant refused unsafe requests. They also tested whether the assistant could be tricked into generating disallowed content or leaking internal prompts. Where failures were found, they tuned retrieval filters, strengthened refusal policies, and improved output sanitization.

Gate 3 evidence included: evaluation results, red-team findings, and remediation status, documented residual risks, and explicit approval for any exceptions. This mirrored the same evidence logic used in traditional secure SDLC, only expanded for AI risk.

Implement phase and Gate 4, monitoring is not optional

NorthPeak's Gate 4 was dominated by one theme: monitoring readiness. Traditional monitoring focuses on availability, errors, and security events. AI monitoring adds model behavior indicators: drift, unusual prompt patterns, repeated refusal triggers, spikes in sensitive-topic queries, and anomalies suggesting misuse.

The operations team asked a practical question: "How do we know the assistant is going wrong before customers tell us?" That became a go-live condition. The system launched with dashboards for safety signals and abuse detection, plus rapid rollback capabilities. The incident response plan included AI-specific playbooks: disable retrieval, restrict scopes, rotate system prompts, and suspend certain user groups if misuse patterns emerged.

Sustain and Gate 5, Continuous Assurance Without Code Changes

AI systems can change because the world changes. Knowledge bases evolve. Policies update. Customer behavior shifts. Vendors update models. Gate 5 required a continuous assurance routine: periodic evaluation re-runs, change control for prompt and retrieval updates, and formal review of incidents and near-misses. Governance required version traceability so the organization could answer a future audit question: "What model and configuration produced that output on that date?"

Case Study 3 lessons

The biggest lesson was not that AI is dangerous. It is that AI is different. If you treat it like a normal feature, you will govern it too lightly. The second lesson was that safe AI requires friction, but it is the right kind of friction. It is the friction of review, monitoring, and accountability, not the friction of late-stage panic.

CROSSS-CASE LESSONS

what repeats across build, buy, and AI

Across all three cases, the difference between success and struggle was governance maturity, expressed in five repeatable behaviors.

First, the teams defined risk tier early and used it to scale evidence requirements. That prevented both extremes: over-governance for low-risk work and under-governance for high-risk work.

Second, the teams treated evidence as a continuous output, not as a phase-ending artifact. Evidence accumulation made gates faster and more objective.

Third, the teams made security requirements testable. They replaced vague statements with acceptance criteria and proofs.

Fourth, the teams treated operational readiness as part of delivery, not as an afterthought. They validated monitoring, response, and rollback capability before approving go-live.

Fifth, the teams made accountability explicit. Risk acceptance was documented, owned, time-boxed, and monitored.

These behaviors align with modern project management principles that emphasize value delivery, risk stewardship, and tailoring, because governance is not a fixed weight, it is a tailored control system that protects value (PMI, 2021). They also align with the CSF 2.0 emphasis that cybersecurity risk management and governance must be integrated into organizational decisions rather than isolated within technical teams (NIST, 2024).

To close, a short dialogue captures the spirit of this chapter.

- Engineer: “We can ship this next week.”
- Security lead: “We can ship next week if we can prove next week.”
- Sponsor: “What do you need to prove it?”

- PMO: "The evidence bundle, the test results, the exceptions with owners, and the operational readiness checks."
- Sponsor: "Then prove it. If we cannot prove it, we are not ready."

That is the discipline Part ¿ is designed to teach. In the next chapter, we translate these patterns into governance anti-patterns and board-ready Go or No-Go signals that help leaders decide with evidence rather than optimism.

♦

> The most resilient organizations are the ones that learn, adapt, and improve in the face of setbacks.
>
> *-Author Unknown-*

♦

Go or No-Go Governance

Secure technology delivery rarely collapses because a team "forgot security." It collapses because governance drifted, quietly at first, then all at once. Drift shows up as small compromises that feel reasonable in the moment, like allowing a temporary service account, skipping a negative test because "we will add it later," or accepting a vendor's assurance without evidence. Each compromise is a single loose thread. Over time, the threads become a tear you cannot hide. That is why mature organizations do not treat governance as a meeting, they treat it as a discipline of decisions, evidence, and accountability across the lifecycle. Frameworks help, but only when they translate into behavior. NIST CSF 2.0 makes this explicit by elevating cybersecurity governance as a first-class function, not an afterthought (NIST, 2024).

This chapter is a practical field guide. It names the governance anti-patterns that repeatedly derail projects, then provides Go or No-Go signals you can use at each ADDIS gate. The intent is not to create fear or bureaucracy. The intent is to create clarity. Clarity is what protects delivery speed, because rework is slower than discipline, and breach response is slower than prevention. If you lead projects, you already know this truth in your bones. A late security surprise is never "one more task." It is a schedule reset, a credibility loss, and sometimes a public incident.

A simple dialogue captures the difference between immature and mature governance.

"Are we ready to proceed?" the sponsor asks.

- The immature answer sounds confident but vague: "Yes, we are on track."
- The mature answer sounds calm but specific: "Yes, and here is the evidence bundle. Risks are within tolerance, exceptions are

documented with owners and dates, security testing is complete for the agreed scope, and operational readiness has passed validation."

That is the point of Go or No-Go signals. They replace optimism with proof.

Why projects derail, governance failures are usually the root cause

When teams talk about failed technology initiatives, they often describe symptoms: missed deadlines, unstable releases, security findings, audit escalations, vendor conflict, user backlash. Under the symptoms, the root cause is commonly a governance breakdown. Decision rights were unclear. Evidence was not produced continuously. Risk acceptance happened by accident. The secure SDLC was treated as optional when the pressure rose.

A high-performing organization treats secure delivery as an operating system with a control spine. That spine includes governance forums, clear roles, traceability, and evidence-based gates. The NIST Secure Software Development Framework (SSDF) reinforces this idea in plain terms, secure development must be built into the way work is planned, designed, built, tested, and released, not bolted on at the end (Souppaya et al., 2022).

For AI-enabled projects, the governance burden increases. The system can be correct today and wrong tomorrow because the world shifts, the data shifts, or user interaction shifts. NIST's AI Risk Management Framework emphasizes lifecycle governance and continuous risk management through mapping, measurement, and management activities (NIST, 2023).

Governance is not "extra." It is how you keep trust intact while delivering change.

The governance pitfalls that quietly kill projects

Governance pitfalls are repeatable breakdowns that disguise themselves as efficiency. They sound practical, and they feel normal. Over time, they become predictable drivers of rework, risk, and loss of trust.

- Pitfall 1- Security treated as a late-stage inspection: Teams postpone threat modeling, security requirements, and control design until testing or go-live. The outcome is expensive rework, or "temporary" exceptions that quietly become permanent. In practice, late security is not security, it becomes negotiation under schedule pressure.
- Pitfall 2 - Vague requirements that cannot be tested: Phrases like "strong authentication," "secure logging," and "privacy compliant" are not requirements. They are intentions. A secure SDLC requires measurable acceptance criteria, test cases, and retained evidence so the team can prove what was built and what was verified.
- Pitfall 3 - Unclear decision rights: When no one can clearly name who approves risk acceptance, exceptions, and compensating controls, governance turns into performance. People nod in meetings and then implement whatever keeps the timeline moving. Later, accountability disappears, and everyone claims they were not informed.
- Pitfall 4 - Evidence assembled at the end: When evidence is created days before the gate review, it will be incomplete, inconsistent, and hard to verify. Reviewers have no time to trace decisions, and gates become political because proof is weak. The correction is simple: produce evidence continuously, then curate it before the gate.
- Pitfall 5 - Vendor assurances replace validation: Statements like "we are ISO certified" do not prove your implementation is secure. "Our platform is compliant" does not prove your configuration is hardened. Supplier risk is real, especially with integrations and

managed services, so governance must require proof in your environment, not marketing claims.

- Pitfall 6 - Exceptions without expiry or monitoring: A risk exception with no owner, no end date, and no monitoring plan is not a decision. It is a slow breach. If residual risk must be accepted, handle it with discipline: define scope, time-box it, monitor it, and require conscious re-approval.
- Pitfall 7 - AI treated as a feature, not a risk class: AI-enabled initiatives often skip data lineage clarity, evaluation rigor, misuse testing, and drift monitoring. That is not a minor oversight, it is governance failure. OWASP's LLM risk categories make the point bluntly: prompt injection and insecure output handling can turn a "chat feature" into a control bypass if downstream actions blindly trust model outputs (OWASP, 2023).
- Pitfall 8 - Go-live defined as deployment, not readiness: Production is not a finish line. It is a contract with users, auditors, regulators, and attackers. That is why Gate 4 exists. Operational readiness is not guaranteed by a successful deployment script, it requires proof of supportability, monitoring, response readiness, and control effectiveness.
- Pitfall 9 - Compliance treated as paperwork, not risk management: Modern regulators increasingly ask about governance, risk management, and oversight. The SEC's cybersecurity disclosure rules emphasize governance and incident disclosure expectations (SEC, 2023). In the EU, NIS2 and DORA reinforce minimum cybersecurity and resilience expectations (European Commission, 2023; European Parliament and Council, 2022).

If you recognize these governance pitfalls, that is progress. Recognition is the first control. The next step is to replace them with clear gate signals, evidence-driven criteria, and decisions that are recorded and enforced.

What "Go or No-Go" really means in ADDIS gate governance

A gate decision is not a morale boost and it is not a schedule checkpoint. It is a control point where leadership confirms readiness to proceed based on evidence, not assurances. Gates exist because optimism is not a control. When an organization approves the next step without proof, it is not moving fast, it is moving blind. ADDIS uses gates to replace blind momentum with disciplined progress, so delivery remains defensible under audit, resilient under stress, and accountable when tradeoffs are required.

Each gate has a distinct purpose and a distinct evidence intent. Gate 1, the Analyze Go or No-Go, confirms the problem is understood, scope is bounded, feasibility is credible, and early risks are identified with owners. Gate 2, Design Approval, confirms Security by Design has been translated into real design decisions, explicit trust boundaries, mapped controls, and a test strategy that can produce traceable evidence. Gate 3, Build or Acquire Release Readiness, confirms controls are implemented and validated, critical findings are resolved or governed, and residual risks are approved explicitly. Gate 4, Implementation Go-Live, confirms production readiness, stable service health, monitoring and logging coverage, alert routing, response capability, and a formal handover posture. Gate 5, the Sustain Review, confirms continuous assurance is operating, maintenance and access governance are disciplined, and the solution remains governable over time.

Think of each gate as a bridge inspection. A bridge can look fine from a distance, but no responsible owner signs off without structural evidence, load testing, and documented accountability. Gates apply the same principle to technology delivery.

Gate 1 signals: Analyze Go or No-Go

Gate 1 is where many organizations lose the plot. They rush into build before the problem is bounded, before security assumptions are documented, and before risk appetite is applied. Gate 1 is the point where you prevent runaway scope, hidden integrations, and unrealistic timelines.

Go signals at Gate 1 include the following conditions:

- The scope and boundary are explicit, including data boundaries and trust boundaries, and the out-of-scope items are documented (ISO, 2022). ISO
- Security, privacy, and compliance requirements exist as testable statements, not vague promises.
- A threat model or preliminary abuse case analysis exists for the core workflows, including third-party and API abuse paths (Souppaya et al., 2022).
- Risk tiering is established, and it drives minimum evidence expectations and independent validation levels.
- Decision rights are defined, including who can approve exceptions and who owns residual risk.

No-Go signals at Gate 1 are often simple:

- Requirements contain security language but no measurable acceptance criteria.
- Vendor selection is effectively "already decided" without due diligence on controls and integration risks.
- The data story is unclear: where data originates, where it flows, what is personal, what is confidential, what is regulated.

- The project plan treats security testing as a late milestone rather than continuous evidence.

For AI-enabled projects, Gate 1 must also establish AI governance basics. If the team cannot clearly state intended use, unacceptable use, and accountability boundaries, the project is not ready to proceed (NIST, 2023).

Gate 2 signals: Design Approval

Gate 2 is the point where Security by Design becomes real. It is also where architecture choices either reduce attack surface or multiply it. If Gate 2 is weak, Gate 3 and Gate 4 become firefighting exercises.

Go signals at Gate 2 include:

- Architecture diagrams show data flows, trust boundaries, and identity flows, not only boxes and arrows.
- Security controls are designed into the architecture with explicit mapping to threats, risks, and requirements (NIST, 2024).
- Logging and monitoring are designed as product features, including required event fields, retention, alert thresholds, and escalation paths.
- Key nonfunctional requirements are defined: availability targets, recovery objectives, encryption expectations, key management boundaries, and segmentation decisions (ISO, 2022).
- The test strategy is defined early enough to influence design, including what must be proven before release (Souppaya et al., 2022).

No-Go signals at Gate 2 include:

- Security controls exist only as generic "must comply" statements with no design decisions attached.
- The design assumes a future control will solve today's risk, such as "we will add monitoring later."
- Integration points are treated as routine, yet no one has defined authentication method, token handling, authorization model, or failure modes.
- The project cannot demonstrate how security requirements will be tested and evidenced.

For AI-enabled systems, Gate 2 must require a stronger design posture: data lineage clarity, model or prompt security considerations, evaluation design, and explicit mitigation for common LLM abuse patterns (OWASP, 2023).

Gate 3 signals: Build or Acquire Release Readiness

Gate 3 is where teams often confuse "working" with "ready." The system may pass functional demos, yet still fail basic security and assurance checks. Gate 3 exists to stop unsafe releases from rolling downhill into production.

Go signals at Gate 3 include:

- Secure SDLC practices have been followed with evidence: code review discipline, vulnerability management, secrets handling, build integrity controls, and security testing results (Souppaya et al., 2022).
- Critical findings are either remediated or have approved exceptions with compensating controls, owners, and expiry dates.

- Traceability exists: requirements to design to controls to tests to results.
- For vendor-acquired solutions, configuration hardening and integration security have been validated, not assumed.
- The evidence set is reviewable by an independent party without relying on verbal explanations.

No-Go signals at Gate 3 include:

- "We will fix that after go-live" appears repeatedly for high-risk issues.
- Penetration testing or security validation is deferred because of schedule pressure.
- The team cannot show what changed since the last review, and cannot show what was re-tested.
- For AI systems, evaluation is shallow: no red-team testing, no misuse testing, no measurement of failure modes, no plan for monitoring drift (NIST, 2023).

A 0.1 percent discipline here is to require teams to quantify residual risk in plain language. Not a score, a story: "If this control fails, what happens, who is affected, what is the blast radius, and how fast can we detect and respond?" This is how governance becomes real.

Gate 4 signals: Implementation Go-Live

Gate 4 is the line between controlled change and public consequences. Once you deploy, you are no longer arguing with your backlog. You are arguing with reality, customers, attackers, and regulators.

Go signals at Gate 4 include:

- Production access is governed: privileged access controls, separation of duties, and break-glass procedures are defined and tested (ISO, 2022).
- Monitoring is operational: alerts route to real responders, on-call coverage exists, runbooks exist, and incident communication paths are clear.
- Backup, recovery, and rollback procedures have been tested, not merely documented.
- Data migration integrity checks are completed, and reconciliation procedures exist.
- Change management and release governance are ready for steady-state operations, including emergency patches.

No-Go signals at Gate 4 include:

- The operations team says, "We have not seen this system before," or "We do not have the logs we need."
- The security team cannot confirm production configuration baselines, key management, and identity enforcement.
- The incident response team has not validated detection coverage or escalation procedures.

Regulatory reality strengthens the case for Gate 4 discipline. For example, DORA's resilience expectations and oversight pressures in the financial sector raise the cost of weak operational readiness, because outages and ICT disruptions are governance events, not only IT events (European Parliament and Council, 2022).

Gate 5 signals: Sustain Review and continuous assurance

Gate 5 is where many organizations relax too soon. They treat the project as finished and move on. Attackers do not move on. Systems age. Dependencies change. AI models drift. Vulnerabilities emerge. Gate 5 exists to confirm that the solution remains governable and safe after the spotlight fades.

Go signals at Gate 5 include:

- Continuous assurance is operating: vulnerability management cadence, patch governance, control monitoring, and periodic validation are defined and active (ISO, 2022).
- Metrics exist that executives can understand: time to patch critical issues, number of high-risk exceptions, incident trends, and control health indicators (NIST, 2024).
- Ownership has shifted cleanly from project teams to operational owners with clear accountability and budget.
- Lessons learned are captured and translated into updated standards, patterns, and future gate criteria.

No-Go signals at Gate 5 include:

- Exceptions remain open with no monitoring and no expiry.
- Monitoring exists but is not actionable, because alerts are noisy, routes are unclear, or responders are not trained.
- For AI systems, there is no drift and misuse monitoring plan, and no triggers for re-evaluation (NIST, 2023).

If Gate 5 is weak, the organization is betting its reputation on hope. Hope is not a control.

A board-level question set that changes outcomes

Governance matures when leaders ask better questions. These questions are short, sharp, and uncomfortable, which is why they work:

- "Show me the evidence, not the plan. What proof exists today?"
- "What risks are we accepting, who approved them, and when will we revisit?"
- "If this fails in production, what is the blast radius and how fast will we detect it?"
- "What third parties are in the control boundary, and what assurance do we have beyond their marketing?"
- "For AI: what is the intended use, what is unacceptable use, and how do we detect misuse?"

These questions align with modern governance expectations across frameworks and regulatory trends. CSF 2.0's emphasis on governance reinforces that oversight and accountability must be explicit, not implied (NIST, 2024).

Special considerations for AI-enabled projects

AI changes the nature of Go or No-Go. In many AI projects, the risk is not only exploitation, it is uncontrolled behavior at scale. A model can produce unsafe outputs, leak sensitive data, or be manipulated through prompt injection. When downstream systems treat model output as trusted instructions, the model becomes a privilege escalation path. OWASP highlights this risk pattern directly through categories like prompt injection and insecure output handling (OWASP, 2023).

In practical terms, AI governance requires four additions to your gate mindset:

First, treat data governance as security governance. If you cannot defend data lineage, consent, retention, and access controls, you cannot defend the system.

Second, require evaluation evidence that matches risk. Accuracy is not enough. You need robustness, misuse resistance, security testing, and failure mode measurement (NIST, 2023).

Third, require monitoring and change control. AI systems evolve through data changes, model updates, and prompt updates. Governance must track and approve those changes with traceability.

Fourth, align with emerging standards where appropriate. ISO/IEC 42001 provides a management-system approach for AI governance that fits well with organizations already using ISO-style assurance models (ISO/IEC, 2023).

Turning signals into habit, the discipline of repeatable decisions

The most effective organizations do not rely on heroic individuals. They build repeatable decision habits. A habit has a trigger, a routine, and a reward. Gate governance provides the trigger. Evidence-based review is the routine. Reduced surprises is the reward.

To build that habit, apply three operational rules:

1. Evidence must be continuous. Do not allow end-of-phase evidence assembly. Require incremental proof throughout the phase.

2. Risk acceptance must be explicit and time-boxed. Every exception has an owner, a rationale, compensating controls, a review date, and monitoring signals.

3. Gate criteria must be right-sized to risk tier. Higher-risk initiatives demand deeper evidence, independent validation, and stronger operational commitments.

This is also where the PMO earns its strategic value. The PMO is not merely a scheduling function. In secure technology project management, the PMO enforces decision rights, standardizes evidence expectations, and ensures governance remains consistent across the portfolio. When the PMO does this well, governance becomes faster, not slower, because teams stop reinventing what "ready" means.

Chapter Summary

Chapter 26 is about avoiding predictable failure. Governance pitfalls do not appear because teams are careless. They appear because teams are pressured. Pressure compresses time, and compressed time tempts shortcuts. ADDIS gate governance exists to prevent shortcuts from becoming incidents.

Go or No-Go signals are not slogans. They are practical thresholds that protect delivery integrity. They make security by design measurable. They make secure SDLC execution provable. They make AI governance operational instead of aspirational. When you apply these signals consistently across Gate 1 through Gate 5, you build something most organizations lack: the ability to deliver modern technology at speed without trading away trust.

REFERENCES

Axelos. (2019). ITIL Foundation: ITIL 4 edition. The Stationery Office.

Beyer, B., Jones, C., Petoff, J., & Murphy, N. R. (2016). Site reliability engineering: How Google runs production systems. O'Reilly Media.

Chandramouli, R. (2022). Implementation of DevSecOps for a microservices-based application with service mesh (NIST Special Publication 800-204C). National Institute of Standards and Technology. https://doi.org/10.6028/NIST.SP.800-204C

European Insurance and Occupational Pensions Authority. (n.d.). Digital Operational Resilience Act (DORA) and ICT risk oversight resources. Retrieved December 17, 2025, from https://www.eiopa.europa.eu/

European Union. (2022). Directive (EU) 2022/2555 of the European Parliament and of the Council of 14 December 2022 on measures for a high common level of cybersecurity across the Union, amending Regulation (EU) No 910/2014 and Directive (EU) 2018/1972, and repealing Directive (EU) 2016/1148 (NIS 2 Directive). Official Journal of the European Union, L 333, 80–152. https://eur-lex.europa.eu/eli/dir/2022/2555/oj/eng EUR-Lex

European Union. (2022). Regulation (EU) 2022/2554 of the European Parliament and of the Council of 14 December 2022 on digital operational resilience for the financial sector and amending Regulations (EC) No 1060/2009, (EU) No 648/2012, (EU) No 600/2014, (EU) No 909/2014 and (EU) 2016/1011 (Text with EEA relevance). Official Journal of the European Union, L 333, 1–79. https://eur-lex.europa.eu/eli/reg/2022/2554/oj/eng EUR-Lex

European Union. (2024). Regulation (EU) 2024/1689 of the European Parliament and of the Council of 13 June 2024 laying down harmonised rules on artificial intelligence and amending Regulations (EC) No 300/2008, (EU) No 167/2013, (EU) No 168/2013, (EU) 2018/858, (EU) 2018/1139 and (EU) 2019/2144 and Directives 2014/90/EU, (EU) 2016/797 and (EU) 2020/1828 (Artificial Intelligence Act). Official Journal of the European Union, L, 2024/1689. https://eur-lex.europa.eu/eli/reg/2024/1689/oj/eng EUR-Lex

International Organization for Standardization. (2015). ISO/IEC 38500:2015: Information technology—Governance of IT for the organization. ISO.

International Organization for Standardization. (2022). ISO/IEC 27001:2022: Information security, cybersecurity, and privacy protection—Information security management systems—Requirements. ISO.

International Organization for Standardization. (2023a). ISO/IEC 42001:2023: Information technology—Artificial intelligence—Management system. ISO.

International Organization for Standardization. (2023b). ISO/IEC 23894:2023: Information technology—Artificial intelligence—Risk management. ISO.

International Organization for Standardization. (2024). ISO/IEC 38500:2024: Information technology—Governance of IT for the organization. ISO.

ISACA. (2018). COBIT 2019 framework: Introduction and methodology. ISACA.

ISACA. (2019). COBIT 2019 framework: Governance and management objectives. ISACA.

Microsoft. (2022a). Threat modeling: The STRIDE model. Microsoft Learn. Retrieved December 17, 2025, from https://learn.microsoft.com/

Microsoft. (2022b). Threat modeling. Microsoft Learn. Retrieved December 17, 2025, from https://learn.microsoft.com/

MITRE. (2025). MITRE ATLAS: Adversarial Threat Landscape for Artificial-Intelligence Systems. Retrieved December 17, 2025, from https://atlas.mitre.org/

National Institute of Standards and Technology. (2023). Artificial Intelligence Risk Management Framework (AI RMF 1.0) (NIST AI 100-1). U.S. Department of Commerce. https://doi.org/10.6028/NIST.AI.100-1

National Institute of Standards and Technology. (2024a). Artificial Intelligence Risk Management Framework: Generative AI Profile (NIST AI 600-1). U.S. Department of Commerce. https://doi.org/10.6028/NIST.AI.600-1

National Institute of Standards and Technology. (2024b). The NIST Cybersecurity Framework (CSF) 2.0 (NIST CSWP 29). U.S. Department of Commerce. https://doi.org/10.6028/NIST.CSWP.29

National Institute of Standards and Technology. (2025). Computer Security Incident Handling Guide (NIST Special Publication 800-61 Rev. 3). U.S. Department of Commerce. https://doi.org/10.6028/NIST.SP.800-61r3 NIST Publications

Open Source Security Foundation (OpenSSF). (n.d.). Supply-chain Levels for Software Artifacts (SLSA). Retrieved December 17, 2025, from https://slsa.dev/

Organisation for Economic Co-operation and Development. (2019). Recommendation of the Council on Artificial Intelligence (OECD/LEGAL/0449). https://legalinstruments.oecd.org/en/instruments/oecd-legal-0449 OECD Legal Instruments

OWASP Foundation. (2023). OWASP Top 10 for Large Language Model Applications. Retrieved December 17, 2025, from https://owasp.org/

Project Management Institute. (2017). Agile practice guide. Project Management Institute.

Project Management Institute. (2021a). A guide to the project management body of knowledge (PMBOK® Guide) (7th ed.). Project Management Institute.

Project Management Institute. (2021b). The standard for project management. Project Management Institute.

Souppaya, M., & Scarfone, K. (2016). Guide to data-centric system threat modeling (NIST Special Publication 800-154). National Institute of Standards and Technology. https://doi.org/10.6028/NIST.SP.800-154

Souppaya, M., Scarfone, K., & Dodson, D. (2022). Secure Software Development Framework (SSDF) Version 1.1: Recommendations for mitigating the risk of software vulnerabilities (NIST Special Publication 800-218). National Institute of Standards and Technology. https://doi.org/10.6028/NIST.SP.800-218

U.S. Securities and Exchange Commission. (2023). Cybersecurity risk management, strategy, governance, and incident disclosure. Federal Register, 88(146), 51896–51981.

www.ingramcontent.com/pod-product-compliance
Lightning Source LLC
LaVergne TN
LVHW052149210926
848482LV00019B/296